# C

# By

# EXAMPLE

## ACADEMIC EDITION

que
*College*

**Greg Perry**

## *C By Example*, **Special Edition**

### © **1994 by Que**

Library of Congress Catalog No: 93-85723

ISBN: 1-56529-453-X

99  98          10  9

Interpretation of the printing code: the rightmost double-digit number is the year of the book's printing; the rightmost single-digit number, the number of the book's printing. For example, a printing code of 93-1 shows that the first printing of the book occurred in 1993.

Screen reproductions in this book were created with Collage Plus from Inner Media, Inc., Hollis, NH.

**Publisher:** *David P. Ewing*

**Associate Publisher:** *Rick Ranucci*

**Director of Publishing:** *Michael Miller*

**Managing Editor:** *Corinne Walls*

**Marketing Manager:** *Ray Robinson*

## Title Manager
*Joseph B. Wikert*

## Production Editors
*J. Christopher Nelson*
*Jodi Jensen*

## Editors
*David F. Noble*
*Judy Brunetti*
*Linda Seifert*

## Technical Editor
*Greg Guntle*

## Book Designer
*Amy Peppler-Adams*

## Production Team
*Jeff Baker*
*Angela Bannan*
*Danielle Bird*
*Ayrika Bryant*
*Paula Carroll*
*Laurie Casey*
*Brad Chinn*
*Charlotte Clapp*
*Meshell Dinn*
*Brook Farling*
*Michelle Greenwalt*

*Carla Hall*
*Michael Hughes*
*Heather Kaufman*
*Bob LaRoche*
*Wendy Ott*
*Ryan Rader*
*Beth Rago*
*Amy L. Steed*
*Tina Trettin*
*Johnna VanHoose*
*Michelle Worthington*

Composed in *Palatino* and *MCPdigital* by Prentice Hall Computer Publishing

# Dedication

*For Mario, Franca, and all the Camerucci family: Your food at Rome's* Monti's *is made even better by your friendship.* Grazie!

# About the Author

Greg Perry is a speaker and writer in both the programming and applications sides of computing. He is known for bringing programming topics down to the beginner's level. Perry has been a programmer and trainer for the past 15 years. He received his first degree in computer science and then received a master's degree in corporate finance. Besides writing, he teaches, consults, and lectures across the country, including at the acclaimed Software Development programming conferences. Perry is the author of 20 other computer books, including *QBasic By Example*, *Access Programming By Example*, and *Turbo C++ By Example* (all published by Que). In addition, he has published articles in several publications such as *Software Development*, *PC World*, and *Data Training*.

# Acknowledgments

I appreciate Joseph Wikert at Prentice Hall/Que for trusting me completely with the direction and style of this book.

The rest of my editors—Jodi Jensen, Chris Nelson, David Noble, Judy Brunetti, and Linda Seifert—kept me on track so that readers can have an accurate and readable text.

Gary Farrar is one of the primary reasons for this book's readability. Gary is an excellent example of the pupil who surpassed the teacher. I am grateful for your help, Gary.

When Dr. Richard C. Burgess and his wonderful wife, Ellen, stepped back into my life, they filled a void. Rick, you are the reason I am who I am today. Ellen, you have always been *simpatica, molta!*

As always, my beautiful bride Jayne, my parents Glen and Bettye Perry, and of course, Luke, the bischon, are my closest daily companions. It is for them that I work.

## Trademark Acknowlegments

All terms mentioned in this book that are known to be trademarks or service marks have been appropriately capitalized. Que Corporation cannot attest to the accuracy of this information. Use of a term in this book should not be regarded as affecting the validity of any trademark or service mark.

ANSI is a registered trademark of American National Standards Institute.

DEC is a registed trademark of Digital Equipment Corporation.

IBM is a registered trademark of International Business Machines Corporation.

Microsoft QuickC and MS-DOS are registered trademarks of Microsoft Corporation.

Turbo C is a registered trademark of Borland International, Inc.

UNIX is a registered trademark of AT&T.

X Window System is a trademark of the Massachusetts Institute of Technology.

# Overview

## VI Arrays and Pointers

## VII Structures and File I/O

# Contents

Contents

Contents

Contents

## Part VI Arrays and Pointers

Contents

## Part VII Structures and File I/O

### 28 Structures     483

### 29 Arrays of Structures     503

### 30 Sequential Files     527

### 31 Random Access Files     545

## A Memory Addressing, Binary, and Hexadecimal Review 561

## B Answers to Review Questions 577

Contents

# Introduction

Every day, more and more people learn and use the C programming language. I have taught C to hundreds of students, and I grow more fond of the language with each course I teach. The C programming language is now the mainstream computer course in colleges. Knowledge of C is an essential prerequisite for employment in the computer industry. I hope this book helps fill a need that the vast number of C books currently in print do not fill: the need for a book with a straightforward, friendly, and comfortable feel that provides a stepping-stone style to C for beginners.

*C By Example,* Special Edition, is an updated version of an outstanding and successful series of *By Example* books. Much of the material in this Special Edition was revised from the earlier *By Example* book, but the strengths of that first book were kept. The philosophy of these books is simple: the best way to teach computer programming concepts is with multiple examples. Command descriptions, format syntax, and language references are not enough to teach a newcomer a programming language. Only by looking at many examples in which new commands are immediately used and by running sample programs can programming students get more than just a feel for the language.

## Who Should Use This Book

This book teaches at three levels: beginning, intermediate, and advanced. Text and numerous examples are aimed at readers on each level. If you are new to C, and even if you are new to computers, this book attempts to put you at ease and gradually build your C programming skills. If you are an expert at C, this book tries to provide a few extras for you along the way.

# The Book's Philosophy

This book focuses on programming *correctly* in C by teaching structured programming techniques and proper program design. Emphasis is always placed on a program's readability rather than "tricks of the trade" code examples. In this changing world, programs should be clear, properly structured, and well documented, and this book does not waver from the importance of this philosophy.

*C By Example* teaches you C by using a holistic approach. In addition to learning the mechanics of the language, you learn some tips and warnings, how to use C for different types of applications, and a little of the history and interesting asides about the computing industry.

Many other books build single applications, adding to them a little at a time with each chapter. The chapters of this book are stand-alone chapters, showing you complete programs that fully demonstrate the commands discussed in the chapter. There is a program for every level of reader, from beginning to advanced.

The book contains almost 200 sample program listings. These programs show ways that you can use C for personal finance, school and business record keeping, math and science, and general-purpose applications that almost everybody with a computer can use. This wide variety of programs shows you that C is a very powerful language that is easy to learn and use.

# Overview

This book is divided into seven parts. Part I introduces you to the C environment, as well as to introductory programming concepts. Starting with Part II, the book presents the C programming language commands and built-in functions. After mastering the language, you then can use the book as a reference. When you need help with a specific C programming problem, turn to the area that describes that part of the language to see various examples of code.

For an idea of the book's layout, here is a description of each part of the book.

## Part I: Introduction to C

Part I explains what C is by presenting a brief history of the C programming language and then outlining C's advantages over other languages. This part describes your computer's hardware, how you develop your C programs, and the steps you follow to enter and run programs. You write your first C programs in Chapter 3.

## Part II: C Operators

Part II teaches the entire set of C operators. The rich assortment of operators (C has more operators than any other programming language except APL) makes up for the fact that the C programming language is very small. The operators and their order of precedence are more important in C than in most programming languages.

## Part III: C Constructs

C data processing is powerful because of the looping, comparison, and selection constructs that C offers. Part III shows you how to write programs that flow correctly and have control computations that produce accurate and readable code.

## Part IV: Variable Scope and Modular Programming

To support true structured programming techniques, C must allow for local and global variables, as well as offer several ways to pass and return variables between functions. Part IV illustrates the strength of C as a structured language that attempts—if the programmer is willing to "listen to the language"—to protect local variables by making them visible only to the parts of the program that need them.

## Part V: Character Input, Output, and Library Functions

C has no commands that perform input or output. To make up for this apparent oversight, C compiler writers supply several useful input and output functions. By separating input and output functions from the language, C achieves better portability between computers; if your program runs on one computer, it should work on any other.

Part V describes these input and output functions. It describes also several of the other built-in math, character, and string functions available with C. These functions keep you from having to write your own routines to perform common tasks.

## Part VI: Arrays and Pointers

C offers single-dimensional and multidimensional arrays. These arrays hold multiple occurrences of repeating data, but do not require much effort on your part to process.

Unlike many other programming languages, C also uses pointer variables frequently. Pointer variables and arrays, the subject of Part VI, work together to give you flexible data storage, which enables you to sort and search data easily.

## Part VII: Structures and File I/O

Variables, arrays, and pointers are not enough to hold the types of data your programs will require. Structures allow for more powerful groupings of many different kinds of data into manageable units.

Your computer would be too limiting if you could not store data to the disk and retrieve that data back into your programs. Disk files are required by most "real world" applications. Part VII describes how C processes sequential- and random-access files and teaches the fundamental principles needed to save data effectively to disk. A new section appears in this edition that explains the mysteries of dynamic memory allocation and deallocation.

## Conventions

The following typographic conventions are used in this book:

- ◆ Command and function names are in `lowercase monospace`. Code lines, variable names, and any text you would see on-screen are also in `monospace`.

- ◆ Placeholders in code are in `italic monospace`. A *placeholder* is a word or phrase that you must replace with more specific text.

- ◆ User input following a prompt is in **`bold monospace`**.

- ◆ File names are in uppercase regular text.

- ◆ New terms, which can be found in the glossary at the back of this book, are in *italic*.

- ◆ All programs in this Special Edition have callouts that pinpoint certain features or nuances of C.

## Index to the Icons

 Beginning information

 Intermediate information

 Advanced information

 Tip

 Caution

 Note

 Pseudocode

➡ Code continuation—indicates that the code line was too long to fit within the margins of this book. Simply leave one space and continue typing the second line.

## Pseudocode

Pseudocode appears in italic and precedes many of the program listings in this book. Pseudocode is a description, written in English, of what tasks you want your program to perform. Writing pseudocode before you write your program can help you conceptualize your program's purpose.

## Companion Disk Offer

If you'd like to save yourself hours of tedious typing, use the order form at the back of this book to order the companion disk for *C By Example*, Special Edition. This disk contains the source code for all complete programs and sample code in the book. Additionally, the answers to many of the review exercise programs are included on this disk.

# Part I

*Introduction to C*

# CHAPTER 1

# Welcome to C

C is one of the most popular programming languages in use today. The C programming language is a high-level, efficient language that has been standardized and made available to work on almost every computer in the world. Whether you are a beginning, an intermediate, or an expert programmer, C has the programming tools you need to make your computer do just what *you* want it to do. This chapter introduces you to C, briefly describes its history, shows you the advantages of using C over other computer languages, and concludes by introducing you to hardware and software concepts.

## What C Can Do for You

Have you ever wanted your computer to perform exactly as you wished? Maybe you have looked for a program that keeps track of your household budget—exactly as you prefer—but haven't found one. Perhaps you want to track the records of a small (or large) business with your computer, but you have found nothing that prints reports exactly as you'd like them. Possibly you have thought of a new use for a computer that no one else has thought of, and you would like to implement your idea. C gives you the power to develop all these uses for your computer.

ANSI C was defined by the American National Standards Institute to achieve uniformity among versions of C.

If your computer could understand English, you would not need to learn a programming language. But because the computer does not, you must learn to write instructions in a language your computer recognizes. C is a small but powerful programming language. Several companies have written different versions of C, but almost all C languages available today conform to the ANSI standard. *ANSI C-compatible* means that the C language in question conforms to the standard defined by the American National Standards Institute (ANSI). This group of computer professionals has attempted to develop a uniform C language. If you program using the ANSI C standard, your program should successfully run on any other computer in the world that also uses ANSI C. Whether something is ANSI C-compatible is important to people who want to write and sell programs that work on many different types of computers.

This book shows you how to program in ANSI C. Whether you use a PC, minicomputer, mainframe, or supercomputer, the C language you learn here should work on them all.

When some people attempt to learn C, even if they are programmers in other computer languages, they find that C can be cryptic and difficult to understand. This does not have to be the case. When you are taught to write clear and concise C code, in an order that builds on fundamental programming concepts, C is no more difficult to learn or use than any other programming language. Actually, after you get started, C's modularity makes it even easier to use.

Even if you've never programmed a computer before, you may soon understand that programming in C is rewarding. Becoming an expert programmer in C—or in any other computer language—takes time and dedication. Nevertheless, you can start writing simple programs with very little effort. After you learn the fundamentals of C programming, you can build on what you learn, and hone your skills as you write more powerful programs. You might also see new uses for your computer and develop programs that others can use.

The importance of C cannot be overly stressed. Throughout the years, several programming languages have been developed that were designed to be "the only programming language you would ever need." PL/I was heralded as such back in the early 1960s. It turned out to be so large and took so many system resources that it simply became another language programmers used, along with COBOL, FORTRAN, and many others. In the mid-1970s, Pascal was developed for smaller computers. Microcomputers had just been invented, and the Pascal language was small enough to fit in their limited memory space while still offering advantages over many other languages. Pascal became very popular and still is used frequently. It never became *the* answer for all programming tasks, however, and failed at being "the only programming language you would ever need."

When C became known to the mass computer markets in the late 1970s, it also was promoted as "the only programming language you would ever need." What surprised so many skeptics (including this author) is that C has almost fulfilled this promise! An incredible number of programming shops have converted to C. The appeal of C's efficiency, combined with its portability between computers, makes it the language of choice. Most of today's familiar spreadsheets, databases, and word processors have been written in C.

C's use seems to be growing. The computer professional help-wanted ads seem to seek more and more C programmers every day. By learning this popular language, you will stay up with the programming crowds and keep your skills current. You have taken the first step: with this book, you learn the C language particulars, as well as many programming tips to use and pitfalls to avoid. This book attempts to make you not just a C programmer, but also a better programmer in general by applying the structured, long-term programming habits that professionals require in today's businesses and industries.

## The Background of C

The UNIX operating system was written almost entirely in C.

Before you jump into C, you might find it helpful to know something about the evolution of the C programming language. Bell Labs first developed this language in the early 1970s, primarily so that Bell programmers could write their UNIX operating system for a new DEC (Digital Equipment Corporation) computer. Until that time, operating systems were written in assembly language, which is tedious, time-consuming, and difficult to maintain. The Bell Labs people knew they needed a higher-level programming language to implement their project more quickly and to make its code easier to maintain.

Because other high-level languages at the time (COBOL, FORTRAN, PL/I, and Algol) were too slow for an operating system's code, the Bell Labs programmers decided to write their own language. They based their new language on Algol and BCPL. Algol is still used in some European markets, but is not used much in America. BCPL strongly influenced C although it did not offer some language features the makers of C required. After a few versions, these Bell programmers developed a language that met their goals very well. C is efficient (it is sometimes called a high low-level language because of its speed of execution) and flexible, and C contains the proper constructs that enable it to be maintained over time.

## C Compared to Other Languages

If you have programmed before, you should understand a little about how C differs from other programming languages on the market. Besides being a very efficient language, C is known also as a *weakly typed* language; that is, the data type you assign to a variable does not necessarily require that same type of data. (Function prototyping under the new ANSI standards, however, helps alleviate this problem.) For example, if you define an integer variable and then decide to put a character value into it, C lets you do this. The data may not be in the format you expect, but C does its best. This is much different from strongly typed languages such as COBOL and Pascal. Although you can get into trouble a little more easily, C enables you to view the same data in different ways.

C's philosophy is this: Trust the programmers—they *must* know what they're doing!

C's being weakly typed places much more responsibility on the programmer. C is an extremely flexible language. It must be flexible to be used to write operating systems. At any one time, an operating system does not know what is coming down the line. If, for example, an operating system expects an integer but instead receives a character, the operating system's language must be flexible enough to handle this different data without aborting.

The added responsibility of the weakly typed, flexible C language adds to the programmer's burden of being careful while programming. The trade-off is worth it, however. The designers of C did not want to hamper C programmers by adding lots of strict rules to the language.

C is a small, block-structured programming language. It has fewer than 40 keywords. To make up for its small vocabulary, C has one of the largest assortments of *operators* (second only to APL). The large number of operators in C could tempt programmers to write cryptic programs that do a lot with a small amount of code. As you learn throughout this book, however, making the program more readable is more important than squeezing out bytes. This book teaches you how to use the C operators to their fullest extent while maintaining readable programs.

C's large number of operators (more than the number of keywords) requires a more judicious use of an *operator precedence* table. The C operator precedence table is provided in Appendix D. Unlike most other languages that have only 4 or 5 levels of precedence, C has 15. As you learn C, you must master each of these 15 levels. This is not as difficult as it sounds, but its importance cannot be overstated.

C also has no input or output statements. You might want to read that sentence again! C has *no* commands that perform input or output. This is one of the most important reasons why C is available on so many different computers. The I/O (input/output) statements of most languages tie those languages to specific hardware. BASIC, for instance, has almost twenty I/O commands—some of which write to the screen, the printer, a modem, and so forth. If you write a BASIC program for a microcomputer, the chances are good that the program cannot run on a mainframe without considerable modification.

C uses built-in functions for I/O.

C's input and output are performed through the abundant use of *function calls*. With every C compiler comes a library of standard I/O functions that your program calls to perform input and output. These standard routines are *hardware independent* because they work on any device and on any compiler that conforms to the ANSI C standard (as most do).

To master C completely, you must be more aware of your computer's hardware than most other languages require you to be. You certainly do not have to be a hardware expert, but understanding the internal data representation makes C much more usable and meaningful. It also helps if you can become familiar with binary and hexadecimal numbers. You might want to read Appendix A for a tutorial on these topics before you start to learn the C language. If you do not want to explore these topics, you can still become a very good C programmer. Knowing what goes on "under the hood," however, can make C more meaningful to you.

## C and Microcomputers

C was a relatively unknown language until it was placed on the microcomputer. With the invention and growth of the microcomputer, C blossomed into a worldwide computer language. Most readers of this book are probably working on a microcomputer-based C system. If you are new to computers, it might help you to know how microcomputers were developed.

In the 1970s, NASA created the *microchip*, a tiny wafer of silicon that occupies a space smaller than a postage stamp. Computer components could be placed on these microchips, so computers required much less space than before. NASA produced these smaller computers in response to its need to send rocket ships to the moon with on-board computers. The computers on Earth could not provide split-second accuracy for rockets because radio waves took several seconds to travel between the Earth and the moon. Through development, these microchips became small enough so that the computers could travel with a rocket and safely compute the rocket's trajectory.

The space program was not the only beneficiary of computer miniaturization. Because microchips became the heart of the *micro*computer, computers could then fit on desktops. These microcomputers cost much less than their larger counterparts, so many people started buying them. Thus, the home and small-business computer market was born.

Today, microcomputers are typically called PCs (for personal computers) from the widespread use of the original IBM PC. The early PCs did not have the memory capacity of the large computers used by government and big business. Nevertheless, PC owners still needed a way to program these machines. The first programming language chosen for PCs was BASIC. Over the years, many other languages were ported from larger computers to the PC. However, no language was as successful as C in becoming the worldwide standard programming language.

Before diving into C, you might take a few moments to familiarize yourself with some of the hardware and software components of your own PC. The next section introduces you to computer components that C interacts with, such as the operating system, memory, disks, and input/output devices. If you are already familiar with your computer's hardware and software, you might want to skip to Chapter 2, "What Is a Program?" and begin using C right away.

# An Overview of Your Computer

Your computer system consists of two parts: *hardware* and *software*. The hardware consists of all the physical parts of the machine. Hardware has been defined as "anything you can kick." Although this definition is coarse, it illustrates that your computer's hardware consists of whatever components you can touch. The software is everything else. Software is made up of programs and data that interact with your hardware. The C language is an example of software. You can use C to create even more software programs and data.

## Hardware

Figure 1.1 shows a typical PC system. Before using C, you should have a general understanding of what hardware is and how your hardware components work together.

**Figure 1.1**

A typical PC system.

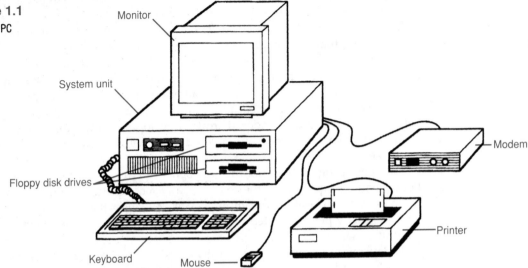

## The System Unit and Memory

The *system unit* is the large, boxlike component of the computer. This unit houses the PC's microchip. You may hear the microchip called the *microprocessor, CPU,* or *central processing unit.* The CPU acts like a traffic cop, directing the flow of information throughout your computer system. The CPU is analogous to the human brain. When you use a computer, you are actually interacting with its CPU. All the other hardware exists so that the CPU can send information to you (through the monitor or printer), and you can give instructions to the CPU (through the keyboard or mouse).

The system unit also houses the computer's internal *memory.* Although the memory has several names, it is commonly referred to as RAM (random-access memory). RAM is where the CPU looks for software and data. When you run a C program, for example, you are instructing your computer's CPU to look in RAM for that program and carry out its instructions. C takes up space in RAM when it is loaded.

RAM is used for many things and is one of the most important components of your computer's hardware. Without RAM, your computer would have no place for its instructions and data. The amount of RAM can also affect the computer's speed. In general, the more RAM your computer has, the more work it can do and the faster it can process data.

A *byte* is a single character of memory.

The amount of RAM is measured by the number of characters it can hold. PCs generally hold approximately 640,000 characters of primary RAM (and can hold additional RAM, discussed a little later). A character in computer terminology is called a *byte*, and a byte can be a letter, number, or special character such as an exclamation point or a question mark. If your computer has 640,000 bytes of RAM, it can hold a total of approximately 640,000 characters.

All the zeros following RAM measurements can get cumbersome. You often see the shortcut notation K (*kilobyte*, which comes from the metric system's *kilo*, meaning 1,000) in place of the last three zeros. In computer terms, K means exactly 1,024 bytes, but this number is usually rounded down to 1,000 to make it easier to remember. That's why 640K means *approximately* 640,000 bytes of RAM.

---

**The Power of Two**

Although K means approximately 1,000 bytes of memory, K equates to 1,024. Computers function using *on* and *off* states of electricity. These are called *binary* states. At the computer's lowest level, it does nothing more than turn electricity on and off with many millions of switches called *transistors*. Because these switches have two possibilities, the total number of states of these switches—and thus the total number of states of electricity—equals a number that is a power of 2.

The closest power of 2 to 1,000 is 1,024 (2 to the 10th power). The inventors of computers designed memory so that it is always added in kilobytes, or multiples of 1,024 bytes at a time. Therefore, if you add 128K of RAM to a computer, you are actually adding a total of 131,072 bytes of RAM (128 times 1,024 equals 131,072).

Because K actually means *more* than 1,000, you always get a little more memory than you bargained for! Even though your computer might be rated at 640K, it really holds more than 640,000 bytes (655,360 to be exact). See Appendix A for a more detailed discussion of memory.

---

The limit of RAM is similar to the limits of audiocassette tapes. If a cassette is manufactured to hold 60 minutes of music, it cannot hold 75 minutes of music. Likewise, the total number of characters that make up your program (the C data) and your computer's system programs cannot exceed the RAM's limit (unless you save some of the characters to disk).

You want as much RAM as possible to hold the C compiler, your program, and the system programs. Generally, 640K is ample room for anything you might want to do in C. Computer RAM is relatively inexpensive, so if your computer has fewer than 640K bytes of memory, you should consider purchasing additional memory to increase the total RAM to 640K. You can put more than 640K in most PCs. There are two types of additional RAM: *extended* memory and *expanded* memory. You can access this extra RAM with some C systems, but most newcomers to C programming have no need to worry about RAM beyond 640K.

The computer stores C programs to RAM as you write them. If you have used a word processor before, you have used RAM. As you type words in your word-processed documents, the words appear on the video screen and also go to RAM for storage.

Despite its importance, RAM is only one type of memory in your computer. RAM is *volatile;* that is, when you turn the computer off, all RAM is erased. Therefore, you must store the contents of RAM to a nonvolatile, more permanent memory device (such as a disk) before you turn off your computer. Otherwise, you lose your work.

## Disk Storage

A *disk* is another type of computer memory, sometimes called *external memory.* Disk storage is nonvolatile. When you turn off your computer, the disk's contents do not go away. This is very important. After typing a long C program into RAM, you do not want to retype the same program every time you turn your computer back on. Therefore, after creating a C program, you save the program to disk, where it remains until you're ready to retrieve it again.

Disk storage differs from RAM in ways other than volatility. Disk storage cannot be processed by the CPU. If you have a program or data on disk that you want to use, you must transfer it from the disk into RAM. That is the only way the CPU can work with the program or data. Luckily, most disks hold many times more data than the RAM's 640K. Therefore, if you fill up RAM, you can store its contents on disk and continue working. As RAM continues to fill up, you or your C program can keep storing the contents of RAM to disk.

This might sound complicated, but all you have to understand is that data must be brought into RAM before your computer can process it and saved to disk before you shut your computer off. Most of the time, a C program runs in RAM and brings in data from the disk as needed. Later in the book, you learn that working with disk files is not difficult.

There are two types of disks: *hard disks* and *floppy disks.* Hard disks (sometimes called *fixed disks*) hold much more data and are many times faster to work with than floppy disks. Most of your C programs and data should be stored on your hard disk. Floppy disks are good for backing up hard disks and transferring data and programs from one computer to another. These removable floppy disks are sometimes called *diskettes.* Figure 1.2 shows two common sizes: 5 1/4-inch and 3 1/2-inch disks. These disks can hold from 360K to 1.4 million bytes of data.

Before using a new box of floppy disks, you need to format them (unless you buy ones that are already formatted). Formatting prepares the disks for use on your computer by writing a pattern of paths, called *tracks,* where your data and programs will be stored. Refer to your operating system's instruction manual for the correct formatting procedure. (PC users must use the DOS FORMAT command.)

Disk drives house the disks in your computer. Usually, the disk drives are stored in your system unit. The hard disk stays sealed inside the hard disk drive, and you never remove it (expect for repairs). In general, the floppy disk drives also are contained in the system unit, but with these drives, you must insert and remove your disks manually.

**Figure 1.2**

A 5 1/4-inch disk
and a 3 1/2-inch
disk.

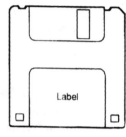

Disk drives have names. The computer's first floppy disk drive is called drive A. The second floppy disk drive, if you have one, is called drive B. The first hard disk (many computers have only one) is called drive C. If you have more than one hard disk, or if your hard disk is logically divided into more than one, the others are named drive D, drive E, and so on.

Disk size is measured in bytes, just as RAM is. Disks can hold many millions of bytes of data. An 80-million-byte hard disk is common. In computer terminology, a million bytes is called a *megabyte* and is abbreviated as M. Therefore, if you have a 60-megabyte hard disk, it can hold approximately 60 million characters of data before it runs out of space.

## The Monitor

The television-like screen is called the *monitor*. Sometimes the monitor is called the CRT (which stands for *cathode ray tube*, the primary component of the monitor). The monitor is one place where the output of the computer can be sent. When you want to look at a list of names and addresses, you can write a C program to list the information on the monitor.

The advantage of screen output over printing is that screen output is faster and does not waste paper. Screen output, however, is not permanent. When text is *scrolled* off-screen (displaced by additional text coming on-screen), it is gone, and you may not always be able to see it again.

All monitors have a *cursor*, which is a character such as a blinking underline or rectangle. The cursor moves when you type letters on-screen and always indicates the location of the *next* character to be typed.

Monitors that can display pictures are called *graphics monitors*. Although most PC monitors are capable of displaying graphics and text, some can display only text.

If your monitor cannot display colors, it is called a *monochrome* monitor. Most of today's monitors are color monitors.

The monitor plugs into a *display adapter* located in the system unit. The display adapter determines the amount of resolution and number of possible on-screen colors. *Resolution* refers to the number of row-and-column intersections. The higher the resolution, the more rows and columns are present on-screen, and the sharper the text and graphics appear. Some common display adapters are MCGA, CGA, EGA, VGA, SVGA, and XGA.

## The Printer

The printer provides a more permanent way of recording your computer's results. It is the "typewriter" of the computer. Your printer can print C program output to paper. Generally, you can print anything that appears on your screen. You can use the printer to print checks and envelopes too because most types of paper have been made to work with computer printers.

The two most common PC printers are the *dot-matrix* printer and the *laser* printer. A dot-matrix printer is inexpensive and fast and uses a series of small dots to represent printed text and graphics. A laser printer is faster but more expensive than a dot-matrix printer. The output of a laser printer is much sharper because a laser beam burns toner ink into the paper. For many people, a dot-matrix printer provides all the speed and quality they need for most applications. C can send output to either type of printer.

## The Keyboard

Figure 1.3 shows typical PC keyboards. Most of the keys are the same as those on a standard typewriter. The letter and number keys in the center of the keyboard produce their indicated characters on-screen. If you want to type an uppercase letter, be sure to press one of the Shift keys before typing the letter. Pressing the Caps Lock key puts the keyboard into an all-uppercase mode, but you still must press the Shift key to type one of the special characters above a number. For instance, to type the percent sign (%), you press Shift-5, even with Caps Lock on.

Like the Shift keys, the Alt and Ctrl keys can be used with other keys. Some C programs require that you press Alt or Ctrl before pressing another key. For instance, if your C program prompts you to press Alt-F, you should press the Alt key, then press F while still holding down Alt, and then release both keys. Do not hold them both down for long, however, or the computer keeps repeating your keystrokes as if you typed them more than once.

The key marked Esc is called the *escape* key. In many C programs, you can press Esc to "escape" out of, or exit from, something you started and then want to stop. For example, if you prompt your C compiler for help and then you no longer need the help message, you can press Esc to remove the help message from the screen.

The group of numbers and arrows on the far right of the keyboard is called the *numeric keypad*. People familiar with a 10-key adding machine usually prefer to enter numbers from the keypad rather than from the top row of the alphabetic key section. The numbers on the keypad work only when you press the Num Lock key. If you press Num Lock a second time, you disable these number keys and make the arrow keys work again. To prevent confusion, many keyboards have separate arrow keys and a keypad used solely for numbers.

**Figure 1.3**
Various PC
keyboards.

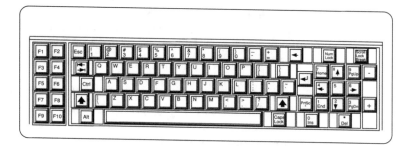

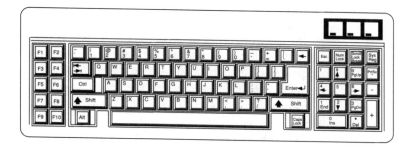

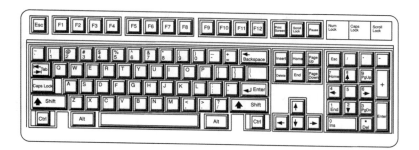

The arrows help you move the cursor from one area of the screen to another. To move the cursor toward the top of the screen, for example, you need to press the up-arrow key repeatedly. To move the cursor to the right, you press the right-arrow key. Do not confuse the Backspace key with the left-arrow key. Pressing Backspace moves the cursor backward one character at a time—erasing everything as it moves. Pressing the left-arrow key moves the cursor backward without erasing.

The keys marked Insert and Delete (Ins and Del on some keyboards) are useful for editing. Your C program editor probably takes advantage of these two keys. Insert and Delete work in C programs the same way they work in a word processor's text. If you do not have separate keys labeled Insert and Delete, you probably need to press Num Lock and use the keypad key 0 (for Insert) and period (for Delete).

PgUp and PgDn are the keys to press when you want to scroll the screen (that is, move your on-screen text either up or down). The screen acts like a camera that pans up and down your C programs. You can move down through text by pressing PgDn, and up through the text by pressing PgUp. (As with Insert and Delete, you may have to use the keypad for these operations.)

The keys labeled F1 through F12 (some keyboards go only to F10) are called *function keys*. The function keys are located either across the top of the alphabetic section or to the left of it. These keys perform advanced functions. When you press one of them, you usually want to issue a complex command, such as searching for a specific word in a program. The function keys in your C program, however, do not necessarily produce the same results as they might in another program, such as a word processor. Functions keys are *application-specific*.

> **Caution:** Computer keyboards have a key for number 1. Do not substitute the lowercase L (*l*) to represent the number 1, as you might on a typewriter. To C, a 1 is very different from the letter *l*. You should be careful also to use 0 when you mean zero, and *O* when you want the uppercase letter *O*.

## The Mouse

The mouse, a relatively new kind of input device, moves the cursor to any location on-screen. If you have never used a mouse before, you should take a little time to become skillful in moving the cursor with it. When you use a C editor (described in the next chapter, "What Is a Program?"), you might use a mouse for selecting commands from the editor's menus.

Mouse devices have two or three buttons. Most of the time, pressing the third button produces the same results as simultaneously pressing both keys on a two-button mouse.

> **For Related Information**
>
> ◆ "Using a Program Editor," p. 31

## The Modem

A PC *modem* enables your PC to communicate with other computers over telephone lines. Some modems, called *external modems*, sit in a box outside the computer. *Internal modems* reside inside the system unit. It does not matter which one you have, because they operate identically.

Some people have modems so that they can share data between their computer and that of a long-distance friend or off-site co-worker. You can write programs in C that communicate with your modem.

---

**A Modem by Any Other Name...**

The term *digital computer* comes from the fact that your computer operates on binary (on and off) digital impulses of electricity. These digital states of electricity are perfect for your computer's equipment, but they cannot be sent over normal telephone lines. Telephone signals are called *analog* signals, which are much different from the binary digital signals in your PC.

Therefore, before your computer can transmit data over a telephone line, the information must be *modulated* (converted) into analog signals. The receiving computer must then have a way to *demodulate*—convert those signals back to digital.

The modem is the means by which computer signals are modulated and demodulated from digital to analog, and from analog to digital. Thus, the device that *modulates* and *demodulates* these signals is called a *modem*.

---

## Software

No matter how fast, large, and powerful your computer's hardware is, its software determines what work gets done and how the computer does it. Software is to a computer what music is to a stereo system. You store software on the computer's disk and load it into your computer's memory when you are ready to process the software, just as you store music on a tape and play it when you want to hear music.

### Programs and Data

No doubt you have heard the phrase *data processing*. This is what computers really do: they take data and manipulate it into meaningful output. The meaningful output is called *information*. Figure 1.4 shows the *input-process-output* model, which is the foundation of everything that happens in the computer.

In Chapter 2, "What Is a Program?," you learn the mechanics of programs. For now, you should know that the programs you write in C process the data that you input into the programs. Both data and programs make up the software. The hardware acts as a vehicle to gather the input and produce the output. Without software, computers would be worthless, just as an expensive stereo would be useless without some way of playing music so that you can hear it.

**Figure 1.4**

Data processing
at its most
elementary level.

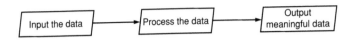

The input comes from input devices, such as keyboards, modems, and disk drives. The CPU processes the input and sends the results to the output devices, such as the printer and the monitor. A C payroll program might get its input (the hours worked) from the keyboard. The program then instructs the CPU to calculate the payroll amount for each employee listed in the disk files. After processing the payroll, the program can then print checks on the printer.

---

**For Related Information**

◆ "Understanding Computer Programs," p. 28
◆ "Considering Program Design," p. 29

---

## MS-DOS

MS-DOS (Microsoft Disk Operating System) is a system that enables your C programs to interact with hardware. MS-DOS (commonly called DOS for short) is always loaded into RAM when you power-up your computer. DOS controls more than just the disks; DOS is there so that your programs can communicate with all the computer's hardware, including the monitor, keyboard, and printer.

Figure 1.5 illustrates the concept of DOS as the "go-between" for your computer's hardware and software. Because DOS understands how to control every device hooked to your computer, it stays in RAM and waits for a hardware request. For instance, printing the words *C is fun!* on your printer takes many computer instructions. However, you do not have to worry about all those instructions. When the C program wants to print something, it tells DOS to print it. DOS always knows how to send information to the printer, so it takes the C program requests and does the work of routing that data to the printer.

Many people program computers for years and never take the time to learn why DOS is there. You do not have to be an expert in DOS, or even know more than a few simple DOS commands, to be proficient with your PC. Nevertheless, DOS does some things that C cannot do, such as formatting disks and copying files to them. As you learn more about the computer, you may see the need to understand DOS better. For a good introduction to using DOS, refer to the book *MS-DOS 6 QuickStart* (Que Corporation).

**Note:** As mentioned, DOS always resides in RAM and is loaded when you start your computer. This is done automatically so that you can use the computer and program in C without worrying about how to get DOS into RAM. It is important to remember that DOS always takes up some of your total RAM.

**Figure 1.5**

DOS interfaces between hardware and software.

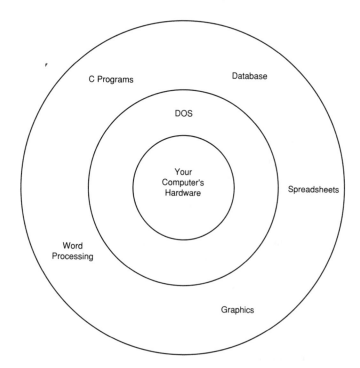

Figure 1.6 shows you the placement of DOS, C, and your remaining data area in RAM. This is a typical way to represent RAM—several boxes stacked on top of each other. Each memory location (each byte) has a unique *address*, just as everyone's residence has a unique address. The first address in memory begins at 0, the second RAM address is 1, and so on, until the last RAM location many thousands of bytes later.

Your operating system (whether you use MS-DOS, PC DOS, DR DOS, or UNIX) takes part of the first few thousand bytes of memory. The amount of RAM that DOS takes varies with each computer's configuration. When you work in C, the C system sits on top of DOS, leaving you with the rest of RAM for your program and data. This explains why you may have a total of 512K of RAM and still not have enough memory to run some programs—DOS is sitting there, taking some of it for itself.

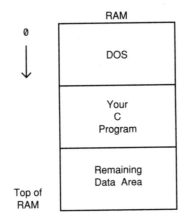

**Figure 1.6**

After MS-DOS and a C program are loaded, there is less RAM for data.

## Summary

C is an efficient, powerful, and popular programming language. Whether you are new to C or an experienced programmer, C is all you need to produce computer programs that make the computer work the way you want it to.

This chapter presented the background of C by walking you through the history of the C programming language. The chapter also compared C with other programming languages and provided an overview of microcomputers, computer hardware, and software.

The rest of this book is devoted to teaching you C. The next chapter explains program concepts so that you can begin to write C programs.

## Review Questions

Answers to review questions are in Appendix B.

1. What is the name of one of the programming languages that C was developed from?

2. In what decade was C developed?

3. True or false: C is too large to fit on many microcomputers.

4. Which usually holds more data: RAM or the hard disk?

5. What device is needed for your PC to communicate over telephone lines?

6. Which of the following device types best describes the mouse?

   a. Storage

   b. Input

   c. Output

   d. Processing

7. What key would you press to turn off the numbers on the numeric keypad?

8. What operating system is written almost entirely in C?

9. Why is RAM considered volatile?

10. True or false: The greater the resolution, the better the appearance of graphics on-screen.

11. Exactly how many bytes is 512K?

12. What does *modem* stand for?

# CHAPTER 2

# What Is a Program?

This chapter introduces you to fundamental programming concepts. The task of programming computers has been described as rewarding, challenging, easy, difficult, fast, or slow. Actually, it is a combination of all these descriptions. Writing complex programs to solve advanced problems can be frustrating and time-consuming, but you can have fun along the way, especially with the rich assortment of features C has to offer.

The concept of programming is described, from a program's inception to its execution on your computer. The most difficult part of programming is breaking up the problem into logical steps the computer can carry out. Before you finish this chapter, you will have typed and executed your first C program.

The following topics are covered:

- ◆ The concept of programming
- ◆ The program's output
- ◆ Program design
- ◆ Using an editor
- ◆ Using a compiler
- ◆ Entering and running a C program
- ◆ Handling errors

After you complete this chapter, you should be ready to learn the C programming language elements in greater detail.

# Understanding Computer Programs

Before you can make C work for you, you must write a C program. You have seen the word *program* used several times in this book. A program is a set of instructions that enables a computer to perform certain tasks.

Keep in mind that computers are only machines. They're not smart; in fact, they're quite the opposite! They don't do anything until they are given very detailed instructions. A word processor, for example, is a program somebody wrote—in a language such as C—that tells your computer exactly how to behave when you type words into it.

If you have ever followed a recipe, you are familiar with the concept of programming. A recipe is a "program," or a set of instructions, telling you how to prepare a certain dish. A good recipe lists these instructions in their correct order and with enough description so that you can carry out the directions successfully, without any need to make assumptions.

The program tells the computer what to do.

If you want your computer to help with your budget, keep track of names and addresses, or compute your gas mileage, it needs a program telling it how to do those things. You can supply that program in two ways: buy a program that somebody else wrote or write the program yourself.

Writing the program yourself has a big advantage for many applications: the program does exactly what *you* want it to do. If you buy one that is already written, you have to adapt your needs to those of whoever wrote the program. This is where C comes in. With the C programming language (and a little study), you can make your computer carry out your own tasks precisely.

To give C programming instructions to your computer, you need an *editor* and a *C compiler*. An editor is similar to a word processor; it is a program that lets you type a C program into memory, make changes (such as moving, copying, inserting, and deleting text), and save the program more permanently in a disk file. After you use the editor to type the program, you must compile it before you can run it.

The C programming language is called a *compiled* language. You cannot write a C program and run it on your computer unless you have a C compiler. The compiler takes your C language instructions and translates them into a form that your computer can read. A C compiler is the tool your computer needs to understand the C language instructions in your programs. Many compilers come with their own built-in editor. If yours does, you probably feel that your C programming is more integrated. A later section in this chapter discusses editors and compilers in more detail.

> **Note:** If you have a C++ compiler, such as Borland's Turbo C++ or Microsoft's Visual C++, you can use the compiler for C programs as long as the program file names end in .C. Later, if you learn C++, the compiler will work for C++ programs as well.

To some beginning programmers, the process of compiling a program before running it may seem like an added and meaningless step. If you first learned programming by using a dialect of the BASIC programming language, you may not have heard of a compiler or understand the need for one. That's because BASIC (also QBasic, APL, and some versions of other computer languages) is not a compiled language but an *interpreted* language. Instead of translating the entire program into machine-readable form (as a compiler does in one step), an interpreter translates each program instruction—and then executes it—before translating the next one. The difference between the two is subtle, but the bottom line is not: compilers produce *much* more efficient and faster-running programs than interpreters do. This seemingly extra step of compiling is worth the effort (and with today's compilers, there is not much extra effort needed).

Because computers are machines that do not think, the instructions you write in C must be very detailed. You cannot assume that your computer understands what to do if some instruction is not in your program, or if you write an instruction that does not conform to C language requirements.

After you write and compile a C program, you must *run* (execute) it. Otherwise, your computer does not know that you want it to follow the instructions in the program. Just as a cook must follow a recipe's instructions before the dish is made, a computer must execute a program's instructions before the computer can accomplish what you want it to do. When you run a program, you are telling the computer to carry out your instructions.

---

**The Program and Its Output**

While you are programming, remember the difference between a program and its output. Your program contains only the C instructions that you write. But the computer follows your instructions only *after* you run the program.

Throughout this book, you often see a *program listing* (that is, the C instructions in the program) followed by the results that occur when you run the program. The results are the output of the program, and they go to an output device, such as the screen, the printer, or a disk file.

---

# Considering Program Design

Design your programs before you type them.

You must plan your programs before typing them into your C editor. When builders construct houses, for example, they don't immediately grab their lumber and tools and start building! They first find out what the owner of the house wants; then they draw up the plans, order the materials, gather the workers, and finally start building the house.

The hardest part of writing a program is breaking it into logical steps the computer can follow. Learning the C language is a requirement, but it is not the only thing to consider. There is a method of writing programs, a formal procedure you should learn, that makes your programming job easier. To write a program, you should follow these steps:

1. Define the problem to be solved with the computer.

2. Design the program's output (what the user should see).

3. Break the problem into logical steps to achieve this output.

4. Write the program (using the editor).

5. Compile the program.

6. Test the program to make sure it performs as you expect.

As you can see from this procedure, the typing of a program occurs toward the end of programming. This is important, because you first need to plan how to tell the computer how to perform each task.

A computer can perform instructions only one step at a time. You must assume that your computer has no previous knowledge of the problem, so it is up to you to provide that knowledge, which, after all, is what a good recipe does. It would be a foolish recipe for baking a cake if the recipe said only to "bake the cake." Why? Because such a short instruction *assumes* too much about the knowledge of the baker. But even if a recipe is written out step-by-step, care must be taken (through planning) to be certain that the steps are in the right order. Wouldn't it be foolish also to instruct a baker to put the ingredients into the oven before stirring them?

Throughout the book, the preceding programming procedure is adhered to as each program is presented. Before you see the actual program, you see it described in pseudocode. The goals of the program are presented first, then these goals are broken down into logical steps, and finally the program is written.

Designing the program in advance makes the entire program structure more accurate and keeps you from having to make many changes later. A builder, for example, knows that a room is much harder to add after the house is built. So, if you do not properly plan every step, it is going to take you longer to create the final, working program. It is always more difficult to make major changes after your program is written.

Planning and developing according to these six steps become much more important as you write longer and more complicated programs. Throughout this book, you learn helpful tips for program design. For now, it's time to launch into C so that you can experience typing your own program and seeing it run.

# Using a Program Editor

The instructions in a C program are called the *source code*. You type source code into the computer's memory by using your program editor. After you type the C source code (your program), you should save it to a disk file before compiling and running the program. Most C compilers expect C source programs to be stored in files with file names ending in .C. For example, the following are valid file names for most C compilers:

MYPROG.C

SALESACT.C

EMPLYEE.C

ACCREC.C

Many C compilers include a built-in editor. Two of the most popular C compilers are Borland's Turbo C++ and Microsoft's Visual C++. Both conform to the ANSI C standard and include their own extended language elements. (Remember that these C++ compilers run C programs.) These two compilers run in fully integrated environments that relieve the programmer from having to worry about finding a separate program editor or learning many compiler-specific commands.

Figure 2.1 shows a Turbo C++ screen. Across the top of the screen are commands for pull-down menus that offer editing, compiling, and running options. The middle of the screen contains the body of the program editor, and this is the area where the program goes. From this screen, you type, edit, compile, and run your C source programs. Without an integrated environment, you would have to start an editor, type your program, save the program to disk, exit the editor, run the compiler, and only *then* run the compiled program from the operating system. With Turbo C++ and Visual C++, you simply type the program into the editor and then—in one step—choose the proper menu option that compiles and runs the program.

If you do not own an integrated environment such as Turbo C++ or Visual C++, you need to find a program editor. Word processors can act as editors, but you must learn how to save and load files in a true ASCII text format. It is often easier to use an editor than it is to make a word processor work like one.

On PCs, all DOS versions starting with 5.0 come with a nice, full-screen editor, called EDIT. It offers menu-driven commands and full cursor-control capabilities. EDIT is a simple program to use and is a good program editor for beginners. Refer to your DOS manual or a good book on DOS, such as *MS-DOS 6 QuickStart* (Que Corporation), for more information on this program editor.

Another editor, called EDLIN, is available for all versions of DOS. EDLIN is a line editor that does not allow full-screen cursor control, and it requires you to learn some cryptic commands. The advantage to learning EDLIN, however, is that it is always included with any PC.

**Figure 2.1**

Turbo C/C++'s
integrated
environment.

```
 ≡  File  Edit  Search  Run  Compile  Debug  Project  Options    Window  Help
 ┌─[■]─────────────────────── \CBOOK\C10AGE.C ────────────────2=[↑]─┐
 /* Filename: C10AGE.C
    Program that helps ensure age values are reasonable */
 #include <stdio.h>
 main()
 {
    int age;

    printf("What is your age");
    if ((age > 10) && (age < 100))
      { printf(" \x07 \x07 \n");    /* Beep twice */
        printf("*** The age must be between 10 and 100 ***\n"); }
    else
        { printf("You entered a valid age."); }
    return;
 ───── 1:1 ─────◄█──────────────────────────────────────────────
 ─────────────────────────────── Message ───────────────────────1─



 F1 Help  F2 Save  F3 Open  Alt-F9 Compile  F9 Make  F10 Menu
```

You can pick from
among the many
available editors.

If you use a computer other than a PC, such as a UNIX-based minicomputer or a mainframe, you need to learn which editors are available. Most UNIX systems include the vi editor. If you program on a UNIX operating system, it is worth your time to learn the vi editor. It is to UNIX what EDLIN is to PC operating systems, and vi is available on almost every UNIX computer in the world.

Mainframe users have other editors available, such as the ISPF editor. You may have to check with your systems department to find an editor accessible from your account.

**Note:** Because this book teaches the ANSI C standard programming language, no attempt is made to tie in specific editor or compiler commands—there are too many on the market to cover them all in one book. As long as you write ANSI C-specific programs, the tools you use to edit, compile, and run those programs are secondary; your goal of good programming is the result of whatever applications you produce.

**For Related Information**

◆ "Looking at a C Program," p. 39

# Using a C Compiler

After you type and edit your C program's source code, you must compile the program. The process you use to compile the program depends on the version of C and the computer you are using. Turbo C++ users need only press Alt-R to compile and run their programs. Most PC C compilers can produce an *executable* file whose name begins with the same name as the source code but ends with an EXE file extension. For example, if your source program were named GRADEAVG.C, the PC would produce a compiled file called GRADEAVG.EXE, which you could execute at the DOS prompt by entering the name GRADEAVG.

> **Note:** Each program in this book contains a comment that specifies a recommended file name for the source program. You do not have to follow the file-naming conventions used in this book; the file names are only suggestions. If you use a mainframe, you need to follow the data-set-naming conventions set up by your system administrator. Each program name on the sample disk (see the order form at the back of the book), however, matches the file name of the corresponding program listing in this book.

UNIX users generally have to use the cc compiler. This produces an executable file whose name (by default) is A.OUT. You can then run the A.OUT file from the UNIX prompt. Mainframe users generally have company-standard procedures for compiling C source programs and storing their results in a test account.

Unlike many other programming languages, a C program must be routed through a *preprocessor* before it is compiled. C source code can contain *preprocessor directives* that control the way programs compile. The preprocessor step is performed automatically by your C compiler, so it requires no additional effort or commands to learn on your part.

You may have to refer to your compiler's reference manuals or to your company's system personnel to learn how to compile programs for your programming environment. Again, learning the programming environment is not as critical as learning the C language. The compiler is just a way to transform your program from a source code file to an executable file.

A program must go through one additional stage after compiling and before running. It is called the *linking*, or *link editing*, stage. When your program is linked, needed run-time information (which is not always available to the compiler) is supplied to the program. You can also combine several compiled programs into one executable program by linking them. Most of the time, however, the compiler initiates the link editing stage (this is especially true with integrated compilers such as Turbo C++ and Visual C++), and you do not have to worry about the process.

Figure 2.2 shows the steps that your C compiler and link editor perform to produce an executable program.

**Figure 2.2**

Compiling C
source code into
an executable
program.

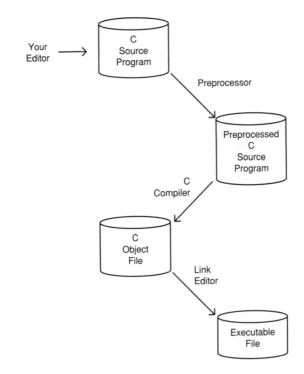

## Running a Sample Program

Before delving into the specifics of the C language, you should take a few moments to become familiar with your editor and C compiler. Starting with the next chapter, "Your First C Program," you should put all your concentration into the C programming language and not worry about using a specific editor or compiling environment.

Following this paragraph is a block of *pseudocode*, which describes in English what you want the program to do. Following the pseudocode is a short program. Start your editor of choice and type the program into your computer. Be as accurate as possible—a single typing mistake can cause the C compiler to generate a series of errors. You do not have to understand the program's content at this point; the goal is simply to give you practice in using your editor and compiler.

*Identify the program and include the necessary header file. This program will print a name five times and then make a beep sound. Define a constant called BELL, which is the character code for a beep. A counter is needed that counts from 1 to 5, so make ctr an integer equal to 0. A variable is needed to hold the user's answer, so make fname a character array that holds 20 elements.*

*Ask the user for his or her first name. Get the user's answer and assign it to fname. If the counter is less than 5, print the user's answer, add 1 to the counter, and repeat. Make a beep sound.*

```
/* Filename: C2FIRST.C
   Requests a name, prints the name 5 times, and rings a bell */

#include <stdio.h>
#define BELL '\a'

main()
{
   int ctr=0;            /* Integer variable to count through loop */
   char fname[20];       /* Define character array to hold name    */

   printf("What is your first name?");     /* Prompt the user */
   scanf(" %s", fname);        /* Get the name from the keyboard */
   while (ctr < 5)                  /* Loop to print the name */
   {                               /* exactly 5 times          */
     printf("%s\n", fname);
     ctr++;
   }
   printf("%c", BELL);              /* Ring the terminals bell */
   return;
}
```

Again, be as accurate as possible. In most programming languages—and especially in C—the characters you type in a program must be accurate. In this sample C program, for instance, you see () (parentheses), [ ] (brackets), and {} (braces), but you cannot use them interchangeably.

The *comments* (words between the symbols /* and */) to the right of some lines do not need to end in the same alignments shown in the listing. However, you should become familiar with your editor and learn to space characters accurately so that you can type this program exactly as shown.

Compile the program and execute it. Granted, the first time you do this, you may have to check your reference manuals or contact someone who already knows your C compiler. But do not worry about damaging your computer: nothing you do from the keyboard can harm the physical computer. The worst thing you can do at this point is erase portions of your compiler software or change the compiler's options—all of which can be easily corrected by reloading the compiler from its original source. (It is only remotely likely that you would do anything harmful like this, even if you are a beginner.)

# Handling Errors

Because you are typing instructions for a machine, you must be very accurate. If you misspell a word, leave out a quotation mark, or make another mistake, your C compiler informs you with an error message. In Turbo C and QuickC, the error probably appears in a separate window, as shown in Figure 2.3. The most common error is a *syntax error* and usually implies a misspelled word.

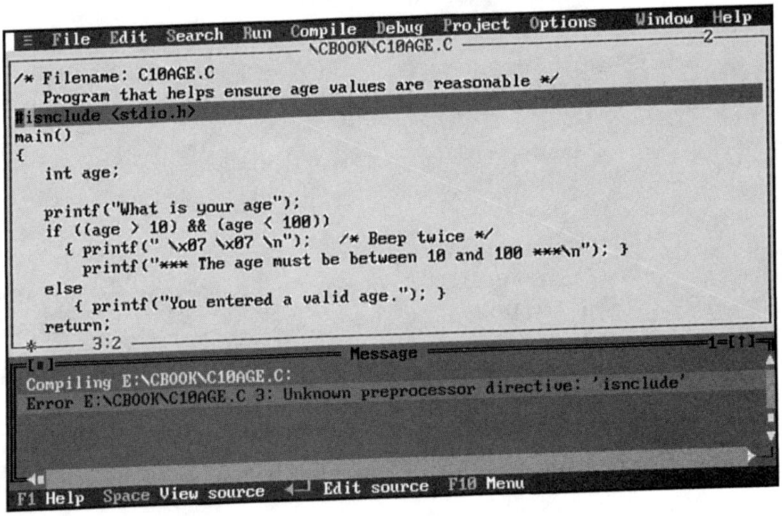

**Figure 2.3**

The compiler reporting a program error.

```
 ≡  File  Edit  Search  Run  Compile  Debug  Project  Options   Window  Help
                          ─ \CBOOK\C10AGE.C ─────────────────────2─
/* Filename: C10AGE.C
   Program that helps ensure age values are reasonable */
#isnclude <stdio.h>
main()
{
    int age;

    printf("What is your age");
    if ((age > 10) && (age < 100))
       { printf(" \x07 \x07 \n");    /* Beep twice */
         printf("*** The age must be between 10 and 100 ***\n"); }
    else
         { printf("You entered a valid age."); }
    return;
 ─ 3:2 ─                                                    1=[↑]─
[■]═══════════════════════ Message ════════════════════════
Compiling E:\CBOOK\C10AGE.C:
Error E:\CBOOK\C10AGE.C 3: Unknown preprocessor directive: 'isnclude'


F1 Help  Space View source  ←┘ Edit source  F10 Menu
```

When you get an error message (or more than one), you must return to the program editor and correct the error. If you don't understand the error, you may have to check your reference manual or scour your program's source code until you find the offending problem.

## Getting the Bugs Out

One of the first computers, owned by the military, refused to print some important data one day. After its programmers tried for many hours to find the problem in the program, a programmer by the name of Grace Hopper decided to check out the printer.

She found a small moth lodged between two important wires. When she removed the moth, the printer started working perfectly (although the moth did not have the same luck).

The late Grace Hopper retired as an admiral from the Navy. Although she was responsible for developing many important computer concepts (she was the author of the original COBOL language), she may be best known for discovering the first computer bug.

Ever since Admiral Hopper discovered that moth, errors in computer programs have been known as *computer bugs*. When you test your programs, you may have to *debug* them—remove the errors by correcting typing mistakes or changing the logic so that your program does exactly what you want it to do.

After you have used the editor to type your program correctly (and you get no compile errors), the program should run correctly by asking for your first name and then printing it five times on-screen. After the program prints your name for the fifth time, you hear the computer's bell ring.

This example helps illustrate the difference between a program and its output. You must type the program (or load one from disk) and then run the program to see its output.

## Summary

After reading this chapter, you should understand the steps necessary to write a C program. You know that planning makes writing the program much easier and that your program's instructions produce the output only after you run the program.

You also learned how to use your program editor and compiler. Some program editors are as powerful as word processors. Now that you know how to run C programs, you are ready to start learning the C programming language itself.

## Review Questions

Answers to review questions are in Appendix B.

1. What is a program?

2. What are the two ways to obtain a program that does what you want?

3. True or false: Computers can think.

4. What is the difference between a program and its output?

5. What do you use for typing C programs into the computer?

6. What file name extension should all C programs have?

7. Why is typing the program one of the *last* steps in the programming process?

**8.** What does the term *debug* mean?

**9.** Why is it important to write ANSI C-compatible programs?

**10.** True or false: You must link a program before compiling it.

# Your First C Program

Before looking at the C language specifically, many people like to "walk through" a few simple programs to get the overall feel of what a C program is like. That is the purpose of this chapter. Along the way, you are introduced to some important C language commands and other elements. The rest of the book covers these commands and elements in more detail.

This chapter introduces the following topics:

♦ An overview of C programs and their structure

♦ Variables and constants

♦ Simple math operators

♦ Screen output format

The chapter also gives you a few general tools to familiarize you with the C programming language. The rest of the book concentrates on more specific areas of the language itself.

## Looking at a C Program

Figure 3.1 shows the outline of a typical small C program. No C commands are shown in the figure. Although there is much more to a program than this outline implies, this is the general format of the beginning examples in this book.

**Figure 3.1**

A skeleton outline of a simple C program.

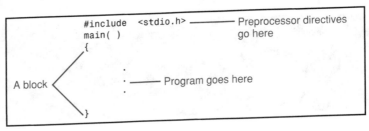

To get acquainted with C programs as quickly as possible, you should look at a C program in its entirety. Here is a listing of a very simple C program. It doesn't do much, but it enables you to see the general format of C programming. The next few sections discuss elements from this program and other programs. You may not understand everything in this program, even after finishing the chapter, but it is a good place to start.

```
/* Filename: C3FIRST.C
    Initial C program that demonstrates the C comments
    and shows a few variables and their definitions */
#include <stdio.h>
main()
{
    int i, j;      /* These 3 lines define 4 variables */
    char c;
    float x;

    i = 4;         /* i and j are assigned integer values */
    j = i + 7;
    c = 'A';       /* All character constants are
                      enclosed in single quotes */

    x = 9.087;     /* x requires a floating-point value since it
                      was defined as a floating-point variable */

    x = x * 4.5; /* Change what was in x with a formula */

    printf("%d %d %c %f", i, j, c, x);
    /* Sends the values of the variables to the screen */

    return;    /* Should end programs and functions with return */

}
```

For now, become familiar with this overall program. See whether you can understand any part or all of it. If you are new to programming, you should know that the computer looks at each line of the program, starting with the first line and working its way down, until the computer has carried out all the instructions in the program. (Of course, you first need to compile and link the program, as described in Chapter 2.)

The output of this program is minimal: it simply displays four values on-screen after performing some assignments and calculations of arbitrary values. Just concentrate on the general format at this point.

## The Format of a C Program

C is a free-form language.

Unlike some other programming languages, such as COBOL, C is a *free-form* language. That is, programming statements can start in any column of any line. You can insert blank lines in a program if you want. This sample program is called C3FIRST.C. (You can find the name of each program in this book in the first line of each program listing.) It contains several blank lines to help separate parts of the program. In a simple program such as this, the separation is not as critical as it might be in a longer, more complex program.

Generally, spaces in C programs are free-form as well. Your goal should be to make your programs not as compact as possible but as readable as possible. For example, the C3FIRST.C program shown in the preceding section could be rewritten as follows:

```
/* Filename: C3FIRST.C Initial C program that demonstrates the
C comments and shows a few variables and their definitions */
#include <stdio.h>
main() {int i, j;
/* These 3 lines define 4 variables */
char c;float x;i=4;/* i and j are assigned integer values  */
j=i+7;c='A';/* All character constants are enclosed in single
quotes */x=9.087;/* x requires a floating-point value since it
was defined as a floating-point variable */x=x*4.5;/* Change
what was in x with a formula */printf("%d %d %c %f",i,j,c,x);
/* Sends the values of the variables to the screen */return;
/* Should end programs and functions with return*/}
```

To the C compiler, the two programs are exactly the same, and they produce the same result. To people who have to read the program, however, the first style is *much* more readable. Granted, this compressed version is an extreme example.

## Readability Is the Key

As long as programs do their job and produce correct output, who cares how well they are written? Even in today's world of fast computers and abundant memory and disk space, *you* should still care. Even if no one else ever looks at your C programs, you might need to make changes at a later date. The more readable you make your programs, the faster you can find what needs changing and then make your changes.

If you work as a programmer for a company, you can almost certainly expect to modify someone else's source code, and others will modify yours. In programming departments, it is said that long-term employees write readable programs. Given the new global economy and all the changes that will face businesses in the years ahead, companies are seeking programmers who write for the future. Consequently, programmers whose programs are straightforward, readable, abundant with *white space* (separating lines and spaces), and devoid of hard-to-read "tricks" that make for messy programs may have the best employment opportunities.

Use lots of white space so that you can have separate lines and spaces throughout your programs. Notice that the first few lines of C3FIRST.C start in the first column, but the body of the program is indented a few spaces. This helps programmers "zero in" on the important code. When you write programs that contain several sections (called *blocks*), your use of white space helps the reader's eye drop down to and recognize the next indented block.

## Uppercase versus Lowercase

Use lowercase abundantly in C.

Uppercase and lowercase letters are much more significant in C than in most other programming languages. You can see that almost all of C3FIRST.C is in lowercase. The entire C language is in lowercase. For example, you must type the keywords `int`, `char`, and `return` into programs by using lowercase letters. If you use uppercase letters, the C compiler will produce many errors and refuse to compile the program until you correct the errors. Appendix E shows a list of every command in the C programming language. You can see that no commands have uppercase letters.

Many C programmers reserve uppercase letters for some words and messages sent to the screen, printer, or disk file; they use lowercase letters for almost everything else. There is, however, one exception to this rule that you will learn more about in Chapter 6, "Preprocessor Directives," which covers the `#define` preprocessor directive.

The line before `main()`, `#include <stdio.h>`, is not actually a C statement but a *preprocessor directive* that instructs the C compiler to prepare for input and output throughout the program.

## Braces and *main()*

All C programs require the following lines:

```
main()
{
```

A C *block* is enclosed between two braces.

The statements that follow `main()` are the first statements executed. The section of a C program that begins with `main()`, followed by an opening brace (`{`), is called the *main function*. A C program is actually a collection of functions (small sections of code). The function called `main()` is always required and always the first function executed.

In the sample program in this chapter, almost the entire program is main() because the matching closing brace that follows main()'s opening brace is at the end of the program. Everything between two matching braces is called a *block*. You learn more about blocks later. For now, just note that this sample program contains only one function, main(), and the entire function is a single block because there is only one pair of braces.

All *executable* C statements must be followed by a semicolon (;) so that C knows where the statements end. Because the computer ignores all comments, do *not* put semicolons after your comments. Notice that the lines containing main() and the braces do not end with semicolons either. These lines simply define the beginning and end of the function and do not execute.

As you become better acquainted with C, you will learn when to include the semicolon and when to leave it off. Many beginning C programmers learn quickly when semicolons are required; your compiler certainly lets you know if you forget to include a semicolon where one is needed.

Figure 3.2 repeats the sample program shown in Figure 3.1. It contains additional markings to help acquaint you with these new terms as well as other items described in the rest of this chapter.

> All executable C statements must end with a semicolon (;).

**Figure 3.2**

The parts of the sample program.

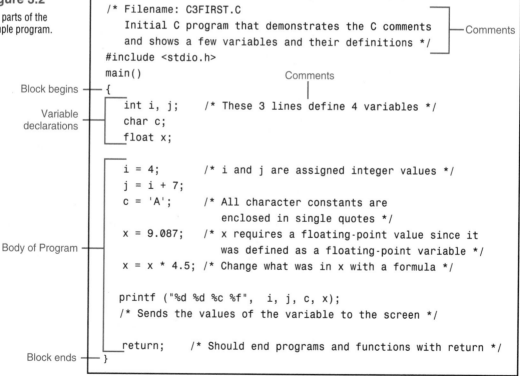

```
/* Filename: C3FIRST.C
   Initial C program that demonstrates the C comments      ── Comments
   and shows a few variables and their definitions */
#include <stdio.h>
main()                                Comments
{
    int i, j;    /* These 3 lines define 4 variables */
    char c;
    float x;

    i = 4;       /* i and j are assigned integer values */
    j = i + 7;
    c = 'A';     /* All character constants are
                    enclosed in single quotes */
    x = 9.087;   /* x requires a floating-point value since it
                    was defined as a floating-point variable */
    x = x * 4.5; /* Change what was in x with a formula */

    printf ("%d %d %c %f",  i, j, c, x);
    /* Sends the values of the variable to the screen */

    return;      /* Should end programs and functions with return */
}
```

Block begins
Variable declarations
Body of Program
Block ends

## Comments in C

In Chapter 2, you learned the difference between a program and its output. Most users of a program do not see the program itself; they see instead the output from the execution of the program's instructions. Programmers, however, look at the program listings and add new routines, change old ones, and update the program for advancements in computer equipment.

As explained earlier, the readability of a program is important so that you and other programmers can look through it easily. But no matter how clearly you write C programs, you can always enhance their readability by adding comments throughout.

*Comments* are messages that you insert in your C programs, explaining what is going on at that point in the program. For example, if you write a payroll program, you might put a comment before the check-printing routine that describes what is about to happen. You never put C language statements inside a comment, because a comment is a message for people—not computers. The C compiler ignores all comments in every program.

Comments tell *people* what the program is doing.

> **Note:** C comments always begin with a /* symbol and end with a */ symbol.

A comment can span more than one line. Notice in the sample program, C3FIRST.C, that the first three lines are actually a single comment. This comment explains the file name and a little about the program.

Comments can also share lines with other C commands. Several comments are to the right of much of the C3FIRST.C program, explaining what the individual lines do. Use abundant comments, but remember whom they're for: people and not computers. Use comments to help explain your code, but do not *over*comment. For example, even though you may not be familiar with C yet, you can guess easily the purpose of the following statement:

```
printf("C By Example");   /* Print C By Example on the screen */
```

It prints "C By Example" on the screen. Actually, the comment is redundant because it adds nothing to your understanding of the line of code. It would be much better, in this case, to leave out the comment. If you sense that a particular comment would merely echo the C code, omit that comment. Not every line of a C program needs a comment. Comment only when code lines need explaining—in plain English—to the people looking at your program.

It does not matter whether you use uppercase, lowercase, or a mixture of both in your comments because C ignores them. Most C programmers capitalize the first letter of sentences in comments, just as you would in everyday writing. Because only people read comments, use whatever case seems appropriate for the letters in your message.

> **Caution:** C comments cannot be *nested*. That is, you cannot put a comment within another comment. If you do, the C compiler gets confused when it sees a second comment begin before the end of the first comment.

The following section of a C program is illegal because one comment resides within another:

```
sales = 3456.54 * bonus;
/* This is an example of a C program
   /* It does NOT
      comment correctly! */
   The first comment did not end before the second began. */
```

This sometimes confuses programmers who are just learning C, but know another programming language. In C, you cannot *comment out* large sections of code just by inserting /* at the beginning of the section and */ at the end if *any* lines within that section already have comments. In some languages, programmers can comment out several lines in a program so that those lines do not execute. This enables the programmer to test remaining lines independently from those commented out. If you try this in C—and create nested comments—your compiler becomes confused.

---

**Comment As You Go**

Insert your comments *as you write your programs*. You are most familiar with your program's logic at the time you are typing the program into the editor. Some people put off adding comments until after the program is written. More often than not, however, those comments never get put in, or else they are written halfheartedly.

If you comment as you write your code, you can glance back at your comments while working on later sections of the program—instead of having to decipher previous code. This is a great help whenever you want to see something earlier in the program.

---

## Examples

**1.** Suppose you want to write a C program that produces a fancy boxed title containing your name with flashing dots around it (like a marquee). The C code to do this might be difficult to understand and may not, by itself, be clear to others who look at your program later. So, before such code, you might want to insert the following comment:

```
/* The following few lines draw a fancy box around
   a name, then display flashing dots around the
   name like a Hollywood movie marquee. */
```

This does not tell C to do anything because a comment is not a command, but it makes the next few lines of code more understandable to you and other readers of the program. The comment explains in plain English what the program is getting ready to do.

2. You should also put the disk file name of the program in one of the first comments. In the C3FIRST.C program shown earlier, the first line is really the beginning of a comment:

```
/* Filename: C3FIRST.C
```

The comment continues to the following two lines, but this part of it tells you in which disk file the program is stored. Throughout this book, programs have comments that include a possible file name under which the program can be stored. The program names provided begin with C*x*, where *x* is the number of the chapter in which the program appears (for example, C6DEF1.C and C10LOGO.C). This helps you find the programs when they are referred to in another section of the book.

> **Tip:** It may be a good idea to put your name in a comment at the top of your program. If people need to modify the program at a later date, they first might want to consult with you, the original programmer, before they change the code.

## Explaining the Sample Program

Now that you have an overview of a C program, its structure, and its comments, the rest of this chapter walks you through the entire sample program. Do not expect to become a C expert just by reading this section—that is what the rest of the book is for! For now, just sit back and follow this walk-through of the program code.

As described earlier, this sample program contains several comments. The first three lines of the program are one comment:

```
/* Filename: C3FIRST.C
   Initial C program that demonstrates the C comments
   and shows a few variables and their definitions */
```

This comment tells you the file name and explains the purpose of the program. This is not the only comment in the program; others appear throughout the rest of the code.

The next two lines (following the blank separating line) are shown here:

```
main()
{
```

This begins the main() function. Basically, the main() function's opening and closing braces enclose the body of this program and the instructions that execute. C programs often contain more than one function, but they *always* contain a function called main(). The main() function does not need to be the first one, but it usually is. The opening brace begins the first and only block of this program.

When this program is compiled and run, the computer looks for main() and starts executing whatever instruction follows main()'s opening brace. Here are the three lines that follow:

```
int i, j;    /* These 3 lines define 4 variables */
char c;
float x;
```

These three lines define *variables*. A variable definition describes all variables used in that block of code.

A C program processes data into meaningful results. All C programs include the following:

♦ Commands

♦ Data

Data is made up of *variables* and *constants*. As the name implies, a *variable* is data that can change (become variable) while the program runs. A *constant* remains the same. In life, a variable might be your salary. It increases over time (if you are lucky). A constant might be your first name or social security number because each remains with you throughout life and does not usually change.

Chapter 4, "Variables and Constants," fully explains these concepts. However, to give you an overview of the sample program's elements, the following discussion explains variables and constants in this program.

C enables you to use several kinds of *constants*. For now, you simply need to understand that a C constant is any number, character, word, or phrase. The following are all valid C constants:

```
5.6     -45     'Q'     "Mary"     18.67643     0.0
```

As you can see, some constants are numeric, and others are character-based. Two of the constants are enclosed within single or double quotation marks, but the quotation marks themselves are not part of the constants. A single-character constant requires single quotation marks around it; a string of characters, such as "Mary", requires double quotation marks.

Look for the constants in the sample program. You can find these:

```
4    7    'A'    9.087    4.5
```

A variable is like a box that holds something inside your computer. That "something" might be a number or character. You can have as many variables as your program needs to hold data that changes in the program. After you put a value into a variable, it stays in that variable until you change it or put something else into it.

Variables have names so that you can tell them apart. You use the assignment operator, the equal sign (=), to assign values to variables. The statement

```
sales=25000;
```

puts the constant value 25000 into the variable named sales. In the sample program, you can find the following variables:

```
i    j    c    x
```

The three lines of code that follow the opening brace of the sample program define these variables. This variable definition lets the rest of the program know that two integer variables named i and j, as well as a character variable called c and a floating-point variable called x, appear throughout the program. The terms *integer* and *floating-point* basically refer to two different types of numbers: integers are whole numbers, and floating-point numbers contain decimal points.

You can see the variables being assigned values in the next few statements of the sample program:

```
i = 4;      /* i and j are assigned integer values */
j = i + 7;
c = 'A';    /* All character constants are
               enclosed in single quotes */
x = 9.087;  /* x requires a floating-point value since it
               was defined as a floating-point variable */
x = x * 4.5; /* Change what was in x with a formula */
```

The first line puts 4 in the integer variable i. The second line adds 7 to the variable i's value to get 11, which then gets assigned to (or put into) the variable called j. The plus sign (+) in C works just as it does on calculators. The other primary math operators are shown in Table 3.1.

**Table 3.1. The primary math operators.**

| Operator | Meaning | Example |
|----------|----------------|----------|
| + | Addition | 4 + 5 |
| - | Subtraction | 7 - 2 |
| * | Multiplication | 12 * 6 |
| / | Division | 48 / 12 |

The character constant A is assigned to the c variable. The number 9.087 is assigned to the variable called x, and then x is immediately overwritten with a new value: itself (9.087) multiplied by 4.5. This helps illustrate why computer designers use an asterisk (*) for multiplication and not a lowercase x as people generally do to show multiplication: the computer would confuse the variable x with the multiplication symbol x if both were allowed.

> **Tip:** If mathematical operators are on the right side of the equal sign, the math is completely carried out before the assignment is performed.

The next line (after the comment) includes the following special—and, at first, confusing—statement:

```
printf("%d %d %c %f", i, j, c, x);
```

When the program runs and gets to this line, it prints the contents of the four variables to the screen. It does *not* print %d %d %c %f, even though it might look as if it does. The "%d %d %c %f" is called a *format string*, which describes the format of what is to follow. The %d means that a decimal integer prints in that location. The %c and %f mean that a character and a floating-point value, respectively, print in those locations. This should make more sense to you later.

For now, you can ignore format strings inside printf lines until Chapter 7 explains them more fully. The important part of this line is that the four values for i, j, c, and x print on-screen.

The output from this line is as follows:

```
4 11 A 40.891499
```

Because this is the only printf in the program, this is the only output the sample program produces. You might think that the program is rather long for such a small output. After you learn more about C, you should be able to write more useful programs.

The printf is not a C command. You might recall from Chapter 2 that C has no built-in input/output commands. The printf is a built-in *function*, not an actual command. You have seen one function already, main(), which is one *you* write the code for. The C programming designers have already written the code for the printf function. At this point, you can think of printf as being a command that outputs values to the screen, but it is really a built-in function.

To differentiate printf from regular C commands, parentheses are used after the name, as in printf(). All function names have parentheses following them in a C program. Sometimes these parentheses have something between them; at other times they are blank.

The following two lines are the end of the program:

```
    return;    /* Should end programs and functions with return */
}
```

Put a return statement at the end of each function.

The return command simply tells C that this function is finished. C returns control to whatever was controlling the program before it started running. In this case, because there was only one function, control is returned to DOS or to the C editing environment.

Actually, the return statement is optional. C would know when it reached the end of the program without this statement. But it is a good programming practice to put a return statement at the end of every function, including main(). Because some functions require a return statement (if you are returning values), it is better to get in the habit of using them rather than run the risk of leaving one out when you really need it.

The closing brace after the return does two things in this program. It signals the end of a block (begun earlier with the opening brace), which is the end of the main() function, and it signals the end of the program.

**For Related Information**

◆ "Naming Variables," p. 54

◆ "Understanding Variable Types," p. 55

◆ "Assigning Values to Variables," p. 61

◆ "Understanding the *printf()* Function," p. 106

◆ "Printing Strings," p. 106

## Summary

This chapter focused on writing helpful and appropriate comments for your programs. You also learned a little about variables and constants, which hold the program's data. Without them, the term *data processing* would no longer be meaningful.

Now that you have a feel for what a C program looks like, it is time to begin looking at specifics of the commands. Starting with the next chapter, you begin to write your own programs. The next chapter picks up where this one leaves off: it takes a detailed look at constants and variables, and better describes their uses and how you choose their names.

## Review Questions

Answers to review questions are in Appendix B.

1. What must go before and after each comment in a C program?

2. What is a variable?

3. What is a constant?

4. True or false: You can put a comment within another comment.

5. What are four C math operators?

6. What operator puts a value into a variable? (Hint: It is called the assignment operator.)

7. True or false: A variable can consist of only two types: integers and characters.

8. What is the built-in function that writes output to the screen?

9. Is the following a variable name or a string constant?

   ```
   city
   ```

10. What, if anything, is wrong with the following C statement?

    ```
    RETURN;
    ```

# Variables and Constants

To understand data processing with C, you must know how C creates, stores, and manipulates data. By introducing the following topics, this chapter shows you how C handles data:

- ◆ The concepts of variables and constants
- ◆ The types of C variables and constants
- ◆ Special constants
- ◆ Naming and using variables
- ◆ Defining variables
- ◆ Assigning values to variables

Now that you have seen an overview of the C programming language, you can start writing C programs. In this chapter, you begin to write your own programs from scratch.

Garbage in, garbage out!

You learned in the last chapter that C programs consist of commands and data. Data is the heart of all C programs; if you do not correctly define or use variables and constants, your data is inaccurate, and your results are going to be inaccurate as well. A computer adage says that if you put garbage in, you are going to get garbage out. This is very true. People usually blame computers for mistakes, but the computers are not always at fault. Instead, their data is often not entered properly into their programs.

This chapter spends a lot of time focusing on numeric variables and numeric constants. If you are not a "numbers" person, do not fret. Working with numbers is the computer's job. You need to understand only how to tell the computer what you want it to do.

# Variables

Variables have characteristics. When you decide that your program needs another variable, you simply define a new variable, and C makes sure you get it. You define all C variables at the top of whatever block of code needs them. To define a variable, you must understand the following possible characteristics:

- Each variable has a name.
- Each variable has a type.
- Each variable holds a value that you assign to the variable.

The following sections explain each of these characteristics.

## Naming Variables

Because you can have many variables in a single program, you must assign names to them so that you can keep track of them. Variable names are unique, just as house addresses are unique. If two variables have the same name, C will not know which variable you mean when you request one of them.

Variable names can be as short as a single letter or as long as 31 characters. The names must begin with a letter of the alphabet but, after the first letter, they can contain letters, numbers, and underscore (_) characters.

> **Tip:** Spaces are not allowed in variable names, so many programmers use the underscore character to separate parts of variable names. Programmers (as in this book) also embed some uppercase letters in a variable name to indicate parts of the name. Never type a variable's name completely in uppercase letters, however, because they are best left for defined constants, described in Chapter 6.

The following variable names are all valid:

```
salary     aug91_sales     i     indexAge     amount
```

Uppercase letters in variable names are different from lowercase letters. For example, each of the following four variables is viewed differently by a C compiler:

```
sales     Sales     SALES     sALES
```

Be very careful with the Shift key when you type a variable name. Do not inadvertently change the case of a variable name in a program. If you do, C thinks that the two different forms of the name are distinct and separate variables.

Do not give variables the same name as a command or built-in function.

Variables cannot have the same name as a C command or function. Appendix E shows a list of all C command and function names that you must watch out for whenever you are naming variables.

The following are *invalid* variable names:

```
81_sales     Aug91+Sales     MY AGE     printf
```

> **Tip:** Although you can call a variable any name that fits the naming rules (as long as it is not the name of another variable in the program), you should always use meaningful variable names. Give your variables names that help describe the values they are holding.

Keeping track of total payroll in a variable called `totalPayroll`, for example, is easier than when using a variable named `XYZ34`. Even though both names are valid, `totalPayroll` is much more descriptive and easier to remember. By looking at its name, you have a good idea of what the variable holds.

## Understanding Variable Types

Variables can hold different *types* of data. Table 4.1 lists the different types of C variables. For instance, if a variable holds an integer, C assumes that no decimal point or fractional part (the part to the right of the decimal point) exists for the variable's value. A very large number of types are possible in C. For now, the most important types you should concentrate on are `char`, `int`, and `float`. You can insert the prefix `long` to make some of the variables hold larger values than they would hold otherwise. Using an `unsigned` prefix enables variables to hold positive numbers only.

**Table 4.1. Some C variable types.**

| Definition Name | Type |
| --- | --- |
| char | Character |
| unsigned char | Unsigned character |
| signed char | Signed character (same as char) |
| int | Integer |
| unsigned int | Unsigned integer |

*continues*

**Table 4.1. Continued**

| Definition Name | Type |
|---|---|
| signed int | Signed integer (same as `int`) |
| short int | Short integer |
| unsigned short int | Unsigned short integer |
| signed short int | Signed short integer (same as `short int`) |
| long | Long integer |
| long int | Long integer (same as `long`) |
| signed long int | Signed long integer (same as `long int`) |
| unsigned long int | Unsigned long integer |
| float | Floating-point |
| double | Double floating-point |
| long double | Long double floating-point |

The next section describes more fully each of these types. For now, you need to concentrate on the importance of defining them before using them.

## Defining Variables

There are two places where you can define a variable:

♦ After the opening brace of a block of code (usually at the top of a function)

♦ Before a function name (such as before `main()` in the program)

The first of these is the more common and is used throughout much of this book. (If you define a variable before a function name, it is called a *global* variable. Later chapters address the pros and cons of global variables.) To define a variable, you must state its type, followed by its name. In the preceding chapter, you saw a program that defined four variables in the following way:

*Define the variables i and j as integers, then define the variable c as a character, and finally define the variable x as a floating-point variable.*

```
main()
{
    int i, j;    /* These 3 lines define 4 variables */
    char c;
    float x;
    /* Rest of program follows */
```

The first line after the opening brace defines two integer variables named i and j. You have no idea what is inside those variables, however. You generally cannot assume that a variable holds zero—or any other number—until you assign it a value. The first line basically tells C the following:

"I am going to use two integer variables somewhere in this program. Be expecting them. I want them named i and j. When I put a value into i or j, I ensure that the value is an integer."

*Define all variables in a C program before you use them.*

Without such a definition, you could not assign i or j a value later. All variables must be defined before you use them. This does not necessarily hold true in other programming languages, such as QBasic, but it does for C. You could define each of these two variables on lines by themselves, as in the following code:

```
main()
{
    int i;
    int j;
    /* Rest of program follows */
```

You do not gain any readability by doing this, however. Most C programmers prefer to define variables of the same type on the same line.

In the example, the second line after the opening brace defines a character variable called c. Only single characters should be placed there. Next, a floating-point variable called x is defined.

---

**For Related Information**

♦ "Global versus Local Variables," p. 297

♦ "Variable Scope," p. 298

---

## Examples

1. Suppose that you had to keep track of a person's first, middle, and last initials. Because an initial is obviously a character, it would be prudent to define three character variables to hold the three initials. In C, you could do that with the following statement:

```
main()
{
    char first, middle, last;
    /* Rest of program follows */
```

This statement could go after the opening brace of main(). It lets the rest of the program know that you require these three character variables.

**2.** You could define these three variables also on three separate lines although doing so does not necessarily improve readability. This definition could be accomplished with the following:

```
main()
{
    char first;
    char middle;
    char last;
    /* Rest of program follows */
```

**3.** Suppose that you want to keep track of a person's age and weight. If you want to store these values as whole numbers, they would probably go in integer variables. The following statement would define those variables:

```
main()
{
    int age, weight;
    /* Rest of program follows */
```

## Looking at Data Types

You might wonder why it is important to have so many variable types. After all, a number is just a number. But C has more data types than almost all other programming languages. The variable's type is critical, but choosing the type among the many offerings is not as difficult as it may first appear.

The character variable is easy to understand. A character variable can hold only a single character; you cannot put more than a single character into a character variable.

> **Note:** Unlike many other programming languages, C does not have a string variable. To store a string of characters, you must use an *aggregate* variable type that combines other fundamental types, such as an array. Chapter 5, "Character Arrays and Strings," explains this more fully.

Integers hold whole numbers. Although mathematicians may cringe at this definition, an integer is really just any number that does not contain a decimal point. All the following expressions are integers:

```
45      -932      0      12      5421
```

Floating-point numbers contain decimal points. They are known as *real* numbers to mathematicians. Any time you need to store a salary, a temperature, or any other number that may have a fractional part (a decimal portion), you must store it in a floating-point variable. All the following expressions are floating-point numbers, and any floating-point variable can hold them:

```
45.12     -2344.5432    0.00    .04594
```

Sometimes you need to keep track of very large numbers; at other times, you need to work with smaller numbers. Table 4.2 shows a list of ranges that each C variable type might hold.

**Caution:** All true ANSI C programmers know that they cannot count on using the exact values in Table 4.2 on every computer that uses C. These ranges are typical on a PC but may be much different on another computer. Use this table only as a guide.

### Table 4.2. Typical ranges that C variables might hold.

| Type | Range* |
| --- | --- |
| char | −128 to 127 |
| unsigned char | 0 to 255 |
| signed char | −128 to 127 |
| int | −32768 to 32767 |
| unsigned int | 0 to 65535 |
| signed int | −32768 to 32767 |
| short int | −32768 to 32767 |
| unsigned short int | 0 to 65535 |
| signed short int | −32768 to 32767 |
| long int | −2147483648 to 2147483647 |
| signed long int | −2147483648 to 2147483647 |
| float | −3.4E+38 to 3.4E+38 |
| double | −1.7E+308 to 1.7E+308 |
| long double | −1.7E+308 to 1.7E+308 |

*Use this table only as a guide; different compilers and different computers may allow different ranges.

> **Note:** The floating-point ranges in Table 4.2 are shown in scientific notation. To determine the actual range, take the number before the E (meaning *Exponent*) and multiply it by 10 raised to the power after the plus sign. For instance, a floating-point number (type `float`) can contain a number as small as $-3.4 \times 10^{38}$.

Notice that long integers and long doubles tend to hold larger numbers (and therefore have a higher precision) than regular integers and regular double floating-point variables. This is due to the larger number of memory locations used by many of the C compilers for these data types. Again, this is usually—but not always—the case.

### Limit Excessive Data Typing

If the long variable types hold larger numbers than the regular ones, you might initially want to use long variables for all your data. This would not be required in most cases and would probably slow your program's execution.

As Appendix A describes, the more memory locations used by data, the larger that data can be. However, every time your computer has to access more storage for a single variable (as is usually the case for long variables), the CPU takes much longer to access it, calculate with it, and store it.

Use the long variables only if you suspect that your data overflows the typical data type ranges. Although the ranges differ among computers, you should have an idea of whether your numbers may exceed the computer's storage ranges. If you are working with extremely large (or extremely small and fractional) numbers, you should consider using the long variables.

Generally, all numeric variables should be signed (the default) unless you know for certain that your data contains only positive numbers. (Some values, such as age and distances, are always positive.) By making a variable an unsigned variable, you gain a little extra storage range (as explained in Appendix A), but that extra range of values must always be positive.

Obviously, you must be aware of what kinds of data your variables hold. You certainly do not always know exactly what all variables are holding, but you can have a general idea. For example, in storing a person's age, you should realize that a long integer variable would be a waste of space because nobody can live to an age that can't be stored by a regular integer.

At first, it may seem strange for Table 4.2 to state that character variables can hold numeric values. In C, integers and character variables frequently can be used interchangeably. As explained in Appendix A, the ASCII table characters each have a unique number that corresponds to their location in the table. If you store a number in a character variable, C treats the data as if it were the ASCII character that matched that number in the table. Conversely, you can store character data in an integer variable. C finds that character's ASCII number and stores that number instead of the character. Examples that help illustrate this follow a little later in the chapter.

---

**Designating Long, Unsigned, and Floating-Point Constants**

When you assign a number to a type, C interprets the type as the smallest type that can hold the number. For example, if you print a number such as **63**, C knows that this number fits into a signed integer memory location. It does not treat the number as a long integer, because **63** is not large enough to warrant a long integer constant size.

However, you can append a suffix character to numeric constants to override the default type. If you put an **L** at the end of an integer, C interprets that integer as a long integer. The number **63** is an integer constant, but the number **63L** is a long integer constant.

Assign the **U** suffix to designate an unsigned integer constant. The number **63** is, by default, a signed integer constant. If you type **63U**, C treats it as an unsigned integer. The suffix **UL** indicates an unsigned long constant.

C interprets all floating-point constants (numbers that contain decimal points) as double floating-point constants. This ensures maximum accuracy in such numbers. If you use the constant **6.82**, C treats it as a double floating-point data type even though it would fit in a regular **float.** You can append the floating-point suffix (**F**) or the long double floating-point suffix (**L**) to constants that contain decimal points to represent a floating-point constant or a long double floating-point constant, respectively, instead of the default double constant value.

You may rarely use these suffixes, but if you need to assign a constant value to an extended or unsigned variable, you may gain a little more accuracy if you add **U**, **L**, **UL**, or **F** (their lowercase equivalents work too) to the end of the constant.

---

## Assigning Values to Variables

Now that you know about the C variable types, you are ready to learn the specifics of putting values into those variables. You do this with the *assignment* statement. The equal sign (=) is used for assigning values to variables. The format of the assignment statement is as follows:

```
variable=expression;
```

The *variable* is any variable you defined earlier. The expression is any variable, constant, expression, or combination that produces a resulting data type that is the same as the *variable*'s data type.

> **Tip:** Think of the equal sign as a left-pointing arrow. Loosely, the equal sign means that you want to take the number, variable, or expression on the right side of the equal sign and put it into the variable on the left side of the equal sign.

## Examples

1. If you want to keep track of your current age, salary, and dependents, you can store these values in three C variables. You first define the variables by deciding on correct types and good names for them. You then assign values to them. Later in the program, these values may change (for example, if the program calculates a new pay increase for you).

   Good variable names would be age, salary, and dependents. If you use these names to define these three variables, the first part of the main() function might look like this:

   ```
   /* Define and store three values */
   main()
   {
       int age;
       float salary;
       int dependents;
   ```

   Notice that you do not need to define all integer variables together. After you have defined these variables, you can assign them values, such as in the following three statements:

   ```
       age=32;
       salary=25000.00;
       dependents=2;
   /* Rest of program follows */
   ```

   This example is not very long and doesn't do much, but it illustrates using and assigning values to variables.

2. Do not put commas in values that you assign to variables. Numeric constants should *never* contain commas. The following statement is *invalid*:

   ```
       salary=25,000.00;  /* NOT allowed! */
   ```

3. You can assign variables or mathematical expressions to other variables. Suppose that you stored your tax rate in a variable called `taxRate` earlier in a program and then decided to use your tax rate for your spouse's rate as well. At the proper point in the program, you could supply the following code:

```
spouseTaxRate = taxRate;
```

(You can put spaces around the equal sign—it's all right with the C compiler—but you don't have to.) At this point in the program, the value in `taxRate` would be copied to a new variable named `spouseTaxRate`. The value in `taxRate` would still be there after this line finishes. This assumes that the variables were defined earlier in the program.

If your spouse's tax rate is going to be 40 percent of yours, you can assign an expression to the spouse's variable, as in the following code:

```
spouseTaxRate = taxR * .40;
```

Any of the four mathematical symbols you learned in the last chapter, as well as the additional ones you learn about later in the book, can be part of the expression you assign to a variable.

4. If you want to assign character data to a character variable, you must enclose the character in single quotation marks. All C character constants must be enclosed in single quotation marks.

The following section of a program defines three variables and then assigns three initials to them. The initials are character constants because they are enclosed in single quotation marks.

```
main()
{
    char first, middle, last;
    first = 'G';
    middle = 'M';
    last = 'P';
    /* Rest of program follows */
```

Because these are variables, you can put other values into them later if the program warrants it.

> **Caution:** Do not mix types. In most cases, C lets you do this, but the results are unpredictable. For instance, in the middle variable presented in the last example, you could have stored the following floating-point constant:
>
> ```
> middle = 345.43244;    /* Do not do this! */
> ```
>
> If you did so, `middle` would hold a strange value that would seem to be meaningless. Make sure that values you assign to variables match the variable's type. The only major exception to this occurs when you assign an integer to a character variable, or a character to an integer variable, as you learn shortly.

# Constants

As with variables, there are several types of C constants. Remember that a constant does not change. Integer constants are whole numbers that do not contain decimal points. Floating-point constants are numbers that contain a fractional portion (a decimal point with an optional value to the right of the decimal point).

## Integer Constants

You already know that an integer is any whole number without a decimal point. C lets you assign integer constants to variables, use integer constants for calculations, and print integer constants in the `printf()` function.

A regular integer constant cannot begin with a leading 0. To C, the number 012 is *not* the number twelve. If you precede an integer constant with a 0, C thinks that it is an *octal* constant. An octal constant is a base-8 number. The octal numbering system is not used much in today's computer systems. The newer versions of C retain octal capabilities for compatibility with previous versions.

An octal integer constant contains a leading 0, and a hexadecimal constant contains a leading 0x.

A special integer in C that *is* still greatly used today is the base-16, or *hexadecimal*, constant. Appendix A describes the hexadecimal numbering system. If you want to represent a hexadecimal integer constant, add the 0x prefix to it. All the following numbers are hexadecimal numbers:

```
0x10    0x2C4    0xFFFF    0X9
```

Notice that it does not matter if you use a lowercase or uppercase letter x after the leading zero, or an uppercase or lowercase hexadecimal digit (for hex numbers A through F). If you write business application programs in C, you may think you never have the need for using hexadecimal, and you might be correct. For a complete understanding of C and your computer in general, however, you should become a little familiar with the fundamentals of hexadecimal numbers.

Table 4.3 shows a few integer constants represented in their regular decimal, hexadecimal, and octal notations. Each row contains the same number in all three bases.

**Table 4.3. Integer constants represented in three different bases.**

| Decimal (Base 10) | Hexadecimal (Base 16) | Octal (Base 8) |
|---|---|---|
| 16 | 0x10 | 020 |
| 65536 | 0x10000 | 0200000 |
| 25 | 0x19 | 031 |

**Note:** Floating-point constants may begin with a leading zero—for example, 0.7. They will be properly interpreted by C. Only integers are hexadecimal or octal constants if preceded by a zero.

**Your Computer's Word Size Is Important**

If you write a lot of system programs that use hexadecimal numbers, you probably want to store those numbers in *unsigned* variables. This keeps C from wrongly interpreting positive numbers as negative numbers.

For example, if your computer stores integers in 2-byte words (as most PCs do), the hexadecimal constant 0xFFFF represents either –1 or 65535, depending on how the sign bit is interpreted. If you defined an unsigned integer, such as

```
unsigned int iNum = 0xFFFF;
```

C knows that you want it to use the sign bit as data and not as the sign. If you defined the same value as a signed integer, however, as in

```
int iNum = 0xFFFF;   /* The word "signed" is optional */
```

C thinks that this is a negative number (–1) because the sign bit is turned on. (If you were to convert 0xFFFF to binary, you would get 16 ones.) Appendix A describes these concepts in more detail.

> **For Related Information**
>
> ◆ "The *sizeof* Operator," p. 189

## String Constants

A string constant is always enclosed in double quotation marks.

One type of C constant, called the string constant, does not have a matching variable. A string constant is *always* enclosed in double quotation marks. Here are examples of string constants:

```
"C Programming"    "123"    " "    "4323 E. Oak Road"    "x"
```

Any string of characters between double quotation marks—even a single character between double quotation marks—is considered to be a string constant. A single space, a word, or a group of words between double quotation marks is a C string constant. If the string constant contains only numeric digits, it is *not* a number; it is a string of numeric digits you cannot use to perform mathematics. You can perform math only on numbers, not on string constants that contain numbers, or even on a character constant that might contain a number (enclosed in single quotation marks).

> **Note:** A string constant is *any* character, digit, or group of characters enclosed in double quotation marks. A character constant is any character enclosed in single quotation marks.

The double quotation marks are never considered part of the string constant. They surround the string and simply inform the C compiler that the constant is a string constant and not another type.

It is easy to print string constants. Simply put the string constants in a `printf()` function. No other `printf()` characters you have seen, such as `"%d"` or `"%c"`, are needed. Here is an example of what you need to type to print a string constant to the screen.

*Print* C By Example *to the screen.*

```
printf("C By Example");
```

## Examples

**1.** The following program displays a simple message on-screen. No variables are needed because no data is stored or calculated.

```
/* Filename: C4ST1.C
   Displays a string on-screen */
#include <stdio.h>
main()
{
   printf("C By Example!");
   return;                          The message
}
```

Remember to make the last line in your C program (before the closing brace) a return statement.

**2.** You probably want to label the output from your programs. Do not print the value of a variable unless you print also a string constant that describes that variable. The following program computes sales tax for a sale and prints the tax. Notice that a message is printed first which tells the program user what the next number means.

```
/* Filename: C4ST2.C
   Computes sales tax and displays it with an appropriate
   message */
#include <stdio.h>
main()
{
   float sale, tax;
   float taxRate = .08;     /* Sales tax percentage */

   /* Determine the amount of the sale */
   sale = 22.54;

   /* Compute the sales tax */
   tax = sale * taxRate; ———— Tax computation

   /* Print the results */
   printf("The sales tax is ");
   printf("%f", tax);

   return;
}
```

## String-Constant Endings

An additional aspect of string constants sometimes confuses beginning C programmers. All string constants end with a zero. You do not see the zero, but C makes sure that it stores the zero at the end of the string in memory. Figure 4.1 shows what the string "C Program" looks like in memory.

**Figure 4.1**

In memory, a string constant always ends with 0.

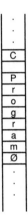

You do not need to worry about putting the zero at the end of a string constant; C does it for you every time it stores a string. If your program contained the string "C Program", for example, the compiler would recognize it as a string constant (from the double quotation marks) and store the zero at the end.

The zero is important to C. It is called the *string delimiter*. Without it, C would not know where the string constant ended in memory. (Remember that the double quotation marks are not stored as part of the string, so C cannot use them to determine where the string ends.)

All string constants end in a null zero (also called a binary zero or ASCII zero).

The string-delimiting zero is *not* the same as the character zero. If you look at the ASCII table in Appendix C, you can see that the first entry, ASCII number 0, is the *null* character. (If you are unfamiliar with the ASCII table, you should read Appendix A for a review.) This differentiates the string-delimiting zero from the character '0', whose ASCII value is 48.

As explained in Appendix A, all memory locations in a computer actually hold bit patterns for characters. If the letter A is stored in memory, an A is not really there; the binary bit pattern for the ASCII A (01000001) is stored there. Because the binary bit pattern for the null zero is 00000000, the string-delimiting zero is also called a *binary zero*.

To illustrate this further, Figure 4.2 shows the bit patterns for the following string constant when stored in memory:

```
"I am 30."
```

**Figure 4.2**

The bit pattern showing that a null zero and a character zero are different.

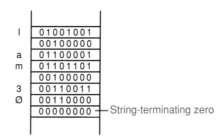

Figure 4.2 shows how a string is stored in your computer's memory at the binary level. It is important for you to recognize that the character 0, inside the number 30, is not the same zero (at the bit level) as the string-terminating null zero. If it were, C would think that this string ended after the 3, which would be incorrect.

This concept is fairly advanced, but you truly need to understand it before continuing. If you are new to computers, reading the material in Appendix A will help you understand this concept.

## String Lengths

The length of a string constant does not include the null zero.

Many times, your program needs to know the length of a string. This becomes critical when you learn how to accept string input from the keyboard. The length of a string is the number of characters up to, but not including, the delimiting null zero. Do *not* include the null character in that count, even though you know that C adds it to the end of the string.

---

**For Related Information**

♦ "Useful String Functions," p. 374

---

## Examples

**1.** All the following are string constants:

```
0"        "C"        "A much longer string constant"
```

**2.** Note the following string constants and their corresponding string lengths:

| String | Length |
|---|---|
| "C" | 1 |
| "0" | 1 |
| "Hello" | 5 |
| " " | 0 |
| "30 oranges" | 10 |

## Character Constants

All C character constants should be enclosed within single quotation marks. The single quotation marks are not part of the character, but they serve to delimit the character. The following are valid C character constants:

```
'w'     'W'     'C'     '7'     '*'     '='     '.'     'K'
```

C does not append a null zero to the end of character constants. You should know that the following are very different to C:

```
'R'    "R"
```

'R' is a single character constant. It is one character long because *all* character constants (and variables) are one character long. "R" is a string constant because it is delimited by double quotation marks. Its length is also one, but it includes a null zero in memory so that C knows where the string ends. Because of this difference, you cannot mix character constants and character strings. Figure 4.3 shows how these two constants are stored in memory.

**Figure 4.3**

The difference in memory between '*R*' as a character constant and "*R*" as a string constant.

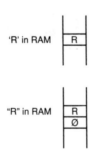

'R' in RAM

"R" in RAM

All the alphabetic, numeric, and special characters on your keyboard can be character constants. Some characters, however, cannot be represented with your keyboard. They include some of the higher ASCII characters (such as the Spanish Ñ). Because you do not have keys for every character in the ASCII table, C lets you represent such a character by typing its ASCII hexadecimal number inside single quotation marks.

For example, the hexadecimal ASCII number for the Spanish Ñ is A5. To store Ñ in a variable, add the prefix \x to A5 and enclose the combination in single quotation marks so that C will know to use the special character. You could do that with the following code:

```
char sn='\xA5';   /* Puts the Spanish N into the variable
                      called sn */
```

This is the way to store (or print) any character from the ASCII table, even if that character does not have a key on your keyboard.

The single quotation marks still tell C that a *single* character is inside the quotation marks. Even though '\xA5' contains four characters inside the quotation marks, those four characters represent a single character, not a character string. If you were to include those four characters inside a string constant, C would treat \xA5 as a single character within the string. The string constant

```
"An accented a is \xA0"
```

is a C string that is 18 characters long, not 21 characters. C interprets the \xA0 character as an *á* just as it should.

**Caution:** If you are familiar with entering ASCII characters by typing their ASCII numbers with Alt- number combinations, using the numeric keypad, do *not* use this method in your C programs. Using keypad numbers might work on your computer, but your programs might not be portable to another computer's C compiler (not all C compilers support this method).

Any character preceded by a backslash (\), as in the preceding examples, is called an *escape sequence*, or *escape character*. Table 4.4 shows some additional escape sequences that come in handy when you want to print special characters.

**Tip:** Include \n in a printf() statement if you want to skip to the next line.

### Table 4.4. Special C escape sequence characters.

| Escape Sequence | Meaning |
| --- | --- |
| \a | Alarm (the terminal's bell) |
| \b | Backspace |
| \f | Formfeed (for the printer) |
| \n | Newline (carriage return and line feed) |
| \r | Carriage return |
| \t | Tab |
| \v | Vertical tab |
| \\ | Backslash (\) |
| \? | Question mark |
| \' | Single quotation mark |
| \" | Double quotation mark |
| \ooo | Octal number |
| \xhh | Hexadecimal number |
| \0 | Null zero (or binary zero) |

---

**Math with C Characters**

Because C links characters so closely with their ASCII numbers, you can perform arithmetic on character data. The code

```
char c;
c = 'T' + 5;      /* Add 5 to the ASCII character */
```

actually stores a Y in c. The ASCII value of the letter T is 84. Adding 5 to 84 produces 89, which is the ASCII value for Y. Because the variable c is not an integer variable but a character variable, C knows to put in c the ASCII character for 89, not the number itself.

Conversely, you can store character constants in integer variables. If you do, C stores the matching ASCII number for that character. The code

```
int i='P';
```

does not put a letter P in i because i is not a character variable. C assigns the number 80 in the variable because 80 is the ASCII number for the letter P.

## Examples

1. To print two names on two different lines, include the \n between them.

   *Print the name* Harry *to the screen; drop the cursor down to a new line and print* Jerry.

   ```
   printf("Harry\nJerry");
   ```

   When the program gets to this line, it prints

   ```
   Harry
   Jerry
   ```

2. The following short program rings the bell on your computer by assigning the \a escape sequence to a variable and then printing that variable:

   ```
   /* Filename: C4BELL.C
      Rings the bell */
   #include <stdio.h>
   main()
   {
      char bell='\a';
      printf("%c", bell);   /* "%c" means print a character
                                value */

      return;
   }
   ```

## Summary

A firm grasp of C's fundamentals is critical to your better understanding of the more detailed material that follows. This is one of the last general-topic chapters in the book. You learned about variable types, constant types, how to name variables, and how to assign variable values. These issues are critical to your understanding of the rest of C.

This chapter taught you how to store almost every type of constant into variables. There is no string variable, so you cannot store string constants in string variables (as you can in other programming languages). However, you can "fool" C into *thinking* it has a string variable by using a character array to hold strings. You learn this important concept in the next chapter.

## Review Questions

Answers to review questions are in Appendix B.

**1.** Which of the following variable names are valid?

```
myName      89sales      sales_89      a-Salary
```

**2.** Which of the following constants are characters, strings, integers, and floating-point constants?

```
0      -12.0      "2.0"      "X"      'X'      65.4      -708      '0'
```

**3.** How many variables do the following statements define, and what are their types?

```
int i, j, k;
char c, d, e;
float x=65.43;
```

**4.** What do all string constants end with?

**5.** True or false: An unsigned variable can hold a larger value than a signed variable can.

**6.** How many characters of storage does the following constant take?

```
'\x41'
```

**7.** How is the following string stored at the bit level?

```
"Order 10 of them."
```

**8.** How is the following string (called a *null string*) stored at the bit level? (Hint: The length is zero, but there is still a terminating character.)

```
""
```

# Review Exercises

**1.** Write C code to store in three variables your weight (you can fib), height in feet, and shoe size. Define the variables and then assign them values in the body of your program.

**2.** Rewrite your program from exercise 1, adding correct `printf()` statements to print the values to the screen. Use appropriate messages (by printing string constants) to describe the numbers that are printed.

**3.** Write a program that converts several temperature values in Fahrenheit degrees to Celsius with this formula:

```
Celsius = (faren - 32) * (5.0 / 9.0);
```

Leave the parentheses in your converison formula. Use these Fahrenheit values for your conversion:

```
32, 100, 85
```

Before printing the converted temperatures, ring the computer's bell (Hint: Look back at Table 4.4) and print a message telling the user what you're about to print.

# CHAPTER 5

# Character Arrays and Strings

Even though C has no string variables, you can use character arrays to make C think that it has string variables. The concept of arrays may be new to you, but this chapter explains how easy they are to define and use. After you define these arrays, they can hold character strings—just as if they were real string variables. This chapter introduces the following topics:

+ Character arrays

+ How character arrays and strings are alike and different

+ Examples of using character arrays and strings

After you master this chapter, you are on your way toward being able to manipulate almost every type of variable that C offers. Manipulating characters and words distinguishes a computer from a powerful calculator and gives computers true data processing capabilities.

## Character Arrays

A string constant can be stored in an array of characters.

Almost every type of data in C has a variable, but there is no variable for holding character strings. The authors of C realized that you need some way to store strings in variables, but instead of storing them in a string variable (as in languages such as BASIC or Pascal), you must store them in an *array* of characters.

If you have never programmed before, an array might be new to you. An *array* is a list (sometimes called a *table*) of variables, and most programming languages allow the use of such lists. Suppose that you had to keep track of the sales records of 100 salespeople. You could make up 100 variable names and assign to each one a different salesperson's sales record.

All those different variable names, however, are difficult to track. If you were to put them in an array of floating-point variables, you would need to keep track of only a single name (the array name) and could reference each of the 100 values by a numeric subscript.

Part VI, "Arrays and Pointers," covers array processing in more detail. However, to work with character string data in your early programs, you need to become familiar with the concept of an array of characters (called a *character array*).

Because a string is simply a list of one or more characters, a character array is the perfect place to hold strings of information. Suppose that you want to keep track of a person's full name, age, and salary in variables. The age and salary are easy because there are variable types that can hold such data. You would write the following code to define those two variables:

```
int age;
float salary;
```

You have no string variable to hold the name, but you can create an appropriate array of characters (which is really one or more character variables next to each other in memory) with the following definition:

```
char name[15];
```

This reserves a character array. An array definition always includes brackets ( [ ] ) that define the storage C needs to reserve for the array. This array is 15 characters long. The array name is name. You can also assign to the character array a value at the time you define it. The following definition statement not only defines the character array but also assigns the name "Michael Jones" at the same time:

*Define the character array called* name *as 15 characters long and assign* Michael Jones *to that array.*

```
char name[15]="Michael Jones";
```

Figure 5.1 shows what this array looks like in memory. Each of the 15 boxes of the array is called an *element*. Notice the null zero (the string-terminating character) at the end of the string. Notice also that the last character of the array contains no data. You filled only the first 14 elements of the array with the data and the data's null zero. The 15th element actually has a value in it, but whatever follows the string's null zero is not important just now.

**Figure 5.1**

A character array
after being defined
and assigned a
string value.

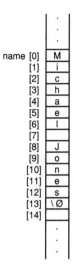

You can access individual elements within an array, or you can access the array as a whole. This is the primary advantage of an array over the use of many differently named variables. You can assign a value to an individual array element by putting the element's location, called a *subscript*, in brackets, as in the following line:

```
name[3]='k';
```

This overwrites the h in the name Michael with a k. The string now looks like the one in Figure 5.2.

**Figure 5.2**

The array contents
after changing one
of the elements.

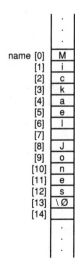

All array subscripts start at zero. Therefore, to overwrite the first element, you must use `0` as the subscript. Assigning `name[3]` (as in Figure 5.2) changes the value of the fourth element in the array.

You can print the entire string—or, more accurately, the entire array—with a single `printf()` function, as

```
printf(name);
```

or

```
printf("%s", name);
```

Notice that when you print an array, you do not put brackets after the array name. Also, as long as a character array holds a string—and it does if you have put a string into the array or ensured that a null zero is at the end of its character data—you can print the array with or without the `"%s"` (string) format code.

But you must be sure to reserve enough characters in the array to hold the entire string. The line

```
char name[5]="Michael Jones";   /* NOT valid! */
```

would be incorrect because it reserves only 5 characters for the array, while the name and its null zero require 14 characters. However, C would *not* give you an error message if you tried to do this; instead, it would overwrite whatever follows the `name` array in memory. This could cause unpredictable results and would never be correct.

Always reserve enough array elements to hold the string, plus its null-terminating character. It is easy to forget the null character, but don't do it. If your string contains 13 characters, it must have also a 14th element for the null zero—or it will never be treated like a string. To help eliminate this error, C gives you a shortcut. The following two character-array statements are the same:

```
char horse[9]="Stallion";
```

```
char horse[]="Stallion";
```

If you assign a value to a character array at the same time you declare the array, C counts the string's length, adds one for the null zero, and reserves that much array space for you automatically.

*Never* define a character array (or any other type of array) with empty brackets if you do not also assign values to that array at the same time. The statement

```
char people[];   /* NOT recommended! */
```

does *not* reserve any space for the array called `people`. Because you did not assign the array a value when you defined it, C assumes that this array contains zero elements. Therefore, you have no room to put values into this array later. Most compilers generate an error if you attempt this.

**For Related Information**

♦ "Useful String Functions," p. 374

♦ "Understanding Array Basics," p. 389

♦ "Initializing Arrays," p. 394

# Character Arrays versus Strings

In the preceding section, you saw how to put a string into a character array. Strings can exist in C only as string *constants* or as strings stored in character arrays. At this point, you need to understand that only strings must be stored in character arrays. As you read through this book and become more familiar with arrays and strings, however, you should become more comfortable with their use.

**Note:** Strings must be stored in character arrays, but not all character arrays contain strings.

Look at the two arrays shown in Figure 5.3. The first one, called cara1, is a character array, but it does not contain a string. Instead of a string, it contains a list of several characters. The second array, called cara2, contains a string because it has a null zero at the end.

**Figure 5.3**

Two character arrays: the one above contains characters, but the one below contains a character string.

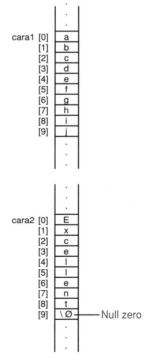

These arrays could be initialized with the following definition statements:

*Define the array* cara1 *with 10 individual characters. Define the array* cara2 *with the character string* "Excellent".

```
char cara1[10]={'a', 'b', 'c', 'd', 'e', 'f', 'g', 'h', 'i','j'};
char cara2[9]="Excellent";  /* No room for null zero */
```

If you want to put only individual characters into an array, you must enclose the list of characters in braces, as shown. You could also initialize cara1 later in the program, using assignment statements, as the following code section does:

```
char cara1[10];
cara1[0]='a';
cara1[1]='b';
cara1[2]='c';
cara1[3]='d';
cara1[4]='e';
cara1[5]='f';
cara1[6]='g';
cara1[7]='h';
cara1[8]='i';
cara1[9]='j';    /* Last element possible with subscript of 9 */
```

Because the cara1 character array does not contain a null zero, it does *not* contain a string of characters. It contains only characters that can be stored in the array and used individually. However, they cannot be treated in a program as if they were a string.

> **Caution:** You cannot assign string values to character arrays in a regular assignment statement, except when you first define them.

Because a character array is not a string variable (it can be used only to hold a string), it cannot go on the left side of an equal sign (=). The program that follows is *invalid*:

```
#include <stdio.h>
main()
{
    char petname[20];      /*  Reserve space for the pet's name */
    petname = "Alfalfa"; /* INVALID! */
    printf(petname);
    return;
}
```

Because the pet's name was not assigned *at the time the character array was defined*, the character array cannot be assigned a value later. The following, however, is allowed because you can assign values individually to a character array:

Defines the array

Fills the array

```
/* Filename: C5PETSTR.C */
#include <stdio.h>
main()
{
    char petname[20];    /* Reserve space for the pet's name */
    petname[0]='A';  /* Assign values one element at a time */
    petname[1]='l';
    petname[2]='f';
    petname[3]='a';
    petname[4]='l';
    petname[5]='f';
    petname[6]='a';
    petname[7]='\0';  /* Needed to ensure this is a string! */
    printf(petname);  /* Now the pet's name prints properly */
    return;
}
```

The petname character array now holds a string because the last character is a null zero. How long is the string in petname? It is seven characters long because the length of a string never includes the null zero.

You cannot assign more than 20 characters to this array because its reserved space is only 20 characters. However, you can store any string of 19 (leaving one for the null zero) or fewer characters to the array. If you put the "Alfalfa" string into the array as shown and then assign a null zero to petname[3], as in

```
petname[3]='\0';
```

the string in petname is now just three characters long. You have, in effect, shortened the string. There are still 20 characters reserved for petname, but the data inside the array is the string "Alf" ending with a null zero.

There are many other ways to assign a value to a string. You can use the strcpy() function, for example. This is a built-in function—like printf()—that lets you copy a string constant into a string. To copy the "Alfalfa" pet name into the petname array, you can type

```
strcpy(petname, "Alfalfa");  /* Copies Alfalfa into the array */
```

The strcpy() function puts string constants into string arrays.

The strcpy() ("string copy") function assumes that the first value in the parentheses is a character array name, and that the second value is a valid string constant or another character array that holds a string. You must be sure that the first character array in the parentheses is long enough (in number of reserved elements) to hold whatever string you copy into it. When you use strcpy(), be sure to insert the line #include <string.h> before main().

Other methods of initializing arrays are explored throughout this book.

## Examples

1. Suppose that you want to keep track of your aunt's name in a program so that you can print it. If your aunt's name is Ruth Ann Cooper, you need to reserve at least 16 elements—15 to hold the name and one to hold the null character. The following statement correctly reserves a character array to hold the name:

```
char auntName[16];
```

2. If you want to put your aunt's name in the array at the same time you reserve the array storage, you can do it like this:

```
char auntName[16]="Ruth Ann Cooper";
```

You can also leave out the array size and let C count the number of elements needed:

```
char auntName[]="Ruth Ann Cooper";
```

3. Suppose that you want to keep track of the names of three friends. The longest name is 20 characters (including the null zero). You simply need to reserve enough character-array space to hold each friend's name. The following would do it:

```
char friend1[20];
char friend2[20];
char friend3[20];
```

These array definitions should go toward the top of the block, along with any integer, floating-point, or character variables you need to define.

4. The next example asks the user for a first and last name. It then prints the user's initials on-screen by printing the first character of each name in the array. The program must print each array's 0 subscript because the first subscript of any array begins at 0, not 1.

```
/* Filename: C5INIT.C
   Prints the user's initials */
#include <stdio.h>
main()
{
   char first[20];   /* Holds the first name */
   char last[20];    /* Holds the last name */
```

```
        printf("What is your first name? ");
        scanf(" %s", first);
        printf("What is your last name? ");
        scanf(" %s", last);
```

The first and
last initials

```
        /* Print the initials */
        printf("Your initials are %c.%c.", first[0], last[0]);
        return;
    }
```

5. The following program takes your three friends' character arrays and assigns them string values, by using the three methods shown in this chapter:

```
/* Filename: C5STR.C
   Stores and initializes 3 character arrays for 3 friends */
#include <stdio.h>
#include <string.h>
main()
{
    /* Define all arrays and initialize the first one */
    char friend1[20]="Jackie Paul Johnson";
    char friend2[20];
    char friend3[20];

/* Use a function to initialize the second array */
    strcpy(friend2, "Julie L. Roberts");

    friend3[0]='A';            /* Initialize the last array, an
                                  element at a time */
    friend3[1]='d';
    friend3[2]='a';
    friend3[3]='m';
    friend3[4]=' ';
    friend3[5]='G';
    friend3[6]='.';
    friend3[7]=' ';
    friend3[8]='S';
    friend3[9]='m';
```

Initialize *friend1*

Initialize *friend2*

Makes *friend3* hold a string

```
friend3[10]='i';
friend3[11]='t';
friend3[12]='h';
friend3[13]='\0';

/* Print all three names */
printf("%s\n", friend1);
printf("%s\n", friend2);
printf("%s\n", friend3);
return;
}
```

The last method of initializing a character array with a string—one element at a time—is not used as often as the other methods.

## Summary

This has been a powerful chapter. You learned about character arrays that hold strings. Even though C has no string variables, character arrays can hold string constants. After you put a string into a character array, you can print or manipulate it as if it were a string.

Starting with the next chapter, you begin to hone the C skills you are building. Chapter 6 introduces preprocessor directives, which are not part of the C language, but help you work with your source code as a whole before your program is compiled.

## Review Questions

Answers to review questions are in Appendix B.

1. How would you define a character array called myName that holds the following string constant?

   ```
   "This is C"
   ```

2. How long is the string in #1?

3. How many bytes of storage does the string in #1 take?

4. What do all string constants end with?

5. How many variables do the following statements define, and what are their types?

```
char name[25];
char address[25];
```

6. True or false: The following statement assigns a string constant to a character array.

```
myname[]="Kim Langston";
```

7. True or false: The following definition puts a string into the character array called city.

```
char city[]={'M', 'i', 'a', 'm', 'i', '\0'};
```

8. True or false: The following definition puts a string into the character array called city.

```
char city[]={'M', 'i', 'a', 'm', 'i'};
```

## Review Exercises

1. Write the C code to store your name, address, city, state, and ZIP code all in character arrays. Define the variables and then assign them values in the body of your program.

2. Rewrite the program in exercise 1, adding correct printf() statements to print the values to the screen. Use appropriate messages (by printing string constants) to describe the values printed.

3. Write a program to store and print the names of your two favorite television shows. Store these names in two character arrays. Initialize one of the strings (assign it the first show's name) at the time you define the array. Initialize the second string in the body of the program with the strcpy() function.

4. Write a program that puts 10 different initials into 10 elements of a single character array. Do not store a null zero. Print the list backward, one initial on each line.

# CHAPTER 6

# Preprocessor Directives

As you may recall from Chapter 2, the C compiler routes your programs through a *preprocessor* before it compiles them. The preprocessor might be called a "precompiler" because it preprocesses and prepares your source code for compiling before your compiler receives it.

Because this *preprocess* is so important to C, you should familiarize yourself with it before learning more specialized commands in the language itself. Regular C commands do not affect the preprocessor. You must supply special non-C commands, called *preprocessor directives*, to control the preprocessor. These directives enable you, for example, to effect changes to your source code before it reaches the compiler. This chapter covers the following topics:

♦ What preprocessor directives are

♦ The `#include` preprocessor directive

♦ The `#define` preprocessor directive

♦ Examples of both

Almost every proper C program contains preprocessor directives. This chapter describes the two most common: `#include` and `#define`.

## Understanding Preprocessor Directives

Preprocessor directives are commands that you supply to the preprocessor. All preprocessor directives begin with a pound sign (#). Never put a semicolon at the end of preprocessor directives, because they are preprocessor commands and not C commands. Preprocessor directives typically begin in column 1 of your source program. They could begin in any column, of course, but you should stay with tradition and start them in the first column wherever they appear. Here is a program that contains three preprocessor directives:

```
/* Filename: C6PRE.C
   C program that demonstrates preprocessor directives */

#include <stdio.h>
#define AGE 28
#define MESSAGE "Hello, world."

main()
{
   int i = 10, age;   /* i is assigned a value at definition */
                      /* age is still UNDEFINED */

   age = 5;           /* Puts 5 in the variable age */

   i = i * AGE;       /* AGE is not the same as the variable age */

   printf("%d %d %d", i, age, AGE);  /* Prints 280 5 28 */
   printf(MESSAGE);   /* "Hello world" gets printed on-screen */

   return;
}
```

Three preprocessor directives

Preprocessor directives temporarily change your source code.

Preprocessor directives cause your C preprocessor to change your source code, but these changes last only as long as the compilation takes. When you look at the source code again, the preprocessor is finished with your file, and its changes are no longer in the file. The preprocessor does not in any way compile your program or look at your actual C commands. Some beginning C students tend to get confused by this, but you shouldn't as long as you realize that your program *has yet to be compiled* when the preprocessor directives execute.

It has been said that a preprocessor does nothing more than text editing to your program. This analogy holds true throughout this chapter.

## Using the *#include* Directive

The #include preprocessor directive *merges* a disk file into your source program. Remember that a preprocessor directive does nothing more than a word processing command might do to your program; word processors are also capable of file merging. The #include preprocessor directive has one of the following formats:

```
#include <filename>

#include "filename"
```

In the #include directive, *filename* must be an ASCII text file (just as your source file must be) that resides on your disk. To see this better, leave C for just a moment. The following example shows the contents of two files on disk. One is called OUTSIDE, and the other is called INSIDE.

The OUTSIDE file contains the following lines:

```
Now is the time for all good men
#include <INSIDE>
to come to the aid of their country.
```

The INSIDE file consists of these lines:

```
A quick brown fox jumps
over the lazy dog.
```

Assume that you can run the OUTSIDE file through the C preprocessor, which would find the #include directive and replace it with the entire file called INSIDE. In other words, the C preprocessor directive would merge the INSIDE file into the OUTSIDE file—at the #include location—and OUTSIDE would expand to include the merged text. After the preprocessing ends, OUTSIDE looks like this:

```
Now is the time for all good men
A quick brown fox jumps
over the lazy dog.
to come to the aid of their country.
```

The INSIDE file remains on disk in its original form. Only the file containing the #include directive is changed. Note, however, that this change is only *temporary*; that is, OUTSIDE is expanded by the included file only for as long as it takes to compile the program.

A few examples that are more usable with C might help. You might want to #include a file containing common code that you frequently use. Suppose that you print your name and address often in your C programs. You *could* type the following few lines of code in every program that prints your name and address:

```
printf("Kelly Jane Peterson\n");
printf("Apartment #217\n");
printf("4323 East Skelly Drive\n");
printf("New York, NY\n");
printf("            10012\n");
```

Instead of having to retype the same five lines everywhere you want your name and address to print, you could just type them *once* and save them in a file called MYADD.C. From then on, you would simply need to type a single line:

```
#include <myadd.c>
```

This approach not only saves typing, but also maintains consistency and accuracy. (Sometimes this kind of repeated text is known as *boilerplate*.)

You usually can use angle brackets (<>) or double quotation marks (" ") around the included file name with the same results. The angle brackets tell the preprocessor to look for the *include* file in a default include directory, set up by your compiler. The double quotation marks tell the preprocessor first to look for the include file in the directory where the source code is stored and, if missing, then to look for it in the system's include directory.

Most of the time, you do see angle brackets around the included file name. If you want to include sections of code in other programs, be sure to store that code in the system's include directory (if you use angle brackets).

Even though #include works well for inserted source code, there are other ways to include common source code that are more efficient. You learn about these methods, called *external functions*, in Chapter 17, "Writing C Functions."

*The #include directive is most often used for system header files.*

This source code #include example serves well to explain what the #include preprocessor directive does. Despite this fact, #include seldom is used to include source code text, but is more often used to include special system files called *header* files. These system files inform C how to interpret the many built-in functions you use. Your C compiler comes with its own header files. When you (or your system administrator) installed your C compiler, these header files were automatically stored on your disk in the system's include directory. Their file names always end in .h to differentiate them from regular C source code.

The most common header file is named stdio.h. This gives your C compiler needed information about the built-in printf() function, as well as other very useful and common built-in routines that perform input and output. The name "stdio.h" stands for *standard input/output header*.

At this point, you don't really need to understand the stdio.h file. You should, however, place this file before main() in every program you write. It is rare that a C program does *not* need stdio.h included, but if it isn't needed, including it does no harm. Your programs can work without stdio.h (you've already seen it happen in this book); nevertheless, your programs are more accurate, and hidden errors come to the surface much faster if you include this file.

Throughout this book, whenever a new built-in function is described, the function's matching header file is also given. Because almost every C program you write includes a printf() to print to the screen, almost every program contains the following line:

*Include the built-in C header file stdio.h.*

```
#include <stdio.h>
```

In the last chapter, you learned about the strcpy() function. Its header file is called string.h. Therefore, if you write a program that contains strcpy(), you should include its matching header file at the same time you include <stdio.h>. These go on separate lines:

```
#include <stdio.h>
#include <string.h>
```

The order of your include files does not matter as long as you include them before the functions that need them. Most C programmers include all of their needed header files before main().

These header files are nothing more than text files. If you like, search your disk with your C editor and find one, such as stdio.h, and look at it. The file may seem very complex at this point, but there is nothing "hidden" about it. If you do look at a header file, however, do *not* change it in any way. If you do, you may have to reload your compiler from scratch to restore the file.

## Examples

1. The following program is very short. It includes the name-and-address printing routine described earlier. After printing the name and address, it ends.

```
/* Filename: C6INC1.C
     Illustrates the #include preprocessor directive */
main()
{
#include "myadd.c"
return;
}
```

File replaces this line ⎯⎯ (points to `#include "myadd.c"`)

The double quotation marks are used because the file named MYADD.C is stored in the same directory as the source file. Remember that if you type this program into your computer (after typing and saving the MYADD.C file) and then compile your program, the MYADD.C file is included only as long as it takes to compile the program. Your compiler does not see this file. Your compiler sees—and "thinks" you typed—the following:

```
/* Filename: C6INCL1.C
     Illustrates the #include preprocessor directive */
#include <stdio.h>
main()
{
printf("Kelly Jane Peterson\n");
printf("Apartment #217\n");
printf("4323 East Skelly Drive\n");
printf("New York, New York\n");
printf("                10012\n");
    return;
}
```

The contents of MYADD.C ⎯⎯ (points to the printf lines through return)

This explains what is meant by a preprocessor: the changes are made to your source code *before* it's compiled. The original source code is restored as soon as the compile is finished. When you look at your program again, it is back in its original form, as originally typed, with the #include statement.

2. Because this program uses printf(), it should also include the standard input/output header file.

```
/* Filename: C6INCL2.C
   Illustrates the #include preprocessor directive */

#include <stdio.h>

main()
{
#include "myadd.c"
    return;
}
```

To help with I/O ⟶ #include <stdio.h>

3. The following program copies a message into a character array and prints it to the screen. Because the printf() and strcpy() built-in functions are used, both of their header files should also be included.

```
/* Filename: C6INCL3.C
   Uses two header files */

#include <stdio.h>
#include <string.h>

main()
{
    char message[20];
    strcpy(message, "This is fun!");
    printf(message);
    return;
}
```

For string functions ⟶ #include <string.h>

## Using the *#define* Directive

The #define preprocessor directive is also commonly used in many C programs. This directive might seem strange at first, but it really does nothing more than a search-and-replace command does on a word processor. The format of #define is as follows:

```
#define ARGUMENT1 argument2
```

The #define
directive replaces
every occurrence
of a first argument
with a second
argument.

*ARGUMENT1* is a single word containing no spaces. Use the same naming rules for the #define statement's first argument as for variables (see Chapter 4). For the first argument, it is traditional to use uppercase letters—one of the only uses of uppercase in the entire C language. At least one space separates *ARGUMENT1* from *argument2*. The *argument2* can be any character, word, or phrase; it can also contain spaces or anything else you can type on the keyboard. Because #define is a preprocessor directive and not a C executable command, do *not* put a semicolon at the end of its expression.

The #define preprocessor directive replaces the occurrence of *ARGUMENT1* everywhere in your program with the contents of *argument2*. In most cases, the #define directive should go before main() (along with any #include directives). Look at the following #define directive:

*Define the AGELIMIT constant to 21.*

```
#define AGELIMIT 21
```

If your program includes one or more occurrences of the term AGELIMIT, the preprocessor replaces every one of them with the number 21. The compiler then reacts as if you actually had typed 21 instead of AGELIMIT, because the preprocessor changes all occurrences of AGELIMIT to 21 before your compiler sees the source code. But, again, the change is only temporary. After your program is compiled, you see it as you originally typed it, with #define and AGELIMIT still intact.

AGELIMIT is *not* a variable because variables are defined and assigned values only when your program is compiled and run. The preprocessor changes your source file *before* it is compiled.

> **Note:** When a variable is said to be *defined*, the term *define* has nothing to do with the #define preprocessor directive. #define defines constants that never change (sometimes called *literals*), but int, float, and the other data type keywords define variables by reserving storage and assigning names to the variables.

You may wonder why you would ever need to go to this much trouble. If you want 21 everywhere AGELIMIT occurs, you could type 21 to begin with! But the advantage of using #define over constants is that if the age limit ever *changes* (perhaps to 18), you need to change only *one* line in the program—and not every single occurrence of the constant 21.

The #define
directive creates
defined constants.

Because #define enables you to define and change constants easily, the replaced arguments of the #define directive are sometimes called *defined constants*. You can define any type of constant, including string constants. The following program contains a defined string constant that replaces a string in two places:

```
/* Filename: C6DEF1.C
   Defines a string constant and uses it twice */

#include <stdio.h>
#define MYNAME "Phil Ward"

main()
{
   char name[]=MYNAME;
   printf("My name is %s\n", name);    /* Prints the array */
   printf("My name is %s\n", MYNAME); /* Prints the defined
                                         constant */
   return;
}
```

*MYNAME* will be replaced

The first argument of `#define` is in uppercase to distinguish it from variable names, which are usually lowercase in a program. If you didn't use uppercase, your preprocessor wouldn't get confused, but people who look at your program might become confused. When the first `#define` argument is in uppercase, other people can tell at a glance which items are defined constants and which are not. They know that when they see an uppercase word (if you follow the recommended standard for this first `#define` argument), they can look at the top of the program and see the argument's actual defined value.

The fact that defined constants are not variables is made even clearer in the following program. This program prints five values. Try to guess what those five values are before you look at the answer following the program. (Don't let the math frighten you away from programming! You'll learn in later chapters how to set up calculations properly so that C can compute them for you.)

```
/* Filename: C6DEF2.C
   Illustrates that #define constants are not variables */

#include <stdio.h>

#define X1 b+c
#define X2 X1 + X1
#define X3 X2 * c + X1 - d
#define X4 2 * X1 + 3 * X2 + 4 * X3

main()
{
   int b = 2;     /* Defines and initializes four variables */
   int c = 3;
```

```
        int d = 4;
        int e = X4;
```
Defined constants
```
        printf("%d  %d  %d  %d  %d", e, X1, X2, X3, X4);
        return;
    }
```

Here is the output from this program:

```
44    5    10    17    44
```

If you had treated X1, X2, X3, and X4 as variables, you would not get the correct answers. X1 through X4 are not variables; they are defined constants. Before your program is compiled, the preprocessor looks at the first line and knows to change every occurrence of X1 to b+c. This occurs before the next #define is processed. Therefore, after the first #define, the source code looks like this:

```
/* Filename: C6DEF2.C
    Illustrates that #define constants are not variables */

#include <stdio.h>
```
X1 was replaced
```
#define X2 b+c + b+c
#define X3 X2 * c + b+c - d
#define X4 2 * b+c + 3 * X2 + 4 * X3

main()
{
    int b=2;       /* Defines and initializes four variables */
    int c=3;
    int d=4;
    int e=X4;

    printf("%d  %d  %d  %d  %d", e, b+c, X2, X3, X4);
    return;
}
```

After the first #define finishes, the second one takes over and changes every occurrence of X2 to b+c + b+c. Your source code at that point becomes the following:

```
/* Filename: C6DEF2.C
    Illustrates that #define constants are not variables */

#include <stdio.h>
```

*X2 was replaced* ───────

```
#define X3 b+c + b+c * c + b+c - d
#define X4 2 * b+c + 3 * b+c + b+c + 4 * X3

main()
{
    int b=2;        /* Defines and initializes four variables */
    int c=3;
    int d=4;
    int e=X4;

    printf("%d  %d  %d  %d  %d", e, b+c, b+c + b+c, X3, X4);
    return;
}
```

After the second #define finishes, the third one takes over and changes every occurrence of X3 to b+c + b+c * c + b+c - d. Your source code then becomes the following:

```
/* Filename: C6DEF2.C
   Illustrates that #define constants are not variables */

#include <stdio.h>

#define X4 2 * b+c + 3 * b+c + b+c + 4 * b+c + b+c * c + b+c - d
```

*X3 was replaced* ───────

```
main()
{
    int b=2;        /* Defines and initializes four variables */
    int c=3;
    int d=4;
    int e=X4;

    printf("%d  %d  %d  %d  %d", e, b+c, b+c + b+c, b+c + b+c *
            c + b+c - d, X4);
    return;
}
```

The source code is growing rapidly! After the third #define finishes, the fourth and last one takes over and changes every occurrence of X4 to 2 * b+c + 3 * b+c + b+c + 4 * b+c + b+c * c + b+c - d. Your source code at this last point becomes this:

```
/* Filename: C6DEF2.C
   Illustrates that #define constants are not variables */

#include <stdio.h>

main()
{
   int b=2;        /* Defines and initializes four variables */
   int c=3;
   int d=4;
   int e=2 * b+c + 3 * b+c + b+c + 4 * b+c + b+c * c + b+c - d;

   printf("%d  %d  %d  %d  %d", e, b+c, b+c + b+c, b+c +
          b+c * c + b+c - d, 2 * b+c + 3 * b+c + b+c +
          4 * b+c + b+c * c + b+c - d);
   return;
}
```

X4 was replaced ——————

This is what your compiler actually sees. You did not type this complete listing; you typed the original listing that was shown first. The preprocessor expanded your source code into this longer form, just as if you *had* typed it this way.

This example may be extreme, but it serves to illustrate how #define works on your source code and doesn't define any variables. The #define really behaves like a word processor's search-and-replace command. Because of this, you can even rewrite the C language itself!

If you are used to BASIC, you might be more comfortable typing PRINT instead of C's printf() when you want to print on-screen. If so, the #define statement

```
#define PRINT printf
```

allows you to print in C with these statements:

```
PRINT("This is a new printing technique\n");
PRINT("I could have used printf() instead."\n);
```

This works because, by the time your compiler sees the program, it sees only the following:

```
printf("This is a new printing technique\n");
printf("I could have used printf() instead."\n);
```

In addition, you cannot replace a defined constant if it resides in another string constant. For example, you could not use the #define statement

```
#define AGE
```

to replace information in

```
printf("AGE");
```

because AGE is a string constant, and it prints literally just as it appears inside the double quotation marks. The preprocessor can replace only defined constants that do not appear within quotation marks.

---

**Do Not Overdo *#define***

Many early C programmers enjoyed redefining parts of the language to suit whatever they were used to in another language. The `printf()` to `PRINT` example is one example of this. You can redefine virtually any C statement or function to "look" any way you like.

But there is a danger to this, and you should be very wary of using `#define` for this purpose. Redefining the language becomes *very* confusing to others who may need to modify your program later. Also, as you become more familiar with C, you should naturally start using the true C language more and more. When you are comfortable with C, older programs that you redefined will be confusing even to *you*!

Therefore, if you are going to program in C, use the language conventions that C provides. Shy away from trying to redefine commands in the language. Think of the `#define` directive as a great way to define numeric and string constants. If those constants ever change, you need to change only one line in your program. Just say no to any temptation to redefine commands and built-in functions.

---

## Examples

1. Suppose that you want to keep track of your company's target sales amount of $55,000.00. That target amount has not changed for the last two years. Because it probably will not change soon (sales are flat), you decide to start using a defined constant to represent this target amount. Then, if target sales do change, you just have to change the amount on the `#define` line. It would look like

```
#define TARGETSALES 55000.00
```

which defines a floating-point constant. You can then assign `TARGETSALES` to floating-point variables and print it, just as if you had typed 55000.00 throughout your program, as these lines show:

```
amt = TARGETSALES;
printf("%f",TARGETSALES);
```

2. If you find yourself defining the same constants in many programs, you might consider putting them in their own file on disk and then `#include`

them. This saves typing your defined constants at the top of every program. If you store these constants in a file called MYDEFS.C in your program's directory, you could include it with the following #include statement:

```
#include "mydefs.c"
```

(To use angle brackets, you would have to store the file in your system's include directory.)

3. Defined constants are good for array sizes. Suppose that you define an array for a customer's name. When you write the program, you know you don't have a customer whose name is longer than 22 characters (including the null). Therefore, you can type

```
#define CNMLENGTH 22
```

When you define the array, you can use this:

```
char custName[CNMLENGTH]
```

Other statements that need to know the array size can also use CNMLENGTH.

4. Many C programmers define a list of error messages. Once they define the messages with an easy-to-remember name, they can print those constants if an error occurs—while still maintaining consistency throughout their programs. Often, you might see something like the following toward the top of C programs:

```
#define DISKERR "Your disk drive seems not to be working"
#define PRNTERR "Your printer is not responding"
#define AGEERR  "You cannot enter an age that small"
#define NAMEERR "You must enter a full name"
```

## Summary

This chapter showed you the #include and #define preprocessor directives. Although these are the only two preprocessor directives you know so far, they are the two used in most C programs. Despite the fact that these directives are not executed like regular C statements, they temporarily change your source code by merging and defining constants into your program.

The next chapter explains printf() in more detail. There are many printf() options that you might want to use as you write programs. You also learn a way to get keyboard input into your C programs.

## Review Questions

Answers to review questions are in Appendix B.

1. True or false: You can define variables with the preprocessor directives.

2. Which preprocessor directive merges another file into your program?

3. Which preprocessor directive defines constants throughout your program?

4. True or false: You can define character, string, integer, and floating-point constants with the #define directive.

5. Which happens first: your program is compiled or preprocessed?

6. When would you use the angle brackets in an #include, and when would you use double quotation marks?

7. Which are easier to change: defined constants or constants that you type throughout a program? Why?

8. Which header file should be included in almost every C program you write?

9. True or false: The #define in the line

```
#define MESSAGE "Please press Enter to continue..."
```

would change the following statement:

```
printf("MESSAGE");
```

10. What is the output from the following program?

```c
/* Filename: C6EXER.C */

#include <stdio.h>
#define AMT1 a+a+a
#define AMT2 AMT1 - AMT1

main()
{
    int a=1;
    printf("Amount is %d", AMT2);
    return;
}
```

# Review Exercises

**1.** Write a program that prints your name to the screen. Use a defined constant for the name. Do not use a character array and don't type your actual name inside the printf().

**2.** Suppose that your boss wanted you to write a program which produced an "exception report." If the company's sales are less than $100,000.00 or more than $750,000.00, your boss wants your program to print the appropriate message. You learn how to produce these types of reports later in the book, but for now, just write the #define statements that define these two floating-point constants.

**3.** Write the printf() statements that print your name and birth date to the screen. Store these statements in a file. Write a second program that includes the first file so that you can print your name and birth date. Be sure to include <stdio.h> because the included file contains printf() statements.

**4.** Write a program that defines the 10 digits 0 through 9 as constants ZERO through NINE. Add these 10 defined digits together and print the result.

# CHAPTER 7

# Simple Input and Output

You have already seen the printf() function, which prints values to the screen. But printf() does much more than that. Because the screen is such a common output device, you must understand how to take advantage of printf()'s various features in order to have it print exactly the way *you* want your data to appear. Your programs also become much more powerful if you learn how to obtain input from the keyboard. The scanf() function mirrors printf(). But instead of sending output values to the screen, scanf() accepts values the user types at the keyboard.

printf() is the basic screen output function, and scanf() is the basic keyboard input function. The printf() and scanf() functions offer beginning C programmers output and input functions they can use with relative ease. Both of these functions are limited—especially scanf()—but they enable your programs to send output and receive input.

This chapter introduces the following topics:

♦ The printf() function

♦ Control strings

♦ Conversion characters

♦ Conversion character modifiers

♦ The scanf() function

You may be surprised at how much more advanced your programs can become after you learn these input/output functions.

# Understanding the *printf()* Function

The printf() function sends output to the screen.

The printf() function sends data to the standard output device, which is generally the screen—unless you redirect the standard output to a different device. If you are unfamiliar with device redirection at the operating system level, you can learn more about it in Part V of this book. But for now, if you do nothing special, printf() sends all output to the screen.

The format of printf() is a little different from that of regular C commands. The values that go inside the parentheses vary, depending on the data you are printing. As a general rule, however, the following printf() format holds true:

```
printf(controlString [, one or more values]);
```

Notice that printf() always requires a controlString. This is a string, or a character array containing a string, that determines how the rest of the values (if any are listed) print. These values can be variables, constants, expressions, or a combination of all three.

**Tip:** Despite its name, printf() sends output to the screen and not to the printer.

# Printing Strings

The easiest data to print with printf() is a string. To print a string constant, you simply put it inside the printf() function. For example, to print the string The rain in Spain, you simply type the following:

*Print the phrase The rain in Spain to the screen.*

```
printf("The rain in Spain");
```

Remember, though, that printf() does *not* perform an automatic carriage return. This means that the screen's cursor remains after the last character printed. Subsequent printf()s begin right next to that last-printed character.

To understand this better, try to predict the output from these three printf() functions:

```
printf("Line 1");
printf("Line 2");
printf("Line 3");
```

These lines produce

```
Line 1Line 2Line 3
```

which is probably not what is intended. Therefore, you must include the newline character (\n) whenever you want to move the cursor to the next line. The following three printf() functions produce a three-line output:

```
printf("Line 1\n");
printf("Line 2\n");
printf("Line 3\n");
```

The output from these printf() functions is

```
Line 1
Line 2
Line 3
```

The \n character sends the cursor to the next line—no matter where you insert it. The following three printf() functions also produce the correct three-line output:

```
printf("Line 1");
printf("\nLine 2\n");
printf("Line 3");
```

The second printf() prints a new line before it prints anything else. It then prints its string followed by another new line. The third string prints on that new line.

You also can print strings stored in character arrays by putting the array name inside the printf(). For example, if you were to store your name in an array defined as

```
char myName[] = "Lyndon Harris";
```

you could print the name with this printf():

```
printf(myName);
```

## Examples

1. The following section of code prints three string constants on three different lines:

```
printf("Nancy Carson\n");
printf("1213 Oak Street\n");
printf("Fairbanks, AK\n");
```

2. The printf() function is often used to label output. Before printing an age, amount, salary, or any other numeric data, you should always print a string constant that tells the user what the number means. The following printf() lets the user know that the next number to be printed is an age. Without this printf(), the user may not recognize that the number is an age.

```
printf("Here is the age that was found in our files:");
```

**3.** All four of these `printf()`s produce different output because all four string constants are different:

```
printf("Come back tomorrow\n");
printf("Come   back   tomorrow\n");
printf("cOME BACK TOMORROW\n");
printf("C o m e   b a c k   t o m o r r o w\n");
```

**4.** You can print a blank line by printing two newline characters next to each other (`\n\n`) after a string, as in

```
printf("Prepare the invoices...\n\n");
```

**5.** The following program assigns a message in a character array and then prints that message:

```
/* Filename: C7PS.C
   Prints a string stored in a character array */
#include <stdio.h>
main()
{
    char message[] = "Please turn on your printer";
    printf(message);
    return;
}
```

Initialize character array

This prints the string stored in `message`—and keeps printing until the null zero is reached. This is why the null zero is so important: it tells C where the string in the array ends.

## Defining Conversion Characters

Inside many of the `printf()`s that you have seen in the last few chapters were several *conversion characters*. These special characters tell `printf()` exactly how the data following the characters is to be interpreted. Table 7.1 shows a list of several conversion characters. Because any type of data can go inside the `printf()`'s parentheses, these conversion characters are needed any time you print more than a string constant. If you don't want to print a string, the string constant must contain at least one of the conversion characters.

**Table 7.1. The *printf()* conversion characters.**

| Conversion Character | Output |
|---|---|
| %s | String of characters (until null zero is reached) |
| %c | Character |
| %d | Decimal integer |
| %f | Floating-point numbers |
| %e | Exponential notation floating-point numbers |
| %g | Use the shorter of %f or %e |
| %u | Unsigned integer |
| %o | Octal integer |
| %x | Hexadecimal integer |
| %% | Percent sign (%) |

**Note:** You can insert an 1 (lowercase *l*) or L before the integer and floating-point conversion characters (such as %ld and %lf) to indicate that a long integer or long double floating-point value is to be printed.

The first four conversion characters are used much more often than the others. Any character not shown in Table 7.1 prints exactly as it appears in the control string. The following sections describe these conversion characters and their uses in printf().

## String Conversion Character %s

If you print a string constant, the string conversion character is not required. The following two printf()s are identical:

*Print the sentence C is fun! and then put the cursor on the next line. Print the same thing, using the string conversion character.*

```
printf("C is fun!\n");
printf("%s", "C is fun!\n");
```

The %s informs the printf() function that a string follows. Because C does not need the %s to print strings, however, the %s is redundant. You can include the %s if you print strings stored in character arrays, but again, the %s is not needed. If cary were a character array containing a valid string, both of the following printf()s would work:

```
printf("%s", cary);   /* Prints the string in cary        */
printf(cary);         /* Works as long as cary is an array */
                      /* that holds a valid string         */
```

C does not need the %s conversion character because anything *not* a conversion character prints exactly as it appears in the control string.

## Character Conversion Character %c

You must, however, use the %c conversion character any time you print single characters, whether they are character constants or character variables. You use the following printf() to print three character constants:

*Print the characters A, B, and C, using the character conversion character.*

```
printf("%c %c %c", 'A','B','C');
```

These three character constants print with one blank space between them. Figure 7.1 shows why this is the case. Each %c informs C that a character appears in its place, and the blank that follows each of the first two %c conversion characters prints as a blank space.

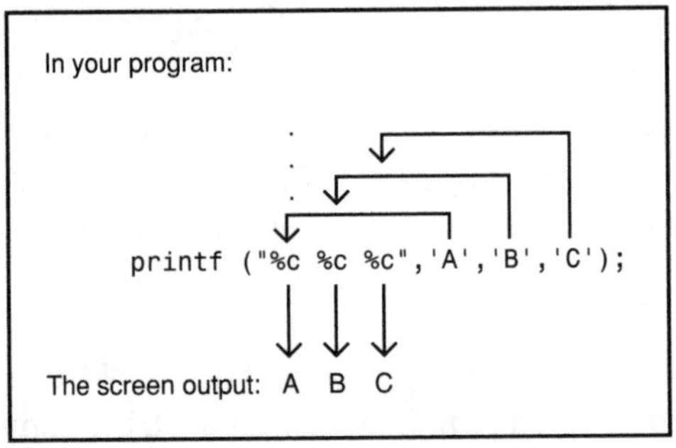

**Figure 7.1**

Conversion characters in action.

You must use the %c conversion character also when you print character variables. This includes single elements (such as c[3]) from a character array. The following program stores the three letters in three character variables and then prints them:

```
/* Filename: C7PC.C
   Stores and prints the contents of 3 variables */
#include <stdio.h>
main()
```

```
{
    char first, second, last;
    first='A';
    second='B';
    last='C';

    printf("%c %c %c", first, second, last);
    return;
}
```

Prints characters

## Integer and Floating-Point Conversion Characters %d and %f

When you want to print a numeric constant or variable, you must include the proper conversion character inside the printf() control string. If i, j, and k are integer variables, you *cannot* print them with this printf():

```
printf(i,j,k);
```

Because printf() is a function and not a command, this printf() function has no way of knowing what type the variables are. The results are unpredictable, and you may see garbage on your screen—if anything appears at all.

When you print numbers, you must first print a control string that includes the format of those numbers. The following printf() prints a string. In the output from the following line, a string appears with an integer (%d) and a floating-point number (%f) printed inside that string:

```
printf("I am Betty, I am %d years old, and I make %f\n",  35,
        34050.25);
```

This produces the following output:

```
I am Betty, I am 35 years old, and I make 34050.25
```

It's okay if your output contains extra decimal places. Later in this chapter, you learn how to limit the number of decimal places printed.

Figure 7.2 shows how C interprets the control string and the variables that follow. Be sure you understand this example before moving on. It is the foundation of the printf() function.

You can also print integer and floating-point variables in the same manner.

**Note:** The %i also works as an integer printf() conversion character. This is easier to remember (%i for *integer*), but it is rarely used by C programmers. You should follow the standard and use %d for printing integers.

**Figure 7.2**

A control string in action.

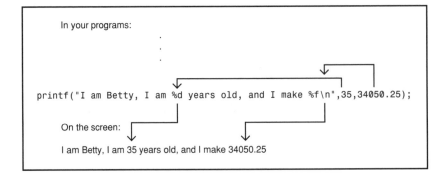

**Examples**

1. The following program stores a few values in three variables and then prints the results:

```
/* Filename: C7PRNT1.C
   Prints values in variables */
#include <stdio.h>

main()
{
    char first='E';        /* Store some character, integer, */
    char middle='W';       /* and floating-point variables   */
    char last='C';
    int age=32;
    int dependents=2;
    float salary=25000.00;
    float bonus=575.25;

    /* Print the results */
    printf("%c%c%c", first, middle, last);
    printf("%d%d", age, dependents);
    printf("%f%f", salary, bonus);
    return;
}
```

Prints characters, integers, and floating-point numbers

2. The preceding program, however, doesn't help the user at all. The output is not labeled, and it prints on a single line. Here is the same program with a few messages printed before the numbers, and some newline characters placed where they are needed:

```
/* Filename: C7PRNT2.C
   Prints values in variables with appropriate labels */
#include <stdio.h>
```

```
main()
{
    char first='E';        /* Store some character, integer, */
    char middle='W';       /* and floating-point variables   */
    char last='C';
    int age=32;
    int dependents=2;
    float salary=25000.00;
    float bonus=575.25;
    /* Print the results */
    printf("Here are the initials:\n");
    printf("%c%c%c\n\n", first, middle, last);
    printf("The age and number of dependents are:\n");
    printf("%d %d\n\n", age, dependents);
    printf("The salary and bonus are:\n");
    printf("%f %f", salary, bonus);
    return;
}
```

Titles for the output

This program produces the following output:

```
Here are the initials:
EWC

The age and number of dependents are:
32    2

The salary and bonus are:
25000.000000 575.250000
```

The floating-point values print with too many zeros, of course, but the numbers are correct. The next section shows you how to limit the number of leading and trailing zeros that are printed.

3. If you need to print a table of numbers, you can use the \t tab character. Place the tab character between the numbers that print. The following program prints a list of baseball team names and the number of hits for each team during the first three weeks of the season:

```
/* Filename: C7TEAM.C
   Prints a table of team names and hits for three weeks */
#include <stdio.h>

main()
{
```

```
        printf("Parrots\tRams\tKings\tTitans\tChargers\n");
        printf("%d\t%d\t%d\t%d\t%d\n", 3,5,2,1,0);
        printf("%d\t%d\t%d\t%d\t%d\n", 2,5,1,0,1);
        printf("%d\t%d\t%d\t%d\t%d\n", 2,6,4,3,0);

        return;
    }
```

\t moves to a tab stop

This program produces the following table. You can see that, even though the names are of different widths, the numbers print correctly beneath them. The \t character forces the next name or value into the next tab position (every eight characters for most C compilers).

```
Parrots Rams    Kings   Titans  Chargers
3       5       2       1       0
2       5       1       0       1
2       6       4       3       0
```

# Hex and Octal Conversion Characters %x and %o

The %x and %o characters are used to print hexadecimal and octal numbers. Even if you store a hexadecimal number in an integer variable (with the leading 0x characters, such as 0x3C1), that variable prints as a decimal value if you use the %d conversion character. To print the value in hex, you must use the %x conversion character.

> **Tip:** You can print any integer value as a hexadecimal number if you use the %x conversion character. You do not need to store the integer as a hex number first.

## Example

Suppose that you are working on a systems program and need to add five hexadecimal values together to test the result. You can write a short C program which does just that. You can then print the answer as a hexadecimal number, by using the %x conversion character, as shown in the following program:

```
/* Filename: C7HEX.C
   Adds five hexadecimal numbers and prints the answer */
#include <stdio.h>
```

```
main()
{
   /* Store the five numbers to add together */
   int num1=0x4c, num2=0x52, num3=0xd1, num4=0xdc, num5=0x1f;
   int hexAns;    /* This will hold the result */
   hexAns = num1 + num2 + num3 + num4 + num5;
   /* Print the answer */
   printf("The hexadecimal numbers add up to: %x \n", hexAns);
   return;
}
```

Initializes five hexadecimal numbers

This program produces the following single line of output:

```
The hexadecimal numbers add up to: 26a
```

## Exponential Conversion Characters %e and %g

The %e exponential conversion character is used to print very large, or very small, floating-point numbers. It prints these numbers in scientific notation format. Scientific notation is a shortcut method for representing extremely large or small values. Many people program in C for years and never use scientific notation. But if you understand it (and it *is* simple), you should feel at home with many language reference manuals and not be surprised if a C program prints a number on your screen in scientific notation.

You can learn scientific notation easily by looking at a few examples. Basically, you can represent any number in scientific notation, but doing so makes sense only with extremely large or small numbers. All scientific notation numbers are floating-point numbers (or double floating-point numbers if they need larger storage). Table 7.2 lists some numbers in scientific notation and their equivalents.

**Table 7.2. Examples of scientific notation.**

| Scientific Notation | Equivalent |
| --- | --- |
| 3.08E+12 | 3,080,000,000,000 |
| −9.7587E+04 | −97,587 |
| +5.164E−4 | 0.0005164 |
| −4.6545E−9 | −0.0000000046545 |
| 1.654E+302 | $1.654 \times 10^{302}$ |

Numbers in scientific notation have the letter E in them. Positive scientific numbers begin with a plus sign (+) or have no sign at all. Negative scientific numbers begin with a minus sign (–).

You can easily figure out the rest. Take the portion of the number at the left and multiply it by 10 raised to the number on the right. In other words, +2.164E+3 means to take 2.164 and multiply it by 1,000 (10 raised to the 3d power, or $10^3$). Similarly, –5.432E–4 means negative 5.432 times .0001 (10 raised to the –4 power, or $10^4$).

You can print any floating-point value or variable in scientific notation if you use the %e conversion character. If you are unsure whether the number needs scientific notation, use the %g conversion character. When C encounters %g, it prints the number as a regular floating-point constant, if it can, and uses scientific notation only if it must, to output the number more accurately.

## Examples

1. The speed of light travels at 186,000 miles per second. To store 186,000 in a floating-point variable by using scientific notation, you type

```
float lightSpeed = 1.86E+5;
```

When you start using C to perform calculations, use the %g conversion character if you suspect that the number may be large or small enough to warrant it. Any number can be printed in scientific notation, but extremely large floating-point values must be. Use the following printf() to print this variable:

```
printf("The speed of light is %g\n", lightSpeed);
```

2. The sun is 93,000,000 miles from the earth. (You are learning a lot of space travel trivia while practicing programming!) The moon is only about 264,000 miles from the earth. To store these two distances in scientific notation, you code them in this manner:

```
float sunDist = 9.3E+7;
float moonDist = 2.64E+5;
```

3. You can combine the preceding definitions into a single statement by separating them with commas:

```
float sunDist = 9.3E+7, moonDist = 2.64E+5;
```

# Using Conversion Character Modifiers

You can modify the way conversion characters print.

You already have seen the need for additional program output control. All floating-point numbers print (using %f) with too many decimal places for most applications. What if you want to print only dollars and cents (two decimal places) or an average with a single decimal place? If you want to control the way these conversion characters produce output, you have to include a modified conversion character.

You can insert a modifying number inside many of the numeric conversion characters. This number tells C how many print positions to use. For example, the following printf() prints the number 456, using three positions (the length of the data):

```
printf("%d", 456);
```

If the 456 were stored in an integer variable, it would still use three positions to print because the number of digits printed is three. However, if you insert a number before the d in the conversion character, you can exactly control how many positions print. The following printf() prints the number 456 in five positions (with two leading spaces):

```
printf("%5d", 456);
```

You typically use the width number when you want to print data in uniform columns. The following program shows you the importance of the width number. Each printf() output is illustrated in the adjacent comment.

```
/* Filename: C7MOD1.C
   Illustrates various integer width printf() modifiers */
#include <stdio.h>
main()
{                                          /* The output appears below */
    printf("%d%d%d \n", 456, 456, 456);    /* 456456456 */
    printf("%5d%5d%5d \n", 456, 456, 456); /*   456  456  456 */
    printf("%7d%7d%7d \n", 456, 456, 456); /*     456    456    456 */
    return;
}
```

No width specified
Prints the integers within 5 spaces each
Prints the integers within 7 spaces each

When you put a width number inside a conversion character, C right justifies the number in the width you specify. In other words, when you specify an 8-digit width, C prints a value inside those 8 digits, padding the number with leading blanks if the number does not fill the full width.

**Note:** If you do not specify a width large enough to hold the number, C ignores your width request and prints the number in its entirety.

If you put a minus sign before the width specifier, C left justifies the number inside the width. For example, the following program prints its numbers to the left of its fields, as shown especially in the final two comments:

```
/* Filename: C7MOD2.C
   Illustrates various integer width printf() modifiers */
#include <stdio.h>
main()
{                                    /* The output appears below */
  printf("%d%d%d \n", 456, 456, 456);        /*456456456*/
  printf("%-5d%-5d%-5d \n", 456, 456, 456); /*456  456  456  */
  printf("%-7d%-7d%-7d \n", 456, 456, 456); /*456    456    456    */
  return;
}
```

Minus sign forces left-justification

You can control the width of strings in the same manner, by using the width modifier in the %s string conversion character. If you do not specify enough width to output the full string, C ignores your width.

The width specifiers become more important when you want to print floating-point numbers. The format of the floating-point width specifier is

```
%width.decimalsf
```

The floating-point conversion character %6.2f tells C to print a floating-point number within six positions, including the decimal point and the fractional part. It also informs C to print two decimal places. If C has to round the fractional part, it does so. The line

```
printf("%6.2f", 134.568767);
```

produces this output:

```
134.57
```

Without the format modifier, C prints

```
134.568767
```

**Tip:** When printing floating-point numbers, C always prints the entire portion to the left of the decimal (to maintain as much accuracy as possible) no matter how many positions you specify. Therefore, many C programmers ignore the width specifier for floating-point numbers and specify only the decimal part, as in %.2f.

## Examples

1. Earlier, you saw how the \t tab character can be used to print columns of data. The tab character is limited to eight columns. If you want more control over the width of your data, specify a width in the output conversion characters. The following program is an altered version of C7TEAM.C, using the width specifier instead of the tab character. The width specifier ensures that each column is 10 characters wide.

```
/* Filename: C7TEAMMD.C
   Prints a table of team names and hits for three weeks,
   using width-modifying conversion characters */
#include <stdio.h>

main()
{
    printf("%10s%10s%10s%10s%10s\n",
    ➥"Parrots","Rams","Kings","Titans","Chargers");
    printf("%10d%10d%10d%10d%10d\n", 3,5,2,1,0);
    printf("%10d%10d%10d%10d%10d\n", 2,5,1,0,1);
    printf("%10d%10d%10d%10d%10d\n", 2,6,4,3,0);

    return;
}
```

The *10* keeps the numbers aligned

2. The following program is a payroll program. The output prints dollar amounts (to two decimal places).

```
/* Filename: C7PAY1.C
   Computes and prints payroll data properly in dollars and
   cents */
#include <stdio.h>

main()
{
    char empName[]="Larry Payton";
    char payDate[]="03/09/93";
    int hoursWorked=40;
    float rate=7.50;              /* Pay per hour */
    float taxRate=.40;            /* Tax percentage rate */
    float grossPay, taxes, netPay;

    /* Compute the pay amount */
    grossPay = hoursWorked * rate;
```

```
        taxes = taxRate * grossPay;
        netPay = grossPay - taxes;

        /* Print the results */
        printf("As of %s\n", payDate);
        printf("%s worked %d hours\n", empName, hoursWorked);
        printf("and got paid %6.2f\n", grossPay);
        printf("After taxes of %5.2f\n", taxes);
        printf("his take-home pay was: $%6.2f\n", netPay);

        return;
}
```

All *floats* print with two decimal places

The following is the output from this program. Remember that the floating-point variables still hold their full precision (to six decimal places). The width-modifying numbers affect only how the variables are output, not what is stored in them.

```
As of: 03/09/93
Larry Payton worked 40 hours
and got paid 300.00
After taxes of 120.00
his take-home pay was $180.00
```

**3.** Most C programmers do not use a width specifier to the left of the decimal point when printing dollars and cents. Here again is the payroll program that uses the shortcut floating-point width method. Notice that the last three `printf()` statements include the `%.2f` modifier. C knows to print the full number to the left of the decimal, but only two places to the right.

```
/* Filename: C7PAY2.C
   Computes and prints payroll data properly, using the
   shortcut modifier */
#include <stdio.h>

main()
{
    char empName[]="Larry Payton";
    char payDate[]="03/09/93";
    int hoursWorked=40;
    float rate=7.50;                /* Pay per hour */
    float taxRate=.40;              /* Tax percentage rate */
    float grossPay, taxes, netPay;
```

```
        /* Compute the pay amount \*/
        grossPay = hoursWorked * rate;
        taxes = taxRate * grossPay;
        netPay = grossPay - taxes;

        /* Print the results */
        printf("As of: %s\n", payDate);
        printf("%s worked %d hours\n", empName, hoursWorked);
        printf("and got paid %.2f\n", grossPay);
        printf("After taxes of %.2f\n", taxes);
        printf("his take-home pay was $%.2f\n", netPay);

        return;
    }
```

No width
specified

This program's output is the same as that of the last one.

## Keeping Count of Output

Make sure that your printed values match the control strings supplied with them. The printf() function cannot fix problems resulting from mismatched values and control strings. Don't try to print floating-point values with character-string control codes. If you list five integer variables in a printf(), be sure to include five %d conversion characters in the printf() as well.

---

**Printing ASCII Values**

There is one exception to the rule of printing with matching conversion characters. If you want to print the ASCII value of a character, you can print that character (whether it is a constant or variable) with the integer %d conversion character. Instead of printing the character, C prints the matching ASCII number for that character.

Conversely, if you print an integer with a %c conversion character, you see the character which matches that integer's value from the ASCII table.

The following two printf()s illustrate this:

```
printf("%c", 65);  /* Prints letter A */
printf("%d", 'A'); /* Prints number 65 */
```

---

Depending on your C compiler, the output may be empty—or produce garbage on-screen—if you mismatch your parameters. The following example illustrates some of the problems that can occur. Because these printf()s are mismatched (the control strings don't always match the variables and constants being printed), you should check the comment to the right for the probable output or error that might occur.

```
/* Filename: C7PROB.C
   Demonstrates possible printf() problems */
#include <stdio.h>
main()
{
  int i, j, k;
  char a, b, c;

  i = 4;
  j = 5;
  k = 6;

  a = 'I';
  b = 'B';                              /*****************************/
  c = 'M';                              /* Output is shown below:    */
                                        /*                           */
  printf("This is a message\n");        /* This is a message       */
  printf("%d %d %d\n", i, j, k);        /* 4 5 6                   */
  printf(i, j, k);                      /* (unpredictable)         */
  printf("\n%c %d  %c %d", a, i, c, j); /* I 4  M 5                */
  printf("\nB%cB%cB%c\n", a, a, a);     /* BIBIBI                  */
  printf(a, b, c);                      /* (unpredictable)         */
  printf("\nHi.\n", a, b, c);           /* Hi.                     */
  printf("%d %d\n", i, j, k);           /* 4 5                     */
  printf("%c %c %c %c\n", a, b, c);     /* I B M  (garbage)        */
  printf("%cc%dd\n", a, i);             /* Ic4d                    */
  printf("%s\n", "No conv. char. needed");
                                        /* No conv. char. needed */
  printf("No conv. char. needed");      /* No conv. char. needed */
  printf("\n%s %c", "A", 'A');          /* A A                     */
  printf("\n%s %c", 'A', "A");          /* (unpredictable)         */
  printf("\nNumber in string %d, see?", i);
                            /* Number in string 4, see?*/
  printf("\nWatch your types! %d %c", b, j);
                            /* Watch your types!(garbage)*/
                            /*****************************/

  return;
}
```

The annotation "Data to be printed" points to the lines:
```
i = 4;
j = 5;
k = 6;

a = 'I';
b = 'B';
c = 'M';
```

The bottom line is this: avoid these types of problems by making sure that every conversion character inside your `printf()` control string matches the data that follows the control string.

## Understanding the *scanf()* Function

The `scanf()` function stores keyboard input in variables.

You now understand how C represents data and variables, as well as how to print that data. But there is another part of this programming you haven't seen: how a user inputs data into your programs.

Until now, every program has had no input of data. All the data you've worked with has been assigned to variables within the programs. However, this is not always the best way to input data; in addition, you rarely know what your data is going to be when you write your programs. Most data becomes known only when you run the programs or when another user runs them.

The `scanf()` function is one way to get input from the keyboard. When a program reaches a line with a `scanf()`, the user at the keyboard can enter values directly into variables. Then the program can process those variables and produce output. Figure 7.3 illustrates the difference between `printf()` and `scanf()`.

**Figure 7.3**

The difference between *printf( )* and *scanf( )*.

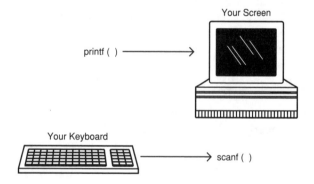

The `scanf()` function has its drawbacks (discussed later in this section); but if you understand the `printf()` function, `scanf()` shouldn't pose too much of a problem. Therefore, the next few chapters make use of `scanf()` until you learn even more powerful (and flexible) input methods.

`scanf()`, which looks very much like `printf()`, contains a control string and one or more variables to the right of the control string. The control string describes to C exactly what the incoming keyboard values look like and what their types are. The format of `scanf()` is

```
scanf(controlString, one or more values);
```

---

**The** *scanf( )* **Function Fills Variables with Values**

There is a major difference between `scanf()` and the assignment statements (such as `i=17;`) that you have seen. Both fill variables with values. However, the assignment statement assigned specific values to variables *at programming time*. When you run a program with assignment statements, you know exactly what values are going into the variables because you wrote the program to store those values there. Every time you run the program, the results are exactly the same because the same values go into (are assigned to) the same variables.

In contrast, when you write programs that use `scanf()`, you have no idea what values are going into the `scanf()`'s variables, because their values are not known *until the program is run and the user enters those values*. This produces much more flexible programs, which can be used by a greater variety of people. Every time the program is run, different results are output, depending on what the user types at each `scanf()` in the program.

---

The stdio.h header file contains the information C needs for `scanf()`, so include the file whenever you use `scanf()`.

The `scanf()` *controlString* uses almost the same conversion characters as the `printf()` *controlString*, with two slight differences. You should never include the newline character \n in a `scanf()` control string. The `scanf()` function "knows" that the input is finished when the user presses Enter. If you supply an additional newline code, `scanf()` gets confused and may not terminate properly. In addition, always put a beginning space inside every `scanf()` control string. This does not affect the user's input, but `scanf()` sometimes requires the space in order to work properly. Later examples clarify this.

The scanf() function requires that the user type correctly. This is not always possible to guarantee!

As mentioned earlier, `scanf()` poses a few problems. The `scanf()` function requires that the user type the input *exactly* the way *controlString* specifies. Because you cannot control your user's typing, accuracy cannot always be ensured. For example, you might want the user to enter an integer value followed by a floating-point value (your `scanf()` control string might expect it too), but your user might decide to enter something else! If this happens, there is not much you can do. The resulting input will be incorrect, but your C program has no reliable method for testing user accuracy—for the benefit of the user—before your program is run.

For the next few chapters, assume that the user knows to enter the correct values. However, for your own programs used by others, be on the lookout for additional methods to get better input.

---

**Caution:** The user's keyboard input values *must* match, in number and type, the control string contained in each `scanf()`.

---

Another problem with scanf() is not as easy to explain at this point in the book. The scanf() function requires that you use pointer variables, not regular variables, in its parentheses. Although this sounds complicated, it doesn't have to be. You should have no problem with scanf()'s pointer requirements if you remember the following two simple rules:

**1.** Always put an ampersand (&) before variable names inside a scanf().

**2.** Never put an ampersand (&) before an array name inside a scanf().

Despite these strange scanf() rules, you can learn this function very quickly by looking at a few examples.

## Examples

**1.** If you want a program that computes a 7-percent sales tax, you can use the scanf() statement to get the sales, compute the tax, and then print the results, as the following program shows:

```
/* Filename: C7SLTX1.C
   Gets a sales amount and prints the sales tax */
#include <stdio.h>
main()
{
    float totalSale;   /* User's sales amount will go here */
    float stax;

    /* Get the sales amount from user */
    scanf(" %f", &totalSale);   /* Don't forget the beginning
                                   space and & */

    /* Calculate sales tax */
    stax = totalSale * .07;

      printf("The sales tax for %.2f is %.2f", totalSale,
              stax);
    return;
}
```

Sales tax computed here ———

If you run this program, the program waits for you to enter a value for the total sale. Remember to use the ampersand in front of the totalSale variable when you put it in the scanf() function. After you press Enter, the program calculates the sales tax and prints the results.

If you enter 10.00 as the sale amount, you see the following output:

```
The sales tax for 10.00 is 0.70
```

2. The preceding program is fine for introducing `scanf()`, but it contains a serious problem. The problem is not in the code itself but in the program's assumption about the user: it does not tell the user what it expects him or her to enter. Because the `scanf()` assumes too much already, your programs that use `scanf()` should inform your users *exactly* what they are to type. The following revision of this program prompts the user with an appropriate message before getting the sale amount:

```
/* Filename: C7SLTX2.C
   Prompts for a sales amount and prints the sales tax */
#include <stdio.h>
main()
{
   float totalSale;   /* User's sales amount will go here */
   float stax;

   /* Display a message for the user */
   printf("What is the total amount of the sale? ");

   /* Get the sales amount from user */
   scanf(" %f", &totalSale);   /* Don't forget the beginning
                                     space and & */

   /* Calculate sales tax */
   stax = totalSale * .07;

   printf("The sales tax for %.2f is %.2f", totalSale,
          stax);
   return;
}
```

Prompt the user ──── printf("What is the total amount of the sale? ");

Because the first `printf()` does not contain a newline character (\n), the user's response to the prompt appears directly to the right of the question mark.

3. Use the string conversion character (%s) to input keyboard strings into character arrays with `scanf()`. You are limited, however, to getting one word at a time, because the `scanf()` does not let you type more than one word into a single character array. The following program asks users for their first and last names. It must store these two names in two different character arrays because `scanf()` cannot get both names at once. The program then prints the names in reverse order.

```
/* Filename: C7PHON.C
   Program that gets the user's name and prints it
   to the screen as it would appear in a phone book. */
#include <stdio.h>
main()
{
   char first[20], last[20];
   printf("What is your first name? ");
   scanf(" %s", first);
   printf("What is your last name? ");
   scanf(" %s", last);
   printf("\n\n");     /* Print 2 blank lines */
   printf("In a phone book, your name would look like
➥this:\n");
   printf(" %s, %s", last, first);
   return;
}
```

*scanf( ) can get only one word at a time*

Figure 7.4 shows a sample run from this program. Notice that you do not include the ampersand before an array name, only before "single" nonarray variables.

**Figure 7.4**

The screen after a user has input her name.

```
What is your first name? Martha
What is your last name? Roberts


In a phone book, your name would like like this:
Roberts, Martha
```

**4.** Suppose that you want to write for your seven-year-old daughter a program that does simple addition. The following program prompts her for two numbers. The program then waits for her to type an answer. When she gives her answer, the program displays the correct result so that she can see how well she did. (Later, you learn how you can immediately let her know whether her answer is correct.)

```
/* Filename: C7MATH.C
   Program to help children with simple addition.
   Prompts child for 2 values, after printing a title
   message */
#include <stdio.h>
main()
{
```

Asks child for
numbers

The child can
verify the
answer

```c
        int num1, num2, ans;
        int herAns;

        printf("*** Math Practice ***\n");
        printf("\n\n");      /* Print 2 blank lines */
        printf("What is the first number? ");
        scanf(" %d", &num1);
        printf("What is the second number? ");
        scanf(" %d", &num2);

        /* Compute answer and give her a chance to wait for it */
        ans=num1+num2;

        printf("\nWhat do you think is the answer? ");
        scanf(" %d", &herAns);    /* Nothing is done with this */

        /* Print answer after a blank line */
        printf("\n%d plus %d is: %d\n", num1, num2, ans);
        printf("\nHope you got it right!");
        return;
}
```

## Summary

After learning the printf() and scanf() functions in this chapter, you should be able to print almost anything on-screen. By studying the conversion characters and how they behave, you can control your output more thoroughly than ever before. And because you now can receive keyboard values, your programs are much more powerful. No longer do you need to know your data values when you write your programs. With scanf(), you can ask the user to enter values into variables for you.

You now have the tools you need to begin writing programs that fit the data processing model of "input-process-output." This chapter concludes the preliminaries of the C programming language. So far, this book has attempted to give you an overview of the language and to show you enough of C's elements so that you can begin writing helpful programs as soon as possible.

The next chapter begins a new type of discussion. You learn how C's math and relational operators work on data, as well as the importance of their table of precedence.

# Review Questions

Answers to review questions are in Appendix B.

1. What is the difference between printf() and scanf()?

2. Why is a prompt message important before using scanf() for input?

3. How many values are entered with the following scanf(), and what are their types?

```
scanf(" %d %d %f %s", &i, &j, &k, l);
```

4. True or false: The %s conversion character is usually not required in printf() control strings.

5. Which types of variables do *not* require the ampersand (&) character in scanf() functions?

6. Because they both put values into variables, is there any difference between assigning values to variables and using scanf() to give them values?

7. What is the output produced by the following printf()?

```
printf("The backslash, \"\\\" character is special");
```

8. What is the output of the following printf()?

```
printf("%8.3f", 123.456789);
```

9. True or false: To print a number in octal, hex, and decimal, you need to store it in three different variables.

10. Convert the following scientific notation numbers to their floating-point equivalents.

```
1.234E+6      1.234E-6      -1.234E+6      -1.234E-6
```

# Review Exercises

1. Write a program that prompts users for name and weight. Store these values in separate variables and print them on-screen.

2. Assume that you are a college professor needing to average grades for 10 students. Write a program that prompts you for 10 different grades and then displays their average.

3. Modify your program in exercise 2 to ask for each student's name and grade. Print the list on-screen with each student's name and grade in two columns. Make sure that the columns align by using a width modifier on

the grade. At the bottom, print the average of all grades. (Hint: Store the 10 names and 10 grades in different variables with different names.) This program is easy, but it takes about 30 lines, plus appropriate comments and prompts. Later, you learn ways to streamline this program.

4. Write a program that first prompts users for their full names (store each—first, middle, and last—in three separate character arrays), hours worked, hourly rates, and tax rates, and then displays taxes and net pay, using the appropriate dollars-and-cents print codes.

5. Modify the child's math program shown earlier in this chapter (C7MATH.C) to include subtraction, multiplication, and division, after the child has finished practicing addition.

6. Test your understanding of the backslash conversion character by writing a program that uses `printf()` functions to produce the following picture on your screen.

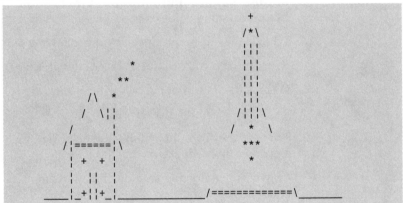

# Part II

*C Operators*

# CHAPTER 8

# Math Operators and Precedence

You may be dreading this chapter if you don't like math—but relax. C does all your math for you! That you must be good at math to understand how to program computers is a misconception. In fact, the opposite is true. Your computer is your "slave"; it follows your instructions and does all calculations for you. In this chapter, you learn how C computes. The following topics are covered:

- ◆ Primary math operators

- ◆ Order of operator precedence

- ◆ Assignment statements

- ◆ Mixed data-type calculations

- ◆ Typecasting

Many people who dislike math actually enjoy learning how the computer handles it. After learning the math operators and a few simple ways in which C uses them, you should feel comfortable putting calculations into your programs. Computers are very fast, and they can perform math operations many times faster than you can!

## C's Primary Math Operators

C *math operators* are symbols for multiplying, dividing, adding, and subtracting, as well as for other operations. C operators are not always mathematical, but many are. Table 8.1 lists these operator symbols.

**Table 8.1. C primary operators.**

| Symbol | Meaning |
|---|---|
| * | Multiplication |
| / | Division and integer division |
| % | Modulus or remainder |
| + | Addition |
| - | Subtraction |

Most of these operators work in the ways that are familiar to you. Multiplication, addition, subtraction, and (usually) division produce the same results you get when you do these math functions with a calculator. Table 8.2 shows four samples that illustrate four of these simple operators.

**Table 8.2. Typical operator results.**

| Formula | Result |
|---|---|
| 4 * 2 | 8 |
| 64 / 4 | 16 |
| 12 + 9 | 21 |
| 80 – 15 | 65 |

Table 8.2 contains examples of *binary operations* performed with the four operators. Don't confuse binary operations with *binary numbers*. When an operator is used between two constants, variables, or a combination of both, the operator is called a *binary operator* because it operates with two values. When you use these operators (such as assigning their results to variables), C does not "care" whether you put spaces around the operators.

> **Caution:** For multiplication, use the asterisk (*), *not* an x, which you might normally use. An x cannot be the multiplication sign because C would confuse it with a variable called x. C would not know whether you mean to multiply or to use the value of a variable called x.

## The Unary Operators

A *unary operator* operates on, or affects, a single value. For instance, you can assign a variable a positive or negative number by using a unary + or –. You can also assign a variable another positive or negative number by using a unary + or –.

### Examples

**1.** The following section of code assigns a positive or negative number to each of four variables. All the plus and minus signs are unary because they are not used between two values.

*Make a equal to negative 25, b equal to positive 25, c equal to negative a, and d equal to positive b.*

```
a = -25;    /* Assign 'a' a negative 25 */
b = +25;    /* Assign 'b' a positive 25 (+ is not needed) */
c = -a;     /* Assign 'c' the negative of 'a' (-25) */
d = +b;     /* Assign 'd' the positive of 'b' (+ is not
               needed) */
```

**2.** You generally do not need to use the unary plus sign. C assumes that a number or variable is positive even if you don't put a plus sign in front of it. The following four statements do not contain plus signs but are equivalent to the preceding four:

```
a = -25;    /* Assign 'a' a negative 25 */
b =  25;    /* Assign 'b' a positive 25 */
c = -a;     /* Assign 'c' the negative of 'a' (-25) */
d =  b;     /* Assign 'd' the positive of 'b' */
```

**3.** The unary negative comes in handy when you want to negate a single number or variable. The following short program assigns a negative number (using the unary –) to a variable and then prints the negative of that same variable. Note that the negative of a negative is a positive. Because the variable had a negative number to begin with, the `printf()` produces a positive result.

```
/* Filename: C8NEG.C
   The negative of a variable that contains a negative value */
#include <stdio.h>
main()
{
   signed int temp=-12;   /* 'signed' is not needed because  */
                          /* that is the default   */
   printf("%d", -temp);   /* Produces a 12 on the screen   */
                  └─ Reverses temp's sign
   return;
}
```

The variable definition does not need the *signed* prefix because all integer variables are signed by default.

4. If you want to subtract the negative of a variable, make sure you put a space before the unary minus sign. For example, the line

```
newTemp = oldTemp - -inversionFactor;
```

temporarily negates `inversionFactor` and then subtracts that negated value from `oldTemp`.

## Division and Modulus

The division sign (/) and the modulus operator (%) may behave in ways unfamiliar to you. They're usually as easy to use, though, as the other operators you have just seen.

The modulus operator (%) computes a remainder of an integer division.

The forward slash (/) always divides. However, it produces an integer division if integer values (constants, variables, or a combination of both) appear on both sides of the slash. If there is a remainder, C discards it.

The percent sign (%) produces a *modulus*, or a *remainder*, of an integer division. The operator requires that integers be on both sides of the symbol, or the operator will not work.

### Examples

1. Suppose that you want to compute your weekly pay. The following program asks for your yearly pay, divides it by 52, and prints the result to two decimal places:

```
/* Filename: C8DIV.C
   Displays user's weekly pay */
#include <stdio.h>
main()
{
   float weekly, yearly;
   printf("What is your annual pay? ");  /* Prompt user */
   scanf("%f", &yearly);
                        ┌ Divide to make weekly
   weekly = yearly / 52;  /* Computes the weekly */
   printf("\n\nYour weekly pay is $%.2f", weekly);
   return;
}
```

Because a floating-point number is used in the division, C produces a floating-point result. Here is a sample run from such a program:

```
What is your annual pay? 38000.00

Your weekly pay is $730.77
```

2. Integer division does not round its results. If you divide two integers and the answer is not a whole number, C ignores the fractional part. The following printf()s help show this. The output that would result from each printf() appears in the comment to the right of each line.

```
printf("%d \n", 10/2);      /* 5  (no remainder) */
printf("%d \n", 300/100);   /* 3  (no remainder) */
printf("%d \n", 10/3);      /* 3  (discarded remainder) */
printf("%d \n", 300/165);   /* 1  (discarded remainder) */
```

# The Order of Precedence

Knowing the meaning of the math operators is the first of two steps toward your understanding of C calculations. You must understand also the *order of precedence*. The order of precedence (sometimes called the *math hierarchy*, or *order of operators*) determines exactly how C computes formulas. The precedence of operators is the same as that used in high school algebra courses. (But don't worry, this is the *easy* part of algebra!) To see how the order of precedence works, try to determine the result of the following simple calculation:

```
2 + 3 * 2
```

If you said 10, you would not be alone; many people would respond with 10. However, 10 is correct only if you interpret the formula from left to right. But what if you calculated the multiplication first? If you took the value of 3 * 2, got an answer of 6, and then added 2 to it, you would end up with an answer of 8—which is exactly the same answer that C computes!

C always performs multiplication, division, and modulus first, and then performs addition and subtraction. Table 8.3 shows the order of the operators you have seen so far. Of course, there are many more levels to C's precedence table of operators than shown in Table 8.3. Unlike most computer languages, C has 15 levels of precedence. Appendix D contains the complete precedence table, and you might notice in this appendix that multiplication, division, and modulus reside on level 3, one level higher than level 4's addition and subtraction. In the next few chapters, you learn how to use the rest of this precedence table in your C programs.

C performs multiplication, division, and modulus *before* addition and subtraction.

## Table 8.3. Order of precedence for primary operators.

| Order | Operator |
|---|---|
| First | Multiplication, division, modulus remainder (*, /, %) |
| Second | Addition, subtraction (+, -) |

## Examples

1. It is easy to follow C's order of operators if you follow the intermediate results one at a time. The three calculations in Figure 8.1 show you how to do this.

**Figure 8.1**

Calculations showing C's order of operators with lines indicating precedence.

```
6 + 2 * 3 - 4 / 2
    V
6 + 6 - 4 / 2
        V
6 + 6 - 2
    V
12 - 2
  V
  10
```

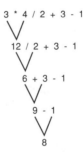

```
3 * 4 / 2 + 3 - 1
  V
12 / 2 + 3 - 1
    V
6 + 3 - 1
    V
9 - 1
  V
  8
```

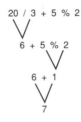

```
20 / 3 + 5 % 2
   V
6 + 5 % 2
      V
6 + 1
  V
  7
```

2. Looking back at the precedence table again, notice that multiplication, division, and modulus are on the same level. This implies that there is no hierarchy on that level. If more than one of these operators appear in a calculation, C performs the math from left to right. The same is true of addition and subtraction—the leftmost operation is done first.

Figure 8.2 illustrates an example.

**Figure 8.2**

C's order of operators from left to right with lines indicating precedence.

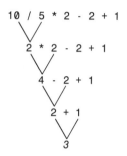

Because the division appears to the left of the multiplication and both are on the same level, division is computed first.

You now should be able to follow the order of these C operators. You really don't need to worry about the math because C does all the work. However, you should understand this order of operators so that you know how to structure your calculations. Now that you have *mastered* this order, it's time to see how you can override it with parentheses!

## Using Parentheses

Parentheses override the usual order of math.

If you want to override the order of precedence, you can put parentheses in the calculation. The parentheses actually reside on a level above the multiplication, division, and modulus in the precedence table. In other words, *any* calculation in parentheses—whether it is addition, subtraction, division, or something else—is always calculated before the rest of the line. The other calculations are then performed in their normal operator order.

The first formula in this chapter, 2 + 3 * 2, produced 8 because the multiplication was performed before addition. However, by adding parentheses around the addition, as in (2 + 3) * 2, the answer becomes 10.

In the precedence table shown in Appendix D, the parentheses reside on level 1 (the highest level in the table). Being higher than the other levels makes parentheses take precedence over multiplication, division, and all other operators.

### Examples

1. Look at the calculations shown in Figure 8.3. These are the same three formulas shown in the last section, but their results are calculated

differently because the parentheses override the normal order of operators.

**Figure 8.3**

The use of parentheses as the highest precedence level with lines indicating precedence.

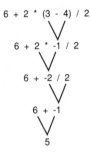

```
6 + 2 * (3 - 4) / 2
       \   /
6 + 2 * -1 / 2
     \   /
6 + -2 / 2
   \   /
6 + -1
 \   /
  5
```

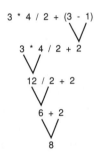

```
3 * 4 / 2 + (3 - 1)
           \   /
3 * 4 / 2 + 2
 \   /
12 / 2 + 2
   \   /
6 + 2
 \   /
  8
```

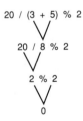

```
20 / (3 + 5) % 2
     \   /
20 / 8 % 2
   \   /
2 % 2
 \   /
  0
```

2. If an expression contains parentheses-within-parentheses, C evaluates the innermost parentheses first. The expressions in Figure 8.4 illustrate this.

3. The following program produces an incorrect result, even though it looks as if it should work. See if you can spot the error.

*Identify the program and include the necessary header file. This program will average some grades. We need variables for the average and each of the three grades, so define avg, grade1, grade2, and grade3 as floating-point variables. Make the average equal to the three grades divided by 3. Print the average to the screen.*

**Figure 8.4**

The use of parentheses within parentheses with lines indicating precedence.

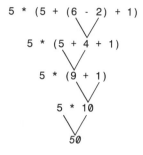

```
5 * (5 + (6 - 2) + 1)
        \_____/
5 * (5 + 4 + 1)
     _____/
5 * (9 + 1)
     \_____/
5 * 10
    \__/
     50
```

```
/* Filename: C8AVG1.C
   Computes the average of three grades */
#include <stdio.h>
main()
{
   float avg, grade1=87.6, grade2=94.8, grade3=74.5;

   avg = grade1 + grade2 + grade3 / 3.0;  ——— Oops! Does not
   printf("The average is %.1f", avg);          compute average!
   return;
}
```

The problem is that division is performed first. Therefore, the third grade is first divided by 3.0, and then the other two grades are added to that result. To correct this problem, you would simply have to add one set of parentheses, as shown here:

```
/* Filename: C8AVG2.C
   Computes the average of three grades */
#include <stdio.h>
main()
{
   float avg, grade1=87.6, grade2=94.8, grade3=74.5;

   avg = (grade1 + grade2 + grade3) / 3.0;  ——— Proper average
   printf("The average is %.1f", avg);
   return;
}
```

**Tip:** Use plenty of parentheses in your C programs to make the order of operators clearer, even when you don't have to override their default order. It sometimes makes the calculations easier to understand later when you might need to modify the program.

**Shorter Is Not Always Better**

When you program computers for a living, it is much more important to write programs that are easy to understand than programs that are short or include tricky calculations.

*Maintainability* is the computer industry's word for changing and updating programs that were written in a simple style earlier. The business world is changing rapidly, and the programs that companies have used for years must often be updated to reflect this changing environment. Businesses do not always have the resources to write programs from scratch. They usually make do by modifying the ones they have.

Years ago when computer hardware was much more expensive, and when computer memories were much smaller, it was important to write small programs, which often relied on clever, individualized tricks and shortcuts. Unfortunately, such programs are often difficult to revise, especially if the original programmers leave and someone else (you!) must step in and modify all their original code.

Companies are realizing the importance of spending time to write programs that are easy to modify and that do not rely on tricks, or "quick-and-dirty" routines that are hard to follow. You can be a much more valuable programmer if you write clean programs, with lots of white space, many remarks, and very straightforward code. Put parentheses around formulas if it makes them clearer, and use variables for storing results in case you need the same answer later in the program. Break long calculations into several smaller ones.

Throughout the rest of this book, you can read tips on writing maintainable programs. You and your colleagues might appreciate these tips when you incorporate them into your own C programs.

# The Assignment Statements

In C, the assignment operator (=) behaves differently from what you might be used to in other languages. So far, you have seen the operator used for simple assignment of values to variables, which is consistent with its use in most other programming languages.

However, the assignment operator *also* can be used in other ways, such as for multiple assignment statements and compound assignments. The following sections illustrate these uses.

## Multiple Assignments

If two or more equal signs appear in an expression, each of them performs an assignment. This introduces a new aspect of the precedence order you should understand. Consider the following expression:

```
a=b=c=d=e=100;
```

This may at first seem confusing, especially if you know other computer languages. To C, the equal sign always means to assign the value on the right to the variable on the left. This right-to-left order is described in Appendix D's precedence table. The third column in that table is labeled *Associativity*, which describes the direction of the operation. The assignment operator associates from right to left, whereas some of the other C operators associate from left to right.

Because the assignment associates from right to left, the preceding expression first assigns 100 to the variable named e. This produces a value, 100, of the expression. In C, all expressions produce values, typically the result of assignments. Therefore, this value, 100, is then assigned to the variable d. The value of that 100 is assigned to c, then to b, and finally to a. Whatever values were in the five variables previous to this statement would be replaced by 100 after the statement finishes.

Because C does not automatically set variables to zero before you use them, you might want to zero them out before you use them with a single assignment statement. The following section of variable definitions and initializations is performed with multiple assignment statements:

```
#include <stdio.h>
main()
{
    int ctr, numEmp, numDep;
    float sales, salary, amount;

    ctr=numEmp=numDep=0;
    sales=salary=amount=0;
    /* Rest of program follows */
```

In C, you can include the assignment statement almost anywhere in a program, even within another calculation. For example, consider the statement

```
value = 5 + (r = 9 - c);
```

which is a perfectly legal C statement. The assignment operator resides on the first level of the precedence table and always produces a value. Because its associativity is right to left, the r is first assigned 9 - c because the rightmost equal sign is evaluated first. The subexpression (r = 9 - c) produces a value (whatever is placed into r) that is added to 5 before that result is stored in value.

## Example

Because C does not initialize variables to zero before you use them, you may want to include a multiple assignment operator to zero them out before using them. The following section of code ensures that all variables are initialized before the rest of the program uses them:

```c
#include <stdio.h>
main()
(
    int numEmp, dependents, age;
    float salary, hrRate, taxrate;

    /* Initialize all variables to zero */
    numEmp=dependents=age=hours=0;
    salary=hrRate=taxrate=0.0;

    /* Rest of program follows */
```

## Compound Assignments

Many times in programming, you may want to update the value of a variable. That is, you need to take a variable's current value, add or multiply that value by an expression, and then assign the value back to the original variable. The following assignment statement demonstrates this:

```c
salary=salary*1.2;
```

This expression multiplies the old value of `salary` by 1.2 (in effect, raising the value in `salary` by 20 percent) and then assigns it back to `salary`. C provides several operators, called *compound operators*, that you can use when the same variable appears on both sides of the equal sign. The compound operators are shown in Table 8.4.

### Table 8.4. C's compound operators.

| Operator | Example | Equivalent |
|---|---|---|
| += | bonus+=500; | bonus=bonus+500; |
| -= | budget-=50; | budget=budget-50; |
| *= | salary*=1.2; | salary=salary*1.2; |
| /= | factor/=.50; | factor=factor/.50; |
| %= | daynum%=7; | daynum=daynum%7; |

The compound operators are low in the precedence table. They typically are evaluated very late in equations that use them.

## Examples

1. You have been storing your factory's production amount in a variable called prodAmt, and your supervisor has just informed you of a new addition that needs to be applied to that production value. You could code this update in a statement that looks like this:

```
prodAmt = prodAmt + 2.6;  /* Add 2.6 to current production */
```

Instead of using this formula, you should use C's compound addition operator by coding it like this:

```
prodAmt += 2.6;  /* Add 2.6 to current production */
```

2. Suppose that you are a high school teacher who wants to adjust your students' grades upward. You gave a test that seemed too difficult, and the grades were not up to your expectations. If you had stored each student's grade in a variable named grade1, grade2, grade3, and so on, you could update the grades from within a program with the following section of compound assignments:

```
grade1*=1.1;     /* Increase each student's grade by 10
                      percent */
grade2*=1.1;
grade3*=1.1;
/* Rest of grade changes follow */
```

3. The precedence of the compound operators requires important consideration when you decide how to code compound assignments. Notice from Appendix D that the compound operators are on level 14, much lower than the regular math operators. This means that you must be careful how you interpret the compound operators.

Suppose that you want to update the value of a sales variable with this formula:

```
4-factor+bonus
```

You could update the sales variable with the following statement:

```
sales += 4 - factor + bonus;
```

This adds the quantity `4-factor+bonus` to `sales`. Although this returns the same value as the following statement, the two are evaluated differently:

```
sales = sales + 4 - factor + bonus;
```

Because the += operator is much lower in the precedence table than + or -, += is performed last, and with right-to-left associativity. Therefore, the following two statements *are* equivalent, from a precedence viewpoint:

```
sales += 4 - factor + bonus;

sales = sales + (4 - factor + bonus);
```

## Mixed Data Types in Calculations

C attempts to convert the smaller data type to the larger one in a mixed data-type expression.

You can mix data types in C, such as adding together an integer and a floating-point value. C generally converts the smaller of the two types to the other. For instance, if you add a double to an integer, C first converts the integer to a double value and then performs the calculation. This produces the most accurate result possible. The automatic conversion of data types is only temporary; the converted value is back in its original data type as soon as the expression is finished.

If C converted two different data types to the smaller value's type, the higher-precision value would be truncated, or shortened too much, and accuracy would be lost. For example, in the following short program, the floating-point value of `sales` is added to an integer called `bonus`. Before C computes the answer, it converts `bonus` to a floating-point value, which results in a floating-point answer.

```
/* Filename: C8DATA.C
   Demonstrates mixed data types in an expression */
#include <stdio.h>
main()
{
   int bonus=50;
   float salary=1400.50;
   float total;

   total=salary+bonus;   /* bonus becomes floating-point
                                  temporarily */
   printf("The total is %.2f", total);
   return;
}
```

Mixed data type calculation ──────── (points to the line `total=salary+bonus;`)

## Typecasting

Most of the time, you don't have to worry about C's automatic conversion of data types. However, problems can occur if you mix unsigned variables with variables of other data types. Because of differences in computer architecture, unsigned variables do not always convert to the larger data type. This can result in loss of accuracy and even incorrect results.

You can override C's default conversions by specifying your own *temporary* type change. This is called *typecasting*. When you typecast, you temporarily change a variable's data type from its defined data type to a new one. The format of a typecast is

```
(data type) expression
```

where `data type` can be any valid C data type, and `expression` can be a variable, a constant, or an expression that combines both. The following code typecasts the integer variable age to a double floating-point variable temporarily so that it can be multiplied by the double floating-point `factor`:

```
ageFactor = (double)age * factor;   /* Temporarily change age */
                                    /* to double            */
```

## Examples

1. Suppose that you want to verify the interest calculation used by your bank on a loan. The interest rate is 15.5 percent, stored as .155 in a floating-point variable. The amount of interest you owe is computed by multiplying the amount of the loan balance by the interest rate and then multiplying that by the number of days in the year since the loan originated. The following program finds the daily interest rate by dividing the annual interest rate by 365, the number of days in a year. C must convert the integer 365 to a floating-point constant automatically because it is used with a floating-point variable.

```
/* Filename: C8INT1.C
   Calculates interest on a loan */
#include <stdio.h>
main()
{
   int days=45;                 /* Days since loan
origination */
   float principal = 3500.00;   /* Original loan amount
*/
   float interestRate=0.155;    /* Annual interest rate
*/
   float dailyInterest;         /* Daily interest rate
*/
                                        ┌Gets daily interest rate
   dailyInterest=interestRate/365;  /* Compute floating-
                                        point value */
```

```
    /* Because days is an integer, it too will be converted
        to float next */
 dailyInterest = principal * dailyInterest * days;
 principal+=dailyInterest;          /* Update the principal
                                         with interest */
 printf("The balance you owe is %.2f", principal);
 return;
}
```

Here is the output of this program:

```
The balance you owe is 3566.88
```

2. Instead of letting C perform the conversion, you may want to typecast all mixed expressions to ensure that they convert to your liking. Here is the same program except that typecasts are used to convert the integer constants to floating-point values before they are used.

```
/* Filename: C8INT2.C
   Calculates interest on a loan, using typecasting */
#include <stdio.h>
main()
{
    int days=45;                    /* Days since loan origina-
                                       tion */
    float principal = 3500.00;  /* Original loan amount */
    float interestRate=0.155;   /* Annual interest rate */
    float dailyInterest;        /* Daily interest rate */

    dailyInterest=interestRate/(float)365;   /* Typecast days
                           └─Explicit typecast  to float */

    /* Since days is integer, convert it to float too */
    dailyInterest = principal * dailyInterest * (float)days;
    principal+=dailyInterest;   /* Update the principal with
                                   interest */
    printf("The balance you owe is %.2f", principal);
    return;
}
```

The output from this program is exactly the same as for the first program.

---

**For Related Information**

♦ "Additional C Operators," p. 181
♦ "Bitwise Operators," p. 195
♦ "Numeric Functions," p. 378

## Summary

You now understand C's primary math operators and the importance of the precedence table. Parentheses group operations together so that they can override the default precedence levels. C differs from some other programming languages in that every operator in C has a meaning, no matter where it appears in an expression. This enables you to use the assignment operator (=) in the middle of other expressions.

When you perform math with C, you also must be aware of how C interprets data types, especially when you mix them within the same expression. Of course, you can temporarily typecast a variable or constant so that you can override its default data type.

This chapter introduced you to C operators. The following two chapters extend this introduction to include relational and logical operators. They enable you to compare data and then compute accordingly.

## Review Questions

Answers to review questions are in Appendix B.

1. What is the result of each of the following expressions?

   a. 1 + 2 * 4 / 2

   b. (1 + 2) * 4 / 2

   c. 1 + 2 * (4 / 2)

2. What is the result of each of the following expressions?

   a. 9 % 2 + 1

   b. (1 + (10 - (2 + 2)))

3. Convert each of the following formulas into its C assignment equivalents:

   a. $a = \dfrac{3 + 3}{4 + 4}$

   b. x = (a - b)*(a - c)2

   c. $d = \dfrac{(8 - x^2)}{(x - 9)} - \dfrac{(4 * 2 - 1)}{x^3}$

4. Write a short program that prints the area of a circle with a radius of 4 inches and pi equal to 3.14159. (Hint: The area of a circle is computed by pi * radius².)

5. Write the assignment and `printf()` statements that print the remainder of 100 / 3.

# Review Exercises

1. Write a program that prints each of the first 8 powers of 2—that is, $2^1$, $2^2$, $2^3$,...$2^8$. Include a comment that indicates your name at the top of the program. Print string constants that describe each answer printed. The first two lines of your output should look like this:

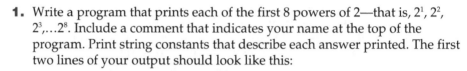

```
2 raised to the first power is: 2
2 raised to the second power is: 4
```

2. Change C8DIV.C so that it computes and prints a bonus of 15 percent of the gross pay. Taxes are not to be taken out of the bonus. After printing the four variables `grossPay`, `taxRate`, `bonus`, and `grossPay`, print a check on the screen that looks like a printed check. Add string constants so that it prints the name of the payee and puts your name as the payer at the bottom of the check.

3. Store in variables the weights and ages of three people. Print a table, with titles, of the weights and ages. At the bottom of the table, print the average of the weights and ages.

4. Assume that a video store employee works 50 hours. She gets paid $4.50 for the first 40 hours; she gets time-and-a-half pay (1.5 times the regular pay rate) for the first five hours over 40; and she gets double-time pay for all hours over 45. Assuming a 28-percent tax rate, write a program that prints her gross pay, taxes, and net pay to the screen. Label each amount with appropriate titles (using string constants) and add appropriate comments in the program.

# CHAPTER 9

# Relational Operators

Sometimes you actually *don't* want every statement in your C program to execute every time the program runs. So far, every program in this book has started executing at the top and has continued, line by line, until the last statement stopped executing. But, depending on your application, you may not always want this to happen.

Such programs are known as *data-driven* programs. That is, the data should dictate what the program does. You would not want the computer to print all paychecks for every pay period, for example, because some employees might have taken a leave of absence, or they might be paid on commission and not have made a sale during that period. Printing paychecks with zero dollars would be ridiculous. You want the computer to print checks only for employees who have pay coming, and for nobody else!

This chapter shows you how to create data-driven programs. These programs do not execute the same way every time they are run. This is possible through the use of *relational* operators that *conditionally* control other statements. Relational operators first "look" at the constants and variables in the program and then operate according to what they "find." This may sound like difficult programming, but it is actually quite straightforward and intuitive.

This chapter introduces the following topics:

♦ Relational operators

♦ The `if` statement

♦ The `else` statement

The chapter not only introduces these comparison commands, but also prepares you for much more powerful programs that become possible once you learn the relational operators.

# Defining Relational Operators

Relational operators compare data.

In addition to the math operators you learned in Chapter 8, operators for data comparisons are available. They are called *relational operators*, and their task is to compare data. They enable you to know whether two variables are equal or not equal, or which one is less or more than the other. Table 9.1 lists the relational operators.

**Table 9.1. The relational operators.**

| Operator | Description |
| --- | --- |
| == | Equal to |
| > | Greater than |
| < | Less than |
| >= | Greater than or equal to |
| <= | Less than or equal to |
| != | Not equal to |

The six relational operators provide the foundation for comparing data in C programming. They always appear with two constants, variables, or expressions (or with some combination of these), with one on each side of the operator. These relational operators are so useful that you should learn them as well as you know the +, -, *, /, and % mathematical operators.

**Note:** Unlike many programming languages, C uses a double equal sign (==) as a test for equality. The single equal sign (=) is reserved for assignment of values only.

## Examples

**1.** Assume that a program initializes four variables:

```
int a=5;
int b=10;
int c=15;
int d=5;
```

The following statements are then True:

a is equal to d, so a == d.

b is less than c, so b < c.

decision. The block of statements following the `if` executes if the decision (the result of the relation) is True, but the block does not execute otherwise.

As with relational logic, you also use `if` logic in everyday life. Consider the statements that follow:

"If the day is warm, I will go swimming."

"If I make enough money, we will build a new house."

"If the light is green, go."

"If the light is red, stop."

Each of these statements is *conditional*. That is, you perform the activity if—*and only if*—the condition is true.

> **Caution:** Do *not* put a semicolon after the parentheses of the relational test. Semicolons go after each statement inside the block.

### Expressions as the Condition

C interprets *any* nonzero value as True, and zero always as False. Therefore, you can insert regular nonconditional expressions within the `if` logic. Consider the following section of code:

```
main()
{
    int age=21;    /* Defines and assigns age as 21 */
    if (age=85)
    {  printf("You have lived through a lot!"); }
    /* Rest of program goes here */
```

At first, it may seem as though `printf()` does not execute, *but it does!* Because a regular assignment operator (=) is used (and not the == relational operator), C performs the assignment of **85** to `age`. This, as with all assignments you saw in Chapter 8, produces a value for the expression of **85**. Because **85** is nonzero, C interprets the `if` condition as True and then performs the body of the `if` statement. Mixing up the relational equality test (==) and the regular assignment operator (=) is a common error made in C programs, and the nonzero True test makes this bug even more difficult to find.

The designers of C didn't intend for this to confuse you. They wanted you to take advantage of this feature whenever you could. Instead of putting an assignment before an `if` and then testing the result of that assignment, you can combine the assignment and `if` into a single statement. Test your understanding of this by considering whether C would interpret the following condition as True or False:

*continues*

> *continued*
>
> ```
> if (10 == 10 == 10)...
> ```
>
> Be careful! At first glance, it seems True, but C "thinks" the expression is False! Because the == operator associates from left to right, the first 10 is compared to the second 10. Because they are equal, the result is 1 (for True), and the 1 is then compared to the third 10—which results in a 0 (for False)!

## Examples

**1.** The following are examples of valid C if statements.

> *Make sales a variable representing the salesperson's sales. Make bonus a variable representing the salesperson's bonus. If the salesperson's sales are greater than 5000, he or she gets a bonus of 500.*

```
if (sales > 5000)
   { bonus = 500; }
```

If the preceding code is part of a C program, the value inside the variable sales determines what happens next. If sales contains more than 5000, the next statement that executes is the one inside the block which initializes bonus. If, however, sales contains 5000 or less, the block does not execute, and the line following the if's block executes.

> *If the person's age is less than or equal to 21:*
> *Tell the user that he or she is a minor.*
> *Ask for the user's grade.*
> *Get the user's answer.*

```
if (age <= 21)
   { printf("You are a minor.\n");
     printf("What is your grade?");
     scanf(" %d", &grade); }
```

If the value in age is less than or equal to 21, the lines of code within the block execute next. Otherwise, C skips the entire block and continues with the remaining program.

> *If the person's current balance is higher than the acceptable overdue amount, print a Pastdue! message.*

```
if (balance > lowBalance)
   {printf("Past due!\n"); }
```

If the value in `balance` is more than that in `lowBalance`, execution of the program continues at the block, and the message `Past due!` prints on-screen. You can compare two variables to each other (as in the preceding example), a variable to a constant (as in the previous examples), a constant to a constant (although this is rarely done), or a constant to any expression in place of any variable or constant. The following `if` statement shows an expression included within the `if`:

> *If an employee's pay times the tax rate equals the minimum salary, assign 1400.60 to a variable.*

```
If (pay * taxRate == minimum)
    { lowSalary = 1400.60; }
```

The precedence table of operators in Appendix D includes the relational operators. They are at levels 6 and 7, lower than the other primary math operators. When you use expressions such as the one shown in the preceding example, you can make these expressions much more readable by enclosing them in parentheses (even though this is not required). Here is a rewrite of this `if` statement with ample parentheses:

```
If ((pay * taxRate) == minimum)
    { lowSalary = 1400.60; }
```

**2.** The following is a simple program that computes a salesperson's pay. The salesperson gets a basic flat rate of $4.10 per hour. In addition, if the sales are more than $8,500, the salesperson receives $500 as a bonus. This is a good introductory example of conditional logic that depends on a relation between two values, `sales` and 8500.

```
/* Filename: C9PAY1.C
   Calculates a salesperson's pay based on his or her sales */
#include <stdio.h>
main()
{
    char salName[20];
    int hours;
    float totalSales, bonus, pay;

    printf("\n\n");                /* Print 2 blank lines */
    printf("Payroll Calculation\n");
    printf("-------------------\n");

    /* Ask the user for needed values */

      printf("What is salesperson's last name? ");
```

```
    scanf(" %s", salName);      /* No & because it's an array */
    printf("How many hours did the salesperson work? ");
    scanf(" %d", &hours);
    printf("What were the total sales? ");
    scanf(" %f", &totalSales);

  bonus = 0;                          /* Initially, there is no bonus */

  /* Compute the base pay */
  pay = 4.10 * (float)hours;   /* Typecast the hours */

  /* Add bonus only if sales were high */
  if (totalSales > 8500.00)
     { bonus = 500.00; }

  printf("%s made $%.2f \n", salName, pay);
  printf("and got a bonus of $%.2f", bonus);

  return;
}
```

Test for bonus ———— (points to `if (totalSales > 8500.00)`)

The following output shows the result of running this program twice, each time with different input values. Notice that the program does two different things: it indicates that one employee got no bonus, but computes a bonus for another employee. The $500 bonus is a direct result of the if statement. The assignment of $500 to bonus is executed only if the value in totalSales is more than $8500.

```
Payroll Calculation
- - - - - - - - - - - - - - - - - -
What is salesperson's last name? Harrison
How many hours did the salesperson work? 40
What were the total sales? 6050.64
Harrison made $164.00
and got a bonus of $0.00

Payroll Calculation
- - - - - - - - - - - - - - - - - -
What is salesperson's last name? Robertson
How many hours did the salesperson work? 40
What were the total sales? 9800
Robertson made $164.00
and got a bonus of $500.00
```

**3.** While programming the way users input data, it is often wise to perform *data validation* on the values they type. If a user enters a bad value (for instance, a negative number when you know the input cannot be negative), you can inform the user of the problem and ask for reentry of the data.

Not all data can be validated, of course, but most of it can be checked for reasonableness. For example, if you write a student record-keeping program to track each student's name, address, age, and other pertinent data, you can check to see whether the age falls within a reasonable range. If the user enters 213 for the age, you know the value is incorrect. If the user enters -4 for the age, you know that this value also is incorrect. Not all erroneous input for age can be checked, however. If the user is 21, for instance, and enters 22, your program would have no way of knowing whether this is correct, because 22 falls within a reasonable age range for students.

The following program is a routine that requests an age and checks to make sure it is more than 10. This test is certainly not foolproof (because the user can still enter incorrect ages), but it takes care of extremely low values. If the user enters an invalid age, the program asks for it again inside the if statement.

```c
/* Filename: C9AGE.C
   Program to help ensure that age values are reasonable */
#include <stdio.h>
main()
{
    int age;

    printf("\nWhat is the student's age? ");
    scanf(" %d", &age);
    if (age < 10)
        { printf("%c", '\x07');    /* BEEP */
          printf("*** The age cannot be less than 10 ***\n");
          printf("Try again...\n\n");
          printf("What is the student's age? ");
          scanf(" %d", &age);
        }

    printf("Thank you. You entered a valid age.");
    return;
}
```

Error message
might print

This routine could also be a section of a longer program. You learn later how to prompt repeatedly for a value until a valid input is given. This program takes advantage of the bell (ASCII 7) to warn the user that an invalid age was entered.

If the entered age is less than 10, the user receives an error message. The program beeps and warns the user about the invalid age before asking for it again.

The following shows the result of running this program. Notice that the program "knows," because of the `if` statement, whether age is more than 10.

```
What is the student's age? 3
*** The age cannot be less than 10 ***
Try again...

What is the student's age? 21
Thank you. You entered a valid age.
```

4. Unlike many languages, C does not include a square math operator. Remember that you "square" a number by multiplying it times itself (3 * 3, for example). Because many computers do not allow for integers to hold more than the square of 180, the following program uses `if` statements to make sure the number fits as an integer answer when it is computed.

The program takes a value from the user and prints its square—unless it is more than 180. The message `Square is not allowed for numbers over 180` appears on-screen if the user types a larger number.

```
/* Filename: C9SQR1.C
   Prints the square of the input value
   if the input value is less than 180 */
#include <stdio.h>
main()
{
   int num, square;

   printf("\n\n");  /* Print 2 blank lines */
   printf("What number do you want to see the square of? ");
   scanf(" %d", &num);

   if (num <= 180)
   { square = num * num;
     printf("The square of %d is %d", num, square);
   }
```

Don't compute square if number is too big

```
    if (num > 180)
    { printf("%c", '\x07');    /* BEEP */
      printf("\n*** Square is not allowed for numbers over
      ➡180***");
      printf("\nRun this program again and try a smaller
      ➡value.");
    }

    printf("\nThank you for requesting square roots.\n");
    return;
}
```

The following output shows a couple of sample runs with this program. Notice that both conditions work: if the user enters a number less than 180, the calculated square appears; but if the user enters a larger number, an error message appears.

```
What number do you want to see the square of? 45
The square of 45 is 2025
Thank you for requesting square roots.

What number do you want to see the square of? 212


*** Square is not allowed for numbers over 180 ***
Run this program again and try a smaller value.
Thank you for requesting square roots.
```

This program is improved when you learn the else statement later in this chapter. This code includes a redundant check of the user's input. The variable num must be checked once to print the square if the input number is less than or equal to 180, and checked again for the error message if it is greater than 180.

**5.** The value of 1 and 0 for True and False, respectively, can help save you an extra programming step, which you are not necessarily able to save in other languages. Examine the following section of code:

```
commission = 0;    /* Initialize commission */

if (sales > 10000)
    { commission = 500.00; }

pay = netPay + commission;    /* Commission is 0 unless high
                                 sales */
```

This program can be streamlined and made more efficient by combining the if's relational test because you know that if returns 1 or 0:

```
pay = netPay + (commission = (sales > 10000) * 500.00);
```

This single line does what it took the previous four lines to do. Because the rightmost assignment has precedence, it gets computed first. The variable sales is compared to 10000. If it is more than 10000, a True result of 1 is returned. That 1 is multiplied by 500.00 and stored in commission. If, however, sales is not more than 10000, a 0 results, and 0 multiplied by 500.00 still returns 0.

Whichever value (500.00 or 0) is assigned to commission also becomes the value of that expression. That value is then added to netPay and stored in pay.

# The *else* Statement

The else statement never appears in a program without an if statement. This section introduces the else statement by showing you the popular if-else combination statement. Its format is

```
if (condition)
    { A block of 1 or more C statements }
else
    { A block of 1 or more C statements }
```

The first part of the if-else is identical to the if statement. If the condition is True, the block of C statements following the if executes. If the condition is False, however, the block of C statements following the else executes instead. Whereas the simple if statement determines what happens only when the condition is True, the if-else also determines what happens if the condition is False. No matter what the outcome is, the statement following the if-else executes next.

The following items describe the nature of the if-else:

◆ If the condition test is True, the entire block of statements following the if is performed.

◆ If the condition test is False, the entire block of statements following the else is performed.

**Note:** In addition to comparing numbers, you can compare characters. When you compare characters, C uses the ASCII table to determine which character is "less than" (lower in the ASCII table) the other. But you cannot compare character strings or arrays of character strings directly with relational operators.

┌─────────────────────────────────────────────────────┐
**For Related Information**

♦ "Logical Operators," p. 169
└─────────────────────────────────────────────────────┘

## Examples

**1.** The following program asks the user for a number. It then prints whether or not the number is greater than zero, using the if-else statement.

```
/* Filename: C9IFEL1.C
   Demonstrates if-else by printing whether an
   input value is greater than zero  */
#include <stdio.h>
main()
{
   int num;

   printf("What is your number? ");
   scanf(" %d", &num);   /* Get the user's number */

   if (num > 0)
      { printf("More than 0\n"); }
   else
      { printf("Less or equal to 0\n"); }

   /* No matter what the number is, the following executes */
   printf("\n\nThanks for your time!");
   return;
}
```

Print the result of the test

There is no need to test for *both* possibilities when you use an else. The if tests to see whether the number is greater than zero, and the else automatically takes care of all other possibilities.

**2.** The following program asks the user for his or her first name and then stores it in a character array. The first character of the array is checked to see whether it falls in the first half of the alphabet. If it does, an appropriate message is displayed.

```
/* Filename: C9IFEL2.C
   Tests the user's first initial and prints a message */
#include <stdio.h>
main()
{
```

163

```
    char last[20];   /* Holds the last name */
    printf("What is your last name? ");
    scanf(" %s", last);

    /* Test the initial */
    if (last[0] <= 'M')
        { printf("Your name is early in the alphabet.\n");}
    else
        { printf("You have to wait awhile for YOUR name to
            ➡be called!");}
    return;
}
```

Letter determines
what is printed

Notice that because a character array element is being compared to a
character constant, you must enclose the character constant inside single
quotation marks. The data types on both sides of each relational operator
must match.

3. The following program is a more complete payroll routine than you have
   seen. It uses if to illustrate how to compute overtime pay. The logic goes
   something like this:

   If employees work 40 hours or fewer, they get paid regular pay (their
   hourly rate times the number of hours worked). If employees work from 41
   through 50 hours, they get one-and-a-half times their hourly rate for the
   hours over 40, in addition to their regular pay for the first 40. All hours
   over 50 are paid at double the regular rate.

```
/* Filename: C9PAY2.C
   Computes the full overtime pay possibilities */
#include <stdio.h>
main()
{
    int hours;
    float dt, ht, rp, rate, pay;

    printf("\n\nHow many hours were worked? ");
    scanf(" %d", &hours);
    printf("\nWhat is the regular hourly pay?");
    scanf(" %f", &rate);

    /* Compute pay here */
    /* Double-time possibility */
    if (hours > 50)
```

```
        { dt = 2.0 * rate * (float)(hours - 50);
          ht = 1.5 * rate * 10.0;   /* Time + 1/2 for 10 hours */ }
    else
        { dt = 0.0; }   /* Either none or double for those hours
                             over 50 */

    /* Time and a half */
    if (hours > 40)
        { ht = 1.5 * rate * (float)(hours - 40); }

    /* Regular Pay */
    if (hours >= 40)
        { rp = 40 * rate; }
    else
        { rp = (float)hours * rate; }

    pay = dt + ht + rp;   /* Add up 3 components of payroll */

    printf("\nThe pay is %.2f", pay);
    return;
}
```

Employee gets
time and a half _____ (points to `{ ht = 1.5 * rate * (float)(hours - 40); }`)

Employee gets
regular pay only _____ (points to `{ rp = (float)hours * rate; }`)

**4.** The block of statements following the `if` can contain any valid C statement—even another `if` statement! This sometimes comes in handy, as this example shows.

The following program could be run to give an award to employees based on their years of service to your company. In this example, you are giving a gold watch to those with more than 20 years of service, a paperweight to those with more than 10 years, and a pat on the back to everyone else!

```
/* Filename: C9SERV.C
   Prints a message depending on years of service */
#include <stdio.h>
main()
{
    int yrs;
    printf("How many years of service? ");
    scanf(" %d", &yrs);   /* Get the years they have worked */

    if (yrs > 20)
```

```
          { printf("Give a gold watch\n"); }
      else
          { if (yrs > 10)
            { printf("Give a paperweight\n"); }
            else
              { printf("Give a pat on the back\n"); }
          }
      return;
  }
```

Only workers under 10 years see this

You should probably not rely on the if within an if to take care of *too many* conditions, because more than three or four conditions can add confusion. You might get into some messy logic, such as: "If this is True, and then if this is also True, then do something; but if not that, but something else is True, then . . ." (and so on). The switch statement that you learn about in Chapter 16 handles these types of multiple if selections much better than a long if within an if statement does.

## Summary

You now have the tools to write powerful data-checking programs. This chapter showed you how to compare constants, variables, and combinations of both by using relational operators. The if and if-else statements rely on such data comparisons to determine which code to execute next. You can now *conditionally execute* statements within your programs.

The next chapter takes you one step further by combining relational operators in order to create logical operators (sometimes called *compound conditions*). These logical operators further improve your program's capability to make selections based on data comparisons.

## Review Questions

Answers to review questions are in Appendix B.

1. Which operator tests for equality?

2. State whether each of these relational tests is True or False:

    a. 4 >= 5

    b. 4 == 4

    c. 165 >= 165

    d. 0 != 25

**3.** True or false: `C is fun` prints on-screen when the following statement is executed.

```
if (54 <= 54)
    { printf("C is fun"); }
```

**4.** What is the difference between an `if` statement and an `if-else` statement?

**5.** Does the following `printf()` execute?

```
if (3 != 4 != 1)
    { printf("This will print"); }
```

**6.** Using the ASCII table (see Appendix C), state whether these character relational tests are True or False:

a. `'C' < 'c'`

b. `'0' > '0'`

c. `'?' > ')'`

# Review Exercises

**1.** Write a weather-calculator program that asks for a list of the previous five days' temperatures and then prints `Brrrr!` every time a temperature falls below freezing.

**2.** Write a program that asks for a number and then prints the square and cube (the number multiplied by itself three times) of the number you input, if that number is more than 1. Otherwise, the program does not print anything.

**3.** In a program, ask the user for two numbers. Print a message telling how the first number relates to the second. In other words, if the user enters 5 and 7, your program prints `5 is less than 7`.

**4.** Write a program that prompts the user for an employee's pretax salary and then prints the appropriate taxes. The taxes are 10 percent if the employee makes less than $10,000; 15 percent if the employee earns from $10,000 to $19,999; and 20 percent if the employee earns $20,000 or more.

# CHAPTER 10

# Logical Operators

C's *logical operators* enable you to combine relational operators into more powerful data-testing statements. The logical operators are sometimes called *compound relational operators*. As C's precedence table shows, relational operators take precedence over logical operators when you combine them. The precedence table plays an important role in the use of these types of operators, as this chapter stresses.

The chapter introduces the following topics:

♦ Logical operators

♦ How logical operators are used

♦ How logical operators take precedence

This chapter concludes your study of the conditional testing you can perform with C and illustrates many examples of `if` statements in programs that work on compound conditional tests.

## Logical Operators Defined

There may be times when you need to test more than one set of variables. You can combine more than one relational test in a *compound relational test* by using C's logical operators, as shown in Table 10.1.

**Table 10.1. Logical operators.**

| Operator | Meaning |
| --- | --- |
| && | AND |
| ¦¦ | OR |
| ! | NOT |

Logical operators enable compound relational tests.

The first two logical operators, && and ¦¦, never appear by themselves. They typically go between two or more relational tests.

Tables 10.2, 10.3, and 10.4 illustrate how each logical operator works. These tables are called *truth tables* because they show how to achieve True results from an if statement that uses these operators. Take a minute to study these tables.

**Table 10.2. The && AND truth table. Both sides of the operator must be True.**

| | | | | |
|---|---|---|---|---|
| True | AND | True | = | True |
| True | AND | False | = | False |
| False | AND | True | = | False |
| False | AND | False | = | False |

**Table 10.3. The ¦¦ OR truth table. One or the other side of the operator must be True.**

| | | | | |
|---|---|---|---|---|
| True | OR | True | = | True |
| True | OR | False | = | True |
| False | OR | True | = | True |
| False | OR | False | = | False |

**Table 10.4. The ! NOT Truth table. Causes an opposite relation.**

| | | |
|---|---|---|
| NOT True | = | False |
| NOT False | = | True |

# Logical Operators and Their Use

The True and False on each side of the operators represent a relational if test. The following statements, for example, are valid if tests that use logical operators (sometimes called *compound relational operators*).

*If a is less than b, and c is greater than d, print* Results are invalid *to the screen.*

```
if ((a < b) && (c > d))
   { printf("Results are invalid."); }
```

The variable a must be less than b and, at the same time, c must be greater than d in order for the `printf()` to execute. The if statement still requires parentheses around its complete conditional test. Consider this portion of a program:

```
if ((sales > 5000) || (hrsWorked > 81))
    { bonus=500; }
```

The || is
sometimes called
*inclusive OR.*

The `sales` must be more than 5000, or the `hrsWorked` must be more than 81, before the assignment executes.

Now consider the use of the ! operator in the following relational test:

```
IF (!(sales < 2500))
    { bonus = 500; }
```

If `sales` is greater than or equal to 2500, `bonus` is initialized. This illustrates an important programming tip: Use ! sparingly. Or, as some professionals wisely put it, "Do *not* use ! or your programs will *not* be !(unclear)." It would be much clearer to rewrite this last example by turning it into a positive relational test:

```
if (sales >= 2500)
    { bonus 500; }
```

But the ! operator is sometimes helpful, especially when you test for end-of-file conditions. Most of the time, however, you can avoid using ! by using the reverse logic shown here:

```
!(var1 == var2) is the same as (var1 != var2)

!(var1 <= var2) is the same as (var1 > var2)

!(var1 >= var2) is the same as (var1 < var2)

!(var1 != var2) is the same as (var1 == var2)

!(var1 > var2) is the same as (var1 <= var2)

!(var1 < var2) is the same as (var1 >= var2)
```

Notice that the overall format of the if statement is retained when you use logical operators, but the relational test is expanded to include more than one relation. You can even have three or more relational tests, as in the following statement:

```
if ((a == B) && (d == f) || (1 = m) || !(k <> 2)) ...
```

This is a little too much, however, and good programming practice dictates using *at most* two relational tests inside a single if statement. If you need to combine more than two relational tests, use more than one if statement to do so.

As with other relational operators, you use the following logical operators in everyday conversation:

"If my pay is high and my vacation time is long, we can go to Italy this summer."

"If you take the trash out or clean your room, you can watch TV tonight."

"If you aren't good, you'll be punished."

---

**Internal Truths**

The True or False result of a relational test occurs internally at the bit level. For example, take the `if` test

```
if (a == 6) ...
```

to determine the truth of the relation (a==6). The computer takes a binary 6, or 00000110, and compares it, bit by bit, to the variable a. If a contains 7, a binary 00000111, the result of this *equal* test would be False, because the right bit (called the *least-significant bit*) is different.

---

# C's Logical Efficiency

C attempts to be more efficient than other languages. If you combine multiple relational tests with one of the logical operators, C does not always interpret the full expression. This ultimately makes your programs run faster, but there are dangers! For example, if your program is given the conditional test

```
if ((5 > 4) || (sales < 15) && (15 != 15))...
```

then C "looks at" only the first condition, (5 > 4), and realizes that it does not need to look further. Because (5 > 4) is True and remains True no matter what follows the || (OR), C does not bother with the rest of the expression.

Similarly, in the statement

```
if ((7 < 3) && (age > 15) && (initial == 'D'))...
```

C looks at only the first condition, which is False. Because of the && (AND), anything else that follows is also going to be False, so C does not interpret the expression to the right of (7 < 3). Most of the time, this doesn't pose any problem, but you should be aware that the following expression may not fulfill your expectations:

```
if ((5 > 4) || (num = 0))...
```

The (num = 0) assignment never executes because C needs to interpret only (5 > 4) to see whether the entire expression is True or False. Because of this danger, do *not* include assignment expressions in the same condition as a logical test. The single `if` condition

```
if ((sales > oldSales) || (inventoryFlag = 'Y'))...
```

should be broken into two statements, such as

```
inventoryFlag = 'Y';
if ((sales > oldSales) || (inventoryFlag))...
```

so that the inventoryFlag is always assigned the 'Y' value, no matter how the (sales
> oldSales) expression tests.

## Examples

1. The summer Olympics are held every four years, during each year that is
divisible evenly by 4. The U.S. Census is taken every 10 years, in each year
that is evenly divisible by 10. The following short program asks for a year
and then tells the user if it is a year of the summer Olympics, a year of the
census, or both. The program uses relational operators, logical operators,
and the modulus operator to determine this output.

```
/* Filename: C10YEAR.C
   Determines whether it is Summer Olympics year,
   U.S. Census year, or both */
#include <stdio.h>
main()
{
   int year;
   /* Ask for a year */
   printf("What is a year for the test? ");
   scanf(" %d", &year);

   /* Test the year */
   if (((year % 4)==0) && ((year % 10)==0))          Only decades
      { printf("Both Olympics and U.S. Census!"); }    divisible by 4
   if ((year % 4)==0)                                Only years divisible by 4
      { printf("Summer Olympics only"); }
   else
      { if ((year % 10)==0)                          Only decades not
         { printf("U.S. Census only"); }              divisible by 4
      }
   return;
}
```

2. Now that you know about compound relations, you can write an age-
checking program like C9AGE.C, presented in Chapter 9. That example
ensured that the age would be above 10. The following program shows
another way you can validate input to be sure that it is reasonable.

**173**

C10AGE.C includes a logical operator in its if, to see whether the age is greater than 10 and less than 100. If either of these is the case, the program knows that the user did not enter a valid age.

```
/* Filename: C10AGE.C
   Program to help ensure that age values are reasonable */
#include <stdio.h>
main()
{
    int age;
    printf("What is your age? ");
    scanf(" %d", &age);
    if ((age < 10) || (age > 100))───Test for extreme values
       { printf(" \x07 \x07 \n");    /* Beep twice */
         printf("*** The age must be between 10 and 100***\n"); }
    else
       { printf("You entered a valid age."); }
    return;
}
```

**3.** The following program might be used by a video store to calculate a discount, based on the number of rentals people transact, as well as their customer status. Customers are classified as either R for Regular or S for Special. Special customers have been members of the rental club for more than one year. They automatically receive a 50-cent discount on all rentals. The store also holds "value days" several times a year. On value days, all customers get the 50-cent discount. Special customers do not receive an additional 50 cents off during value days, because every day is a discount for them.

The program asks for each customer's status and whether today is a value day. It then uses the || relation to test for the discount. Even before you started learning C, you would probably have looked at this problem with the following idea in mind:

"If a customer is Special or if it is a value day, deduct 50 cents from the rental."

That's basically the idea of the if decision in the following program. Even though Special customers do not get an additional discount on value days, there is one final if test for them that prints an extra message at the bottom of the screen's indicated billing.

```
/* Filename: C10VIDEO.C
   Program to compute video rental amounts and give
   appropriate discounts based on the day or customer
   status. */
#include <stdio.h>
main()
{
   float tapeCharge, discount, rentalAmt;
   char firstName[15];
   char lastName[15];
   int numTapes;
   char valDay, spStat;

   printf("\n\n *** Video Rental Computation ***\n");
   printf("------------\n"); /* Underline title */

   tapeCharge = 2.00;    /* The before-discount tape fee per
                            tape */

   /* Get input data */
   printf("\nWhat is customer's first name? ");
   scanf(" %s", firstName);
   printf("What is customer's last name? ");
   scanf(" %s", lastName);

   printf("\nHow many tapes are being rented? ");
   scanf(" %d", &numTapes);

   printf("Is this a Value day (Y/N)? ");
   scanf(" %c", &valDay);

   printf("Is this a Special Status customer (Y/N)? ");
   scanf(" %c", &spStat);

   /* Calculate rental amount */
   discount = 0.0;    /* Apply the discount IF customer is
                         eligible */
   if ((valDay == 'Y') || (spStat == 'Y'))—Only some get discount
     { discount = 0.5; }
   rentalAmt = (numTapes * tapeCharge) - (discount * numTapes);
```

```
/* Print the bill */
printf("\n\n** Rental Club **\n\n");
printf("%s %s rented %d tapes\n", firstName, lastName,
        numTapes);
printf("The total was %.2f\n", rentalAmt);
printf("The discount was %.2f per tape\n", discount);


/* Print extra message for Special Status customer */
if (spStat == 'Y')
   { printf("\nThank the customer for being a Special
➥ Status customer");}
return;
}
```

Figure 10.1 shows the output from a sample run of this program. Notice that Special customers have the extra message at the bottom of the screen. This program, because of its if statements, performs differently depending on the data entered. No discount is applied for Regular customers on nonvalue days.

**Figure 10.1**

Logical *if* giving special discounts to certain customers.

```
*** Video Rental Computation ***
-----------------------------

What is customer's first name? Diane
What is customer's last name? Moore

How many tapes are being rented? 3
Is this a Value day (Y/N)? N
Is this a Special Status customer (Y/N)? Y


** Rental Club **

Diane Moore rented 3 tapes
The total was 4.50
The discount was 0.50 per tape

Thank them for being a Special Status customer
```

# Logical Operators and Their Precedence

Don't forget about the precedence of all operators.

The math precedence order you read about in Chapter 8 did not include the logical operators. To be fully informed, you should be familiar with the entire order of precedence, as presented in Appendix D. As you can see, the math operators take precedence over the relational operators, and the relational operators take precedence over the logical operators.

You might wonder why the relational and logical operators are included in a precedence table. The following statement helps show you why:

```
if ((sales < minSal * 2 && yrsEmp > 10 * sub) ...
```

Without the complete order of operators, it would be impossible to determine how such a statement would execute. According to the precedence order, this `if` statement would execute in this manner:

```
if ((sales < (minSal * 2)) && (yrsEmp > (10 * sub))) ...
```

This still may be confusing, but it is less so. The two multiplications would be performed first, followed by the relational tests < and >. The && is performed last because it is lowest in the precedence order of operators.

To avoid such ambiguous problems, be sure to use ample parentheses—even if the default precedence order is still your intention. It is also wise to resist combining too many expressions inside a single `if` relational test.

Notice that ¦¦ (OR) has lower precedence than && (AND). Therefore, the following `if` tests are equivalent:

```
if ((firstInitial == 'A') && (lastInitial == 'G') ¦¦
    (id == 321)) ...
```

```
if (((firstInitial == 'A') && (lastInitial == 'G')) ¦¦
    (id == 321)) ...
```

The second if test is clearer because of the parentheses, but the precedence table makes them identical.

## Summary

This chapter extended the `if` statement to include the &&, ¦¦, and ! logical operators. These operators enable you to combine several relational tests into a single test. C does not always need to look at every relational operator when you combine them in an expression.

This chapter concludes the explanation of the `if` statement. The next chapter explains the remaining C operators. As you saw in this chapter, the precedence table is still very important to the C language. Whenever you are evaluating expressions, keep the precedence table in the back of your mind (or at your fingertips) at all times.

## Review Questions

Answers to review questions are in Appendix B.

1. What are the three logical operators?

2. The following compound relational tests produce True or False comparisons. Determine which are True and which are False.

a. ! (True || False)

b. (True && False) && (False || True)

c. ! (True && False)

d. True || (False && False) || False

**3.** Given the statement

```
int i=12, j=10, k=5;
```

what are the results (True or False) of the following statements? (Hint: Remember that C interprets *any* nonzero statement as True.)

a. i && j

b. 12 - i || k

c. j != k && i != k

**4.** What is the value printed in the following program? (Hint: Don't be misled by the assignment operators on both sides of the ||.)

```
/* Filename: C10LOGO.C
   Logical operator test */
#include <stdio.h>
main()
{
    int f, g;

    g = 5;
    f = 8;
    if ((g = 25) || (f = 35))
        { printf("f is %d and g got changed to: %d", f, g); }
    return;
}
```

**5.** Using the precedence table, determine whether each of the following statements produces a True or False result. After this, you should *really* appreciate the abundant use of parentheses!

a. 5 == 4 + 1 || 7 * 2 != 12 - 1 && 5 == 8 / 2

b. 8 + 9 != 6 - 1 || 10 % 2 != 5 + 0

c. 17 - 1 > 15 + 1 && 0 + 2 = 1 == 1 || 4 != 1

d. 409 * 0 != 1 * 409 + 0 || 1 + 8 * 2 >= 17

**6.** Does the following `printf()` execute?

```
if (((first intial =='A') && (last initial == 'G')) ||
     (id == 321)))
```

# Review Exercises

**1.** Using a single compound `if` statement, write a program to determine whether the user enters an odd positive number.

**2.** Write a program that asks the user for two initials. Print a message telling the user whether the first initial falls alphabetically before the second.

**3.** Write a number-guessing game. Assign a value to a variable called `number` at the top of the program. Give a prompt that asks for five guesses. Get the user's five guesses with a single `scanf()`. See whether any of the guesses matches the `number` and then print an appropriate message if one does.

**4.** Write a tax calculation routine. A family pays no tax if its income is less than $5,000. The family pays a 10-percent tax if the combined salaries are from $5,000 through $9,999, or a 20-percent tax if the combined salaries are from $10,000 through $19,999. Otherwise, the family pays a 30-percent tax.

# CHAPTER 11

# Additional C Operators

C also has several other operators that you should learn. In fact, C has more operators than most programming languages. Unless you become familiar with C's operators, you might think that C programs are cryptic and difficult to follow. But C's heavy reliance on its operators and operator precedence produces the efficiency that enables your programs to run more smoothly and quickly.

This chapter describes the following operators:

- The ?: conditional operator
- The ++ increment operator
- The - - decrement operator
- The sizeof operator
- The (,) comma operator

Most of the operators discussed in this chapter are unlike those found in any other programming language. Even if you have programmed in other languages for many years, you still may be surprised by the power of these C operators.

# The Conditional Operator

The conditional operator is a ternary operator.

The *conditional operator* is C's only *ternary* operator, which requires three operands (compared to the unary operator's single and the binary operator's double operand requirements). The conditional operator is used to replace if-else logic in some situations. The conditional operator is a two-part symbol, ?:, with the following format:

```
conditionalExpression ? expression1 : expression2;
```

The conditionalExpression is any expression in C that results in a True (nonzero) or False (0) answer. If the result of the conditionalExpression is True, expression1 executes. If the result of the conditionalExpression is False, expression2 executes. Only one of the expressions following the question mark executes. You put a single semicolon at the end of expression2. The internal expressions, such as expression1, should not have a semicolon.

Figure 11.1 illustrates the conditional operator a little more clearly.

**Figure 11.1**

Format of the conditional operator.

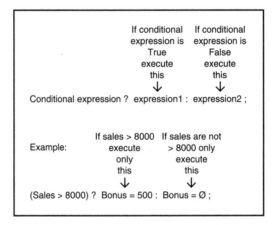

If you require simple if-else logic, the conditional operator usually provides a more direct and succinct method, although you should *always* prefer readability over compact code.

To get a glimpse of the conditional operator at work, consider this section of code:

```
if (a > b)
    { ans = 10; }
else
    { ans = 25; }
```

You can easily rewrite this kind of if-else code by using a single conditional operator:

*If the variable a is greater than the variable b, make the variable ans equal to 10; otherwise, make ans equal to 25.*

```
a > b ? (ans = 10) : (ans = 25);
```

Although parentheses are not required around the `conditionalExpression` to make it work, they usually improve readability. This statement's readability could be improved by using parentheses, as in the following line:

```
(a > b) ? (ans = 10) : (ans = 25);
```

Because each C expression has a value—in this case, the value being assigned—this statement can be made *even more* succinct, without loss of readability, by moving ans to the left of the conditional operation and assigning ans the answer directly like this:

```
ans = (a > b) ? (10) : (25);
```

This expression says, "If a is greater than b, assign 10 to ans; otherwise, assign 25 to ans." Almost any `if-else` statement can be rewritten as a conditional, and vice versa. You should practice converting one to the other, in order to acquaint yourself with the conditional operator's purpose.

> **Note:** Any valid `if` C statement can be a `conditionalExpression`, including all relational and logical operators as well as any of their possible combinations.

---

**For Related Information**

♦ "The *if* Statement," p. 154

♦ "The *else* Statement," p. 162

---

## Examples

**1.** Suppose that you are looking over your early C programs and you notice the following section of code:

```
if (production > target)
    { target *= 1.10; }
else
    { target *= .90; }
```

You realize that such a simple if-else statement can be rewritten, using a conditional operator, and that more efficient code would result. You could therefore change it to the following single statement:

```
(production > target) ? (target *= 1.10) : (target *= .90);
```

2. Using a conditional operator, you can write a routine to find the minimum value between two variables. This is sometimes called a *minimum routine*. The statement to do this is

```
minimum = (var1 < var2) ? var1 : var2;
```

If var1 is less than var2, the value of var1 is assigned to minimum. If var2 is less, the value of var2 is assigned to minimum. If the variables are equal, the value of var2 is assigned to minimum because it does not matter which is assigned.

3. You can write a *maximum routine* just as easily:

```
maximum = (var1 > var2) ? var1 : var2;
```

4. Taking the preceding examples a step further, you can test also for the sign of a variable. The following conditional expression assigns –1 to the variable called sign if testvar is less than 0; 0 to sign if testvar *is* zero; and +1 to sign if testvar is 1 or more:

```
sign = (testvar < 0) ? -1 : (testvar > 0);
```

It may be easy to spot why the less-than test results in a –1, but the second part of the expression might be confusing. This works well because of C's 1 and 0 return values (for True and False, respectively) from a relational test. If testvar is 0 or greater, sign is assigned the answer of (testvar > 0). The value of (testvar > 0) is 1 if True (therefore, testvar is more than 0) or 0 if testvar is equal to 0.

The preceding statement shows C's efficient conditional operator very well. It may also help you to write this by using typical if-else logic. Here is the same problem written with a typical if-else statement:

```
if (testvar < 0)
   { sign = -1; }
else
   { sign = (testvar > 0); }   /* testvar can  be only
                                  0 or more here */
```

# The Increment and Decrement Operators

The ++ operator adds 1 to a variable. The -- operator subtracts 1 from a variable.

C offers two unique operators that add or subtract 1 to or from variables. These are the *increment* and *decrement* operators, ++ and --. Table 11.1 shows how these operators relate to other types of expressions you have seen. Notice that the ++ and -- can go on either side of the modified variable. If the ++ or -- appears on the left, it is known as a *prefix* operator. If it appears on the right, it is a *postfix* operator.

**Table 11.1. The ++ and -- operators.**

| Operator | Example | Description | Equivalent | Statements |
|----------|---------|-------------|------------|------------|
| ++ | i++; | postfix | i = i + 1; | i += 1; |
| ++ | ++i; | prefix | i = i + 1; | i += 1; |
| -- | i--; | postfix | i = i - 1; | i -= 1; |
| -- | --i; | prefix | i = i - 1; | i -= 1; |

When you need to add 1 to a variable or subtract 1 from a variable, you can use these two operators. As Table 11.1 shows, if you need to increment or decrement only a single variable, these operators enable you to do so.

**Increment and Decrement Efficiency**

The increment and decrement operators, ++ and --, are straightforward, efficient methods for adding 1 to a variable and subtracting 1 from a variable. You often need to do this during counting or processing loops, as shown in Part III of this book.

These two operators compile directly into their assembly language equivalents. Almost all computers include, at their lowest binary machine-language commands, increment and decrement instructions. If you use C's increment and decrement operators, you ensure that they compile into these low-level equivalents.

If, however, you *code* expressions to add or subtract 1 (as you would in other programming languages), such as the expression i = i - 1, you *do not* actually ensure that C compiles this instruction into its efficient machine-language equivalent.

Whether you use a prefix or postfix operator does not matter—if you are incrementing or decrementing single variables on lines by themselves. However, when you combine these two operators with other operators in a single expression, you must be aware of their differences. Consider the following program section. Here, all variables are integers because the increment and decrement operators work only on integer variables.

*Make a equal to 6. Increment a, subtract 1 from it, and then assign the result to b.*

```
a = 6;
b = ++a - 1;
```

What are the values of a and b after these two statements finish? The value of a is easy to determine: it is incremented in the second statement, and so it is 7. However, b is either 5 or 6 depending on *when* the variable a increments. To determine when a increments, consider the following rules:

- ◆ If a variable is incremented or decremented with a *prefix* operator, the increment or decrement occurs *before* the variable's value is used in the rest of the expression.

- ◆ If a variable is incremented or decremented with a *postfix* operator, the increment or decrement occurs *after* the variable's value is used in the rest of the expression.

In the preceding code, a contains a prefix increment. Therefore, its value is first incremented to 7, then 1 is subtracted from 7, and the result (6) is assigned to b. But if a postfix increment is used, as in

```
a = 6;
b = a++ - 1;
```

a is 6; therefore, 5 is assigned to b because a does not increment to 7 until after its value is used in the expression. The precedence table in Appendix D shows that prefix operators contain much higher precedence than almost every other operator, especially low-precedence postfix increments and decrements.

> **Tip:** If the order of prefix and postfix operators confuses you, break your expressions into two lines of code, putting the increment or decrement before or after the expression that uses it.

By taking advantage of this tip, you can rewrite the preceding example in the following way:

```
a = 6;
b = a - 1;
a++;
```

There is now no doubt as to when a gets incremented: a increments after b is assigned to a -1.

Even parentheses cannot override the postfix rule. Consider the following statement:

```
x = p + (((amt++)));
```

There are too many unneeded parentheses here, but even the redundant parentheses are not enough to increment amt before adding its value to p. Postfix increments and decrements *always* occur after their variables are used in the surrounding expression.

> **Caution:** Do not attempt to increment or decrement an expression. You can apply these operators only to variables. The following expression is *invalid*:
>
> ```
> sales = ++(rate * hours);   /* Not allowed! */
> ```

## Examples

1. As with all other C operators, keep the precedence table in mind when you evaluate expressions that increment and decrement. Figure 11.2 shows you some examples that illustrate these operators.

**Figure 11.2**

C operators incrementing (above) and decrementing (below) by order of precedence.

```
int i=1;
int j=2;
int k=3;
ans = i++ * j - --k;

       i++ * j -  2
            \/
          2   -  2
            \____/
               0
```
ans = 0, then i increments by 1 to its final value of 2.

```
int i=1;
int j=2;
int k=3;
ans = ++i * j - k--;

      2  * j - k--
         \/
         4  - k--
            \___/
              1
```
ans = 1, then k decrements by 1 to its final value of 2.

**2.** The precedence table takes on even more meaning when you see a section of code such as that shown in Figure 11.3.

**Figure 11.3**

Another example of C operators and their precedence.

```
int i=0;
int j=-1;
int k=0;
int m=1;
ans = i++ && ++j || k || m++;
         |
         |
   i++ && 0  || k || m++
      \  /
       0      || k || m++
           \  /
            0        || m++
                \  /
                 1
```

ans = 1, then i increments by 1 to its final value of 1, and m increments by 1 to its final value of 2.

**3.** Considering the precedence table—and, more important, what you know about C's relational efficiencies—what is the value of the ans in the following section of code?

```
int i=1, j=20, k=-1, l=0, m=1, n=0, o=2, p=1;
ans = i || j-- && k++ || ++l && ++m || n-- & !o || p-- ;
```

This, at first, seems to be extremely complicated. Nevertheless, you can simply glance at it and determine the value of ans, as well as the ending value of the rest of the variables.

Recall that when C performs a relational test with || (OR), it ignores the right side of the || if the left value is True (any nonzero value is True). Because True or any other value is still True, C does not "think" it needs to look at the values on the right. Therefore, C performs this expression as shown:

```
ans = i || j-- && k++ || ++l && ++m || n-- & !o || p--;

      | (TRUE)
```

> **Note:** Because i is True, C "knows" the entire expression is True and ignores the rest of it after the first ¦¦. Therefore, *every other increment and decrement expression is ignored*. The result is that only **ans** is changed by this expression; the rest of the variables, j through p, are never incremented or decremented, even though several of them contain increment and decrement operators. If you use relational operators, be aware of this problem and break out all increment and decrement operators into statements by themselves, placing them on lines before the relational statements that use their values.

## The *sizeof* Operator

There is another operator in C that does not look like an operator at all. It looks like a built-in function, but it is called the sizeof operator. In fact, if you think of sizeof as a function call, you may not get too confused because it works in a similar way. sizeof has one of the following formats:

```
sizeof data
```

or

```
sizeof(data type)
```

The sizeof operator is unary because it operates on a single value. This operator produces a result that represents the size, in bytes, of the *data* or *data type* specified. Because most data types and variables require different amounts of internal storage on different computers, the sizeof operator is provided to enable programs to maintain consistency on different types of computers.

> **Tip:** Most C programmers use parentheses around the sizeof argument, whether that argument is *data* or *data type*. Because you *must* use parentheses around *data type* arguments and *can* use them around *data* arguments, it's simpler to use parentheses always for both kinds of arguments.

The sizeof
operator returns
its argument's size
in bytes.

The sizeof operator is sometimes called a *compile-time operator*. At compile time, instead of run time, the compiler replaces each occurrence of sizeof in your program with an unsigned integer value. Because sizeof is more for advanced C programming, this operator is better used later in the book for more advanced programming requirements.

If you use an array as the sizeof argument, C returns the number of bytes you originally reserved for that array. Data inside the array has nothing to do with the array's returned sizeof value—even if it's only a character array containing a very short string.

## Example

Suppose that you want to know the size, in bytes, of floating-point variables for your computer. You can determine this by putting the keyword float in parentheses—after sizeof—as shown in the following program:

```
/* Filename: C11SIZE1.C
   Prints the size of floating-point values */
#include <stdio.h>
main()
{
   printf("The size of floating-point variables \n");
   printf("on this computer is %d ", (int) sizeof(float));
   return;
}
```

Finds storage size of floating-point values

This program may produce different results on different computers. You can use any valid data type as the sizeof argument. When you directly print sizeof results, as shown here, you should typecast sizeof to an integer in order to print it properly with %d. On PCs, this program most likely produces this output:

```
The size of floating-point variables
on this computer is 4
```

# The Comma Operator

Another C operator, sometimes called a *sequence point*, works a little differently. This is the *comma operator* (,), which does not directly operate on data but produces a left-to-right evaluation of expressions. This operator enables you to put more than one expression on a single line by separating them with commas.

You have already seen one use of the sequence point comma when you learned how to define and initialize variables. In the following section of code, the comma separates statements. Because the comma associates from left to right, the first variable, i, is defined and initialized before the second variable:

```
main()
{
   int i=10, j=25;
   /* Rest of program follows */
```

However, the comma is *not* a sequence point when it is used inside function parentheses. Then it is said to *separate* arguments. Consider this `printf()`:

```
printf("%d %d %d", i, i++, ++i);
```

You may get one of many results from such a statement. The commas serve only to separate arguments of the `printf()`, and do not generate the left-to-right sequence that they would otherwise when they aren't used in functions. With the statement shown here, you are not assured of *any* order! The postfix `i++` might possibly be performed before the prefix `++i`, even though the precedence table does not explain this. Here, the order of evaluation depends on how your compiler sends these arguments to the `printf()` function.

> **Tip:** Do not put increment or decrement operators in function calls.

## Examples

1. You can put more than one expression on a line, using the comma for a sequence point, as in the following program:

```
/* Filename: C11COM1.C
   Illustrates the sequence point */
#include <stdio.h>
main()
{
   int num, sq, cube;
   num = 5;

   /* Calculate the square and cube of the number */
   sq = (num * num), cube = (num * num * num);

   printf("The square of %d is %d, and the cube is %d",
          num, sq, cube);
   return;
}
```

Sequence point comma ——— [points to the line `sq = (num * num), cube = (num * num * num);`]

This use of the comma, however, is not necessarily recommended, because it doesn't add anything to the program and actually decreases its readability. In this example, the square and cube are probably better computed on two separate lines.

2. The comma makes possible some interesting statements. Consider the following section of code:

```
i = 10
j = (i = 12, i + 8);
```

When this code finishes executing, j has the value of 20—even though this is not necessarily clear. In the first statement, i is assigned 10. In the second statement, the comma causes i to be assigned a value of 12; then j is assigned the value of i + 8, or 20.

3. In the following section of code, ans is assigned the value of 12 because the assignment *before* the comma is performed first. Despite this right-to-left associativity of the assignment operator, the comma's sequence point forces the assignment of 12 to x, before x is assigned to ans.

```
ans = (y = 8, x = 12);
```

When this finishes, y contains 8, x contains 12, and ans also contains 12.

## Summary

Now you have learned almost every operator in the C language. As explained in this chapter, the conditional, increment, and decrement operators enable C to stand apart from many other programming languages. You must always be aware of the precedence table whenever you use these, as you must with *all* operators.

The sizeof and sequence point operators act unlike most others. sizeof is a compile-time operator, and it works in a manner similar to the #define preprocessor directive in being replaced by its value at compile time. The sequence point operator enables you to put multiple statements on the same line—or within a single expression—but you should reserve it only for defining variables, because it may be unclear if it is combined with other expressions.

The next chapter explains the bitwise operators. They operate on a very low binary level on your computer's variables. Some people have programmed in C for years but have not yet learned the bitwise operators. If you are just learning C and are not interested in doing bit-level operations, you may want to skim the next chapter and come back to it later when you need those operators.

## Review Questions

Answers to review questions are in Appendix B.

1. What set of statements does the conditional operator replace?

2. Why is the conditional operator called a "ternary" operator?

**3.** Can the following conditional operator be rewritten as an if-else statement? If so, rewrite it as one.

```
ans = (a == b) ? c + 2 : c + 3;
```

**4.** True or false: The statement

```
var++;
```

and the statement

```
var = var + 1;
```

produce the same result.

**5.** Why is using the increment and decrement operators more efficient than using the addition and subtraction operators?

**6.** What is a sequence point?

**7.** Can the output of the following code be determined?

```
age = 20;
printf("You are now %d, and will be %d in one year",
       age, age++);
```

**8.** What is the output of the following code?

```
char name[20] = "Mike";
printf("The size of name is %d", (int) sizeof(name) );
```

# Review Exercises

**1.** Write a program that prints the numerals from 1 to 10. Use 10 different printf()s and only one variable, called result, to hold the value before each printf(). Use the increment operator to add 1 to result before each printf().

**2.** Write a program that asks users for their ages. Using a single printf() that includes a conditional operator, print on-screen the following sentence if the input age is over 21:

```
You are not a minor.
```

Otherwise, print this:

```
You are still a minor.
```

The printf() may be long, but it helps to illustrate how the conditional operator can work within other statements where if-else logic might not.

**3.** Use the conditional operator—and *no* `if-else` statements—to write the following tax calculation routine: A family pays no tax if its annual salary is less than $5,000. It pays a 10-percent tax if the salary range is from $5,000 through $9,999, a 20-percent tax if the salary range is from $10,000 through $19,999, and a 30-percent tax if the salary is $20,000 or more. This exercise is similar to one in Chapter 10, except for the conditional operator.

# CHAPTER 12

# Bitwise Operators

This chapter introduces the *bitwise operators*, which manipulate internal representations of data and not just "values in variables" as the other operators do. These bitwise operators require an understanding of Appendix A's binary numbering system, as well as a computer's memory. If you don't think you're ready to tackle these operators right now, of course, you could always skim this chapter and come back to it later.

Some people program in C for years and never learn the bitwise operators. Nevertheless, understanding them can help you improve a program's efficiency and enable you to operate at a deeper level than many other programming languages allow.

This chapter describes the following bitwise operators:

♦ Logical operators

♦ Compound operators

♦ Shift operators

This chapter concludes the discussion on C operators for a while. After you master the bitwise operators, you can perform almost any operation on your C variables and constants.

## Bitwise Logical Operators

There are four bitwise logical operators, and they are shown in Table 12.1. These operators work on the binary representations of integer data. This enables systems programmers to manipulate internal bits in memory and in variables. The bitwise operators are not just for systems programmers, however. Application programmers also can improve their programs' efficiency in several ways.

**Table 12.1. Bitwise logical operators.**

| Operator | Meaning |
|---|---|
| & | Bitwise AND |
| ¦ | Bitwise inclusive OR |
| ^ | Bitwise exclusive OR |
| ~ | Bitwise 1's complement |

Bitwise operators make bit-by-bit comparisons of internal data.

Each of the bitwise operators makes a bit-by-bit comparison of internal data. Bitwise operators apply only to character and integer variables and constants, and not to floating-point data. Because binary numbers consist of 1s and 0s, these 1s and 0s (called *bits*) are compared to each other in order to produce the desired result for each bitwise operator.

Before you study the examples, you should understand Table 12.2. It contains truth tables that describe the action of each bitwise operator on integer—or character—internal bit patterns.

**Table 12.2. Truth tables.**

*Bitwise AND (&)*

```
0 & 0 = 0
0 & 1 = 0
1 & 0 = 0
1 & 1 = 1
```

*Bitwise inclusive OR (¦)*

```
0 ¦ 0 = 0
0 ¦ 1 = 1
1 ¦ 0 = 1
1 ¦ 1 = 1
```

*Bitwise exclusive OR (^)*

```
0 ^ 0 = 0
0 ^ 1 = 1
1 ^ 0 = 1
1 ^ 1 = 0
```

---

*Bitwise 1's complement (~)*

```
~0 = 1

~1 = 0
```

---

In bitwise truth tables, you can replace the 1 and 0 with True and False, respectively, if it helps you to understand the result better. For the bitwise AND (&) truth table, both bits being compared by the & operator must be True for the result to be True. In other words, "True AND True results in True."

> **Tip:** By replacing the 1s and 0s with True and False, you might be able to relate the bitwise operators to the regular logical operators, && and ¦¦, which you use for `if` comparisons.

The ¦ bitwise operator is sometimes called the *bitwise inclusive OR* operator. If one side of the ¦ operator is 1 (True)—or if both sides are 1—the result is 1 (True).

The ^ operator is called *bitwise exclusive OR*. It means that either side of the ^ operator must be 1 (True) for the result to be 1 (True), but both sides cannot be 1 (True) at the same time.

For bitwise ^, one side or the other—but not both sides—must be 1.

The ~ operator, called *bitwise 1's complement*, reverses each bit to its opposite value.

> **Note:** Bitwise 1's complement does *not* negate a number. As Appendix A shows, most computers use a 2's complement to negate numbers. The bitwise 1's complement reverses the bit pattern of numbers, but it doesn't add the additional 1 as the 2's complement requires.

You can test and change individual bits inside variables in order to check for patterns of data. The following examples help to illustrate each of the four bitwise operators:

> **For Related Information**
>
> ♦ "Binary Negative Numbers," p. 571
>
> ♦ "How Binary and Addressing Relate to C," p. 576

## Examples

1. If you apply the bitwise & operator to numerals 9 and 14, you get a result of 8. Figure 12.1 shows why this is so. When the binary values of 9 (1001) and

14 (1110) are compared on a bitwise & basis, the resulting bit pattern is 8 (1000).

**Figure 12.1**

Performing bitwise & on 9 and 14.

```
  1   0   0   1   (9)
  ↓   ↓   ↓   ↓
  &   &   &   &
  1   1   1   0   (14)
= 1   0   0   0   (8)
```

In a C program, you could code this bitwise comparison in the following manner:

*Make* result *equal to the binary value of 9 (1001) ANDed to the binary value of 14 (1110).*

```
result = 9 & 14;
```

The result variable holds 8, which is the result of the bitwise &. The 9 or 14 (or both) could also be stored in variables, with the same outcome.

**2.** When you apply the bitwise ¦ operator to the numbers 9 and 14, you get 15. When the binary values of 9 (1001) and 14 (1110) are compared on a bitwise ¦ basis, the resulting bit pattern is 15 (1111) because result's bits are 1 (True) in every position where a bit is 1 in either of the two numbers.

In a C program, you could code this bitwise comparison in the following way:

```
result = 9 ¦ 14;
```

The result variable holds 15, which is the result of the bitwise ¦. The 9 or 14 (or both) could also be stored in variables.

**3.** The bitwise ^ applied to 9 and 14 produces 7. Bitwise ^ sets the resulting bits to 1 if one number or the other's bit is 1, but not if both of the matching bits are on at the same time.

In a C program, you could code this bitwise comparison like this:

```
result = 9 ^ 14;
```

The result variable holds 7 (binary 0111), which is the result of the bitwise ^. The 9 (binary 1001) or 14 (binary 1110)—or both—could also be stored in variables, with the same effect.

**4.** The bitwise ~ simply negates each bit. It is a unary bitwise operator because you can apply it to only a single value at any one time. The bitwise ~ applied to 9 results in 6, as shown in Figure 12.2.

**Figure 12.2**

Performing
bitwise ~ on the
number 9.

```
~ 1  0  0  1  (9)
= 0  1  1  0  (6)
```

In a C program, you could code this bitwise operation like this:

```
result = ~9;
```

The `result` variable holds 6, which is the result of the bitwise ~. The 9 could
have been stored in a variable with the same consequence.

5. You can take advantage of the bitwise operators to perform tests on data
that you could not do as efficiently in other ways.

Suppose that you want to know whether the user typed an odd or even
number (assuming that integers are being input). You could use the
modulus operator (%) to see whether the remainder—after dividing the
input value by 2—is 0 or 1. If the remainder is 0, the number is even. If the
remainder is 1, the number is odd.

The bitwise operators are more efficient than other operators because they
directly compare bit patterns without using any mathematical operations.
Because a number is even if its bit pattern ends in a 0, and odd if its bit
pattern ends in 1, you also can test for odd or even numbers by applying
the bitwise & to the data and to a binary 1. This is more efficient than using
the modulus operator. The following program uses this technique to
inform users that their input value is odd or even:

*Identify the file and include the necessary header file. This program will
test for odd or even input. You need a place to put the user's number, so
define the* input *variable as an integer.*

*Ask the user for the number to be tested. Put the user's answer in* input*.
Use the bitwise operator* & *to test the number. If the rightmost bit in* input
*is 1, tell the user that the number is odd. If the rightmost bit in* input *is 0,
tell the user that the number is even.*

```
/* Filename: C12ODEV.C
   Uses a bitwise & to see whether a number is odd or even */
#include <stdio.h>
main()
{
   int input;                    /* Will hold user's number */
   printf("What number do you want me to test? ");
   scanf(" %d", &input);
```

Tests the
rightmost bit

```
if (input & 1)                  /* True if result is 1;
                                   otherwise, it is false (0) */
    { printf("The number %d is odd", input); }
else
    { printf("The number %d is even", input); }
return;
}
```

6. The only difference between the bit patterns for uppercase and lowercase characters is bit number 6 (the third bit from the left, as shown in Appendix A). For lowercase letters, bit 5 is a 1. For uppercase letters, bit 5 is a 0. Figure 12.3 shows how *A* and *B* differ from *a* and *b* by a single bit.

**Figure 12.3**

Bitwise difference between two uppercase and two lowercase ASCII letters.

```
                    ASCII  A  is  01000001   (hex 41, decimal 65)
                    ASCII  a  is  01100001   (hex 61, decimal 97)
Only bit 5 is different ─────────────────┘

                    ASCII  B  is  01000010   (hex 42, decimal 66)
                    ASCII  b  is  01100010   (hex 62, decimal 98)
                                 └───────────── Only bit 5 is different
```

To convert a character to uppercase, you have to turn off (change to a 0) bit number 5. You can apply a bitwise & to the input character 223 (which is 11011111 in binary) to turn off bit 5 and convert any input character to its uppercase equivalent. If the number is already in uppercase, this bitwise & does not change it.

The 223 (binary 11011111) is called a *bitmask* because it acts to mask off (just as masking tape masks off areas to be painted) bit 5 so that it becomes 0, if it is not already. The following program does this to ensure that users type uppercase characters when asked for their initials:

```
/* Filename: C12UPCS1.C
   Converts the input characters to uppercase
   if they aren't already */
#include <stdio.h>
main()
{
    char first, middle, last;   /* Will hold user's initials */
    int bitmask=223;                        /* 11011111 in binary */

    printf("What is your first initial? ");
    scanf(" %c", &first);
    printf("What is your middle initial? ");
    scanf(" %c", &middle);
```

```
        printf("What is your last initial? ");
        scanf(" %c", &last);

        /* Ensure that initials are in uppercase */
        first = first & bitmask;        /* Turn off bit 5 if*/
        middle = middle & bitmask;      /* it is not already*/
        last = last & bitmask;          /* turned off*/

        printf("Your initials are: %c %c %c", first, middle,
            last);
        return;
}
```

Masks bit numbers

The following lines show what happens when two of the initials are typed with lowercase letters. The program converts them to uppercase before printing them again. Although there are other ways to convert to lowercase, none is as efficient as using the & bitwise operator.

```
What is your first initial? g
What is your middle initial? M
What is your last initial? p
Your initials are: G M P
```

# Bitwise Compound Operators

As with most of the mathematical operators, you can combine the bitwise operators with the equal sign (=) to form *compound bitwise operators*. When you want to update the value of a variable, using a bitwise operator, you can shorten the expression by using the compound bitwise operators shown in Table 12.3.

**Table 12.3. Compound bitwise operators.**

| Operator | Description |
| --- | --- |
| &= | Compound bitwise AND assignment |
| ¦= | Compound bitwise inclusive OR assignment |
| ^= | Compound bitwise exclusive OR assignment |

You could rewrite the preceding example, which converted initials to their upper-case equivalents, by using compound bitwise & operations:

```
/* Filename: C12UPCS2.C
   Converts the input characters to uppercase
   if they aren't already */
#include <stdio.h>
main()
{
   char first, middle, last;   /* Will hold user's initials */
   int bitmask=223;                     /* 11011111 in binary */

   printf("What is your first initial? ");
   scanf(" %c", &first);
   printf("What is your middle initial? ");
   scanf(" %c", &middle);
   printf("What is your last initial? ");
   scanf(" %c", &last);

   /* Use compound bitwise operators to ensure
      that initials are in uppercase */
   first &= bitmask;                 /* Turn off bit 5 if */
   middle &= bitmask;                /* it is not already */
   last &= bitmask;                  /* turned off        */

   printf("Your initials are: %c %c %c", first, middle, last);
   return;
}
```

Masks bit number 5

## Bitwise Shift Operators

The bitwise shift operators are shown in Table 12.4. They left-shift or right-shift bits inside a number. The number of bits shifted depends on the value to the right of the bitwise shift operators.

**Table 12.4. Bitwise shift operators.**

| Operator | Description |
| --- | --- |
| << | Bitwise left-shift |
| >> | Bitwise right-shift |

The bitwise shift operators use one of the following fonts:

```
value << numberOfBits

value >> numberOfBits
```

The `value` can be an integer or character variable or a constant. The `numberOfBits` determines how many bits are shifted. Figure 12.4 shows what happens when the number 29 (binary 00011101) is left-shifted 3 bits with the bitwise left-shift (<<) operator. Notice that each bit "shifts over" to the left 3 times, and 0s fill in from the right. If this were a bitwise right-shift (>>) operator, the 0s would fill in from the left as the rest of the bits are shifted right 3 times.

**Figure 12.4**

Shifting the bits in binary 29 to the left.

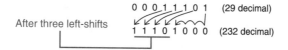

After three left-shifts

0 0 0 1 1 1 0 1    (29 decimal)

1 1 1 0 1 0 0 0    (232 decimal)

**Caution:** The results of bitwise shift operators are not consistent when applied to signed values. On many computers, the sign bit *propagates* with each shift. That is, for every shift position, the sign bit shifts, but the original sign is retained as well. The end result is that negative numbers fill in from the left with 1s, and not with 0s, when a bitwise right-shift operator is applied to them.

## Examples

**1.** The following program takes two values and shifts them three bits to the left and then three bits to the right. This program illustrates how to code the bitwise left-shift and right-shift operators.

```
/* Filename: C12SHFT1.C
   Demonstrates bitwise left- and right-shift operators */
#include <stdio.h>
main()
{
    int num1=25;                        /* 00011001 binary */
    int num2=102;                       /* 01100110 binary */
    int shift1, shift2;        /* Will hold shifted numbers */

    shift1 = num1 << 3;                 /* Bitwise left-shift */
    printf("25 shifted left 3 times is %d \n", shift1);
    shift2 = num2 << 3;                 /* Bitwise left-shift */
    printf("102 shifted left 3 times is %d \n", shift2);
```

Shifts left

```
        shift1 = num1 >> 3;              /* Bitwise right-shift */
        printf("25 shifted right 3 times is %d \n", shift1);
        shift2 = num2 >> 3;              /* Bitwise right-shift */
        printf("102 shifted right 3 times is %d \n", shift2);

        return;
}
```

(Shifts right annotation pointing to the two shift lines above.)

Here is the output from this program:

```
25 shifted left 3 times is 200
102 shifted left 3 times is 816
25 shifted right 3 times is 3
102 shifted right 3 times is 12
```

You may get different results, depending on your computer's architecture.

**2.** Bitwise shifting has a useful feature. If you bitwise left-shift a numeral by a certain number of bit positions, the result is the same as multiplying that number by a power of two. In other words, 15 left-shifted four times results in the same value as 15 times $2^4$, or 15 times 16, which equals 240.

If you bitwise right-shift a numeral by a certain number of bit positions, the result is the same as dividing that number by a power of two. In other words, 64 right-shifted two times results in the same value as 64 divided by $2^2$, or 64 divided by 4, which equals 16.

If you need to multiply or divide a variable by a power of two, you can do it much faster simply by shifting the number. The following program illustrates this:

```
/* Filename: C12SHFT2.C
   Demonstrates multiplication and division
   by bitwise shifting */
#include <stdio.h>
main()
{
    int num1 = 15;                       /* Numbers to be shifted */
    int num2 = 64;
    int shift1, shift2;

    shift1 = num1 << 4;                  /* Multiply num1 by 16 */
    shift2 = num2 >> 2;                  /* Divide num2 by 4 */
```

(Shift to multiply and divide annotation pointing to the two shift lines above.)

```
    printf("15 multiplied by 16 is %d \n", shift1);
    printf("64 divided by 4 is %d \n", shift2);
    return;
}
```

## Summary

The bitwise operators are not often used in application programs because they work at the bit level. You must be comfortable with the binary numbering system before you can fully understand their operations. However, they offer a very efficient method for changing individual bits, or groups of bits, within variables. By using these operators, you can test for odd and even numbers, multiply and divide by powers of two, and perform other tasks for which you would normally use less-efficient operators and commands.

Bitwise operators, despite their efficiency, do not always lend themselves to readable code. Generally, most people reserve bitwise operators for systems-level programming, while using the easier-to-read, higher-level operators for data processing.

## Review Questions

Answers to review questions are in Appendix B.

**1.** What are the four bitwise logical operators, the three compound bitwise logical operators, and the two bitwise shift operators?

**2.** What is the result of each of the following bitwise True-False expressions?

a. 1 ^ 0 & 1 & 1 ¦ 0

b. 1 & 1 & 1 & 1

c. 1 ^ 1 ^ 1 ^ 1

d. ~(1 ^ 0)

**3.** True or false: 7 (binary 111) can be used as a bitmask to test whether the rightmost three bits in a variable are 1s.

**4.** What is the difference between the bitwise ~ (1's complement) and 2's complement?

## Review Exercises

1. Write a program that converts an entered uppercase letter to a lowercase letter by applying a bitmask and one of the bitwise logical operators. If the character is already in lowercase, do not change it.

2. Write a program that asks users for a number. Multiply that number by every power of 2, from $2^1$ to $2^7$; and then divide that number by every power of 2, from $2^1$ to $2^7$. Use only shift operators, but no math operators!

# Part III

*C Constructs*

# CHAPTER 13

# The *while* Loop

The repetitive capabilities of computers make them good tools for processing large amounts of information. The next few chapters introduce you to C constructs, which are the control and looping commands of programming languages. C constructs include powerful, but succinct and efficient, looping commands similar to those of other languages you may already know.

The `while` loop enables your programs to repeat a series of statements, over and over, as long as a certain condition is always met. Computers do not get "bored" while performing the same tasks repeatedly. This is one reason why computers are important in business-data processing.

This chapter covers the following topics:

◆ The `while` statement

◆ The concept of loops

◆ The `do-while` loop

◆ Differences between `if` and `while` loops

◆ The `exit()` function

◆ The `break` statement

◆ Counters and totals

After completing this chapter, you should know the first of several methods C makes available for repeating program sections. This chapter's discussion of loops includes one of the most important uses for looping: creating counter and total variables.

# The *while* Statement

The while statement is one of several C *construct statements*. Each construct (from *construction*) is a programming language statement—or a series of statements—that controls looping. The while, like other such statements, is a *looping statement* that controls the execution of a series of other statements. Looping statements cause parts of a program to execute repeatedly, as long as a certain condition is being met.

The format of the while statement is

```
while (test expression)
    { block of one or more C statements; }
```

The parentheses around `test expression` are required. As long as the `test expression` is True (nonzero), the `block of one or more C statements` executes, repeatedly, until the `test expression` becomes False (evaluates to zero). Braces are required before and after the body of the while loop, unless you want to execute only one statement. Each statement in the body of the while loop requires a semicolon at the end.

The `test expression` usually contains relational, and possibly logical, operators. These operators provide the True-False condition checked in the `test expression`. If the `test expression` is False when the program reaches the while loop for the first time, the body of the while loop does not execute at all. Regardless of whether the body of the while loop executes not at all, one time, or many times, the statements following the while loop's closing brace execute if and when the `test expression` becomes False.

Because the `test expression` determines when the loop finishes, the body of the while loop *must* change the variables used in the `test expression`. Otherwise, the `test expression` never changes, and the while loop repeats forever. This is known as an *infinite loop*, and you should avoid it.

> The body of a while loop executes repeatedly as long as the *test expression* is True.

> **Tip:** If the body of the while loop contains only one statement, the braces surrounding it are not required. It is a good habit to enclose all while loop statements in braces, however. If you must add more statements to the body of the while loop later, your braces are already there.

**For Related Information**

◆ "Defining Relational Operators," p. 152

# The Concept of Loops

You use the loop concept in everyday life. Any time you need to repeat the same procedure, you are performing a loop—just as your computer does with the while construct. Suppose that you are wrapping holiday gifts. The following statements represent the looping steps (in `while` format) that you go through while gift wrapping:

> *while (there are still unwrapped gifts)*
>    *{ Get the next gift;*
>        *Cut the wrapping paper;*
>        *Wrap the gift;*
>        *Put a bow on the gift;*
>        *Fill out a name card for the gift;*
>        *Put the wrapped gift with the others; }*

Whether you have 3, 15, or 100 gifts to wrap, you would go through this procedure (loop) repeatedly until every gift is wrapped. For an example that might be more easily computerized, suppose that you want to total all the checks you wrote last month. You could perform the following loop:

> *while (there are still checks from the last month to be totaled)*
>    *{ Add the amount of the next check to the total; }*

The body of this pseudocode `while` loop has only one statement, but that single statement must be performed until you have added each one of last month's checks. When this loop ends (that is, when no more checks from last month remain to be totaled), you have the total you want.

The body of a `while` loop can contain one or more C statements, including additional `while` loops. Your programs will be more readable if you indent the body of a `while` loop a few spaces to the right. The following examples illustrate this.

## Examples

1. Some programs presented earlier in the book require user input with `scanf()`. If users do not enter appropriate values, these programs display an error message and ask the user to enter another value. This approach is fine, but now that you understand the `while` loop construct, you should put the error message inside a loop. In this way, users see the message continually (rather than once) until they type the correct input values.

   The following program is short, but it demonstrates a `while` loop being used to ensure valid user keyboard input. The program asks whether the user wants to continue. You might want to incorporate this program into a larger one that requires user permission to continue. Put a prompt, such as the one presented here, at the bottom of a screen that is full of text. The text remains on-screen until the user tells the program to continue executing.

   > *Identify the file and include the necessary header file. In this program, you want to ensure that the user enters Y or N. You need to store the user's answer, so define the ans variable as a character. Ask whether the user wants to continue, and prompt for a response. If the user doesn't type Y or N, ask the user for another response.*

```
/* Filename: C13WHIL1.C
   Input routine to ensure that user types a
   correct response. This routine might be part
   of a larger program. */
#include <stdio.h>
main()
{
   char ans;

   printf("Do you want to continue (Y/N)? ");
   scanf(" %c", &ans);                    /* Get user's answer */

   while ((ans != 'Y') && (ans != 'N'))   Make sure that user enters
     { printf("\nYou must type a Y or an N\n");  /* Warn
                                                     and ask*/
        printf("Do you want to continue (Y/N)? "); /* again */
        scanf(" %c", &ans); }             /* Body of while loop
                                              ends here */

   return;
}
```

Make sure that user enters correct answer

Notice that the two scanf() functions do the same thing. An initial scanf(), outside the while loop, must be done to get an answer that the while loop can check. If a user types something other than Y or N, the program prints an error message, asks for another answer, and then loops back to check the answer again. This method of data-entry validation is better than giving users only one additional chance to get it right.

The while loop tests the test expression at the top of the loop. This is why the loop may never execute. If the test is initially False, the loop does not execute even once. Here is the output from this program:

```
Do you want to continue (Y/N)? k

You must type a Y or an N
Do you want to continue (Y/N)? c

You must type a Y or an N
Do you want to continue (Y/N)? s
```

```
You must type a Y or an N

Do you want to continue (Y/N)? 5

You must type a Y or an N
Do you want to continue (Y/N)? Y
```

Note that the program repeats indefinitely until the relational test is True (that is, as soon as the user types either Y or N).

**2.** The following program is an example of an *invalid* while loop. See whether you can find the problem.

```
/* Filename: C13WHBAD.C
   Bad use of a while loop */
#include <stdio.h>
main()
{
   int a=10, b=20;
   while (a > 5) —— a is always more than 5
      { printf("a is %d, and b is %d \n", a, b);
         b = 20 + a; }
   return;
}
```

This while loop is an infinite loop. It is important that at least one statement inside the while changes a variable in the *test expression* (in this example, the variable a); otherwise, the condition is always True. Because the variable a does not change inside the while loop, this program will never end without the user's intervention.

> **Tip:** If you inadvertently write an infinite loop, you must stop the program yourself. If you are using a PC, this typically means pressing Ctrl-Break. If you are using a UNIX-based system, your system administrator may have to stop your program's execution.

**3.** The following program asks the user for a first name and then has a while loop that counts the number of characters in the name. This is a *string length program*; that is, it counts characters until it reaches the null zero. Remember that the length of a string is equal to the number of characters in the string up to—but not including—the null zero.

```
/* Filename: C13WHIL2.C
   Counts the number of letters in the user's first name */
#include <stdio.h>
main()
{
    char name[15];              /* Will hold user's first name */
    int count=0;        /* Will hold total characters in name */

    /* Get the user's first name */
    printf("What is your first name? ");
    scanf(" %s", name);
                              ┌─Eventually false
    while (name[count] > 0) /* Loop until null zero reached */
        { count++; }                    /* Add 1 to the count */

    printf("Your name has %d characters", count);
    return;
}
```

The loop continues as long as the value of the next character in the name array is more than zero. Because the last character in the array is a null zero, the test is False on the name's last character, and the statement following the body of the loop continues.

> **Note:** A built-in string function called `strlen()` determines the length of strings. You learn about this function in Chapter 22, "Character, String, and Numeric Functions."

**4.** The preceding string length program's `while` loop is not as efficient as it could be. Because a `while` loop fails when its test expression is zero, there is no need for the greater-than test. By changing the test expression, you can improve the efficiency of the string length count:

```
/* Filename: C13WHIL3.C
   Counts the number of letters in the user's first name */
#include <stdio.h>
main()
{
```

```
char name[15];               /* Will hold user's first name */
int count=0;        /* Will hold total characters in name */

/* Get the user's first name */
printf("What is your first name? ");
scanf(" %s", name);
                          ┌─No need to test for zero equality
while (name[count])  /* Loop until null zero is reached */
   {  count++; }                   /* Add 1 to the count */

printf("Your name has %d characters", count);
return;
}
```

# The *do-while* Loop

The body of the
do-while loop
executes at least
once.

The do-while statement controls the do-while loop, which is similar to the while loop except that the relational test occurs at the *bottom* (rather than the top) of the loop. This ensures that the body of the loop executes at least once. The do-while tests for a positive relational test; that is, as long as the test is True, the body of the loop continues to execute.

The format of the do-while is

```
do
    { block of one or more C statements; }
while (test expression)
```

The *test expression* must be enclosed within parentheses, just as with a while statement.

### Examples

1. The following program is just like the first one you saw with the while loop (C13WHIL1.C) except that the do-while is used instead. Notice the placement of the *test expression*. Because this expression concludes the loop, user input does not need to appear before the loop and then again in its body.

```
/* Filename: C13WHIL4.C
   Input routine to ensure that user types a
   correct response. This routine might be part
   of a larger program. */
#include <stdio.h>
main()
{
   char ans;

   do ──── The loop always executes at least once
     { printf("\nYou must type a Y or an N\n");    /* Warn
                                                      and ask */
       printf("Do you want to continue (Y/N) ?"); /* again */
       scanf(" %c", &ans);              /* Body of do-while loop
                                           ends here */
     } while ((ans != 'Y') && (ans != 'N'));

     return;
}
       also on 212
```

**2.** Suppose that you are entering sales amounts into the computer in order to calculate extended totals. You want the computer to print the quantity sold, part number, and extended total (quantity times the price per unit). The following program does that:

```
/* Filename: C13INV1.C
   Gets inventory information from user and prints
   an inventory detail listing with extended totals */
#include <stdio.h>
main()
{
   int partNo, quantity;
   float cost, extCost;

   printf("*** Inventory Computation ***\n\n");    /* Title */

   /* Get inventory information */
   do
     { printf("What is the next part number (-999 to end)? ");
       scanf(" %d", &partNo);
       if (partNo != -999) ──Continue only if correct port number is entered
```

```
              { printf("How many were bought? ");
                scanf(" %d", &quantity);
                printf("What is the unit price of this item? ");
                scanf(" %f", &cost);
                extCost = cost * quantity;
                printf("\n%d of # %d will cost %.2f", quantity,
                        partNo, extCost);
                printf("\n\n\n");          /* Print two blank lines */
              }
          } while (partNo != -999);          /* Loop only if part
                                               number is not -999 */


      printf("End of inventory computation\n");
      return;
}
```

Figure 13.1 shows the output from this program.

**Figure 13.1**

Displaying
extended inventory
totals on-screen.

```
*** Inventory Computation ***

What is the next part number (-999 to end)? 123
How many were bought? 4
What is the unit price of this item? 5.43

4 of # 123 will cost 21.72


What is the next part number (-999 to end)? 523
How many were bought? 26
What is the unit price of this item? 1.25

26 of # 523 will cost 32.50


What is the next part number (-999 to end)? -999
End of inventory computation
```

The do-while loop controls the entry of the customer sales information. Notice the "trigger" that ends the loop. If the user enters -999 for the part number, the do-while loop quits because no part numbered –999 exists in the inventory.

However, this program could be improved in several ways. The invoice could be printed to the printer instead of the screen. You learn how to direct your output to a printer in Part V. In addition, the inventory total (the total amount of the entire order) could be computed. You learn how to total such data in the section "Producing Totals" later in this chapter.

# The *if* Loop versus the *while* Loop

Some beginning programmers confuse the if statement with loop constructs. The while and do-while loops repeat a section of code more than once, depending on the condition being tested. The if statement may or may not execute a section of code; if it does, it executes that section only once.

Use an if statement when you want a section of code to execute conditionally *once*, but use a while or do-while loop if you want the section to execute *more than once*. Figure 13.2 shows differences between the if statement and the two while loops.

**Figure 13.2**

Differences between the *if* statement and the *while* and *do-while* loops.

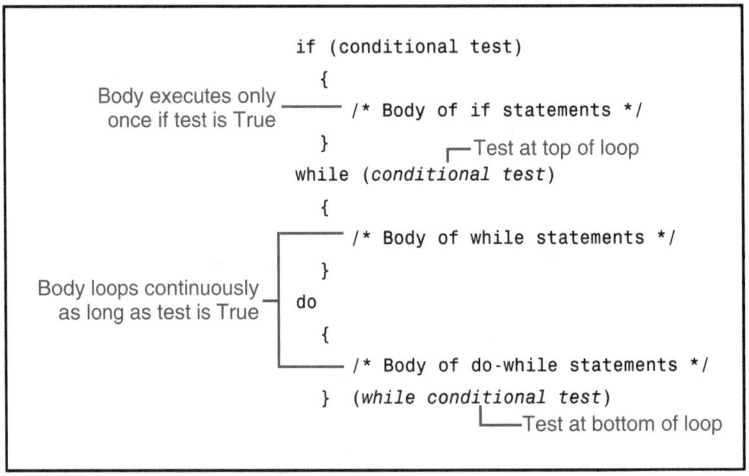

# The *exit()* Function and *break* Statement

The exit() function provides an early exit from your program.

C provides the exit() function as a way to leave a program early (before its natural finish). The format of exit() is

```
exit(status);
```

where *status* is an integer variable or constant. If you are familiar with your operating system's return codes, *status* enables you to test the results of C programs. In DOS, *status* is sent to the operating system's errorlevel *environment variable*, where it can be tested by batch files. You don't have to do anything with the exit() value when control returns to the operating system if you don't want to.

Many times, something happens in a program that requires the program's termination. It may be a major problem, such as a disk drive error. Perhaps users indicate that they want to quit the program—you can tell this by giving users a special value to type in scanf(). The exit() function can be put on a line by itself, or anywhere else that a C statement or function can appear. Typically, exit() is placed in the body of an if statement to end the program early, depending on the result of some relational test.

You should include the stdlib.h header file when you use exit(). This file describes the operation of exit() to your program. Whenever you use a function in a program, you should know its corresponding #include header file, which is usually listed in the compiler's reference manual.

The break statement ends the current loop.

Instead of exiting an entire program, however, you can use the break statement to exit the current loop. The format of break is

```
break;
```

The break statement can go anywhere in a C program that any other statement can go, but usually appears in the body of a while or do-while loop in order to leave the loop early. The following examples illustrate the exit() function and the break statement.

> **Note:** The break statement exits only the most current loop. If you have a while loop in another while loop, break exits only the internal loop.

## Examples

1. Here is a simple program that shows you how the exit() function works. This program looks as though it prints several messages on-screen, but that is misleading. Because exit() appears early in the code, the program quits immediately after main()'s opening brace.

```
/* C13EXIT1.C
   Quits very early because of exit() function */
#include <stdio.h>
#include <stdlib.h>                    /* Required for exit() */
main()
{
   exit(1);                    /* Forces program to end here */

   printf("C programming is fun.\n");
   printf("I like learning C by example!\n");
   printf("C is a powerful language that is not difficult to
   ➥learn.");

   return;
}
```

This code never executes

2. The break statement is not intended to be as strong a program exit as the exit() function. Whereas exit() ends the entire program, break quits only the loop that is currently active. In other words, break is usually placed inside a while or do-while loop to make the program think that the loop is

finished. The statement following the loop executes after a break occurs, but the program does not quit as it does with exit().

The following program appears to print C is fun! until the user enters N to stop it. The message prints only once, however, because the break statement forces an early exit from the loop.

```
/* Filename: C13BRK.C
   Demonstrates the break statement */
#include <stdio.h>
main()
{
   char userAns;

   do
     { printf("C is fun! \n");
       break;                          /* Causes early exit */
       printf("Do you want to see the message again (N/Y)? ");
       scanf(" %c", &userAns);
     } while (userAns == 'Y');

   printf("That's all for now\n");
   return;
}
```

Keeps rest of program from executing

This program always produces the following output:

```
C is fun!
That's all for now
```

You can tell from this program's output that the break statement does not enable the do-while loop to reach its natural conclusion, but causes it to finish early. The final printf() prints because only the current loop—and not the entire program—exits with the break statement.

**3.** Unlike the use of break in the preceding program, break is usually placed after an if statement. This location makes break a *conditional* break, which occurs only if the relational test of the if statement is True.

A good illustration of this use of break is the inventory program you saw earlier (C13INV1.C). Even though the users enter –999 when they want to quit the program, an additional if test is needed inside the do-while. The –999 ends the do-while loop, but the body of the do-while still needs an if test, so the remaining quantity and cost prompts are not given.

If you insert a break after testing for the end of the user's input, as shown
in the following program, the do-while does not need the if test. The break
quits the do-while as soon as the user signals the end of the inventory by
entering –999 as the part number.

```
/* Filename: C13INV2.C
   Gets inventory information from user and prints
   an inventory detail listing with extended totals */
#include <stdio.h>
main()
{
   int partNo, quantity;
   float cost, extCost;

   printf("*** Inventory Computation ***\n\n");    /* Title */

   /* Get inventory information */
   do
    { printf("What is the next part number (-999 to end)? ");
      scanf(" %d", &partNo);       Stops the
      if (partNo == -999)          do-while loop
        { break; }                          /* Exit the loop if
                                               no more part numbers */
      printf("How many were bought? ");
      scanf(" %d", &quantity);
      printf("What is the unit price of this item? ");
      scanf(" %f", &cost);
      extCost = quantity * cost;
      printf("\n%d of # %d will cost %.2f",
               quantity, partNo, extCost);
      printf("\n\n\n");                  /* Print two blank lines */
    } while (partNo != -999);        /* Loop only if part
                                         number is not -999 */

   printf("End of inventory computation\n");
   return;
}
```

**4.** The following program might be used to control two other programs. It illustrates how C can pass information to DOS with exit(). This is your first example of a menu program. Similar to a restaurant menu, a C menu program lists possible user choices. The users decide what they want the computer to do from the menu's available options.

This program returns either a 1 or a 2 to its operating system, depending on the user's selection. It is then up to the operating system to test the (exit) value and run the proper program.

```
/* Filename: C13EXIT2.C
   Asks user for a selection and returns
   that selection to the operating system with exit() */
#include <stdio.h>
#include <stdlib.h>
main()
{
   int ans;

   do
     { printf("Do you want to:\n\n");
       printf("\t1. Run the word processor \n\n");
       printf("\t2. Run the database program \n\n");
       printf("What is your selection? ");
       scanf(" %d", &ans);
     } while ((ans != 1) && (ans != 2));   /* Ensures that user
                                              enters 1 or 2 */
   exit(ans);  /* Return value to operating system */
   return;
}
```

Keeps asking until user enters correct value

## Counters

Counting is important for many applications. You may need to know how many customers you have or how many people scored over a certain average in your class. You might want to count how many checks you wrote last month with your computerized checkbook system.

Before you develop C routines to count occurrences, think of how you count in your own mind. If you were adding a total number of something, such as the stamps in your stamp collection or the number of wedding invitations you sent out, you would probably do the following:

*Start at 0 and add 1 for each item being counted. When you are finished, you should have the total number (or the total count).*

This is all you do when you count with C: assign 0 to a variable and add 1 to it every time you process another data value. The increment operator (++) is especially useful for counting.

## Examples

1. For an illustration of using a counter, the following program prints Comput-ers are fun! 10 times on the screen. You could write a program that has 10 printf() functions, but that would not be very elegant. It would also be too cumbersome to have 5000 printf() functions if you wanted to print that same message 5000 times.

   By adding a while loop and a counter that stops after a certain total is reached, you can control this printing, as the following program shows:

```
/* Filename: C13CNT1.C
   Program to print a message 10 times */
#include <stdio.h>
main()
{
    int ctr = 0;    /* Holds the number of times printed */

    do
      { printf("Computers are fun!\n");
        ctr++;                        /* Add one to the count,
                                         after each printf() */
      } while (ctr < 10);             /* Print again if fewer
                                         than 10 times */

    return;
}
```

*ctr* keeps loop executing

The output from this program is shown here (notice that the message prints exactly 10 times):

```
Computers are fun!
Computers are fun!
Computers are fun!
Computers are fun!
Computers are fun!
Computers are fun!
Computers are fun!
Computers are fun!
Computers are fun!
Computers are fun!
```

The heart of the counting process in this program is the following statement:

```
ctr++;
```

You learned earlier that the increment operator adds 1 to a variable. In this program, the counter variable is incremented each time do-while loops. Because the only operation performed on this line is the increment of ctr, using the prefix increment (++ctr) would produce the same results.

2. The preceding program not only added to the counter variable but also performed the loop a specific number of times. This is a common method of conditionally executing parts of a program for a fixed number of times.

The following program is a password program. A password is stored in an integer variable. The user must correctly enter the matching password within three attempts. If the user does not type the correct password in that time, the program ends. This is a common method that dial-up computers use. They enable a caller to try the password a fixed number of times, and then hang up the phone if that limit is exceeded. This approach helps deter people from trying hundreds of different passwords at any one sitting.

If users guess the correct password in three tries, they see the secret message.

```
/* Filename: C13PASS1.C
   Program to prompt for a password and
   check it against an internal one */
#include <stdio.h>
#include <stdlib.h>
/* stdlib.h for exit() function */
main()
{
    int storedPass = 11862;
    int numTries = 0;      /* Counter for password attempts */
    int userPass;

    while (numTries < 3)                    /* Loop only 3 times */
        { printf("\nWhat is the password (You get 3 tries...)? ");
          scanf(" %d", &userPass);
          numTries++;                       /* Add 1 to counter */
          if (userPass == storedPass)
              { printf("You entered the correct password.\n");
                printf("The cash safe is behind the picture of the
                ➡ship.\n");
```

Keeps track of attempts

```
                exit(0);
           }
        else
          { printf("You entered the wrong password.\n");
           if (numTries == 3)
           { printf("Sorry, you get no more chances"); }
           else
           { printf("You get %d more tries...\n",
                   3-numTries); }
          }
        }                                  /* End of while loop */
     return;
   }
```

This program gives users three chances—in case they make one or two typing mistakes. But after three unsuccessful attempts, the program quits without displaying the secret message.

**3.** The following program is a letter-guessing game. It includes a message telling users how many tries they made before guessing the correct letter. A counter counts the number of tries.

```
/* Filename: C13GUES.C
   Letter-guessing game */
#include <stdio.h>
main()
{
   int tries = 0;
   char compAns, userGuess;

   /* Save the computer's letter */
   compAns = 'T';                   /* Change to a different
                                        letter if desired */

   printf("I am thinking of a letter...");
   do
      { printf("What is your guess? ");
        scanf(" %c", &userGuess);
        tries++;   /* Add 1 to the guess-counting variable */
        if (userGuess > compAns)
           { printf("Your guess was too high\n");
             printf("\nTry again...");
           }
```

```
            if (userGuess < compAns)
              { printf("Your guess was too low\n");
                printf("\nTry again...");
              }
          } while (userGuess != compAns); /* Quit when a
                                            match is found */


      /* They got it right--let them know */
      printf("*** Congratulations!  You got it right! \n");
      printf("It took you only %d tries to guess.", tries);
      return;
  }
```

Loop stops at correct guess ———

Figure 13.3 shows a sample output of this program.

**Figure 13.3**

Counting guesses in a letter-guessing game.

```
I am thinking of a letter...What is your guess? A
Your guess was too low

Try again...What is your guess? Z
Your guess was too high

Try again...What is your guess? N
Your guess was too low

Try again...What is your guess? W
Your guess was too high

Try again...What is your guess? S
Your guess was too low

Try again...What is your guess? T
*** Congratulations! You got it right!
It took you only 6 tries to guess.
```

# Totals

Writing a routine to add values is as easy as counting. Instead of adding 1 to the counter variable, you add a value to the total variable. For instance, if you want to find the total dollar amount of checks you wrote during December, you can start at nothing (0) and add to that the amount of every check written in December. Instead of building a count, you are building a total.

When you want C to add values, just initialize a total variable to zero and then add each value to the total until you have included all the values.

**For Related Information**

◆ "The *for* Statement," p. 233

## Examples

1. Suppose that you want to write a program which adds your grades for a class you are taking. The teacher has informed you that you earn an A if you can accumulate over 450 points.

   The following program keeps asking you for values until you type –1. The –1 is a signal that you are finished entering grades and now want to see the total. This program also prints a congratulatory message if you have enough points for an A.

```
/* Filename: C13GRAD1.C
   Adds up grades and determines whether an A was made */
#include <stdio.h>
main()
{
   float totalGrade=0.0;
   float grade;                 /* Holds individual grades */

   do
   { printf("What is your grade? (-1 to end) ");
     scanf(" %f", &grade);
     if (grade >= 0.0)
       { totalGrade += grade; }        /* Add to total */
   } while (grade >= 0.0);      /* Quit when -1 entered */

   /* Control begins here if no more grades */
   printf("\n\nYou made a total of %.1f points\n",
           totalGrade);
   if (totalGrade >= 450.00)
      { printf("** You made an A!!"); }

   return;
}
```

Add the grades

Notice that the -1 response does not get added to the total number of points. This program checks for the -1 before adding to totalGrade. Figure 13.4 shows the output from this program.

**Figure 13.4**

Computing the
total grade.

```
What is your grade? (-1 to end) 87
What is your grade? (-1 to end) 89
What is your grade? (-1 to end) 96
What is your grade? (-1 to end) 78
What is your grade? (-1 to end) 99
What is your grade? (-1 to end) 87
What is your grade? (-1 to end) 89
What is your grade? (-1 to end) -1


You made a total of 625.0 points
** You made an A!!
```

**2.** The following program is an extension of the grade-calculating program. It not only totals the points, but also computes their average.

For calculating an average, the program must be able to determine the number of grades that are entered for a particular set of grades. This is a subtle problem because the number of grades to be entered is unknown in advance. Therefore, every time the user enters a valid grade (not –1), the program must add 1 to a counter as well as add that grade to the `total` variable. This is a combination counting and totaling routine, which is common in many programs.

```
/* Filename: C13GRAD2.C
   Adds up grades, computes average,
   and determines whether an A was made */
#include <stdio.h>
main()
{
   float totalGrade=0.0;
   float gradeAvg = 0.0;
   float grade;
   int gradeCtr = 0;

   do
   { printf("What is your grade? (-1 to end) ");
     scanf(" %f", &grade);
     if (grade >= 0.0)
       { totalGrade += grade;              /* Add to total */
         gradeCtr ++; }                     /* Add to count */
   } while (grade >= 0.0);          /* Quit when -1 entered */

   /* Control begins here if no more grades */
   gradeAvg = (totalGrade / gradeCtr);        /* Compute
                                                 average */
```

Count the
grades
entered

```
printf("\nYou made a total of %.1f points.\n",
        totalGrade);
printf("Your average was %.1f \n", gradeAvg);
if (totalGrade >= 450.0)
    { printf("** You made an A!!"); }
return;
}
```

Figure 13.5 shows the output of this program. Congratulations! You are on your way to becoming a master C programmer.

**Figure 13.5**

Computing total points and the average.

```
What is your grade? (-1 to end) 88
What is your grade? (-1 to end) 98
What is your grade? (-1 to end) 97
What is your grade? (-1 to end) 87
What is your grade? (-1 to end) 94
What is your grade? (-1 to end) 96
What is your grade? (-1 to end) -1

You made a total of 560.0 points.
Your average was 93.3
** You made an A!!
```

## Summary

This chapter showed you two ways to produce a C loop: the while loop and the do-while loop. These two variations of while loops differ in where they test their *test condition* statements. The while tests at the top of its loop, and the do-while tests at the bottom. The result is that the body of a do-while loop always executes at least once. You also learned that the exit() function and break statement add flexibility to while loops. The exit() function terminates the program, but the break statement terminates only the current loop.

This chapter explained two of the most important applications of loops: counters and totals. Your computer can be a wonderful tool for adding and counting, because of the repetitive capabilities offered with while loops.

The next chapter extends your knowledge of loops by showing you how to create a *determinate* loop, called the for loop. This feature is useful when you want a section of code to loop for a specified number of times.

## Review Questions

Answers to review questions are in Appendix B.

1. What is the difference between a while loop and a do-while loop?

2. What is the difference between a total variable and a counter variable?

3. Which C operator is most useful for counting?

4. True or false: Braces are not required around the body of while and do-while loops.

5. What is wrong with the following code?

```
while (sales > 50)
    printf("Your sales are very good this month.\n");
    printf("You will get a bonus for your high sales\n");
```

6. What file must you include as a header file if you use exit()?

7. How many times does this printf() print?

```
int a=0;
do
    { printf("Careful \n");
       a++; }
while (a > 5);
```

8. How can you inform DOS of the program exit status?

9. What is printed to the screen in the following section of code?

```
a = 1;
while (a < 4)
    { printf("This is the outer loop\n");
      a++;
      while (a <= 25)
         { break;
           printf("This prints 25 times\n"); }
    }
```

## Review Exercises

1. Write a program with a do-while loop that prints the numerals from 10 through 20, with a blank line after each number.

2. Write a weather-calculator program that asks for a list of the previous 10 days' temperatures, computes the average, and prints the results. You have to compute the total as the input occurs, then divide that total by 10 to find the average. Use a while loop for the 10 repetitions.

3. Rewrite the program in exercise 2 by using a do-while loop.

4. Write a program, similar to the weather calculator in exercise 2, but make it more general so that it computes the average of any number of days' temperatures. (Hint: You need to count the number of temperatures to compute the final average.)

5. Write a program that produces your own ASCII table on-screen. Don't print the first 31 characters, because they are nonprintable. Print the codes numbered 32 through 255 by storing their numbers in integer variables and then printing their ASCII values, using the "%c" format code.

# CHAPTER 14

# The *for* Loop

The for loop enables you to repeat sections of your program a specific number of times. Unlike the while and do-while loops, the for loop is a *determinate loop*. This means that when you write your program, you can usually determine how many times the loop takes place. The while and do-while loops execute only until a condition is met. The for loop does this and more: it continues looping until a count (or countdown) is reached.

After the final for loop count is reached, execution continues with the next statement in sequence. This chapter focuses on the for loop construct. The following topics are covered:

♦ The for statement

♦ The concept of for loops

♦ Nested for loops

The for loop is a helpful way of looping through a section of code when you want to count, or total, specified amounts. This loop does not replace the while and do-while loops, however.

## The *for* Statement

The for statement encloses one or more C statements that form the body of the loop. These statements in the loop are executed repeatedly a certain number of times. You, as programmer, control the number of loop repetitions.

The format of the for loop is

```
for (start expression; test expression; count expression)
    { Block of one or more C statements; }
```

C evaluates the start expression before the loop begins. Typically, the start expression is an assignment statement (such as ctr=1;), but it can be any legal expression you specify. C looks at and evaluates the start expression only once, at the top of the loop.

> **Caution:** Do not put a semicolon after the right parenthesis. If you do, the for loop "thinks" that the body of the loop is zero statements long! It would continue looping—doing *nothing* each time—until the **test expression** becomes False.

The for loop will loop for a specified number of times.

Every time the body of the loop repeats, the count expression executes, usually incrementing or decrementing a variable. The test expression evaluates to True (nonzero) or False (zero) and then determines whether the body of the loop repeats again.

> **Tip:** If only one C statement resides in the for loop's body, braces are not required, but they are recommended. If you supply them and add more statements later, the braces will be in place, and you will not leave them out inadvertently.

> **For Related Information**
>
> ◆ "Defining Relational Operators," p. 152

# The Concept of *for* Loops

You use the concept of for loops throughout your day-to-day life. Any time you need to repeat a certain procedure a specified number of times, that repetition becomes a good candidate for a computerized for loop.

To examine the concept of a for loop further, suppose that you are putting up 10 new shutters on your house. You must do the following steps for each shutter:

1. Move the ladder to the location of the shutter.

2. Take a shutter, hammer, and nails up the ladder.

3. Hammer the shutter to the side of the house.

4. Climb down the ladder.

You must perform each of these steps exactly 10 times because you have 10 shutters. After 10 times, you don't put another shutter up because the job is finished. You are looping through a procedure that has several steps. These steps are the body, or the block, of the loop. It is not an endless loop because there are a fixed number of shutters; you run out of shutters only after you have gone through all 10 of them.

For a less physical example that might be more easily computerized, suppose that you need to fill out three tax returns for each of your teenage children. (If you have three teenagers, you probably need more than just a computer to help you get through the day!) For each teenager, you must perform the following steps:

1. Add up the total income.

2. Add up the total deductions.

3. Fill out a tax return.

4. Put it in an envelope.

5. Mail it.

You then must repeat this entire procedure two more times.

Notice how the sentence before these steps began: *For each teenager*. This signals an idea similar to the `for` loop construct.

**Note:** The `for` loop tests at the top of the loop. If the *test expression* is False when the `for` loop begins, the body of the loop never executes.

**The Choice of Loops**

Any loop construct can be written with a `for` loop, a `while` loop, or a `do-while` loop. Generally, you use the `for` loop when you want to count or loop a specific number of times, and you reserve the `while` and `do-while` loops for looping until a False condition is met.

**For Related Information**

♦ "The *while* Statement," p. 210

## Examples

1. To give you a glimpse of the `for` loop's capabilities, this example shows you two programs: one that uses a `for` loop and one that does not. The first program is a counting program. Before studying its contents, look at the output. The results basically speak for themselves and illustrate the `for` loop very well.

Here is the program with a for loop:

*Identify the program and include the necessary header file. You need a counter, so make ctr an integer variable.*

    a.  *Add 1 to the counter.*

    b.  *If the counter is less than or equal to 10, print its value and repeat step a.*

The program with a for loop follows.

```
/* Filename: C14FOR1.C
   Introduces the for loop */
#include <stdio.h>
main()
{
    int ctr;
    for (ctr=1; ctr<=10; ctr++)    /* Start ctr at 1,
                                       increment through loop */
        { printf("%d \n", ctr); }  /* Body of for loop */

    return;
}
```

Loop control ————

> **Tip:** Notice how the body of the for loop is indented. This is a good habit to develop because it makes it easier to see the beginning and end of the loop's body.

This program's output is

```
1
2
3
4
5
6
7
8
9
10
```

Here is the same program but with a do-while loop:

*Identify the program and include the necessary header file. You need a counter, so make ctr an integer variable.*

    *a. Add 1 to the counter.*

    *b. Print the value of the counter.*

    *c. If the counter is less than or equal to 10, repeat step a.*

```
/* Filename: C14WHI1.C
   Simulating a for loop with a do-while loop */
#include <stdio.h>
main()
{
   int ctr=1;
   do
      { printf("%d \n", ctr); /* Body of do-while loop */
        ctr++; }
   while (ctr <= 10);

   return;
}
```

Determines when
loop ends

Notice that the for loop is a cleaner way of controlling the looping process. The for loop does several things that require extra statements in a while loop. With for loops, you do not need to write extra code to initialize variables and increment or decrement them. You can see at a glance (in the expressions in the for statement) exactly how the loop executes, unlike the do-while, which forces you to look at the *bottom* of the loop to see how the loop stops.

**2.** Both of the following sample programs add the numbers from 100 to 200. The first program uses a for loop, but the second one doesn't. The first example begins with a *start expression* other than 1, starting the loop with a bigger *count expression*.

This program has a for loop:

```
/* Filename: C14FOR2.C
   Demonstrates totaling that uses a for loop */
#include <stdio.h>
main()
{
   int total, ctr;

   total = 0;                    /* Will hold total of 100 to 200 */
```

From 100
to 200

```
        for (ctr=100; ctr<=200; ctr++)      /* ctr is 100, 101,
                                                102,...200     */
          { total += ctr; }   /* Add value of ctr each iteration */

          printf("The total is %d", total);
          return;
        }
```

Here is the same program but without a for loop:

```
/* Filename: C14WHI2.C
   A totaling program that uses a do-while loop */
#include <stdio.h>
main()
{
    int total=0;              /* Initialize total */
    int num=100;              /* Starting value */

    do
      { total += num;          /* Add to total */
        num++;                 /* Increment counter */
      } while (num <= 200);
    printf("The total is %d", total);
    return;
}
```

From 100... ────────────── int num=100;

...to 200 ────────────── } while (num <= 200);

Both programs produce this output:

```
The total is 15150
```

The body of the loop in both programs executes 100 times. The starting value is 100, not 1 as in the program in the first example. Notice that the for loop is less complex than the do-while because the initializing, testing, and incrementing are performed in the single for statement.

The following is the last example that compares the for loop with an equivalent program without a for loop.

**3.** The body of the for loop can have more than one statement. This program requests five pairs of data values: children's first names and their ages. It prints the name of the teacher assigned to each child, based on the child's age. This program illustrates a for loop with printf() functions, a scanf() function, and an if statement in its body. Because exactly five children are checked, the for loop ensures that the program ends after the fifth child.

```
/* Filename: C14FOR3.C
   Program that uses a loop to input and print the
   name of the teacher assigned to each child */
#include <stdio.h>
main()
{
   char child[25];         /* Holds child's first name */
   int age;                     /* Holds child's age */
   int ctr;              /* The for loop counter variable */

   for (ctr=1; ctr<=5; ctr++)
     { printf("What is the next child's name? ");
       scanf(" %s", child);
       printf("What is the child's age? ");
       scanf(" %d", &age);
       if (age <= 5)
          { printf("\n%s has Mrs. Jones for a teacher\n",
                    child);}
       if (age == 6)
          { printf("\n%s has Miss Smith for a teacher\n",
                    child); }
       if (age >= 7)
          { printf("\n%s has Mr. Anderson for a teacher\n",
                    child); }
     }  /* Quits after 5 times */

   return;
}
```

Loops 5 times ──────

Figure 14.1 shows the output from this program. You can improve this program further after you learn to use the switch statement in the next chapter.

**1 2**

**4.** The preceding examples used an increment as the *count expression*. You can make the for loop increment the loop variable by any value. It does not need to increment by 1.

The following program prints the even numbers from 1 to 20. It then prints the odd numbers from 1 to 20. To do this, 2 is added to the counter variable (instead of 1 as shown in the previous examples) each time the loop executes.

**Figure 14.1**

Inputting values
inside a *for* loop.

```
What is the next child's name? Jim
What is the child's age? 6

Jim has Miss Smith for a teacher

What is the next child's name? Linda
What is the child's age? 3

Linda has Mrs. Jones for a teacher

What is the next child's name? Elizabeth
What is the child's age? 7

Elizabeth has Mr. Anderson for a teacher

What is the next child's name? Bob
What is the child's age? 5

Bob has Mrs. Jones for a teacher

What is the next child's name? Walter
What is the child's age? 3

Walter has Mrs. Jones for a teacher
```

```c
/* Filename: C14EVOD.C
   Prints the even numbers from 1 to 20,
   then the odd numbers from 1 to 20 */
#include <stdio.h>
main()
{
   int num;                              /* The for loop variable */

   printf("Even numbers below 20\n");              /* Title */
   for (num=2; num<=20; num+=2)
     { printf("%d ", num); }  /* Prints every other number */

   printf("\nOdd numbers below 20\n");   /* A second title */
   for (num=1; num<=20; num+=2)
     { printf("%d ", num); }  /* Prints every other number */

   return;
}
```

Prints only even

Prints only odd

There are two loops in this program. The body of each one consists of a single printf() function. In the first half of the program, the loop variable, num, is 2 and not 1. If it were 1, the number 1 would print first, as it does in the odd number section.

The two `printf()` functions that print the titles are not part of either loop. If they were, the program would print a title before each number. The following shows the result of running this program:

```
Even numbers below 20
2 4 6 8 10 12 14 16 18 20
Odd numbers below 20
1 3 5 7 9 11 13 15 17 19
```

**5.** You can decrement the loop variable as well. If you do, the value is subtracted from the loop variable each time through the loop.

The following example is a rewrite of the counting program, producing the reverse effect by showing a countdown:

```
/* Filename: C14CNTD1.C
   Countdown to the lift-off */
#include <stdio.h>
main()
{
   int ctr;

   for (ctr=10; ctr!=0; ctr--)
      { printf("%d \n", ctr); }    /* Print ctr as it
                                      counts down */
   printf("*** Blast off! ***");
   return;
}
```

Makes loop count down

When you decrement a loop variable, you should make the initial value larger than the end value being tested. In this example, the loop variable, `ctr`, counts down from 10 to 1. Each time through the loop (each iteration), `ctr` is decremented by 1. By looking at the following output of this program, you can see how easy it is to control a loop:

```
10
9
8
7
6
5
4
3
2
1
*** Blast Off! ***
```

> **Tip:** This program's `for` loop illustrates a redundancy that you can eliminate thanks to C. The *test expression*, `ctr!=0;`, tells the `for` loop to continue looping until `ctr` is not equal to zero. However, if `ctr` becomes zero, that is a False value in itself; there is no reason to add the additional `!=0` except for clarity. The `for` loop can be rewritten as
>
> ```
> for (ctr=10; ctr; ctr--)
> ```
>
> without loss of meaning. This is more efficient and is such an integral part of C that you should become comfortable with it. There is little loss of clarity once you get used to it.

**6.** You can also make a `for` loop test for something other than a constant value. The following program combines much of what you have learned so far. It asks for student grades and computes an average. Because there may be a different number of students each semester, the program first asks the user for the number of students. Next, the program loops until the user enters that many scores. It then computes the average based on the total and the number of student grades entered.

```c
/* Filename: C14FOR4.C
   Computes a grade average with a for loop */
#include <stdio.h>
main()
{
    float grade, avg;
    float total=0.0;
    int num;                    /* Total number of grades */
    int loopvar;                /* Used to control for loop */

    printf("\n*** Grade Calculation ***\n\n");  /* Title */
    printf("How many students are there? ");
    scanf(" %d", &num);         /* Get total number to enter */

    for (loopvar=1; loopvar<=num; loopvar++)
      { printf("\nWhat is the next student's grade? ");
        scanf(" %f", &grade);
        total += grade;  }      /* Keep a running total */

    avg = total / num;
    printf("\n\nThe average of this class is %.1f", avg);
    return;
}
```

The number of students controls the loop

Because of the for loop, the total and the average calculations do not need to be changed if the number of students changes.

**7.** Because characters and integers are so closely associated in C, you can increment character variables in a for loop. The following program prints the letters A through Z with a simple for loop.

```
/* Filename: C14FOR5.C
   Prints the alphabet with a simple for loop */
#include <stdio.h>
main()
{
   char letter;

   printf("Here is the alphabet:\n");
   for (letter='A'; letter<='Z'; letter++) /* Loops A to Z */
      { printf("%c ", letter); }

   return;
}
```

Loop controlled by character data

This program produces the following output:

```
Here is the alphabet:
A B C D E F G H I J K L M N O P Q R S T U V W X Y Z
```

**8.** When a for expression is blank, it is considered a *null expression*. In the following for loop, all the expressions are blank:

```
for (;;)
   { printf("Over and over..."); }
```

This loops forever. Although you should avoid infinite loops, your program might dictate that you make a for loop expression blank. If you already initialized the *start expression* earlier in the program, you would be wasting computer time to repeat it in the for loop—and C does not require it.

The following program omits the *start expression* and the *count expression*, leaving only the for loop's *test expression*. Most of the time, you need to omit only one of them. If you use a for loop without two of its expressions, consider replacing it with a while or do-while loop.

```
/* Filename: C14FOR6.C
   Uses only the test expression in
   the for loop to count by 5s */
#include <stdio.h>
main()
{
   int num=5;                              /* Starting value */

   printf("\nCounting by 5s: \n");              /* Title */
   for (; num<=100;)  /* Contains only the test expression */
     { printf("%d\n", num);
        num+=5;      /* Increment expression inside the loop */
     }                          /* End of the loop's body */

   return;
}
```

Defines initial value

Initial value is already defined

Increments loop value

Here is the output from this program:

```
Counting by 5s:
5
10
15
20
25
30
35
40
45
50
55
60
65
70
75
80
85
90
95
100
```

# Nested *for* Loops

Use nested loops
when you want to
repeat a loop more
than once.

Any C statement can go inside the body of a for loop—even another for loop! When you put a loop within a loop, you are creating a *nested loop*. The clock in a sporting event works like a nested loop. You might think that this is stretching an analogy a little too far, but it truly works. A football game counts down from 15 minutes to 0. It does this four times. The first countdown loops from 15 to 0 (for each minute). That countdown is nested in another loop that loops from 1 to 4 (for each of the four quarters).

If your program needs to repeat a loop more than one time, it is a good candidate for a nested loop. Figure 14.2 shows two outlines of nested loops. You can think of the inside loop as looping "faster" than the outside loop. In the first example, the inside for loop counts from 1 to 10 before the outside loop (the variable out) can finish its first iteration. When the outside loop finally does iterate a second time, the inside loop starts over.

**Figure 14.2**

Outlines of two
nested loops.

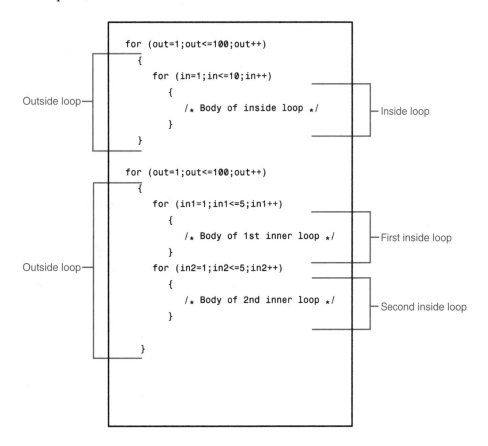

```
for (out=1;out<=100;out++)
  {
    for (in=1;in<=10;in++)
      {
        /* Body of inside loop */
      }
  }

for (out=1;out<=100;out++)
  {
    for (in1=1;in1<=5;in1++)
      {
        /* Body of 1st inner loop */
      }
    for (in2=1;in2<=5;in2++)
      {
        /* Body of 2nd inner loop */
      }
  }
```

Outside loop — (first example)
Inside loop

Outside loop — (second example)
First inside loop
Second inside loop

The second nested loop outline shows two loops within an outside loop. Both of these loops execute in their entirety before the outside loop finishes its first iteration. When the outside loop starts its second iteration, the two inside loops repeat again.

Notice the order of the braces in each example. The inside loop *always* finishes, and therefore its ending brace must come before the outside loop's ending brace. Indention makes this much clearer because you can "line up" braces of each loop.

Nested loops become important later when you use them for array and table processing.

> **Note:** In nested loops, the inside loop (or loops) executes completely before the outside loop's next iteration.

## Examples

**1.** The following program contains a nested loop—a loop within a loop. The inside loop counts and prints from 1 to 5. The outside loop counts from 1 to 3. Therefore, the inside loop repeats, in its entirety, three times. In other words, this program prints the values 1 to 5 and does so three times.

```
/* Filename: C14NEST1.C
   Print the numbers 1 to 5 three times
   using a nested loop */
#include <stdio.h>
main()
{
    int times, num;  /* Outer and inner for loop variables */

    for (times=1; times<=3; times++)
    {
        for (num=1; num<=5; num++)
            { printf("%d", num); }       /* Inner loop body */
        printf("\n");
    }                                     /* End of outer loop */

    return;
}
```

Outer loop — (bracket on for (times...) block)

Inner loop — (bracket on for (num...) block)

The indention follows the standard of `for` loops; every statement in each loop is indented a few spaces. Because the inside loop is already indented, its body is indented another few spaces. The program's output follows:

```
12345
12345
12345
```

**2.** The outside loop's counter variable changes each time through the loop. If one of the inside loop's control variables is the outside loop's counter variable, you see effects such as those shown in the following program:

```c
/* Filename: C14NEST2.C
   An inside loop controlled by the outer loop's
   counter variable */
#include <stdio.h>
main()
{
   int outer, inner;

   for (outer=5; outer>=1; outer—)
      { for (inner=1; inner<=outer; inner++)
           { printf("%d", inner); }    /* End of inner loop */
      printf("\n");
      }
   return;
}
```

Inner loop controlled by outer loop's value

Here is the output from this program:

```
12345
1234
123
12
1
```

Notice that the inside loop repeats five times (as outer counts down from 5 to 1) and prints from five numbers to one number.

Sometimes you need to "play computer" when learning a new concept such as nested loops. By executing a line at a time, writing down each variable's contents, you produce the following table.

| The outer variable | The inner variable |
| --- | --- |
| 5 | 1 |
| 5 | 2 |
| 5 | 3 |
| 5 | 4 |
| 5 | 5 |
| 4 | 1 |
| 4 | 2 |
| 4 | 3 |
| 4 | 4 |
| 3 | 1 |
| 3 | 2 |
| 3 | 3 |
| 2 | 1 |
| 2 | 2 |
| 1 | 1 |

---

**Tip for Mathematicians**

The `for` statement is identical to the mathematical summation symbol. When you write programs to simulate the summation symbol, the `for` statement is an excellent candidate. A nested `for` statement is good for double summations.

For example, the summation

```
i = 30
S (i / 3 * 2)
i = 1
```

can be rewritten as

```
total = 0;
for (i=1; i<=30; i++)
{ total += (i / 3 * 2); }
```

---

**4.** A *factorial* is a mathematical number used in probability theory and statistics. A factorial of any number is the multiplied product of every number from 1 to that number.

For instance, the factorial of 4 is 24 because 4 * 3 * 2 * 1 = 24. The factorial of 6 is 720 because 6 * 5 * 4 * 3 * 2 * 1 = 720. The factorial of 1 is 1 by definition.

Nested loops are good candidates for writing a factorial number-generating program. The following program asks the user for a number and then prints every factorial up to, and including, that number.

```
/*Filename: C14FACT.C
  Computes the factorial of numbers through
  the user's number */
#include <stdio.h>
main()
{
   int outer, num, fact, total;

   printf("What factorial do you want to see? ");
   scanf(" %d", &num);

   for (outer=1; outer <= num; outer++)
     { total = 1;    /* Initialize total for each factorial */
       for (fact=1; fact<= outer; fact++)
         { total *= fact; }       /* Compute each factorial */
     }

   printf("The factorial for %d is %d", num, total);

   return;
}
```

Computed from each inner loop's iteration

The following output shows the factorial of 7. You can run this program, entering different values when asked, and see various factorials. Be careful: factorials multiply quickly. (A factorial of 11 won't fit in an integer variable.)

```
What factorial do you want to see? 7
The factorial for 7 is 5040
```

## Summary

This chapter showed you how to control loops. Instead of writing extra code around a while loop, you can use the for loop to control the number of iterations at the time you define the loop. All for loops contain three parts: a *start expression*, a *test expression*, and a *count expression*.

You have now seen C's three loop constructs: the while loop, the do-while loop, and the for loop. They are similar, but behave differently in how they test and initialize variables. No loop is better than the others. The programming problem should dictate which loop to use. The next chapter shows you more methods for controlling loops.

## Review Questions

Answers to review questions are in Appendix B.

1. What is a loop?

2. True or false: The body of a for loop contains at most one statement.

3. What is a nested loop?

4. Why might you want to leave one or more expressions out of the for statement's parentheses?

5. Which loop "moves" fastest: the inner loop or the outer loop?

6. What is the output from the following program?

```
for (ctr=10; ctr>=1; ctr-=3)
    { printf("%d \n", ctr); }
```

7. True or false: A for loop is better to use than a while loop when you know in advance exactly how many iterations a loop requires.

8. What happens when the *test expression* becomes False in a for statement?

9. True or false: The following program contains a valid nested loop.

```
for (i=1; i<=10; i++);
  { for (j=1; j<=5; j++)
      { printf("%d %d \n". i. j); }
  }
```

**10.** What is the output of the following section of code?

```
 i=1;
start=1;
end=5;
step=1;

for (; start>=end;)
      { printf("%d \n", i);
        start+=step;
        end--;}
```

# Review Exercises

**1.** Write a program that prints the numbers from 1 to 15 on the screen. Use a `for` loop to control the printing.

**2.** Write a program that prints the values from 15 to 1 on the screen. Use a `for` loop to control the printing.

**3.** Write a program that uses a `for` loop to print every odd number from 1 to 100.

**4.** Write a program that asks the user for his or her age. Use a `for` loop to print `Happy Birthday!` for every year of the user's age.

**5.** Write a program that uses a `for` loop to print the ASCII characters from 32 to 255 on the screen. (Hint: Use the `%c` conversion character to print integer variables.)

**6.** Using the ASCII table numbers and a nested `for` loop, write a program that prints the following output:

```
A
AB
ABC
ABCD
ABCDE
```

(Hint: The outside loop should loop from 1 to 5, and the inside loop's start variable should be 65, the value of ASCII *A*.)

CHAPTER *15*

# Other Loop Options

Now that you have mastered the looping constructs, you should learn some loop-related statements. This chapter explains two additional looping commands, the `break` statement and the `continue` statement, which control the way loops operate. These statements work with `while` loops and `for` loops.

The chapter introduces the following topics:

♦ The `break` statement with `for` loops

♦ The `continue` statement with `for` loops

When you master these concepts, you will be well on your way toward writing powerful programs that process large amounts of data.

## The *break* and *for* Statements

The `for` loop was designed to execute for a specified number of times. Occasionally, the `for` loop should quit before the counting variable has reached its final value. As with `while` loops, you use the `break` statement to quit a `for` loop early.

The `break` statement goes in the body of the `for` loop. Programmers rarely put `break` on a line by itself, and it almost always comes after an `if` test. If the `break` were on a line by itself, the loop would always quit early, defeating the purpose of the `for` loop.

### Examples

1. The following program shows what can happen when C encounters an *unconditional* `break` statement—that is, one not preceded by an `if` statement:

*Identify the program and include the necessary header files. You need a variable to hold the current number, so make num an integer variable.*

*Print a "Here are the numbers" message.*

   a. *Make num equal to 1. If num is less than or equal to 20, add 1 to it each time through the loop.*

   b. *Print the value of num.*

   c. *Break out of the loop.*

*Print a good-bye message.*

```
/* Filename: C15BRAK1.C
   A for loop defeated by a break statement */
#include <stdio.h>
main()
{
    int num;

    printf("Here are the numbers from 1 to 20\n");
    for(num=1; num<=20; num++)
      { printf("%d \n", num);
        break; }    /* This exits the for loop immediately */

    printf("That's all, folks!");
    return;
}
```

*break* exits a *for* loop

Here is the result of running this program:

```
Here are the numbers from 1 to 20
1
That's all, folks!
```

Notice that the break immediately terminates the for loop. The for loop might as well not be in this program.

 **2.** The following program is an improved version of the preceding example. It asks whether the user wants to see another number. If so, the for loop continues its next iteration. If not, the break statement terminates the for loop.

```
/* Filename: C15BRAK2.C
   A for loop running at the user's request */
```

```
#include <stdio.h>
main()
{
   int num;    /* Loop counter variable */
   char ans;

   printf("Here are the numbers from 1 to 20\n");

   for (num=1; num<=20; num++)
     { printf("%d \n", num);
       printf("Do you want to see another (Y/N)? ");
       scanf(" %c", &ans);
       if ((ans == 'N') || (ans == 'n'))
          { break; }    /* Will exit the for loop
                            if user wants */
     }

   printf("\nThat's all, folks!");
return;
  }
```

User's answer determines the number of times the numbers print

The following display shows a sample run of this program:

```
Here are the numbers from 1 to 20
1
Do you want to see another (Y/N)? Y
2
Do you want to see another (Y/N)? Y
3
Do you want to see another (Y/N)? Y
4
Do you want to see another (Y/N)? Y
5
Do you want to see another (Y/N)? Y
6
Do you want to see another (Y/N)? Y
7
Do you want to see another (Y/N)? Y
8
Do you want to see another (Y/N)? Y
9
Do you want to see another (Y/N)? Y
10
```

```
Do you want to see another (Y/N)? N

That's all, folks!
```

The for loop prints 20 numbers, as long as the user does not answer N to the prompt. Otherwise, the break takes over and terminates the for loop early. The statement after the body of the loop always executes next if the break occurs.

If you nest one loop inside another, the break terminates the "most active" loop—that is, the innermost loop in which the break statement resides.

3. Use the *conditional* break (an if statement followed by a break) when you are missing data. For example, when you process data files, or large amounts of user data entry, you might expect 100 input numbers and get only 95. You could use a break to terminate the for loop before it cycles through the 96th iteration.

Suppose that the teacher using the grade-averaging program in the preceding chapter (C14FOR4.C) entered an incorrect total number of students. Maybe she typed 16, but there are only 14 students. The previous for loop looped 16 times, no matter how many students there are, because it relies on the teacher's count.

The following grade-averaging program is more sophisticated than that. It asks the teacher for the total number of students, but if the teacher wants, she can enter –99 as a student's score. The –99 does not get averaged; it is used as a trigger value to break out of the for loop before its normal conclusion.

```
/* Filename: C15BRAK3.C
   Computes a grade average with a for loop,
   allowing an early exit with a break statement */
#include <stdio.h>
main()
{
   float grade, avg;
   float total=0.0;
   int num, count=0; /* Total number of grades and counter */
   int loopvar;                    /* Used to control for loop */

   printf("\n*** Grade Calculation ***\n\n");      /* Title */
```

```
     printf("How many students are there? ");
     scanf(" %d", &num);          /* Get total number to enter */

     for (loopvar=1; loopvar<=num; loopvar++)
        { printf("\nWhat is the next student's grade? (-99 to
          ➡ quit) ");
          scanf(" %f", &grade);
          if (grade < 0.0)                   /* A negative number
                                                  triggers break */
             { break; }                 /* Leave the loop early */
          count++;
          total += grade;  }           /* Keep a running total */

     avg = total / count;
     printf("\n\nThe average of this class is %.1f", avg);
     return;
  }
```

Teacher might not have as many students as she thought

Notice that grade is tested for less than 0, not –99.0. You cannot reliably use floating-point values to compare for equality (because of their bit-level representations). Because no grade is negative, *any* negative number triggers the break statement. The following lines show how this program works:

```
*** Grade Calculation ***

How many students are there? 10

What is the next student's grade? (-99 to quit) 87

What is the next student's grade? (-99 to quit) 97

What is the next student's grade? (-99 to quit) 67

What is the next student's grade? (-99 to quit) 89

What is the next student's grade? (-99 to quit) 94
```

```
What is the next student's grade? (-99 to quit) -99


The average of this class is 86.8
```

# The *continue* Statement

The continue
statement causes
C to skip all
remaining
statements in a
loop.

The break statement exits a loop early, but the continue statement forces the computer to perform another iteration of the loop. If you put a continue statement in the body of a for loop or while loop, the computer ignores any statement in the loop that follows continue.

The format of continue is

```
continue;
```

You use the continue statement when data in the body of the loop is bad, out of bounds, or unexpected. Instead of acting on the bad data, you might want to go back to the top of the loop and get another data value. The following examples help illustrate this use of the continue statement.

> **Tip:** The continue statement forces a new iteration of any of the three loop constructs: the for loop, the while loop, and the do-while loop.

Figure 15.1 shows the difference between the break statement and the continue statement.

**Figure 15.1**

The difference between *break* and *continue*.

```
for (i=0;i<=10;i++)
   {
      break;
      Printf("Loop it\n");/*never prints!*/      break terminates loop immediately
   }

/*Rest of program */


for (i=0;i<=10;i++)
   {                                             continue causes loop to perform another iteration
      continue;
      Printf("Loop it\n");/*never prints!*/
   }

/*Rest of program*/
```

## Examples

1. Although the following program appears to print the numbers 1 through 10, each followed by C Programming, it does not. The continue in the body of the for loop causes an early finish to the loop. The first printf() in the for loop executes, but the second does not—because of the continue.

```
/* Filename: C15CON1.C
   Demonstrates use of a continue statement */
#include <stdio.h>
main()
{
   int ctr;

   for (ctr=1; ctr<=10; ctr++)         /* Loop 10 times */
     { printf("%d ", ctr);
        continue;              /* Causes body to end early */
        printf("C Programming\n");
     }
   return;
}
```

This never prints

This program produces the following output:

```
1 2 3 4 5 6 7 8 9 10
```

On some compilers, you get a warning message when you compile this type of program. The compiler recognizes that the second printf() is *unreachable* code—that is, it never executes because of the continue statement.

Because of this response, most programs do not use a continue except after an if statement. This makes it a conditional continue statement, which is more useful. The following two examples demonstrate the conditional use of continue.

2. This program asks users for five lowercase letters, one at a time, and prints their uppercase equivalents. It uses the ASCII table (see Appendix C) to ensure that users enter lowercase letters. (These are the letters whose ASCII numbers range from 97 to 122.) If users do not type a lowercase letter, the program ignores the input with the continue statement.

```
/* Filename: C15CON2.C
   Prints uppercase equivalents of 5 lowercase letters */
#include <stdio.h>
```

```
main()
{
   char letter;
   int ctr;

   for (ctr=1; ctr<=5; ctr++)
     { printf("Please enter a lowercase letter ");
       scanf(" %c", &letter);
       if ((letter < 97) || (letter > 122))  /* See if out-
                                                 of-range */
          { continue; }                      /* Go get another */
       letter -= 32;       /* Subtract 32 from ASCII
                              value to get uppercase */
       printf("The uppercase equivalent is %c \n", letter);
       }
   return;
}
```

Make sure that lowercase was entered

Because of the `continue` statement, only lowercase letters are converted to uppercase.

**3.** Suppose that you want to average the salaries of employees in your company who make over $10,000 a year, but you have only their monthly gross pay figures. The following program might be useful. It prompts for each monthly employee salary, annualizes it (multiplying by 12), and computes an average. The `continue` statement ensures that salaries less than or equal to $10,000 are ignored in the average calculation. The `continue` enables the other salaries to "fall through."

If you enter **-1** as a monthly salary, the program quits and prints the result of the average.

```
/* Filename: C15CON3.C
   Averages salaries over $10,000 */
#include <stdio.h>
main()
{
   float month, year;       /* Monthly and yearly salaries */
   float avg=0.0, total=0.0;
   int count=0;
```

```
        do
          { printf("What is the next monthly salary (-1 to quit)?
     ");
            scanf(" %f", &month);
            if ((year=month*12.00) <= 10000.00)  /* Do not add */
               { continue; }                      /* low salaries */
            if (month < 0.0)
               { break; }            /* Quit if user entered -1 */
            count++;                  /* Add 1 to valid counter */
            total += year;       /* Add yearly salary to total */
          } while (month > 0.0);

        avg = total / (float)count;          /* Compute average */
        printf("\n\nThe average of high salaries is $%.2f", avg);
        return;
      }
```

Loop while there are salaries

Notice that this program uses both a `continue` statement and a `break` statement. The program does one of three things, depending on each user's input. It adds to the total, continues another iteration if the salary is too low, or exits the `while` loop (and the average calculation) if the user types a -1.

Here is the output from this program:

```
What is the next monthly salary (-1 to quit)? 500.00
What is the next monthly salary (-1 to quit)? 2000.00
What is the next monthly salary (-1 to quit)? 750.00
What is the next monthly salary (-1 to quit)? 4000.00
What is the next monthly salary (-1 to quit)? 5000.00
What is the next monthly salary (-1 to quit)? 1200.00
What is the next monthly salary (-1 to quit)? -1


The average of high salaries is $36600.00
```

## Summary

In this chapter, you learned several additional ways to use and modify your program's loops. By adding `continue` and `break` statements, you can better control how each loop behaves. Being able to exit early (with the `break` statement) or continue the next loop iteration early (with the `continue` statement) gives you more freedom when processing different types of data.

The next chapter shows you a construct of C that does not loop but relies on the break statement to work properly. This is the switch statement, and it makes your program choices much easier to write.

## Review Questions

Answers to review questions are in Appendix B.

1. Why do continue statements and break statements rarely appear without an if statement controlling them?

2. What is the output from the following section of code?

```
for (i=1; i<=10; i++)
  { continue;
    printf("***** \n");
  }
```

3. What is the output from the following section of code?

```
for (i=1; i<=10; i++)
  { printf("***** \n");
    break;
  }
```

## Review Exercises

1. Write a grade-averaging program for a class of 20 students. Ignore any grade less than 0 and continue until all 20 student grades are entered, or until the user types –99 to end the program early.

2. Write a program that prints the numerals from 1 to 15 in one column. To the right of the even numbers, print each number's square. To the right of the odd numbers, print each number's cube (the number raised to its third power).

# CHAPTER 16

# The *switch* and *goto* Statements

This chapter focuses on the switch statement. It improves on the if and else-if constructs by streamlining the multiple-choice decisions your programs make. The switch statement does not replace the if statement but is better to use when your programs must perform one of many different actions.

The switch and break statements work together. Almost every switch statement you use includes at least one break statement in the body of the loop. Later in this chapter—and to conclude this part of the book on C constructs—you learn the goto statement for completeness, although it is rarely used.

This chapter introduces the following topics:

- The switch statement for selection

- The goto statement for branching from one part of your program to another

Use switch when your program makes a multiple-choice selection.

If you have mastered the if statement, you should have little trouble with the concepts presented here. By learning the switch statement, you should be able to write menus and multiple-choice, data-entry programs with ease.

## The *switch* Statement

The switch statement is sometimes called the *multiple-choice statement*. It lets your program choose from several alternatives. The format of the switch statement is a little longer than the format of other statements you have seen. Here is the format of the switch statement:

```
switch (expression)
   { case (expression1): { one or more C statements; }
     case (expression2): { one or more C statements; }
     case (expression3): { one or more C statements; }

       .

       .

       .

     default: { one or more C statements; }
   }
```

The *expression* can be an integer expression, a character, a constant, or a variable. The subexpressions (*expression1*, *expression2*, and so on) can be any other integer expression, character, constant, or variable. The number of case expressions following the switch line is determined by your application. The *one or more C statements* can be any block of C code. If the block is only one statement long, you do not need the braces, but they are recommended.

The default line is optional; most (but not all) switch statements include the default. The default line does not have to be the last line of the switch body.

If *expression* matches *expression1*, the statements to the right of *expression1* execute. If *expression* matches *expression2*, the statements to the right of *expression2* execute. If none of the expressions matches the switch *expression*, the default case block executes. The case expression does not need parentheses, but they sometimes make the value easier to find.

**Tip:** Use a **break** statement after each **case** block to keep execution from "falling through" to the remaining **case** statements.

Using the switch statement is easier than its format might lead you to believe. Anywhere an if-else-if combination of statements can go, you can usually put a clearer switch statement instead. The switch statement is much easier to follow than an if-within-an-if-within-an-if, as you've had to write previously.

However, the if and else-if combinations of statements are not bad to use or difficult to follow. When the relational test that determines the choice is complex and contains many && and || operators, the if may be a better candidate. The switch statement is preferred whenever multiple-choice possibilities are based on a single constant, variable, or expression.

**Tip:** Arrange **case** statements in the most-often to least-often executed order to improve your program's speed.

The following examples clarify the switch statement. They compare the switch statement to if statements to help you see the difference.

> **For Related Information**
> ♦ "Defining Relational Operators," p. 152
> ♦ "The *if* Statement," p. 154

## Examples

1. Suppose that you are writing a program to teach your child how to count. Your program should ask the child for a number. It then beeps (rings the computer's alarm bell) as many times as necessary to match that number.

The following program assumes that the child presses a number key from 1 to 5. This program uses the if-else-if combination to accomplish this counting-and-beeping teaching method.

*Identify the program and include the necessary header file. You want to sound a beep and move the cursor to the next line, so define a global variable called BEEP that does this. You need a variable to hold the user's answer, so make num an integer variable.*

*Ask the user for a number. Get the user's number and assign it to num. If num is 1, call BEEP once. If num is 2, call BEEP twice. If num is 3, call BEEP three times. If num is 4, call BEEP four times. If num is 5, call BEEP five times.*

```
/* Filename: C16BEEP1.C
   Beeps a certain number of times */
#include <stdio.h>

/* Define a beep printf() to save repeating printf()s
   throughout the program */
#define BEEP printf("\a \n")
main()
{
   int num;

   /* Get a number from the child (you may have to help) */
   printf("Please enter a number ");
   scanf(" %d", &num);
```

```
                 /* Use multiple if statements to beep */
                 if (num == 1)
                   { BEEP; }
                 else if (num == 2)
                      { BEEP; BEEP; }
                    else if (num == 3)
                         { BEEP; BEEP; BEEP; }
                       else if (num == 4)
                            { BEEP; BEEP; BEEP; BEEP; }
                          else if (num == 5)
                               { BEEP; BEEP; BEEP; BEEP; BEEP; }
                 return;
               }
```

A number of nested *if* statements

No beeps are sounded if the child enters something other than 1 to 5. This program takes advantage of the #define preprocessor directive to define a shortcut to an alarm print() function. In this case, the BEEP is a little clearer to read, as long as you remember that BEEP is not a command but gets replaced with the printf() everywhere it appears.

One drawback to this type of if-within-an-if program is its readability. By the time you indent the body of each if and else, the program is shoved too far to the right. There is no room for more than five or six possibilities. More important, this type of logic is difficult to follow. Because it involves a multiple-choice selection, a switch statement is much better to use, as you can see with the following improved version:

```
/* Filename: C16BEEP2.C
   Beeps a certain number of times using a switch */
#include <stdio.h>

/* Define a beep printf() to save repeating printf()s
   throughout the program */
#define BEEP printf("\a \n")
main()
{
   int num;

   /* Get a number from the child (you may have to help) */
   printf("Please enter a number ");
   scanf(" %d", &num);
```

```
    switch (num)
    { case (1): { BEEP;
                    break; }
      case (2): { BEEP; BEEP;
                    break; }
      case (3): { BEEP; BEEP; BEEP;
                    break; }
      case (4): { BEEP; BEEP; BEEP; BEEP;
                    break; }
      case (5): { BEEP; BEEP; BEEP; BEEP; BEEP;
                    break; }
    }
    return;
}
```

*switch* cleans up nested *if*s

This example is much clearer than the preceding one. The value of num controls the execution—only the case that matches num executes. The indention helps separate each case.

If the child enters a number other than 1 to 5, no beeps are sounded because there is no case expression to match any other value and there is no default case.

Because the BEEP preprocessor directive is short, you can put more than one on a single line. This is not a requirement, however. The block of statements following a case can also be more than one statement long.

If more than one case expression is the same, only the first expression executes.

2. If the child does not type a 1, 2, 3, 4, or 5, nothing happens in the last program. What follows is the same program modified to take advantage of the default option. The default block of statements executes if none of the preceding cases matches:

```
/* Filename: C16BEEP3.C
   Beeps a certain number of times using a switch */
#include <stdio.h>

/* Define a beep printf() to save repeating printf()s
   throughout the program */
#define BEEP printf("\a \n")
main()
{
   int num;
```

```
                      /* Get a number from the child (you may have to help) */
                      printf("Please enter a number ");
Child determines      scanf(" %d", &num);
the beeps

                      switch (num)
                      { case (1): { BEEP;
                                        break; }
                        case (2): { BEEP; BEEP;
                                        break; }
                        case (3): { BEEP; BEEP; BEEP;
                                        break; }
                        case (4): { BEEP; BEEP; BEEP; BEEP;
                                        break; }
                        case (5): { BEEP; BEEP; BEEP; BEEP; BEEP;
                                        break; }
                        default:  { printf("You must enter a number from 1 to
                                      ➥5\n");
                                    printf("Please run this program again\n");
                                    break; }
                      }
                      return;
                    }
```

The break at the end of the default case might seem redundant. After all, no other case statements execute by "falling through" from the default case. It is a good habit to put a break after the default case anyway. If you move the default higher in the switch (it doesn't have to be the last switch option), you are more inclined to move the break with it (where it is then needed).

**3.** To show the importance of using break statements in each case expression, here is the same beeping program without any break statements:

```
/* Filename: C16BEEP4.C
   Incorrectly beeps using a switch */
#include <stdio.h>

/* Define a beep printf() to save repeating printf()s
   throughout the program */
#define BEEP printf("\a \n")
main()
{
    int num;
```

```
/* Get a number from the child (you may have to help) */
printf("Please enter a number ");
scanf(" %d", &num);

switch (num)                              /* Warning! */
{ case (1): { BEEP; }        /* Without a break, this code */
  case (2): { BEEP; BEEP; }       /* falls through to the */
  case (3): { BEEP; BEEP; BEEP; } /* rest of the beeps! */
  case (4): { BEEP; BEEP; BEEP; BEEP;}
  case (5): { BEEP; BEEP; BEEP; BEEP; BEEP;}
  default:  { printf("You must enter a number from 1 to
                ➥ 5\n");
                printf("Please run this program again\n"); }
}
return;
}
```

No *break* statements

If the user types a 1, the program beeps 15 times! The break is not there to stop the execution from falling through to the other cases. Unlike other programming languages, such as Pascal, C's switch statement requires that you insert break statements between each case if you want only one case executed. This is not necessarily a drawback. The trade-off of having to specify break statements gives you more control in how you handle specific cases, as shown in the next example.

**4.** This program controls the printing of end-of-day sales totals. The program first asks for the day of the week. If the day is Monday through Thursday, a daily total is printed. If the day is Friday, a weekly total and a daily total are printed. If the day happens to be the end of the month, a monthly sales total is printed as well.

In a real application, these totals would come from the disk drive rather than be assigned at the top of the program. In addition, instead of individual sales figures being printed, a full daily, weekly, and monthly report of many sales totals would probably be printed. You are on your way to learning more about expanding the power of your C programs. But for now, concentrate on the switch statement and its possibilities.

The daily sales figures; the daily and weekly sales figures; and the daily, weekly, and monthly sales figures are handled through a hierarchy of case statements. Because the daily amount is the last case, it is the only report printed if the day of the week is Monday through Thursday. If the day of the week is Friday, the second case prints the weekly sales total and then falls through to the daily total (because Friday's daily total must be printed as well). If it is the end of the month, the first case executes, falling through to the weekly total, then to the daily sales total as well. In this example, the use of a break statement would be harmful. Other languages that do not offer this "fall through" flexibility are more limiting.

```
/* Filename: C16SALE.C
   Prints daily, weekly, and monthly sales totals */
#include <stdio.h>
main()
{
   float daily=2343.34;    /* Later, these figures will */
   float weekly=13432.65;  /* come from a disk file     */
   float monthly=43468.97; /* instead of being assigned */
                           /* as they are here          */
   char ans;
   int day;           /* Day value to trigger correct case */

   /* Day is assigned 1 through 5 (for Monday through
      Friday) or 6 if it is the end of the month. Assume
      that a weekly AND a daily print if it is the end of
      the month, no matter what the day is. */
   printf("Is this the end of the month? (Y/N) ");
   scanf(" %c", &ans);
   if ((ans=='Y') || (ans=='y'))
     { day=6; }                          /* Month value */
   else
     { printf("What day number, 1 through 5 (for Mon-Fri)
       ➡ is it? ");
       scanf(" %d", &day); }

   switch (day)
     { case (6): printf("The monthly total is $%.2f \n",
                        monthly);
       case (5): printf("The weekly total is $%.2f \n",
                        weekly);
       default:  printf("The daily total is $%.2f \n",
                        daily);
     }
   return;
}
```

Prints monthly ——————————————————————

Prints weekly ——————————————————————

Prints daily ——————————————————————

**5.** The order of the `case` statements is not fixed. You can rearrange them to make them more efficient. If only one or two cases are being selected most of the time, put those cases near the top of the `switch` statement.

For example, assume that most of a company's employees are engineers. By arranging the `case` statements so that Engineering is at the top, you can speed up this program because C will not have to scan through `case` expressions that it rarely executes:

```
/* Filename: C16DEPT2.C
   Prints message depending on the department entered */
#include <stdio.h>
main()
{
   char choice;

   do   /* Display menu and ensure that user enters a
           correct option */
     { printf("\nChoose your department: \n");
       printf("S - Sales \n");
       printf("A - Accounting \n");
       printf("E - Engineering \n");
       printf("P - Payroll \n");
       printf("What is your choice? ");
       scanf(" %c", &choice);
       /* Convert choice to uppercase (if they
          entered lowercase) with the ASCII table */
       if ((choice>=97) && (choice<=122))
         { choice -= 32; }          /* Subtract enough to make
                                        uppercase */
     } while ((choice!='S')&&(choice!='A')&&
              (choice!='E')&&(choice!='P'));

   /* Put Engineering first because it occurs most often */
   switch (choice)
   { case ('E') : { printf("\n Your meeting is at 2:30");
                     break; }
     case ('S') : { printf("\n Your meeting is at 8:30");
                     break; }
     case ('A') : { printf("\n Your meeting is at 10:00");
                     break; }
     case ('P') : { printf("\n Your meeting has been
                    ➥ canceled");
```

*switch* based on character data  — (annotation pointing to `switch (choice)`)

```
                                  break; }
            }
        return;
    }
```

# The *goto* Statement

goto causes
execution to jump
to a statement
other than the next
one.

Early programming languages did not offer the flexible constructs that C gives you, such as for loops, while loops, and switch statements. The only means of looping and comparing was with the goto statement. C still includes a goto, but the other constructs are more powerful, flexible, and easier to follow in a program. Use goto sparingly, if at all. The goto statement lends itself to unstructured and difficult to maintain programs.

The goto statement causes your program to jump to a different location rather than execute the next statement in sequence. The format of the goto statement is

```
goto statement label
```

A *statement label* is named just as variables are (see Chapter 4). A *statement label* cannot have the same name as a C command, a C function, or another variable in the program. If you use a goto statement, there must be elsewhere in the program a *statement label* to which the goto branches. Execution then continues at the statement with the *statement label*.

The *statement label* precedes a line of code. Follow all *statement labels* with a colon (:) so that C knows they are labels and doesn't get them confused with variables. You have not seen statement labels in the C programs so far in this book because none of the programs needed them. A *statement label* is optional unless you have a goto that branches to one.

Each of the following lines of code has a different *statement label*. This code is not a program but individual lines that might be included in a program. Notice that the *statement labels* are to the left of the lines:

```
pay: printf("Place checks in the printer \n");
Again: scanf(" %s", name");
EndIt: printf("That is all the processing. \n");
CALC: amount = (total / .5) * 1.15;
```

The *statement labels* are not intended to replace comments, although a label's name should reflect the code that follows. Statement labels give goto statements a tag *to go to*. When your program gets to the goto, it branches to the statement labeled by the statement label. The program then continues to execute sequentially until the next goto changes the order again (or until the program ends).

> **Tip:** Use identifying line labels. A repetitive calculation deserves a label such as `CalcIt` and not `x15z`. Even though both are allowed, the first one is a better indication of the code's purpose.

---

**Use *goto* Judiciously**

The `goto` is not considered a good programming statement when overused. There is a tendency, especially for beginning programmers, to include too many `goto` statements in a program. When a program branches all over the place, it becomes difficult to follow. Some people call programs with many `goto` statements "spaghetti code."

To eliminate `goto` statements and write better-structured programs, use the other looping and `switch` constructs discussed in the last few chapters.

But the `goto` is not necessarily a bad statement—if used judiciously. Starting with the next chapter, you begin to break your programs into smaller modules called functions, and the `goto` becomes less and less important as you write more and more functions.

For now, become familiar with `goto` so that you can understand programs which use it. Some day, you might be called on to correct the code of someone who used the `goto`.

---

## Examples

1. The following program has a problem that is a direct result of the `goto`, but it is still one of the best illustrations of the `goto` statement. The program consists of an *endless loop* (or an infinite loop). The first three lines (after the opening brace) execute; then the `goto` in the fourth line causes execution to loop back to the beginning and repeat the first three lines. The `goto` continues to do this until you press Ctrl-Break or ask your system administrator to cancel the program.

*Identify the program and include the necessary header file. You want to print a message but to split it over three lines. You want the message to keep repeating, so label the first line. Then use a goto to jump back to that line.*

```
/* Filename: C16GOTO1.C
   Program to show use of goto. This program ends
   only when the user presses Ctrl-Break. */
#include <stdio.h>
main()
```

```
{
   Again: printf("This message \n");
   printf("\t keeps repeating \n");
   printf("\t\t over and over \n");

   goto Again;    /* Repeat continuously */

   return;
}
```

Notice that the statement label has a colon to separate it from the rest of the line, but you never add the colon to the label at the goto statement. Figure 16.1 shows the result of running this program.

**Figure 16.1**

A repeating
printing program.

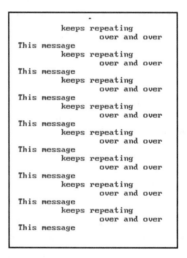

2. It is sometimes easier to read your program's code when you put the statement labels on lines by themselves. Remember that writing maintainable programs is the goal of every good programmer. Making your programs easier to read should be a prime consideration when you write them. The following program is the same repeating program shown in the preceding example except that the statement label is placed on a line by itself:

```
/* Filename: C16GOTO2.C
   Program to show use of goto. This program ends
   only when the user presses Ctrl-Break. */
#include <stdio.h>
main()
```

```
{
Again:
   printf("This message \n");
   printf("\t keeps repeating \n");
   printf("\t\t over and over \n");

   goto Again;    /* Repeat continuously */
   return;
}
```

Statement label ⎯

The line following the statement label is the one that executes next, after control is passed (by the goto) to the label.

Of course, these are silly examples. You really don't want to write programs with infinite loops. The goto is a statement best preceded with an if so that the goto eventually stops branching without intervention from the user.

3. The following program is one of the worst programs ever written. It is the epitome of spaghetti code! However, do your best to follow it and understand its output. By understanding the flow of this output, you can hone your understanding of the goto. You might also appreciate the fact that the rest of this book uses the goto only when needed to make the program clearer.

```
/* Filename: C16GOTO3.C
   This program demonstrates the overuse of goto */
#include <stdio.h>
main()
{
   goto Here;

   First:
   printf("A \n");
   goto Final;

   There:
   printf("B \n");
   goto First;

   Here:
   printf("C \n");
   goto There;
```

Too many
gotos ⎯

```
        Final:
        return;
}
```

At first glance, this program appears to print the first three letters of the alphabet, but the goto statements make them print in reverse order: C, B, A. Although the program is not well designed, some indention of the lines without statement labels makes it a little more readable. This enables you to separate quickly the statement labels from the rest of the code, as you can see from the following program:

```
/* Filename: C16GOTO4.C
   This program demonstrates the overuse of goto */
#include <stdio.h>
main()
{
    goto Here;

First:
    printf("A \n");
    goto Final;

There:
    printf("B \n");
    goto First;

Here:
    printf("C \n");
    goto There;

Final:
    return;
}
```

Still too unorganized because of overuse of *goto*

This program's listing is slightly easier to follow than the preceding one, even though both do the same thing. The remaining programs in this book that use statement labels also use such indention.

You certainly realize that this output would be better produced by the following three lines:

```
printf("C \n");
printf("B \n");
printf("A \n");
```

The goto warning is worth repeating: Use goto sparingly and *only* when its use would make your program more readable and maintainable. Usually, you can use much better commands.

## Summary

You now have seen the switch statement and all its options. With it, you can improve the readability of a complicated if-else-if selection. The switch is especially good when several outcomes are possible, based on the user's choice.

The goto statement causes an unconditional branch and can be difficult to follow at times. The goto is not used much these days, and you can almost always use a better construct. However, you should be acquainted with as much C as possible in case you have to work on programs that others have written.

This ends the part of the book that focuses on program control. The next part introduces user-written functions. So far, you have been using C's built-in functions, such as printf() and scanf(). Now it's time to write your own functions.

## Review Questions

Answers to review questions are in Appendix B.

1. How does goto change the order in which a program normally executes?

2. What statement can substitute for an if-else-if construct?

3. Which statement almost always ends each case statement in a switch?

4. True or false: The order of your case statements has no bearing on the efficiency of your program.

5. Rewrite the following code, using a switch statement:

```
if (num == 1)
    { printf("Alpha"); }
else if (num == 2)
        { printf("Beta"); }
    else if (num == 3)
            { printf("Gamma"); }
        else
            { printf("Other"); }
```

6. Rewrite the following program. using a do-while loop:

```
Ask:
    printf("What is your first name? ");
    scanf(" %s", name);
    if ((name[0] < 'A') || (name[0] > 'Z'))
        { goto Ask; }   /* Keep asking until the user
                            types a valid letter */
```

## Review Exercises

1. Write a program with a switch statement that asks a user for his or her age and then prints a message saying "You can vote!" if the user is 18, "You can adopt!" if the user is 21, or "Are you REALLY that young?" for any other age.

2. Write a program, driven by a menu, for your local TV cable company. Here is how to assess charges: If you are within 20 miles outside the city limits, you pay $12.00 a month; 21 to 30 miles outside the city limits, you pay $23.00 a month; 31 to 50 miles outside the city limits, you pay $34.00. No one beyond 50 miles gets the service. Prompt the user with a menu for the distance of the user's residence from the city limits.

3. Write a program that calculates parking fees for a multilevel parking garage. Ask whether the driver is in a car or a truck. Charge the driver $2.00 for the first hour, $3.00 for the second hour, and $5.00 for more than 2 hours. If the vehicle is a truck, add $1.00 to the total fee. (Hint: Use one switch and one if statement.)

4. Modify the preceding parking problem so that the charge depends on the time of day the vehicle is parked. If the vehicle is parked before 8 a.m., charge the fees in exercise 3. If the vehicle is parked after 8 a.m. and before 5 p.m., charge an extra usage fee of 50 cents. If the vehicle is parked after 5 p.m., deduct 50 cents from the computed price. You must use a menu to prompt users for the following starting times:

```
1. Before 8 a.m.
2. Before 5 p.m.
3. After 5 p.m.
```

# Part IV

*Variable Scope and Modular Programming*

# CHAPTER 17

# Writing C Functions

Computers never get bored. They perform the same input, output, and computations your program requires—for as long as you want them to do it. You can take advantage of their repetitive natures by looking at your programs in a new way: as a series of small routines that execute whenever you need them, however many times you require.

This chapter approaches its subject a little differently than previous chapters. It concentrates on explaining the need for writing your own *functions*, which are *modules* of code that you execute and control from your main() function. So far, all programs in this book have consisted of a single long function called main(). As you learn here, the main() function's primary purpose is to control the execution of other functions that follow it.

This chapter introduces the following topics:

♦ The need for functions

♦ How to trace functions

♦ How to write functions

♦ How to call and return from functions

The chapter stresses the use of *structured programming*, sometimes called *modular programming*. C was designed to make it easy to write your programs in several modules instead of as one long program. By breaking the program into several smaller routines (functions), you can isolate problems, write correct programs faster, and produce programs that are easier to maintain.

# Understanding Function Basics

When you approach an application that needs to be programmed, it is best not to sit down at the keyboard and start typing. Instead, you should first *think* about the program and what it is supposed to do. One of the best ways to attack a program is to start with the overall goal and then divide this goal into several smaller tasks. You should never lose sight of the overall goal, but you should think also of how individual pieces can fit together to accomplish such a goal.

When you finally do sit down to begin coding the problem, continue to think in terms of those pieces fitting together. Don't approach a program as if it were one giant problem, but continue to write those small pieces individually.

This does not mean that you must write separate programs to do everything. You can keep individual pieces of the overall program together—if you know how to write functions. Then you can use the same functions in many different programs.

*C programs should consist of many small functions.*

C programs are not like BASIC or FORTRAN programs. Good C programmers write programs that consist of many small functions, even if their programs execute one or more of these functions only once. But those functions work together to produce a program more quickly and easily than if the program had to be written from scratch.

**Tip:** Rather than code *one* very long program, you should write several smaller routines, called functions. One of these functions must be called `main()`. The `main()` function is always the first to execute. It doesn't need to be first in a program, but it usually is.

# Breaking Down Problems

If your program does very much, break it into several functions. Each function should do *one* primary task. Suppose that you were writing a C program to get a list of characters from the keyboard, alphabetize them, and then print them to the screen. You could—but shouldn't—write all that into one big `main()` function, as the following C *skeleton* (program outline) shows:

```
main()
{
    /* :
      C code to get a list of characters
      :
      C code to alphabetize the characters
      :
      C code to print the alphabetized list on the screen
      : */
    return;
}
```

This skeleton is *not* a good way to write this program. Even though you could type this program in only a few lines of code, it would be much better to get in the habit of breaking up every program into distinct tasks. You should not use main() to do everything—in fact, you should use main() to do little except call each of the functions that do the work.

A better way to organize this program is to write a separate function for each task the program is supposed to do. This doesn't mean that each function should be only one line long. It means that you should make every function a building block which performs only one distinct task in the program.

The following program outline shows you a better way to write the program just described:

```c
main()
{
   getletters();   /* Calls a function to get the letters */
   alphabetize();  /* Calls a function to alphabetize
                      letters */
   printletters(); /* Calls a function to print letters
                      on-screen */
   return;         /* Return to the operating system */
}

getletters()
{
   /* :
      C code to get a list of characters
      : */
   return;   /* Returns to main() */
}

alphabetize()
{
   /* :
      C code to alphabetize the characters
      :   /*
   return;   /* Returns to main() */
}

printletters()
{
   /* :
      C code to print the alphabetized list on the screen
      : */
   return;   /* Returns to main() */
}
```

The program outline shows you a much better way of writing this program. It is longer to type, but much better organized. The only thing the main() function does is control the other functions by showing in one place the order in which they are called. Each separate function executes its instructions and then returns to main(), which calls the next function until no more functions remain. The main() function then returns control of the computer to the operating system.

> **Tip:** A good rule of thumb is that a function should not be more than one screen in length. If it is longer, you are probably doing too much in that function and should therefore break it into two or more functions.

The main() function is usually a calling function that controls the rest of the program.

The first function called main() is what you previously used to hold the entire program. From this point, in all but the smallest of programs, main() simply controls other functions that do the work.

These listings are not examples of real C programs; instead, they are skeletons, or outlines, of programs. From these outlines, it is easier to develop the actual full program. But before going to the keyboard to write a program such as this, you should know that there will be four distinct sections: a primary function-calling main() function, a keyboard data-entry function, an alphabetizing function, and a printing function.

You should never lose sight of the original programming problem. With the approach just described, you never do! Look again at the main() calling routine in the preceding program. Notice that you can glance at main() and get a feel for the overall program, without the remaining statements getting in the way. This is a good example of structured, modular programming. A large programming problem has been broken down into distinct, separate modules called functions, and each function performs one primary job in a few C statements.

## Considering More Function Basics

Little has been said about naming and writing functions, but you probably understand much of the goals of the preceding listing already. C functions generally adhere to the following rules:

1. Every function must have a name.

2. Function names are made up and assigned by the programmer (you!) according to the same rules that apply to naming variables: they can contain up to 31 characters; they must begin with a letter; and they can consist of letters, numbers, and the underscore (_) character.

**3.** All function names have one set of parentheses immediately following them. This helps you (and C) differentiate them from variables. The parentheses may or may not contain something. So far, all such parentheses in this book have been empty.

**4.** The body of each function, starting immediately after the closing parenthesis of the function name, must be enclosed by braces. This means that a block containing one or more statements makes up the body of each function.

Use meaningful function names: `CalcBalance()` is more descriptive than `xy3()`.

Although the outline shown in the preceding listing is a good example of structured code, it can be further improved—and not only by putting the actual C statements inside the program to make it work.

The following listing shows you an example of a C function. You can already tell quite a bit about this function. You know, for instance, that it isn't a complete program, because it has no `main()` function. (All programs *must* have a `main()` function.) You know also that the function name is `calcIt` because parentheses follow this name. These parentheses happen to have something in them. You know also that the body of the function is enclosed in a block of braces. Inside that block is a *smaller* block, the body of a `while` loop. Finally, you recognize that the `return` statement is the last line of the function.

All programs must have a `main()` function.

```
calcIt(int n)
{
   /* Function to print the square of a number */
   int square;

   while (square <= 250)
     { square = n * n;
       printf("The square of %d is %d \n", n, square);
       n++; }     /* A block within the function */

   return;
}
```

**Tip:** Not all functions require a `return` statement for their last line, but it is recommended that you always include one, because it helps to show your intention to return to the calling function at that point. Later in the book, you learn when the `return` statement is required. For now, you should just get in the habit of including a `return` statement.

# Calling and Returning Functions

A function call is like a temporary program detour.

You have been reading much about "function calling" and "returning control." Although you may already understand these phrases from their context, you can probably learn them better through an illustration of what is meant by a function call.

A function call in C is like a detour on a highway. Imagine that you are traveling along the "road" of the primary function called main() and then run into a function-calling statement. You must temporarily leave the main() function and go execute the function that was called. After that function finishes (its return statement is reached), program control reverts to main(). In other words, when you finish a detour, you end up back on the "main" route and continue the trip. Control continues as main() calls other functions.

> **Note:** Generally, the primary function that controls function calls and their order is called a *calling function*. Functions controlled by the calling function are called the *called functions*.

A complete C program, with functions, should make this clear. The following program prints several messages to the screen. Each message printed is determined by the order of the functions. Before worrying too much about what this program does, take a little time to study its structure. You should be able to see three functions defined in the program: main(), nextFun(), and thirdFun(). A fourth function is used also, but it is the built-in C printf() function. The three defined functions appear sequentially, one after the other. The body of each is enclosed in braces, and each has a return statement at its end.

```
/* Filename: C17FUN1.C
   The following program illustrates function calls */
#include <stdio.h>
main()  /* main() is always the first C function executed */
{
    printf("First function called main() \n");
    nextFun();              /* Second function is called here */
    thirdFun();             /* This function is called here */
    printf("main() is completed \n");        /* All control
                                                returns here */

    return;                 /* Control is returned to
                                the operating system    */
}                           /* This brace concludes main() */


nextFun()                               /* Second function;
                             parentheses always required */

{
```

Calls 2 functions

A function definition ———

```
        printf("Inside nextFun() \n");      /* No variables are
                                              defined in the program */
     return;              /* Control is now returned to main() */
  }
```

A function definition ———

```
thirdFun()                          /* Last function in the program */
{
   printf("Inside thirdFun() \n");
   return;                 /* Always return from all functions */
}
```

Here is the output of this program:

```
First function called main()
Inside nextFun()
Inside thirdFun()
main() is completed
```

Figure 17.1 shows a tracing of this program's execution. Notice that `main()` controls which of the other functions is called, as well as the order of the calling. Control *always* returns to the calling function after the called function finishes.

**Figure 17.1**

Tracing function calls.

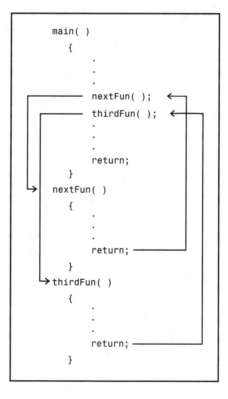

To call a function, simply type its name—including the parentheses—and follow it with a semicolon. Remember that semicolons follow all executable statements in C, and a function call (sometimes called a *function invocation*) is an executable statement. The execution is the function's code being called. Any function can call any other function. It just happens that `main()` is the only function that calls other functions in this program.

Now you can tell that the following statement is a function call:

```
printTotal();
```

Because `printTotal` is not a C command or built-in function name, it must be a variable or a written function's name. Only function names end with the parentheses, so it must be a function call or the start of a function's code. Of the last two possibilities, it must be a call to a function because it ends with a semicolon. If it didn't have a semicolon, it would have to be the start of a function definition.

When you define a function (that is, when you type the function name and its subsequent code inside braces), you *never* follow the name with a semicolon. Notice in the preceding program that `main()`, `nextFun()`, and `thirdFun()` have no semicolons when they appear in the body of the program. A semicolon follows their names only in `main()`, where these functions are called.

> **Caution:** Never define a function within another function. All function code must be listed sequentially, one after the other, throughout the program. A function's closing brace *must* appear before another function's code can be listed.

## Examples

1. Suppose that you are writing a program that does the following. First, it asks users for their departments. Then, if they are in accounting, they should receive the Accounting department's report. If they are in engineering, they should receive the Engineering department's report. And if they are in marketing, they should receive the Marketing department's report.

   The skeleton of such a program follows. The code for `main()` is shown in its entirety, but only a skeleton of the other functions is shown. The `switch` statement is a perfect function-calling statement for such multiple-choice selections.

```
/* Skeleton of a departmental report program */
#include <stdio.h>
main()
{
```

```
    int choice;

    do
      { printf("Choose your department from the following
        ➥ list\n");
        printf("\t1. Accounting \n");
        printf("\t2. Engineering \n");
        printf("\t3. Marketing \n");
        printf("What is your choice? ");
        scanf(" %d", &choice);
      } while ((choice<1) || (choice>3));  /* Ensure 1, 2,
                                               or 3 */


    switch (choice)
    { case(1): { acctReport(); /* Call accounting function */
               break; }            /* Don't fall through */
      case(2): { engReport(); /* Call engineering function */
               break; }
      case(3): { mtgReport();   /* Call marketing function */
               break; }
    }
    return;  /* Program returns to the operating system
              when finished */
}

acctReport()
{
  /* :
     Accounting report code goes here */
     :  */
  return;
}

engReport()
{
  /* :
     Engineering report code goes here */
     :  */
  return;
}
```

```
mtgReport()
{
   /* :
      Marketing report code goes here */
      :  */
   return;
}
```

The bodies of switch statements normally contain function calls. You can tell that these case statements execute functions. For instance, acctReport(); (which is the first line of the first case) is not a variable name or a C command. It is the name of a function defined later in the program. If users enter 1 at the menu, the function called acctReport() executes. When it finishes, control returns to the first case body, whose break statement causes the switch statement to end. The main() function returns to DOS (or to your integrated C environment if you are using one) when its return statement executes.

2. In the preceding example, the main() routine is not very modular. It displays the menu, but that should be done in a separate function. Remember that main() should do very little except control the other functions, which do all the work.

Here is a rewrite of this sample program, with a fourth function to print the menu to the screen. This is truly a modular example, with each function performing a single task. Again, the last three functions show only skeleton code because the goal here is simply to illustrate function calling and returning.

```
/* Second skeleton of a departmental report program */
#include <stdio.h>
main()
{
   int (choice);

   do
      { menuPrint();  /* Call function to print the menu */
        scanf(" %d", &choice);
      } while ((choice<1) || (choice>3));   /* Ensure 1, 2,
                                               or 3 */

   switch choice
      { case(1): { acctReport(); /* Call accounting function */
                   break; }             /* Don't fall through */
```

```
      case(2): { engReport(); /* Call engineering function */
                  break; }
      case(3): { mtgReport();   /* Call marketing function */
                  break; }
    }
    return;   /* Program returns to the operating system
                 when finished */
}

menuPrint()
{
    printf("Choose your department from the following
    ➥list\n");
    printf("\t1. Accounting \n");
    printf("\t2. Engineering \n");
    printf("\t3. Marketing \n");
    printf("What is your choice? ");
    return;    /* Return to main() */
}

acctReport()
{
    /* :
       Accounting report code goes here */
       :  */
    return;
}

engReport()
{
    /* :
       Engineering report code goes here */
       :  */
    return;
}

mtgReport()
{
    /* :
       Marketing report code goes here */
       :  */
    return;
}
```

The menu-printing function doesn't have to follow main(). Because it's the first function called, however, it seems best to define it there.

3. Readability is the key, so programs broken into separate functions result in better-written code. You can write and test each function, one at a time. After you write a general outline of the program, you can list a lot of function calls in main() and define their skeletons after main().

The body of each function initially should consist of a single return statement so that the program compiles in its skeleton format. As you complete each function, you can compile and test the program. This enables you to develop more accurate programs faster. The separate functions let others (who might later modify your program) "zero in" on whatever code they need to change, without affecting the rest of the program.

Another useful habit, popular with many C programmers, is to separate functions from each other with a comment consisting of a line of asterisks (*) or hyphens (-). This makes it easy, especially in longer programs, to see where a function begins and ends. What follows is another listing of the preceding program, but now with its four functions more clearly separated by this type of comment line.

```c
/* Third skeleton of a departmental report program */
#include <stdio.h>
main()
{
   int choice;

   do
     { menuPrint();  /* Call function to print the menu */
        scanf(" %d", &choice);
     } while ((choice<1) || (choice>3));  /* Ensure 1, 2,
                                             or 3 */

   switch (choice)
   { case(1): { acctReport(); /* Call accounting function */
              break; }              /* Don't fall through */
     case(2): { engReport(); /* Call engineering function */
              break; }
     case(3): { mtgReport();   /* Call marketing function */
              break; }
   }
   return;  /* Program returns to the operating system
                when finished */
}
```

```
/************************************************************/
menuPrint()
{
   printf("Choose your department from the following
   ➥ list\n");
   printf("\t1. Accounting \n");
   printf("\t2. Engineering \n");
   printf("\t3. Marketing \n");
   printf("What is your choice? ");
   return;   /* Return to main() */
}

/************************************************************/
acctReport()
{
   /* :
      Accounting report code goes here */
      :  */
   return;
}

/************************************************************/
engReport()
{
   /* :
      Engineering report code goes here */
      :  */
   return;
}

/************************************************************/
mtgReport()
{
   /* :
      Marketing report code goes here */
      :  */
   return;
}
```

Because of space limitations, not all program listings in this book separate the functions in this manner. You might find, however, that your listings are easier to follow if you put these separating comments between your functions.

**4.** You can execute a function more than once simply by calling it from more than one place in a program. If you put a function call in the body of a loop, the function executes repeatedly until the loop finishes.

The following program prints the message C is Fun! several times on-screen—forward and backward—using functions. Notice that main() does not make every function call. The second function, namePrint(), calls the function named reversePrint(). Trace the execution of this program's printf()s. Figure 17.2 shows the program's output to help you trace its execution.

```
/* Filename: C17FUN2.C
   Prints C is fun! several times on the screen */
#include <stdio.h>
main()
{
   int ctr;  /* To control loops */

   for (ctr=1; ctr<=5; ctr++)
      { namePrint(); }              /* Calls function 5 times */

   onePerLine();                    /* Calls last function once */
   return;

}


/************************************************************/
namePrint()
{
   /* Prints C is Fun! across a line, separated by tabs */
   printf("C is Fun!\tC is Fun!\tC is Fun!\tC is Fun!\n");
   printf("C  i s  F u n !\tC  i s  F u n !  \tC  i s  F u n
   ➡!\n");

   reversePrint();        /* Calls next function from here */
   return;                          /* Returns to main() */
}
```

Function is called each time through loop

```
/*************************************************************/
reversePrint()
{
   /* Prints several C is Fun! messages, */
   /*    in reverse, separated by tabs    */
   printf("!nuF si C\t!nuF si C\t!nuF si C\t\n");

   return;                              /* Returns to namePrint() */
}


/*************************************************************/
onePerLine()
{
   /* Prints C is Fun! down the screen */
   printf("C\n \ni\ns\n \nF\nu\nn\n!\n");
   return;   /* Returns to main() */
}
```

**Figure 17.2**

Printing a
message several
times, forward and
backward.

```
C is Fun!        C is Fun!        C is Fun!        C is Fun!
C  i s  F u n ! C  i s  F u n ! C  i s  F u n !
!nuF si C        !nuf si C        !nuf si C
C is Fun!        C is Fun!        C is Fun!        C is Fun!
C  i s  F u n ! C  i s  F u n ! C  i s  F u n !
!nuF si C        !nuf si C        !nuf si C
C is Fun!        C is Fun!        C is Fun!        C is Fun!
C  i s  F u n ! C  i s  F u n ! C  i s  F u n !
!nuF si C        !nuf si C        !nuf si C
C is Fun!        C is Fun!        C is Fun!        C is Fun!
C  i s  F u n ! C  i s  F u n ! C  i s  F u n !
!nuF si C        !nuf si C        !nuf si C
C is Fun!        C is Fun!        C is Fun!        C is Fun!
C  i s  F u n ! C  i s  F u n ! C  i s  F u n !
!nuF si C        !nuf si C        !nuf si C
C

i

s

F
u
n
!
```

# Summary

You now have been exposed to truly structured programs. Instead of typing a long
program, you can break it up into separate functions. This isolates your routines
from each other so that surrounding code doesn't get in the way when you are
concentrating on one section of your program.

Functions introduce just a little more complexity, involving the way variable values are recognized by all the program's functions. The next chapter shows you how variables are handled between functions and helps strengthen your structured programming skills.

## Review Questions

Answers to review questions are in Appendix B.

1. True or false: A function should always include a return statement as its last command.

2. What is the name of the first function executed in a C program?

3. Which is better: one long function or several smaller functions? Why?

4. How do function names differ from variable names?

5. How can you use comments to help separate functions visually from each other?

6. What is wrong with the following program section?

```
calcIt()
{
    printf("Getting ready to calculate the square of 25 \n");

    sq25()
    {
        printf("The square of 25 is %d", (25*25));
        return;
    }

    printf("That is a big number! \n");
    return;
}
```

7. Is the following a variable name, a function call, a function definition, or an expression?

```
scanNames();
```

8. True or false: The following line in a C program is a function call.

```
printf("C is Fun! \n");
```

# CHAPTER 18

# Variable Scope

The concept of *variable scope* is most important when you write functions. Variable scope determines which functions recognize certain variables. If a function recognizes a variable, the variable is *visible* to that function. Variable scope protects variables in one function from other functions that might overwrite them. If a function doesn't need access to a variable, that function shouldn't be able to see or change the variable. In other words, the variable should not even be "visible" to that particular function.

This chapter introduces you to

♦ Global and local variables

♦ Passing arguments

♦ Automatic and static variables

♦ Passing parameters

The preceding chapter introduced the concept of using a different function for each task. This concept is much more useful when you learn about local and global variable scope.

## Global versus Local Variables

If you have programmed only in BASIC, the concept of local and global variables may be new to you. In many interpreted versions of BASIC, all variables are *global*. That is, the entire program knows what every variable is and has the capability to change any of them. If you use a variable called SALES at the top of the program, even the last line in the program can use SALES. (If you don't know BASIC, don't despair—there is one less habit you have to break!)

Global variables
are visible across
many program
functions.

Global variables can be dangerous. Parts of a program can inadvertently change a variable that shouldn't be changed. For example, suppose you are writing a program that keeps track of a grocery store's inventory. You might keep track of sales percentages, discounts, retail prices, wholesale prices, produce prices, dairy prices, delivered prices, price changes, sales tax percentages, holiday markups, post-holiday markdowns, and so on.

Local variables are
visible only in the
block where they
are defined.

The huge number of prices in such a system is confusing. When writing a program to keep track of each these prices, you might mistakenly call both the dairy prices and the delivered prices dPrices. Either C disallows it (does not let you define the same variable twice) or you overwrite a value used for something else. Whatever happens, keeping track of all of these different—but similarly named—prices make this program confusing to write.

Global variables can be dangerous because code can inadvertently overwrite a variable initialized elsewhere in the program. It is better to make every variable *local* in your programs. Then only functions that should be able to change the variables can do so.

You can access (and change) local variables only from the functions in which they are defined. Therefore, if a function defines a variable as local, that variable's scope is protected. The variable cannot be used, changed, or erased by any other function—without special programming that you learn about shortly.

If you use only one function, main(), the concept of local and global is academic. But you know from the last chapter that single-function programs are not recommended. It is best to write modular, structured programs made up of many smaller functions. Therefore, you should know how to define variables as local to only those functions that need them.

## Variable Scope

When you first learned about variables in Chapter 4, "Variables and Constants," you learned that you can define variables in two places:

◆ After the opening brace of a block of code (usually at the top of a function)

◆ Before a function name, such as main()

All examples in this book so far have defined variables using the first method. You have yet to see an example of the second method. Because most of these programs have consisted entirely of a single main() function, there has been no reason to differentiate the two methods. It is only after you start using several functions in one program that these two variable definition methods become critical.

The following rules, specific to local and global variables, are very important:

◆ A variable is local if and only if you define it after the opening brace of a block, usually at the top of a function.

◆ A variable is global if and only if you define it outside a function.

All variables you have seen so far have been local. They have all been defined immediately after the opening braces of `main()`. Therefore, they have been local to `main()`, and only `main()` can use them. Other functions have no idea these variables even exist because they belong to `main()` only. When the function (or block) ends, all its local variables are destroyed.

**Tip:** All local variables disappear (lose their definition) when their block ends.

Global variables are visible from their definition downward throughout the rest of the program.

Global variables are visible ("known") from their point of definition *downward* in the source code. That is, if you define a global variable, *any* line throughout the rest of the program—no matter how many functions and code lines follow it—is able to use that global variable.

## Examples

**1.** The following section of code defines two local variables, `i` and `j`.

```
main()
{
    int i, j;                       /* Local because they're
                                        defined after the brace */
    /* Rest of main() goes here */
}
```

These variables are visible to `main()`, but not to any other function that might follow or be called by `main()`.

**2.** The following section of code defines two global variables, `g` and `h`.

```
#include <stdio.h>
int g, h;                       /* Global because they're
                                    defined before a function */
main()
{
    /* main()'s code goes here */
}
```

It really doesn't matter whether your `#include` lines go before or after global variable definitions.

**3.** Global variables can appear before any function. In the following program, `main()` uses no variables. However, both of the two functions after `main()` can use `sales` and `profit` because these variables are global.

```
/* Filename: C18GLO.C
   Program that contains two global variables */
#include <stdio.h>
main()
{
   printf("No variables defined in main() \n\n");
   doFun();                    /* Call the first function */
   return;
}

float sales, profit;                 /* Two global variables */
doFun()
{
   sales = 20000.00;          /* This variable is visible   */
                              /* from this point down.      */
   profit = 5000.00;          /* So is this one. They are   */
                              /* both global.               */

   printf("The sales in the second function are: %.2f \n",
          sales);
   printf("The profit in the second function is: %.2f \n\n",
          profit);

   thirdFun();                /* Call the third function to
                                 show that globals are visible */

   return;
}

thirdFun()
{
   printf("In the third function: \n");
   printf("The sales in the third function are: %.2f \n",
          sales);
   printf("The profit in the third function is: %.2f \n",
          profit);
   /* If sales and profit were local, they would not be
      visible by more than one function */
   return;
}
```

Known for entire program → `float sales, profit;`

**Note:** If your C compiler sends you a warning saying that there is not a *prototype*, ignore the warning for now. In Chapter 20, you'll learn how to correct this problem.

Note that the main() function can never use sales and profit because they are not visible to main()—even though they are global. Remember, global variables are visible only from their point of definition downward in the program. Statements that appear before global variable definitions cannot use those variables. Figure 18.1 shows the result of running this program.

**Figure 18.1**

Demonstrating the visibility of global variables.

```
No variables defined in main()

The sales in the 2nd function is: 20000.00
The profit in the 2nd function is: 5000.00

In the third function:
The sales in 3rd function is: 20000.00
The profit in 3rd function is: 5000.00
```

**Tip:** Define all global variables at the top of your programs. Even though you can define them later (between any two functions), you can spot them faster if you define them at the top.

4. The following program uses both local and global variables. You should recognize now that j and p are local and i and z are global.

```
/* Filename: C18GLLO.C
   Program with both local and global variables
   Local Variables          Global Variables
       j, p                      i, z              */
#include <stdio.h>
int i = 0;                      /* Global variable because it's
                                        defined outside main() */

main()
{
    float p ;                       /* Local to main() only */
    p = 9.0;                /* Put value in global variable */
    printf("%d  %f\n", i, p);        /* Prints global i
                                            and local p */

    prAgain();                  /* Calls next function */
    return;                          /* Returns to DOS */

}

float z = 9.0;              /* Global variable because it's
                                defined before a function */
```

Known only in *main()*

```
prAgain()
{
    int j = 5;                      /* Local to only prAgain() */
    printf("%d %f %d", j, z, i); /* This couldn't print p! */
    return;                         /* Return to main() */
}
```

Known only
in *prAgain()*

Even though j is defined in a function that main() calls, main() cannot use j because j is local to prAgain(). When prAgain() finishes, j is no longer defined. The variable z is global from its point of definition down. This is why main() cannot print z. Also, the function prAgain() cannot print p because p is local to main() only.

Make sure you can recognize local and global variables before you continue. A little study here makes the rest of this chapter very easy to understand.

5. Two variables can have the same name, as long as they are local to two different functions. They are distinct variables, even though they are named identically.

The following short program uses two variables, both named age. They have two different values, and they are considered to be two different variables. The first age is local to main(), and the second age is local to getAge().

```
/* Filename: C18LOC2.C
    Two different local variables with the same name */
#include <stdio.h>
main()
{
    int age;
    printf("What is your age? ");
    scanf(" %d", &age);

    getAge();                       /* Call the second function */
    printf("main()'s age is still: %d", age);

    return;
}

getAge()
{
    int age;                        /* A different age. This one
                                        is local to getAge() */
    printf("What is your age again? ");
    scanf(" %d", &age);
    return;
}
```

Two different
variables with
the same name

The output of this program follows. Study this output carefully. Notice that main()'s last printf() does not print the newly changed age. Rather, it prints only the age known to main()—the age that is local to main(). Even though they are named the same, main()'s age has nothing to do with getAge()'s age. They might as well have two different variable names.

```
What is your age? 28
What is your age again? 56
main()'s age is still 28
```

You should be careful when naming variables. Having two variables with the same name is misleading. It is easy to become confused while changing this program later. If these variables truly need to be separate, name them differently, such as oldAge and newAge, or age1 and age2. This helps you remember that the variables are different.

6. There are a few times when overlapping local variable names does not add confusion, but be careful about overdoing it. Programmers often use the same variable name as the counter variable in a for loop. For example, the two local variables in the following program have the same name.

```c
/* Filename: C18LOC3.C
   Using two local variables with the same name
   as counting variables */
#include <stdio.h>
main()
{
   int ctr;                              /* Loop counter */
   for (ctr=0; ctr<=10; ctr++)
      { printf("main()'s ctr is %d \n", ctr); }
   doFun();                              /* Call second function */

   return;
}

doFun()
{
   int ctr;
   for (ctr=10; ctr>=0; ctr--)
      { printf("doFun()'s ctr is %d \n", ctr); }
   return;                              /* Return to main() */
}
```

A different *ctr* than the one local to *main()*

Although this is a nonsense program that simply prints 0 through 10 and then prints 10 through 0, it shows that the use of `ctr` in both functions is not a problem. These variables do not hold important data that must be processed; rather, they are `for` loop counting variables. Calling them both `ctr` leads to little confusion because their use is limited to controlling `for` loops. Because a `for` loop initializes and increments variables, the functions never rely on the other one's `ctr` to do anything.

**7.** Be careful about creating local variables with the same name in the same function. If you define a local variable early in a function and then define another local variable with the same name inside a new block, C uses only the innermost variable, until its block ends.

The following example helps clarify this confusing problem. The program contains one function with three local variables.

```
/* Filename: C18MULI.C
   Program with multiple local variables called i */
#include <stdio.h>
main()
{
    int i;                                      /* Outer i */
    i = 10;

    { int i;                                /* New block's i */
      i = 20;                        /* Outer i still holds a 10 */
      printf("%d %d \n", i, i);              /* Prints 20 20 */

    { int i;      /* Another new block and local variable */
      i = 30;                                /* Innermost i only */
      printf("%d %d %d \n", i, i, i); /* Prints 30 30 30 */
    }                            /* Innermost i is now gone forever */

    }         /* Second i is gone forever (its block ended) */

    printf("%d %d %d", i, i, i);           /* Prints 10 10 10 */
    return;
}                        /* main() ends and so do its variables */
```

Three variables inside *main()*, all named i

All local variables are local to the block in which they are defined. This program has three blocks, each one nested within another. Because you can define local variables immediately after an opening brace of a block, there are three distinct `i` variables in this program.

The local i disappears completely when its block ends (that is, when the closing brace is reached). C always prints the variable that it sees as the most local—the one that resides within the innermost block.

## Use Global Variables Sparingly

You may be asking yourself, "Why do I need to know about global and local variables?" At this point, that is an understandable question, especially if you have been programming mostly in BASIC. Here is the bottom line: global variables can be *dangerous*. Code can inadvertently overwrite a variable that was initialized in another place in the program. It is better to have every variable in your program be *local to the function that needs to access it*.

Read that last sentence again. Even though you now know how to make variables global, you should avoid doing so! Try never to use another global variable. It may seem easier to use global variables when you write programs having more than one function: when you make every variable used by every function global, you never have to worry whether one is visible to any given function. On the other hand, a function can accidentally change a global variable when it has no right to change it. If you keep variables local only to functions that need them, you protect their values, and you also keep your programs, both the code and all your data, fully modular.

## The Need for Passing Variables

You just learned the difference between local and global variables. You saw that by making your variables local, you protect their values because the function that sees the variable is the only one that can modify it.

What do you do, however, if you have a local variable you want to use in *two or more* functions? In other words, you may need a variable to be input from the keyboard in one function and printed in another function. If the variable is local only to the first function, how can the second one access it?

You have two solutions if more than one function needs to share a variable. One, you can define the variable globally. This is bad because you want *only* those two functions to "see" the variable, but all other functions can "see" it when it is global. The other alternative—and the better one by far—is to *pass* the local variable from one function to another. This approach has a big advantage: the variable is known only to those two functions. The rest of the program still has no access to it.

**Caution:** Never pass a global variable because C will get confused. There is no reason to pass global variables anyway because they are already visible to all functions.

You pass an argument when you pass one local variable to another function.

When you pass a local variable from one function to another, you *pass an argument* from the first function to the next. You can pass more than one argument (variable) at a time if you want several local variables sent from one function to another. The receiving function *receives a parameter* (variable) from the function that sends it. You shouldn't worry too much about what you call these passed variables—either arguments or parameters. The important thing to remember is that you are sending local variables from one function to another.

> **Note:** You have already passed arguments to functions; you did so when you passed data to the `printf()` function. The constants, variables, and expressions in the `printf()` parentheses are arguments. The built-in `printf()` function receives these values (called parameters on the receiving end) and displays them.

A little more terminology is needed before you see some examples. When a function passes an argument, it is called the *passing function*. The function that receives the argument (called a parameter when it is received) is called the *receiving function*. Figure 18.2 explains these terms.

**Figure 18.2**

The calling and receiving functions.

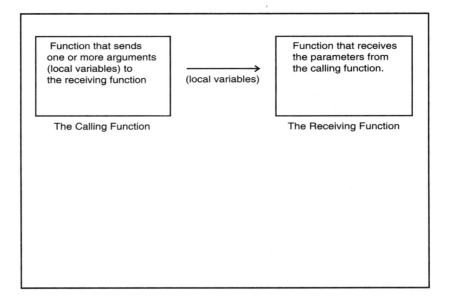

If a function name has empty parenthesis, nothing is being passed to it.

To pass a local variable from one function to another, you must place the local variable in parentheses in both the calling function and the receiving function. For example, the local and global examples presented earlier did not pass local variables from `main()` to `doFun()`. If a function name has empty parentheses, nothing is being passed to it. Given this, the following line passes two variables, total and discount, to a function called doFun().

```
doFun(total, discount);
```

It is sometimes said that a variable or function is *defined*. This has *nothing* to do with the #define preprocessor directive, which defines constants. You define variables with statements such as the following:

```
int i, j;
int m=9;
float x;
char ara[] = "Tulsa";
```

These statements tell the program that you need these variables and want them reserved. A function is defined when the C compiler reads the first statement in the function that describes the name and reads also any variables that may have been passed to that function. Never follow a function definition with a semicolon, but always follow the statement that calls a function with a semicolon.

The following program contains two function definitions, main() and prIt().

*You want to practice passing a variable to a function, so define i as an integer variable and make it equal to 5. The passing (or calling) function will be main(), and the receiving function will be prIt(). Pass the i variable to the prIt() function, and then go back to main().*

```
main()                      /* The main() function definition */
{
   int i=5;                 /* Define an integer variable */
   prIt(i);                 /* Calls the prIt()
                               function and passes it i */
   return;                  /* Return to the operating system */
}

prIt(int i)                 /* The prIt() function definition */
{
    printf("%d \n", i);     /* Calls the printf() function */
    return;                 /* Returns to main() */
}
```

*i* is passed... ⟶ prIt(i);

...to here ⟶ prIt(int i)

Because a passed parameter is treated like a local variable in the receiving function, the printf() in prIt() prints a 5, even though the main() function initialized this variable.

When you pass arguments to a function, the receiving function has no idea about the data types of the incoming variables. Therefore, you must include each parameter's data type in front of the parameter's name. In the previous example, the definition of `prIt()` (the first line of the function) contains the type, `int`, of the incoming variable `i`. Notice that the `main()` calling function does not need to indicate the variable type. In this example, `main()` already knows the type of variable `i` (an integer); only `prIt()` needs to know that `i` is an integer.

> **Tip:** Always define the parameter types in the receiving function. Precede each parameter in the function's parentheses with `int`, `float`, or whatever each passed variable's data type happens to be.

## Examples

1. Here is a `main()` function that contains three local variables. `main()` passes one of these variables to the first function and two of them to the second function.

```
/* Filename: C18LOC4.C
   Pass three local variables to functions */
#include <stdio.h>
prInit(char initial);
prOther(int age, float salary); /* Prototype */
main()
{
   char initial;           /* 3 variables local to main() */
   int age;
   float salary;

   /* Fill these variables in main() */
   printf("What is your initial? ");
   scanf(" %c", &initial);
   printf("What is your age? ");
   scanf(" %d", &age);
   printf("What is your salary? ");
   scanf(" %f", &salary);

   prInit(initial);                    /* Call prInit() and
                                           pass it initial */
   prOther(age, salary);    /* Call prOther() and pass
                                it age and salary */

   return;
}
```

Receives
*main( )*'s initial

```
prInit(char initial)              /* Never put a semicolon in
                                      the function definition */
{
   printf("Your initial is really %c? \n", initial);
   return;                         /* Return to main() */
}

prOther(int age, float salary)            /* Must type both
                                             parameters */
{
   printf("You look young for %d \n", age);
   printf("And $%.2f is a LOT of money!", salary);
   return;                         /* Return to main() */
}
```

Receives
two variables
from *main( )*

**Note:** The line before main() with the /* Prototype */ comment is
required for this program to compile correctly. For now, concentrate on
the arguments being passed and received between functions.

2. A receiving function can contain its own local variables. As long as the names
are not the same, these local variables do not conflict with the passed ones. In
the following program, the second function receives a passed variable from
main() and also defines its own local variable called pricePer.

```
/* Filename: C18LOC5.C
   Second function has its own local variable */
#include <stdio.h>
computeSale(int gallons);
main()
{
   int gallons;

   printf("Richard's Paint Service \n");
   printf("How many gallons of paint did you buy? ");
   scanf(" %d", &gallons);         /* Get gallons in main() */

   computeSale(gallons);    /* Compute total in function */
   return;
}
```

A local variable that is visible only in—
*computeSale()*

```
computeSale(int gallons)
{
    float pricePer = 12.45;        /* Local to computeSale() */

    printf("The total is: $%.2f \n",
            (pricePer*(float)gallons) );
        /* Had to type cast gallons because it was integer */
    return;                          /* Return to main() */
}
```

**3.** The following sample code lines test your skill at recognizing calling functions and receiving functions. Being able to recognize the difference is half the battle of understanding them.

```
doIt()
```

This must be the first line of a new function because it does not end with a semicolon.

```
doIt2(sales);
```

This calls a function called doIt2(). The calling function passes the variable called sales to doIt2().

```
prIt(float total)
```

This is the first line of a function that receives a floating-point variable from another function that called it. All receiving functions must specify the type of each variable being passed.

```
prThem(float total, int number)
```

This is the first line of a function that receives two variables—one is a floating-point variable and the other is an integer. This line cannot be calling the function prThem because there is no semicolon at the end of the line.

## Automatic versus Static Variables

The terms *automatic* and *static* describe what happens to local variables when a function returns to the calling procedure. By default, all local variables are automatic, meaning that they are erased when their function ends. To define a variable as an automatic variable, prefix its definition with the term auto. The auto keyword is optional with local variables because they are automatic by default.

The two statements after `main()`'s opening brace define automatic local variables:

```
main()
{
    int i;
    auto float x;
    /* Rest of main() goes here */
```

Because `auto` is the default, you do not need to include the term `auto` with `x`.

> **Note:** C programmers rarely use the `auto` keyword with local variables because they are automatic by default.

**Automatic variables are local and disappear when their function ends.**

The opposite of an automatic variable is a static variable. All global variables are static and, as mentioned, all static variables retain their values. Therefore, if a local variable is static, it retains its value when its function ends—in case the function is called a second time. To define a variable as static, place the `static` keyword in front of the variable when you define it. The following code section defines three variables, `i`, `j`, and `k`. The variable `i` is automatic, but `j` and `k` are static.

```
myFun()              /* Start of new function definition */
{
    int i;
    static j=25;    /* Both j and k are static variables */
    static k=30;
```

**If local variables are static, their values remain in case the function is called again.**

Always assign an initial value to a static variable when you define it, as shown here in the last two lines. This initial value is placed in the static variable only the first time `myFun()` executes. If you don't assign a static variable an initial value, C initializes it to zero.

> **Tip:** Static variables are good to use when you write functions that keep track of a count or add to a total when called. If the counting or total variables are local and automatic, their values disappear when the function finishes—thus destroying the totals.

## Examples

**1.** Consider this program:

```
/* Filename: C18STA1.C
    Tries to use a static variable
```

```
   without a static definition */
#include <stdio.h>
main()
{
   int ctr;                          /* Used in the for loop to
                                         all a function 25 times */

   for (ctr=1; ctr<=25; ctr++)
     { tripleIt(ctr); }              /* Pass ctr to a function
                                         called tripleIt() */

   return;
}

tripleIt(int ctr)
{
   int total, ans;              /* Local automatic variables */
   /* Triples whatever value is passed to it
       and adds the total */

   total=0;        /* Will hold total of all numbers tripled */

   ans = ctr * 3;                    /* Triple number passed */
   total += ans;    /* Add triple numbers as this is called */

   printf("The number %d, multiplied by 3 is: %d \n",
          ctr, ans);

   if (total > 300)
     { printf("The total of the triple numbers is
        ➥over 300 \n"); }
   return;
}
```

Zeroes total —————— *(pointing to `total=0;` line)*

---

**Automatic and Static Rules for Local Variables**

Local automatic variables disappear when their block ends. All local variables are automatic by default. You can prefix a variable (when you define it) with the `auto` keyword, or you can omit it; the variable is still automatic and its value is destroyed when the block it is local to ends.

Local static variables do not lose their values when their function ends. They remain local to that function. When the function is called after the first time, the static variable's value is still in place. You define a static variable by placing the static keyword before the variable's definition.

This is a nonsense program that doesn't do much, yet you may sense something is wrong. The program passes numbers from 1 to 25 to the function called `tripleIt`. The function triples the number and prints it.

The variable called `total` is initially set to 0. The idea here is to add each tripled number and print a message when the total is larger than 300. However, the `printf()` *never* executes. For each of the 25 times that this subroutine is called, `total` is reset to 0. The `total` variable is an automatic variable whose value is erased and initialized every time its procedure is called. The next example corrects this.

**2.** If you want `total` to retain its value after the procedure ends, you must make it static. Because local variables are automatic by default, you need to include the `static` keyword to override this default. Then the value of the `total` variable is retained each time the subroutine is called.

The following corrects the mistake in the previous program:

```
/* Filename: C18STA2.C
   Uses a static variable with the static definition */
#include <stdio.h>
main()
{
   int ctr;                        /* Used in the for loop to
                                      call a function 25 times */
   for (ctr=1; ctr<=25; ctr++)
     { tripleIt(ctr); }            /* Pass ctr to a function
                                      called tripleIt() */

   return;
}

tripleIt(int ctr)
{
   static int total=0;                /* Local and static */
   int ans;                           /* Local and automatic */
   /* total will be set to 0 only the first time this
      function is called. */

   /* Triples whatever value is passed to it and add
      the total */

   ans = ctr * 3;                     /* Triple number passed */
   total += ans;  /* Add triple numbers as this is called */
```

*total* is not zeroed except for the first time that *tripleIt()* runs

```
        printf("The number %d, multiplied by 3 is: %d \n",
               ctr, ans);

        if (total > 300)
            { printf("The total of the triple numbers is
               ➥over 300 \n"); }
        return;
    }
```

Figure 18.3 shows this program's output. Notice that the function's printf() is triggered, even though total is a local variable. Because total is static, its value is not erased when the function finishes. When the function is called a second time by main(), total's previous value (when you left the routine) is still there.

**Figure 18.3**

Using a static variable to retain a value.

```
The number 1, multiplied by 3 is: 3
The number 2, multiplied by 3 is: 6
The number 3, multiplied by 3 is: 9
The number 4, multiplied by 3 is: 12
The number 5, multiplied by 3 is: 15
The number 6, multiplied by 3 is: 18
The number 7, multiplied by 3 is: 21
The number 8, multiplied by 3 is: 24
The number 9, multiplied by 3 is: 27
The number 10, multiplied by 3 is: 30
The number 11, multiplied by 3 is: 33
The number 12, multiplied by 3 is: 36
The number 13, multiplied by 3 is: 39
The number 14, multiplied by 3 is: 42
The total of the triple numbers is over 300
The number 15, multiplied by 3 is: 45
The total of the triple numbers is over 300
The number 16, multiplied by 3 is: 48
The total of the triple numbers is over 300
The number 17, multiplied by 3 is: 51
The total of the triple numbers is over 300
The number 18, multiplied by 3 is: 54
The total of the triple numbers is over 300
The number 19, multiplied by 3 is: 57
The total of the triple numbers is over 300
The number 20, multiplied by 3 is: 60
The total of the triple numbers is over 300
```

This does not mean that local static variables become global. The main program cannot refer, use, print, or change total because it is local to the second function. Static simply means that the local variable's value is still there if the program calls the function again.

# Three Issues of Parameter Passing

To have a complete understanding of programs with several functions, you need to learn three additional concepts:

- ◆ Passing arguments (variables) by value (also called "by copy")

- ◆ Passing arguments (variables) by address

- ◆ Returning values from functions

The first two concepts deal with the way local variables are passed and received. The third concept describes how receiving functions send values back to the calling functions. The next chapter, "Passing Values," concludes this discussion by explaining these three methods for passing parameters and returning values.

## Summary

Parameter passing is necessary because local variables are better than global. Local variables are protected in their own routines, but sometimes they must be shared with other routines. If local data is to remain in those variables (in case the function is called again in the same program), the variables should be static because otherwise their automatic values disappear.

Most of the information in this chapter should become more obvious as you use functions in your own programs. The next chapter goes into more detail on the actual passing of parameters and shows you two different ways to do it.

## Review Questions

Answers to review questions are in Appendix B.

1. True or false: A function should always include a `return` statement as its last command, even though `return` is not required.

2. When a local variable is passed, is it called an argument or a parameter?

3. True or false: A function that is passed variables from another function cannot also have its own local variables.

4. What must appear inside the receiving function's parentheses besides the variables passed to it?

5. If a function keeps track of a total or count every time it is called, should the counting or totaling variable be automatic or static?

6. When would you pass a global variable to a function? (Be careful—this may be a trick question!)

7. How many arguments are there in the following statement?

```
printf("The rain has fallen %d inches.", rainf);
```

## Review Exercises

**1.** Write a program that asks, in main(), for the age of the user's dog. Write a second function called people() that computes the dog's age in human years (by multiplying the dog's age by 7).

**2.** Write a function that counts the number of times it is called. Name the function countIt(). Do not pass it anything. In the body of countIt(), print the following message:

```
The number of times this function has been called is: ##
```

where ## is the number. (Hint: Because the variable must be local, make it static and initialize it to zero when you first define it.)

**3.** The following program contains several problems. Some of these problems produce errors. One problem is not an error, but a bad location for a variable definition. (Hint: Find all global variables.) See if you can spot some of the problems, and rewrite the program so that it works better.

```c
/* Filename: C18BAD.C
   Program with bad uses of variable definitions */
#include <stdio.h>
#define NUM 10

char city[] = "Miami";
int count;

main()
{
    int abc;

    count = NUM;
    abc = 5;
    doVarFun();

    printf("%d %d %d %c", abc, count, pgmVar, xyz);
    return;
}

int pgmVar = 7;

doVarFun()
{
    char xyz = 'A';

    xyz = 'b';
    printf("%c %d %d %s", xyz, pgmVar, abc, city);
    return;
}
```

# CHAPTER 19

# Passing Values

C passes variables between functions using two different methods. The one you use depends on how you want the passed variables to be changed. This chapter explores these two methods. The concepts discussed here are not unique to the C language. Other programming languages, such as Pascal, FORTRAN, and QBasic, pass parameters using similar techniques. A computer language must have the capability to pass information between functions before it can be called truly structured.

This chapter introduces you to the following:

♦ Passing variables by value

♦ Passing arrays by address

♦ Passing nonarrays by address

Pay close attention because most of the programs in the remainder of the book rely on the methods described in this chapter.

## Passing by Value (by Copy)

The two wordings "passing by value" and "passing by copy" mean the same thing in computer terms. Some textbooks and C programmers say that arguments are passed *by value*, and some say they are passed *by copy*. Both of these phrases describe one of the two methods by which arguments are passed to receiving functions. (The other method is called "by address." This method is covered later in the chapter.)

When you pass by value, a copy of the variable's value is passed to the receiving function.

When an argument (local variable) is passed by value, a copy of the variable's value is sent to—and is assigned to—the receiving function's parameter. If more than one variable is passed by value, a copy of each of their values is sent to—and is assigned to—the receiving function's parameters.

Figure 19.1 shows the *passing by copy* in action. The value of i—not the variable itself—is passed to the called function, which receives it as a variable i. There are two variables called i, not one. The first is local to main(), and the second is local to prIt(). They both have the same names, but because they are local to their respective functions, there is no conflict. The variable does not have to be called i in both functions, and because the value of i is sent to the receiving function, it does not matter what the receiving function calls the variable that receives this value.

**Figure 19.1**

Passing the
variable by value.

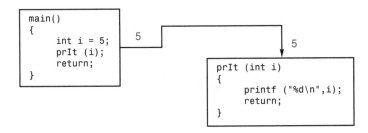

In this case, when passing and receiving variables between functions, it is wisest to retain the *same* names. Even though they are not the same variables, they hold the same value. In this example, the value 5 is passed from main()'s i to prIt()'s i.

Because a copy of i's value (and not the variable itself) is passed to the receiving function, if prIt() changes i, it changes only its copy of i and not main()'s i. This makes for true separation of functions and variables. You now have the technique for passing a copy of a variable to a receiving function, with the receiving function being unable to modify the calling function's variable.

All of C's nonarray variables that you have seen so far are passed by value. You do not have to do anything special to pass variables by value, except to pass them in the calling function's argument list and receive them in the receiving function's parameter list.

**Note:** The default method for passing parameters is by value, as just described, unless you pass arrays. You always pass arrays by the other method, by address, as described later in this chapter.

**For Related Information**

◆ "Calling and Returning Functions," p. 286

## Examples

**1.** The following program asks users for their weight. It then passes that weight to a function that calculates the equivalent weight on the moon. Notice that the second function uses the passed value and calculates with it. After the weight is passed to the second function, that function can treat it as though it were a local variable.

*Identify the program and include the necessary header file. You want to calculate the user's weight on the moon. Because you need to hold the user's weight somewhere, define the variable* weight *as an integer. You also need a function that does the calculations, so create a function called* moon().

*Ask the user how much he or she weighs. Get the user's answer and put it in* weight. *Now pass the user's weight to the* moon() *function, which divides the weight by 6 to get the equivalent weight on the moon. Display the user's weight on the moon. You're finished, so leave the* moon() *function and then leave the* main() *function.*

```
/* Filename: C19PASS1.C
   Calculate the user's weight in a second function */
#include <stdio.h>
main()
{
   int weight;                      /* main()'s local weight */
   printf("How many pounds do you weigh? ");
   scanf(" %d", &weight);

   moon(weight);            /* Call the moon() function and
                               pass it the weight            */
   return;                  /* Return to the operating system */
}

moon(int weight)           /* Define the passed parameter  */
{
   /* Moon weights are 1/6th earth's weights */
   weight /= 6;                     /* Divide the weight by 6 */

   printf("You weigh only %d pounds on the moon!", weight);
   return;                              /* Return to main() */
}
```

Pass *weight* to *moon*()

The output of this program follows:

```
How many pounds do you weigh? 120
You weigh only 20 pounds on the moon!
```

2. You can rename passed variables in the receiving function. They are distinct from the passing function's variable. The following is the same program as in Example 1, except the receiving function calls the passed variable earthWeight. A new variable, called moonWeight, is local to the called function and is used for the moon's equivalent weight.

```
/* Filename: C19PASS2.C
   Calculate the user's weight in a second function */
#include <stdio.h>
main()
{
   int weight;                          /* main()'s local weight */
   printf("How many pounds do you weigh? ");
   scanf(" %d", &weight);

   moon(weight);           /* Call the moon() function and
                              pass it the weight          */
   return;                 /* Return to the operating system */
}

moon(int earthWeight)      /* Define the passed parameter   */
{
   int moonWeight;                    /* Local to this function */

   /* Moon weights are 1/6th earth's weights */
   moonWeight = earthWeight / 6;   /* Divide weight by 6   */

   printf("You only weigh %d pounds on the moon!",
          moonWeight);
   return;                            /* Return to main() */
}
```

Doesn't have to be named *weight*

The resulting output is identical to that of the previous program. Renaming the passed variable changes nothing.

3. The next example passes three variables—of three different types—to the called function. In the receiving function's parameter list, each of these variable types must be defined.

This program prompts users for three values in the main() function. The main() function then passes these variables to the receiving function, which calculates and prints values related to those passed variables. When the called function modifies a variable passed to the function, notice again that this does *not* affect the calling function's variable. When variables are passed by value, the value—not the variable itself—is passed.

```c
/* Filename: C19PASS3.C
   Get grade information for a student */
#include <stdio.h>
checkGrade(char lgrade, float average, int tests);
main()
{
   char lgrade;                              /* Letter grade */
   int  tests;              /* Number of tests not yet taken */
   float average; /* Student's average based on 4.0 scale */

   printf("What letter grade do you want? ");
   scanf(" %c", &lgrade);
   printf("What is your current test average? ");
   scanf(" %f", &average);
   printf("How many tests do you have left? ");
   scanf(" %d", &tests);

   checkGrade(lgrade, average, tests);  /* Call function
                          and pass three variables by value */
   return;
}
```

*main()* passed these three values ———

```c
checkGrade(char lgrade, float average, int tests)
{
   switch (tests)
   {
      case (0): { printf("You will get your current grade
                   ➥ of %c", average);
                 break; }
      case (1): { printf("You still have time to bring
                   ➥ your average ");
                 printf("of %.1f up. Study hard!", average);
                 break; }
```

```
        default:  { printf("Relax. You still have plenty of
                        ➡ time.");
                    break; }
        }
    return;
}
```

# Passing by Address

The previous section described passing arguments by value (or by copy). This section describes how to pass arguments by address.

When you pass by address, the address of the variable is passed to the receiving function.

When you pass an argument (local variable) *by address*, the variable's address is sent to—and is assigned to—the receiving function's parameter. (If you pass more than one variable by address, each of their addresses is sent to—and is assigned to—the receiving function's parameters.)

## Variable Addresses

All variables in memory (RAM) are stored at memory addresses (see Figure 19.2.) If you want more information on the internal representation of memory, refer to Appendix A.

**Figure 19.2**

Memory addresses.

| Memory | Address | |
|---|---|---|
| | 0 | (If you have 640K of RAM, as many microcomputers do, you have exactly 655,360 characters of RAM. |
| | 1 | |
| | 2 | |
| | . | Each of those memory locations has a separate address, just as each house and building have separate addresses.) |
| | . | |
| | . | |
| | 655,358 | |
| | 655,359 | |

When you tell C to define a variable (such as `int i;`), you are requesting that C find an unused place in memory and assign that place (or memory address) to `i`. When your program uses the variable called `i`, C knows to go to `i`'s address and use whatever is there.

If you define five variables as follows:

```
int i;
float x=9.8;
char ara[2] = {'A', 'B'};
int j=8, k=3;
```

C might arbitrarily place them in memory at the addresses shown in Figure 19.3.

**Figure 19.3**

Storing variables in memory.

| Variable Name | Memory | Address |
|---|---|---|
| | | 0 |
| | | 1 |
| | | 2 |
| | . | . |
| i | . | . |
| x | 9.8 | . |
| ara[0] | A | 34,566 |
| ara[1] | B | 34,568 |
| j | 8 | 34,572 |
| k | 3 | 34,573 |
| | . | 34,574 |
| | . | 34,576 |
| | . | . |

You don't know what is contained in the variable called i because you haven't put anything in it yet. Before you use i, initialize it with a value. (All variables—except character variables—usually take up more than one byte of memory.)

## Sample Program

All C arrays are passed by address.

The address of the variable, not its value, is copied to the receiving function when you pass a variable by address. In C, *all arrays are passed by address*. (Actually, a copy of their address is passed, but you will understand this better when you learn more about arrays and pointers.) The following important rule holds true for programs that pass by address:

> Every time you pass a variable by address, if the receiving function changes the variable, it is changed also in the calling function.

Therefore, if you pass an array to a function and the function changes the array, those changes are still with the array when it returns to the calling function. Unlike passing by value, passing by address gives you the ability to change a variable in the *called* function and keep those changes in effect in the *calling* function. The following sample program should help to illustrate this concept.

```
/* Filename: C19ADD1.C
   Passing by address example */
#include <stdio.h>
main()
{
    char name[4]="ABC";

    changeIt(name);          /* Passes by address because
                                       it is an array */
```

```
        printf("%s \n", name);              /* Called function can
                                                change array        */

        return;
    }
```

Same variable
as in *main()*

```
    changeIt(char c[4])         /* You must tell the function
                                        that c is an array */

    {
        printf("%s \n", c);         /* Print as it is passed */
        strcpy(c, "USA");           /* Change the array, both
                                        here and in main() */

        return;
    }
```

Here is the output from this program:

```
ABC
USA
```

At this point, you should have no trouble understanding that the array is passed from main() to the function called changeIt(). Even though changeIt() calls the array c, it refers to the same array passed by the main() function (name).

Figure 19.4 shows how the array is passed. Although the address of the array—and not its value—is passed from name to c, both arrays are the same.

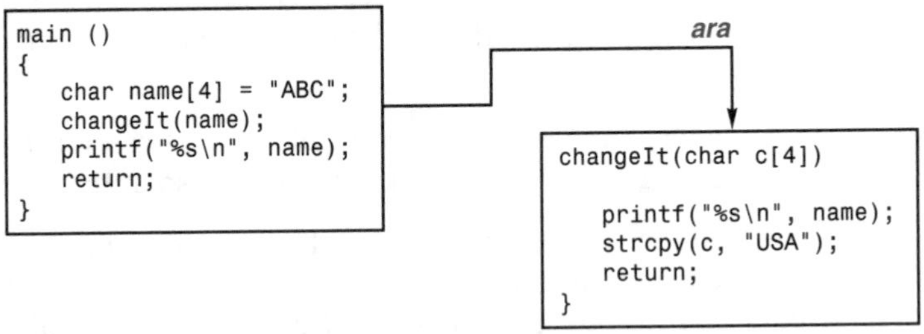

**Figure 19.4**

Passing an array
by address.

```
main ()                                                ara
{
    char name[4] = "ABC";
    changeIt(name);
    printf("%s\n", name);
    return;
}
                                changeIt(char c[4])

                                    printf("%s\n", name);
                                    strcpy(c, "USA");
                                    return;
                                }
```

Before going any further, a few additional comments are in order. Because the address of name is passed to the function—even though the array is called c in the receiving function—it is still the same array as name. Figure 19.5 shows how C accomplishes this at the memory-address level.

**Figure 19.5**

The array being passed is the same array in both functions.

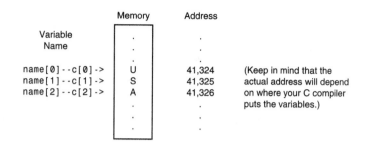

```
                              Memory      Address

         Variable               .            .
          Name                  .            .
                                .            .
    name[0]--c[0]->             U         41,324      (Keep in mind that the
    name[1]--c[1]->             S         41,325      actual address will depend
    name[2]--c[2]->             A         41,326      on where your C compiler
                                .            .        puts the variables.)
                                .            .
                                .            .
```

The variable array is referred to as name in main() and as c in changeIt(). Because the address of name is copied to the receiving function, the variable gets changed no matter what it is called in either function. Because changeIt() changes the array, the array is changed also in main().

## Examples

1. You can now use a function to fill an array with user input. The following function asks users for their first name in the function called getName(). As users type the name in the array, it is also entered in main()'s array. The main() function then passes the array to printName(), where it is printed. (If arrays were passed by value, this program would not work. Only the array value would be passed to the called functions.)

```c
/* Filename: C19ADD2.C
   Get a name in an array, then print it using
   separate functions */
#include <stdio.h>z
main()
{
   char name[25];
   getName(name);                    /* Get the user's name */
   printName(name);                  /* Print the user's name */
   return;
}


getName(char name[25])       /* Pass the array by address */
{
   printf("What is your first name? ");
   scanf(" %s", name);
   return;
```

*main()* will know what the user types

```
          }

          printName(char name[25])
          {
              printf("\n\n Here it is: %s", name);
              return;
          }
```

Save as *main()*'s

When you pass an array, be sure to specify the array's type in the receiving function's parameter list. If the previous program defines the passed array with

```
          getName(char name)
```

the function `getName()` thinks it is being passed a single character variable, *not* a character array. You never need to put the array size in brackets. The following statement also works as the first line of `getName()`:

```
          getName(char name[])
```

Most C programmers put the array size in the brackets even though the size is not needed.

2. Many programmers pass character arrays to functions in order to erase them. Following is a function called `clearIt()`. It expects two parameters: a character array and the total number of elements defined for that array. The array is passed by address (as are all arrays), and the number of elements, `numEls`, is passed by value (as are all nonarrays). When the function finishes, the array is cleared (that is, all its elements are reset to null zero). Subsequent functions that use it can then have an empty array.

```
          clearIt(char ara[10], int numEls)
          {
              int ctr;
              for (ctr=0; ctr<numEls; ctr++)
                { ara[ctr] = '\0'; }
              return;
          }
```

The brackets after ara do not need to contain a number, as described in the previous example. The `10` in this example is simply a placeholder for the brackets. Any value (or no value) would work as well.

## Nonarrays Passed by Address

You can pass nonarrays by address.

You now should see the difference between passing variables by address and by value. You can pass arrays by address and nonarrays by value. You also can override the *by value* default for nonarrays. This is helpful sometimes, but it is not always recommended because the called function can damage values in the calling function.

If you want a nonarray variable changed in a receiving function and also want the changes kept in the calling function, you must override the default and pass the variable by address. (You should understand this section better after you learn how arrays and pointers relate.) To pass a nonarray by address, you must do the following:

**1.** Precede the variable in the calling function with an ampersand (&).

**2.** Precede the variable in the receiving function with an asterisk (*), everywhere the variable appears.

This might sound strange to you (and it is, at this point). Few C programmers override the default of passing by value. When you learn about pointers later, you should have little need for this. Most C programmers don't like to clutter their code with these extra ampersands and asterisks, but they know they can do this if necessary.

The following examples demonstrate how to pass nonarray variables by address.

## Examples

**1.** The following program passes a variable by address from main() to a function. The function changes it and returns to main(). Because the variable is passed by address, main() recognizes the new value.

```
/* Filename: C19ADD3.C
   Demonstrate passing nonarrays by address */
#include <stdio.h>
main()
{
   int amt;

   amt = 100;                    /* Assign a value in main() */
   printf("In main(), amt is %d \n", amt);

   doFun(&amt);          /* The & means pass it by address */
   printf("After return, amt is %d in main() \n", amt);
   return;
}

doFun(int *amt)                          /* Inform function of
                                            passing by address */
```

& makes *amt* pass by address ⎯

Receives a variable by address ⎯

```
{
    *amt = 85;                       /* Assign new value to amt */
    printf("In doFun(), amt is %d \n", *amt);
    return;
}
```

The output from this program follows:

```
In main(), amt is 100
In doFun(), amt is 85
After return, amt is 85 in main()
```

Notice that amt changed in the called function. Because it was passed by address, it gets changed also in the calling function.

---

**How *scanf()* Passes Values**

You can now understand some of the strangeness of the built-in `scanf()` function. This function passes arguments to its internal code. The arguments are control strings and variables that fill up with keyboard input.

Recall that you must put an ampersand (&) before each nonarray variable in the `scanf()` list. For example, to input three integers from the keyboard, you have to code `scanf()` as follows:

```
scanf("%d %d %d", &i1, &i2, &i3);
```

Think about what is happening. If you did not force these variables to be passed by address, the calling function would not be able to access the values typed from the keyboard! When a user types in values, the `scanf()` function fills its parameters with those typed values because you pass the variables by address. The calling program also recognizes those values because they get changed in both places.

No ampersand is needed in front of `scanf()` array variables. To get a name from the keyboard, you type the following `scanf()` statement:

```
scanf(name);
```

The ampersand is not needed because all arrays are automatically passed by address. When `scanf()` gets the keyboard values into the array, the calling program (your program) recognizes them because the array is changed in both places.

---

**2.** You can use a function to get the user's keyboard values. The main()
function recognizes those values as long as you pass them by address. The
following program calculates the cubic feet in a swimming pool. In one
function, it requests the width, length, and depth. In another function, it
calculates the cubic feet of water. Finally, in a third function, it prints the
answer. The main() function is clearly a controlling function, passing
variables between these functions by address.

```
/* Filename: C19POOL.C
   Calculate the cubic feet in a swimming pool */
#include <stdio.h>
main()
{
   int length, width, depth, cubic;

   getValues(&length, &width, &depth);
   calcCubic(&length, &width, &depth, &cubic);
   printCubic(&cubic);

   return;
}
```

All three received
by address

```
getValues(int *length, int *width, int *depth)
{
   printf("What is the pool's length? ");
   scanf(" %d", &*length);
   printf("What is the pool's width? ");
   scanf(" %d", &*width);
   printf("What is the pool's average depth? ");
   scanf(" %d", &*depth);
   return;
}
```

All four received
by address

```
calcCubic(int *length, int *width, int *depth, int *cubic)
{
   /* This may look confusing, but you must
      precede each variable with an asterisk */
   *cubic = (*length) * (*width) * (*depth);
   return;
```

```
    }

printCubic(int *cubic)
{
    printf("\nThe pool has %d cubic feet\n", *cubic);
    return;
}
```

The output follows.

```
What is the pool's length? 16
What is the pool's width? 32
What is the pool's average depth? 6

The pool has 3072 cubic feet
```

Notice the strange scanf() parameters. All variables in a function must be preceded with an asterisk if they are to be passed by address. Because scanf() requires an ampersand before its nonarray variables, this technique adds confusion to the scanf() statement. As you learn later, in Chapter 26, & and * cancel each other. If you find yourself using scanf() in functions (on nonarray variables passed by address), you can omit &*. For example, you can write the first scanf() as follows without any change in the program's output:

```
scanf(" %d", length);
```

## Summary

You now have a complete understanding of the various methods for passing data to functions. Because you will be using local variables as much as possible, you need to know how to pass local variables between functions, but also keep the variables away from functions that don't need them.

You can pass data in two ways: by value and by address. When you pass data by value, which is the default method for nonarrays, only a copy of the variable's contents is passed. If the called function modifies its parameters, those variables are not modified in the calling function. When you pass data by address, as is done with arrays and nonarray variables preceded by an ampersand, the receiving function can change the data in both functions.

Whenever you pass values, you must ensure that they match in number and type. If you don't match them, you can have problems. For example, suppose you pass an array and a floating-point variable, but in the receiving function, you receive a floating-point variable followed by an array. The data is not getting to the receiving function properly because the parameter data types do not match the variables being passed. The next chapter shows you how to protect against such disasters by prototyping all your functions.

# Review Questions

Answers to review questions are in Appendix B.

**1.** What kind of variables are usually passed by address?

**2.** What kind of variables are usually passed by value?

**3.** True or false: If a variable is passed by value, it is passed also by copy.

**4.** If a variable is passed to a function by value and the function changes the variable, is it changed in the calling function?

**5.** If a variable is passed to a function by address and the function changes the variable, is it changed in the calling function?

**6.** What is wrong with the following function?

```
doFun(x, y, z)
{
   printf("The variables are: %d, %d, and %d", x, y, z);
   return;
}
```

**7.** Suppose you pass a nonarray variable and an array to a function at the same time. What is the default?

a. Both are passed by address.

b. Both are passed by value.

c. One is passed by address and the other is passed by value.

# Review Exercises

**1.** Write a main() function and a second function that main() calls. Ask users for their annual income in main(). Pass the income to the second function and print a congratulatory message if the user makes more than $50,000 or an encouragement message if the user makes less.

**2.** Write a three-function program, consisting of the following functions:

```
main()
fun1()
fun2()
```

Define a 10-element character array in main(), fill it with the letters A through J in fun1(), and then print that array backwards in fun2().

**3.** Write a program whose main() function passes a number to a function called printAster(). The printAster() function prints that many asterisks on a line, across the screen. If printAster() is passed a number greater than 80, display an error because most screens cannot print more than 80 characters on the same line. When execution is finished, return control to main() and then return to the operating system.

**4.** Write a function that is passed two integer values by address. The function should define a third local variable. Use the third variable as an intermediate variable and swap the values of both integers passed. For example, suppose the calling function passes it oldPay and newPay as in

```
swapIt(oldPay, newPay);
```

The swapIt() function should reverse the two values so that when control is returned to the calling function, the values of oldPay and newPay are swapped.

# Function Return Values and Prototypes

So far, you have passed variables to functions in only one direction—a calling function passed data to a receiving function. You have yet to see how data is passed back *from* the receiving function to the calling function. When you pass variables by address, the data gets changed in both functions—but this is different from passing data back. This chapter focuses on writing function return values that improve your programming power.

After you learn to pass and return values, you need to *prototype* the functions you write—as well as C's built-in functions, such as printf() and scanf(). By prototyping your functions, you ensure the accuracy of passed and returned values.

This chapter introduces you to the following:

♦ Returning values from functions

♦ Prototyping functions

♦ Understanding header files

This chapter concludes the coverage on functions. After this chapter, your programs will be truly modular. You should write better, more powerful, and more accurate programs after you finalize your understanding of functions and how to use them.

# Function Return Values

Until now, all functions in this book have been *subroutines* or *subfunctions*. A C subroutine is a function that is called from another function, but it does not return any values. The difference between subroutines and functions is not as critical in C as it is in other languages. All functions, whether they are subroutines or functions that return values, are defined in the same way. You can pass variables to each of them, as you have seen throughout Part 4.

Put the return value at the end of the `return` statement.

Functions that return values offer you a new approach to programming. In addition to passing data one way, from calling to receiving function, you can pass data back from a receiving function to its calling function. When you want to return a value from a function to its calling function, put the return value after the `return` statement. To make the return value clearer, many programmers put parentheses around the return value, as shown in the following syntax:

```
return (return value);
```

> **Caution:** Do not return global variables because their values are already known throughout the code.

The calling function must have a use for the return value. For example, suppose you wrote a function that calculated the average of any three integer variables passed to it. If you return the average, the calling function has to receive that return value. The following sample program helps to illustrate this principle.

```c
/* Filename: C20AVG.C
   Calculates the average of three input values */
#include <stdio.h>
main()
{
   int num1, num2, num3;
   int avg;                    /* Will hold the return value */

   printf("Please type three numbers (such as 23, 54, 85) ");
   scanf(" %d, %d, %d", &num1, &num2, &num3);

   /* Call the function, passing the numbers,
      and accept the return value */
   avg = calcAv(num1, num2, num3);

   printf("\n\nThe average is %d", avg);       /* Print the
                                                  return value */

   return;
}
```

```
int calcAv(int num1, int num2, int num3)
{
   int localAvg;   /* Holds the average for these numbers */
   localAvg = (num1+num2+num3) / 3;

   return (localAvg);
}                    ——— main()
```

Here is a sample output from the program:

```
Please type three numbers (such as 23, 54, 85) 30, 40, 50
The average is 40
```

Study this program carefully. It is similar to many you have seen, but a few additional points should be considered now that the function returns a value. It may help to walk through this program a few lines at a time.

The first part of main() is similar to many programs you have seen. It defines its local variables: three for user input and one for the calculated average. The printf() and scanf() are familiar to you. The function call to calcAv() is also familiar; it passes three variables (num1, num2, and num3) by value to calcAv(). (If it passed them by address, an ampersand (&) would have to precede each argument, as discussed in the previous chapter.)

The receiving function, calcAv(), seems similar to others you have seen, except the first line, the function's definition line, has one addition—the int before its name. This is the *type* of the return value. You must always precede a function name with its return data type. If you do not specify a type, C assumes a type of int. Therefore, if this example had no return type, it would work just as well because an int return type would be assumed.

> Put the function's return type before its name.

Because the variable being returned from calcAv() is an integer, the int return type was placed before calcAv()'s name.

You can also see that the return statement of calcAv() includes the return value, localAvg. This is the variable being sent back to the calling function, main(). You can return only a single variable to a calling function.

This introduces a rule for returning variables. Even though a function can receive more than one parameter, it can return only a single value to the calling function. If a receiving function will be modifying more than one value from the calling function, you must pass the parameters by address; you cannot return multiple values using a return statement.

After the receiving function, calcAv(), returns the value, main() must do something with that returned value. So far, you have seen function calls on lines by themselves. Notice in main() that the function call appears on the right side of the following assignment statement:

```
avg = calcAv(num1, num2, num3);
```

When the calcAv() function returns its value—the average of the three numbers—that value *replaces* the function call. If the average computed in calcAv() is 40, the C compiler "sees" the following statement in place of the function call:

```
avg = 40;
```

You typed a function call to the right of the equal sign, but the program replaces a function call with its return value when the return takes place. In other words, a function that returns a value *becomes* that value. You *must* put such a function anywhere you would put any variable or constant, usually to the right of an equal sign, or in an expression, or in printf(). The following is an *incorrect* way of calling calcAv():

```
calcAv(num1, num2, num3);
```

If you did this, C would have nowhere to put the return value of 40 (or whatever it happens to be).

> **Caution:** Function calls that return values seldom appear on lines by themselves. Because the function call is replaced by the return value, you should do something with that return value (such as assign it to a variable or use it in a expression). Return values can be ignored, but doing so usually defeats the purpose of using them.

> **For Related Information**
>
> ◆ "The Need for Passing Variables," p. 305

## Examples

**1.** The following program passes a number to a function called doub(). The function doubles the number and returns the result.

```
/* Filename: C20DOUB.C
   Doubles the user's number */
#include <stdio.h>
main()
{
    int number;                      /* Holds user's input */
    int dNumber;      /* Will hold double the user's input */
    printf("What number do you want doubled? ");
    scanf(" %d", &number);

    dNumber = doub(number);          /* Assign return value */
```

Receives *doub()*'s value

```
        printf("%d doubled is %d", number, dNumber);
        return;
    }

    int doub(int num)
    {
        int dNum;
        dNum = num * 2;                    /* Double the number */
        return (dNum);                     /* Return the result */
    }
```

The program produces output such as this:

```
What number do you want doubled? 5
5 doubled is 10
```

**2.** Function return values can be used *anywhere* that other values—such as constants, variables, and expressions—can be used. The following program is similar to the last. The difference is in main().

The function call is performed not on a line by itself, but from a printf(). This is a nested function call. You call the built-in function printf() using the return value from one of the program's functions named doub(). Because the call to doub() is replaced by its return value, the printf() has enough information to proceed as soon as doub() returns. This gives main() less overhead because it no longer needs a variable called dNumber, although you must use your own judgment as to whether this program is easier to maintain. Sometimes it is wise to include function calls within other expressions; other times it is clearer to call the function and assign its return value to a variable before using it.

```
/* Filename: C20DOUB2.C
   Doubles the user's number */
#include <stdio.h>
main()
{
    int number;                          /* Holds user's input */
    printf("What number do you want doubled? ");
    scanf(" %d", &number);

    /* The third printf() parameter is
       replaced with a return value */
    printf("%d doubled is %d", number, doub(number));

    return;
}
```

Prints the
returned value

```
int doub(int num)
{
    int dNum;
    dNum = num * 2;                    /* Double the number */
    return (dNum);                     /* Return the result */
}
```

**3.** The following program asks the user for a number. That number is then passed to a function called sum(), which adds the numbers from 1 to that number. In other words, if the user types a 6, the function returns the result of the following calculation:

```
1 + 2 + 3 + 4 + 5 + 6
```

This is known as the *sum of the digits* calculation, and it is sometimes used for depreciation in accounting.

```
/* Filename: C20SUMD.C
   Compute the sum of the digits */
#include <stdio.h>
main()
{
    int num, sumd;

    printf("Please type a number: ");
    scanf(" %d", &num);

    sumd = sum(num);
    printf("The sum of the digits is %d", sumd);
    return;
}

int sum(int num)
{
    int ctr;                           /* Local loop counter */
    int sumd=0;                        /* Local to this function */
    if (num <= 0)   /* Check whether parameter is too small */
       { sumd = num; }     /* Returns parameter if too small */
    else
       { for (ctr=1; ctr<=num; ctr++)
             { sumd += ctr; }
       }
    return(sumd);
}
```

A number of calculations make up the returned value

The following is a sample output from this program:

```
Please type a number: 6
The sum of the digits is 21
```

**4.** The following program contains two functions that return values. The first function, maximum(), returns the larger of two numbers entered by the user. The second one, minimum(), returns the smaller.

```
/* Filename: C20MINMX.C
   Finds minimum and maximum values in functions */
#include <stdio.h>
main()
{
   int num1, num2;                    /* User's two numbers */
   int min, max;

   printf("Please type two numbers (such as 46, 75) ");
   scanf(" %d, %d", &num1, &num2);

   max = maximum(num1, num2);    /* Assign the return    */
   min = minimum(num1, num2);    /* value of each        */
                                 /* function to variables */

   printf("The minimum number is %d \n", min);
   printf("The maximum number is %d \n", max);
   return;
}

int maximum(int num1, int num2)
{
   int max;                 /* Local to this function only */
   max = (num1 > num2) ? (num1) : (num2);
   return (max);
}

int minimum(int num1, int num2)
{
   int min;                 /* Local to this function only */
   min = (num1 < num2) ? (num1) : (num2);
   return (min);
}
```

*maximum( )*'s return value ⎯⎯⎯⎯ `max = maximum(num1, num2);`

*minimum( )*'s return value ⎯⎯⎯ `min = minimum(num1, num2);`

Here is a sample output from this program:

```
Please type two numbers (such as 46, 75) 72, 55
The minimum number is 55
The maximum number is 72
```

If the user types the same number, minimum and maximum are the same.

These two functions can be passed any two integer values. In such a simple example as this one, the user already knows which number is lower or higher. The point of such an example is to show how to code return values. You might want to use similar functions in a more useful application, such as finding the highest paid employee from a payroll disk file.

# Function Prototypes

The word *prototype* is sometimes defined as a model. In C, a function prototype models the actual function. Before completing your study of functions, parameters, and return values, you must understand how to prototype each function in your program.

You should prototype each function in your program. By prototyping, you inform C of the function's parameter types and its return value, if any. You do not always need to prototype functions, but it is recommended. Sometimes, a prototype is mandatory before your functions can work properly.

A simple example should help to clarify the need for prototyping. The following simple program asks the user for a temperature in Celsius, then converts it to Fahrenheit. The parameter and the return type are both floating-point. You know the return type is floating-point due to the word float before the convert() function's definition. See if you can follow this program. Other than the Celsius calculation, it is similar to others you have seen.

```
/* Filename: C20TEMP.C
   Converts Celsius temperature to Fahrenheit */
#include <stdio.h>
main()
{
   float cTemp;              /* Holds Celsius temperature
                                           from the user */
   float fTemp;            /* Holds converted temperature */
   printf("What is the Celsius temperature to convert? ");
   scanf(" %f", &cTemp);

   fTemp = convert(cTemp);   /* Convert the temperature */
```

```
    printf("The Fahrenheit equivalent is %.1f", fTemp);
    return;
}
```

Must declare
*float*'s return ——— 
data type

```
float convert(float cTemp) /* The return var and parameter are
                                both floating-point values */
{
    float fTemp;                        /* Local variable */
    fTemp = cTemp * (9.0 / 5.0) + 32.0;
    return (fTemp);
}
```

You must
prototype all
functions that
return a data type
other than `int`.

If you run this program, your C compiler will refuse to compile it or you will get incorrect results, at best. Yet this program seems similar to many you have seen previously. The primary difference is the return type; when you return a data type that is not `int`, you must prototype the function to ensure that it works.

Although prototyping is not required for functions that return integers, you should prototype them as well. Taking this one step further, you should prototype *all* functions, whether they return a value or not.

To prototype a function, copy the function's definition line to the top of your program (immediately before or after the `#include <stdio.h>` line is fine). Place a semicolon at the end of it, and you have the prototype. The definition line (the function's first line) contains the return type, the function name, and the type of each argument, so the function prototype serves as a model of the function that will follow.

If a function does not return a value, or if that function has no arguments passed to it, you should still prototype it. Place the keyword `void` in place of the return type or the parameters. The following listing shows the corrected version of the previous program—now with the prototype lines. Because there is a `convert()` function, there is a prototype for it.

Must prototype
when returning ——— 
a *float*

```
/* Filename: C20TEMP2.C
   Converts Celsius to Fahrenheit */
#include <stdio.h>
float convert(float cType);      /* convert()'s prototype */

main()
{
    float cTemp;              /* Holds Celsius temperature
                                  from the user */
    float fTemp;              /* Holds converted temperature */
    printf("What is the Celsius temperature to convert? ");
    scanf(" %f", &cTemp);
```

```
    fTemp = convert(cTemp);    /* Convert the temperature */

    printf("The Fahrenheit equivalent is %.1f", fTemp);
    return 0;
}

float convert(float cTemp)         /* The return var and
                                      parameter are both
                                      floating-point values */


{
    float fTemp;                        /* Local variable */
    fTemp = cTemp * (9.0 / 5.0) + 32.0;
    return (fTemp);
}
```

All functions must match their prototypes. You have to list only the data types of each parameter—not the individual parameter names—in the parentheses of the function's prototype.

Rarely is main() prototyped. Because main() executes first, and no other C function calls main(), main() is known as a self-prototyping function, or a function that doesn't need a prototype (the only one). To maintain ANSI C compatibility, don't use a return type for main(). Some operating systems (not PC operating systems) require return values from the program. To maintain the ANSI C standard on all sizes of computers, ANSI C programs must either specify an int return type for main() or completely leave off the return type in which case int is assumed. Although main() doesn't have to return value, C programmers generally return 0 from main() as this book will do, but the 0 is not required.

You can look at a statement and tell whether it is a prototype or a function definition (the function's first line) by the semicolon at the end.

## Prototype for Safety

Prototyping protects you from programming mistakes. Suppose you write a function that expects two arguments: an integer followed by a floating-point value. Here is the definition line of such a function:

```
myFun(int num, float amount)
```

What if you passed incorrect data types to myFun()? If you were to call this function by passing it two constants, a floating-point followed by an integer, as in

```
myFun(23.43, 5);          /* Call the myFun() function */
```

the function would *not* receive correct parameters. It is expecting an integer followed by a floating-point, but you did the opposite and sent it a floating-point followed by an integer.

Despite the power of your C compiler, *you don't get an error* if you do this. C lets you pass such incorrect values if you don't prototype first. By prototyping such a function at the top of the program, such as

```
void myFun(int num, float amount);        /* Prototype */
```

*Prototyping protects your programs from function programming errors.*

you tell the compiler to check this function for accuracy. You inform the compiler to expect nothing after the return statement (due to the void keyword) and to expect an integer followed by a floating-point in the parentheses.

If you break any of the prototype's rules, the compiler informs you of the problem and you can correct it. Without the prototype, the program would compile but the results would be wrong. Such a program would be difficult to debug, at best.

## Prototype All Functions

You should prototype every function in your program, except main(). As just described, the prototype defines (for the rest of the program) which functions follow, their return types, and their parameter types. You should also prototype C's built-in functions, such as printf() and scanf().

Think about how you would prototype printf(). You don't always pass it the same types of parameters because you print different data with each printf(). Prototyping functions that you write is easy: the prototype is basically the first line in the function. Prototyping functions that you do not write may seem difficult, but it isn't—you have already done it with every program in this book!

*Header files contain built-in function prototypes.*

The designers of C realized that all functions should be prototyped. They realized also that you cannot prototype built-in functions, so they did it for you and placed the prototypes in header files on your disk. You have been including the printf() and scanf() prototypes in each program with the following statement:

```
#include <stdio.h>
```

Inside the stdio.h file is a prototype of many of C's input and output functions. By having prototypes of these functions, you ensure that they cannot be passed bad values. If someone attempts to pass incorrect values, C catches the problem.

Prototyping is the primary reason why you should always include the matching header file when you use C's built-in functions. The strcpy() function you saw in previous chapters requires the following line:

```
#include <string.h>
```

This is the header file for the `strcpy()` function. Without it, the program may or may not work, depending on how careful you are with the data you pass to `strcpy()`. It is best to be safe and prototype. If you want values other than `int` to be returned from a function, a prototype is required.

## Examples

1. You should prototype all program functions. The following program includes a prototype for `printf()` and `scanf()`:

```
/* Filename: C20PRO1.C
   Calculates sales tax on a sale */
#include <stdio.h>              /* Prototype built-in functions */
main()
{

   float totalSale;
   float taxRate = .07;                  /* Assume 7% tax rate */

   printf("What is the total sale? ");
   scanf(" %f", &totalSale);

   totalSale += (taxRate * totalSale);
   printf("The total sale is %.2f", totalSale);
   return 0;
}
```

For *print()* and *scanf()*

2. The following program asks the user for a number in `main()`, and passes that number to `ascii()`. The `ascii()` function returns the ASCII character that matches the user's number. This illustrates a `char` return type. Functions can return any data type.

```
/* Filename: C20ASC.C
   Prints the ASCII character of the user's number */
/* Prototypes follow */
#include <stdio.h>
char ascii(int num);

main()
{
   int num;
   char ascChar;
```

```
        printf("Enter an ASCII number? ");
        scanf(" %d", &num);

        ascChar = ascii(num);
        printf("The ASCII character for %d is %c", num, ascChar);
        return;
    }
```

Returns a *char* value ——— 
```
char ascii(int num)
    {
        char ascChar;
        ascChar = (char)num;
        return (ascChar);
    }
```

The output from this program follows:

```
Enter an ASCII number? 67
The ASCII character for 67 is C
```

**3.** Suppose you need to calculate net pay for a company. You find yourself multiplying the hours worked by the hourly pay, then deducting taxes to compute the net pay. The following program includes a function that does this for you. It requires three arguments: the hours worked, the hourly pay, and the tax rate (as a floating-point decimal, such as .30 for 30%). The function returns the net pay. The main() calling program tests the function by sending three different payroll values to the function and printing the three return values.

```
/* Filename: C20NPAY.C
   Defines a function that computes net pay */
#include <stdio.h>
float netpayfun(float hours, float rate, float taxrate);

main()
{
    float netPay;

    netPay = netpayfun(40.0, 3.50, .20);
    printf("The pay for 40 hours at $3.50/hr., and a 20%
    ➥tax rate is:");
    printf("$%.2f\n", netPay);
```

```
      netPay = netpayfun(50.0, 10.00, .30);
      printf("The pay for 50 hours at $10.00/hr., and a 30%
      ➡tax rate is:");
      printf("$%.2f\n", netPay);

      netPay = netpayfun(10.0, 5.00, .10);
      printf("The pay for 10 hours at $5.00/hr., and a 10%
      ➡tax rate is:");
      printf("$%.2f\n", netPay);

      return 0;
   }
```

Receives three *floats* ── `float netpayfun(float hours, float rate, float taxrate)`
and returns a *float*

```
   {
      float grossPay, taxes, netPay;
      grossPay = (hours * rate);
      taxes = (taxrate * grossPay);
      netPay = (grossPay - taxes);
      return (netPay);
   }
```

# Summary

You learned how to build your own collection of functions. When you write a function, you might want to use it in more than one program—there is no need to reinvent the wheel. Many programmers write useful functions and use them in more than one program.

You understand the importance of prototyping functions. You should prototype all your own functions and include the appropriate header file when you use one of C's built-in functions. Furthermore, when a function returns a value other than an integer, you must prototype for C to recognize the noninteger return value.

The rest of this book incorporates concepts presented in this part to take advantage of separate, modular functions and local data. You are ready to learn more about how C performs input and output. The next chapter teaches you the theory behind I/O in C and introduces more built-in functions.

# Review Questions

Answers to review questions are in Appendix B.

1. How do you define function return types?

2. What is the maximum number of return values a function can return?

3. What are header files for?

4. What is the default function return type?

5. True or false: A function that returns a value can be passed only a single parameter.

6. How do prototypes protect the programmer from bugs?

7. Why don't you need to return global variables?

8. What is the return type, given the following function prototype?

   ```
   float myFun(char a, int b, float c);
   ```

   How many parameters are passed to myFun()? What are their types?

# Review Exercises

1. Write a program that contains two functions. The first function returns the square of the integer passed to it, and the second function returns the cube. As with all programs from this point on, be sure to prototype all functions, including main().

2. Write a function that returns the double-precision area of a circle, given that a double-precision radius is passed to it. The formula for calculating the area of a circle is

   ```
   area = 3.14159 * radius * radius
   ```

3. Write a function that returns the value of a polynomial given this formula:

   $$9x^4 + 15x^2 + x^1$$

   Assume that x is passed from main() and that it is supplied by the user.

# Part V

*Character Input, Output, and Library Functions*

# CHAPTER 21

# Device and Character I/O

Unlike many programming languages, C contains no input or output commands. C is an extremely *portable* language, meaning that a C program compiled and run on one computer can compile and run also on another computer. Most incompatibilities between computers reside in their input/output (I/O) mechanics. Each different device requires a different method of performing I/O.

By putting all I/O capabilities in common functions supplied with each computer's compiler—and not in C statements—the designers of C ensured that programs were not tied to specific hardware for input and output. A compiler must be modified for every computer for which it is written. This ensures that the compiler works with any specific computer and all of its devices. The compiler programmers write input/output functions for each machine. When your C program writes a character to the screen, the program works whether you have a color PC screen or a UNIX X/Windows terminal.

This chapter shows you additional ways to perform data input and output, besides using the scanf() and printf() functions you have seen throughout the book. By providing character-based I/O functions, C gives you the basic I/O functions you need to write powerful data entry and printing routines.

This chapter introduces you to

♦ Stream and character I/O

♦ Buffered and nonbuffered I/O

♦ Standard device I/O

♦ Redirecting I/O from MS-DOS and UNIX

♦ Printing formatted output

By the time you finish this chapter, you should understand the standard built-in I/O functions that are available in C. Performing character input and output, one character at a time, may sound like a slow method of handling data I/O. You soon learn, however, that character I/O gives you the ability to create more powerful I/O functions than you can by using scanf() or printf().

# Character Stream I/O

C views input and output from all devices as a stream of characters.

C views all input and output as streams of characters. Whether your program gets input from the keyboard, a disk file, a modem, or a mouse, C sees only a stream of characters. C does not "know" or "care" what type of device is supplying the input. C lets the operating system take care of the device specifics. The designers of C want your programs to operate on characters of data without regard to whatever physical method is taking place.

This stream I/O means that the functions you use to get input from the keyboard can be used to get input also from the modem or any other input device. You can use the same functions to write to a disk file, a printer, or the screen. You must have some way of routing that stream input or output to the proper device, but each program's I/O functions work in a similar manner. Figure 21.1 illustrates this concept.

**Figure 21.1**

I/O consists of streams of characters.

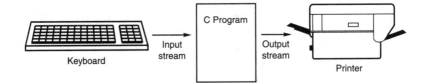

**The Newline Character: \n**

Portability is the key to C's success. Few companies have the resources to rewrite every program they use when they change computer equipment. They need a programming language that works on many platforms (hardware combinations). C achieves true portability better than almost all other programming languages.

It is because of portability that C uses the generic newline character, \n, instead of the specific carriage return and line feed sequences that other languages use. This is also why C uses \t for tab and all the other control characters utilized in I/O functions.

If C relied on a specific ASCII code to represent these special characters, your programs would not be portable. Suppose you wrote a C program on one computer and used a carriage return value such as 12—12 may not be the carriage return value on another type of computer. By using the newline character and the other control characters available in C, you ensure that your program works on any computer on which it is compiled. The specific compilers substitute their computer's actual codes for the control codes in your programs.

# Standard Devices

Table 21.1 shows a listing of standard I/O devices. C always assumes that input comes from stdin, or the *standard input device*. This is usually the keyboard, although you can reroute this default. C assumes that all output goes to stdout, or the *standard output device*. There is nothing magic in the words *stdin* and *stdout*, but many people see these words for the first time in the C language.

### Table 21.1. Standard I/O devices in C.

| I/O Device | C Name | MS-DOS Name | UNIX Name |
|---|---|---|---|
| Screen | stdout | CON: | stdout |
| Keyboard | stdin | CON: | stdin |
| Printer | stdprn | PRN: or LPT1: | lpr |
| Serial port | stdaux | AUX: or COM1: | machine dependent |
| Error messages | stderr | CON: | stderr |
| Disk files | none | filename | filename |

Take a moment to study Table 21.1. MS-DOS users might think that three devices named CON: are confusing. MS-DOS knows the difference between the screen device called CON: (which stands for *console*) and the keyboard device called CON: from the context of the data stream. If you send an output stream (a stream of characters) to CON:, MS-DOS routes it to the screen. If you request input from CON:, MS-DOS gets it from the keyboard. (These defaults hold true as long as you have not redirected these devices.) MS-DOS sends all error messages to the screen (CON:) as well.

**Note:** If you want to route I/O to a second printer or serial port, read Chapter 30, "Sequential Files."

UNIX users may understand the standard C device names already because many of these names are the same as their equivalent UNIX device names. If you use a print spooler, your UNIX printing device may be different from lpr.

If you program on a mainframe, you must use *JCL* (Job Control Language) to route C's standard devices, such as stdin and stdout, to your preferred local or remote I/O devices. If you are new to programming, you may have to contact your system administrator to help you with setting up a JCL file that connects C programs to the appropriate I/O devices.

## Redirecting Devices from MS-DOS and UNIX

The operating system gives you control over devices.

The reason printf() goes to the screen is simply because stdout is routed to the screen by default on most computers. The reason scanf() gets input from the keyboard is because most computers consider the keyboard to be the standard input device, stdin. After compiling your program, C does *not* send data to the screen or get it from the keyboard. Instead, the program sends output to stdout and gets input from stdin. The operating system routes the data to the appropriate device.

Most PC- and UNIX-based operating systems let you reroute I/O from their default locations to other devices with the *output redirection symbol*, >, and the *input redirection symbol*, <. The goal of this book is certainly not to delve into operating system redirection. You might want to get a good book on your operating system (such as Que's *Using MS-DOS 6*, Special Edition or *Using UNIX*) to learn more about how your operating system handles I/O.

Basically, the output redirection symbol informs the operating system that you want standard output to go to a device other than the default (the screen). The input redirection symbol routes input away from the keyboard to another input device. The following examples illustrate how to do this in MS-DOS.

### Examples

1. Suppose you write a program that uses only scanf() and print() for input and output. You want the program to get input from a file called MYDATA, instead of from the keyboard. Because scanf() receives input from stdin, you must redirect stdin. After compiling the program to a file called MYPGM.EXE, you can redirect its input away from the keyboard with the following DOS command:

```
C:>MYPGM < MYDATA
```

You can include a full path name before either the program name or the file name. There is a danger, however, in redirecting all output such as this. *All* output, including screen prompts for keyboard input, goes to MYDATA. This is probably unacceptable in most cases; you will still want prompts and some messages to go to the screen. In the next section, you read how to separate I/O, sending some output to one device such as the screen and the rest to another device such as a file or a printer.

**2.** You can route the program's output to the printer by typing the following line:

```
C:>MYPGM > PRN:
```

This uses the DOS device name for the printer. UNIX users must use `lpr` or the print spooler's device name in place of `PRN:` in these examples.

**3.** If the program requires much input, and that input is stored in a file called ANSWERS, you can override the keyboard default device that `scanf()` uses, as follows:

*When `scanf()` requires input, have the program read from the file named ANSWERS.*

```
C:>MYPGM < ANSWERS
```

**4.** You can also combine redirection symbols. To get input from the AN- SWERS disk file and send the output to the printer, you can use the following code:

```
C:>MYPGM < ANSWERS > PRN:
```

> **Tip:** MS-DOS users can reroute output to a serial printer or a second parallel printer port by substituting **COM1:** or **LPT2:** in place of **PRN:** in these examples.

## Printing Formatted Output

The `fprintf()` function enables your program to write to the printer.

It is easy to send program output to the printer using the `fprintf()` function. The format of `fprintf()` follows:

```
fprintf(device, controlString [, one or more values]);
```

You might notice that the format of `fprintf()` is similar to that of `printf()`. The only difference between `fprintf()` and `printf()` (besides the names) is that `fprintf()` requires a *device* as its first argument. Usually, this device is the standard printer, `stdprn`. In Chapter 30, "Sequential Files," you learn how to write formatted data to a disk file by using `fprintf()`.

The following examples show how you can combine `printf()` and `fprintf()` to write to both the screen and the printer.

> **Caution:** Some compilers, despite being compatible with ANSI C, do not let `fprintf()` print to a printer using the `stdprn` device. If yours does not, you need to learn more about file I/O. See Part 7, "Structures and File I/O," to learn how to route output to the printer using a file pointer.

## Example

The following program asks users for their first and last names. It then prints the full name—last name first—to the printer.

```
/* Filename: C21FPR1.C
   Prints a name on the printer */
#include <stdio.h>
main()
{
   char first[20];
   char last[20];

   printf("What is your first name? ");
   scanf(" %s", first);

   printf("What is your last name? ");
   scanf(" %s", last);

   /* Send names to the printer */
   fprintf(stdprn, "In a phone book, your name");
   fprintf(stdprn, " looks like this: \n");
   fprintf(stdprn, " %s, %s", last, first);
   return;
}
```

Prints to the printer

> **Note:** If you get an undefined symbol error when you compile this program, you'll have to send output to your printer as described in Chapter 30.

---

**For Related Information**

◆ "Understanding the *printf()* Function," p. 106

◆ "Conversion Characters," p. 108

◆ "Writing to a Printer," p. 538

# Character I/O Functions

Because all I/O is actually character I/O, C provides many functions that perform character input and output. The printf() and scanf() functions, however, are not character I/O functions. The printf() and scanf() functions are called *formatted I/O functions* because they give you formatting control (using conversion characters) over your input and output.

There is nothing wrong with using printf() for formatted output, but scanf() has many problems, some of which you have seen. In this section, you learn how to write your own character input routines that replace scanf(). To prepare you for the upcoming chapters on disk files, you also learn how to use character output functions. These functions are generally easier to use than scanf() and printf() because they don't require formatting codes.

# The *getc()* and *putc()* Functions

The getc()
and putc()
functions handle
character I/O with
any standard
device.

The most fundamental character I/O functions are getc() and putc(). The putc() function writes a single character to the standard output device, which is the screen, unless you redirect it from your operating system. The getc() function inputs a single character from the standard input device, which is the keyboard, unless you redirect it.

The format for getc() follows:

```
intVar = getc(device);
```

Don't let the integer *intVar* confuse you. Even though getc() is a character function, you use an integer variable to store the getc() input value. getco() returns a –1 when an end-of-file condition occurs. If you are using getc() to read information from a disk file, the –1 is read when the end of the file is reached. If you used a character variable, the –1 would be interpreted as 255. You learn more about end-of-file conditions in Chapter 30, "Sequential Files." As with all integer variables, you can use the integer input value as though it were a character.

The getc() *device* can be any C standard input device. If you are getting character input from the keyboard, use stdin as the *device*. If you initialize your modem and want to receive characters from it, use stdaux for the *device*.

The format of putc() follows:

```
putc(intVal, device);
```

The *intVal* can be an integer variable, expression, or constant. You output character data with putc(). The *device* can be any standard output C device. To write a character to your printer, use stdprn for the *device*.

> **Note:** Most of the character I/O functions, including `getc()` and `putc()`, are actually called *macros*. These are not true functions, but rather a form of preprocessor directives. Most C programmers program for years and never notice the difference, and you probably won't either. As a precaution, however, be sure you do not include an expression in `putc()`, such as `putc(mychar++);`. A macro may not evaluate this properly.

## Examples

**1.** The following program asks users for their initials, one character at a time. Notice that the program uses both `printf()` and `putc()`. The `printf()` is still useful for formatted output, such as messages to the user. Writing individual characters is best achieved with `putc()`.

The program must call two `getc()` functions for each character typed. When you answer a `getc()` prompt, by typing a character and pressing Enter, C sees that input as a stream of two characters. The `getc()` first gets the letter you typed, then it gets the \n (newline, supplied to C when you press Enter). Examples that follow correct this double `getc()` problem.

```
/* Filename: C21CH1.C
   Introduces getc() and putc() */
#include <stdio.h>
main()
{
   int inChar;                    /* Holds incoming initial */
   char first, last;             /* Holds converted first
                                     and last initial     */

   printf("What is your first name initial? ");
   inChar = getc(stdin);         /* Wait for first initial */
   first = inChar;
   inChar = getc(stdin);              /* Ignore newline */

   printf("What is your last name initial? ");

   inChar = getc(stdin);         /* Wait for last initial */
   last = inChar;
   inChar = getc(stdin);              /* Ignore newline */

   printf("\nHere they are: \n");
   putc(first, stdout);
   putc(last, stdout);
   return;
}
```

Gets characters

Here is the output from this program:

```
What is your first name initial? G
What is your last name initial? P

Here they are:
GP
```

2. You can add carriage returns to better space the output. To print the two initials on two separate lines, use putc() to send a newline character to stdout. The following program uses putc() to separate the characters printed.

```
/* Filename: C21CH2.C
   Introduces getc() and putc() and uses
   putc() to output newline */
#include <stdio.h>
main()
{
   int inChar;                    /* Holds incoming initial */
   char first, last;             /* Holds converted first
                                     and last initial    */

   printf("What is your first name initial? ");
   inChar = getc(stdin);         /* Wait for first initial */
   first = inChar;
   inChar = getc(stdin);              /* Ignore newline */

   printf("What is your last name initial? ");

   inChar = getc(stdin);             /* Wait for last initial */
   last = inChar;
   inChar = getc(stdin);               /* Ignore newline */

   printf("\nHere they are: \n");
   putc(first, stdout);
   putc('\n', stdout);                /* A newline is output */
   putc(last, stdout);
   return;
}
```

Puts a *newline* to the output ——— putc('\n', stdout);

3. It may be clearer to define the newline character as a constant. At the top of the program, you can have

```
#define NEWLINE '\n'
```

The putc() can then read

```
putc(NEWLINE, stdout);
```

Some programmers prefer to define their character formatting constants and refer to them by name. You can decide whether you think this is clearer, or whether you want to continue using the \n character constant in putc().

## The *getchar()* and *putchar()* Functions

Both getchar() and putchar() use stdin and stdout as their target devices.

When you perform character I/O, the getchar() and putchar() functions are easier to use than getc() and putc(). The getchar() and putchar() functions are identical to getc() and putc(), except you do not specify a device because they assume the standard input and output devices, stdin and stdout (typically, the screen and the keyboard) will be used. In the following:

```
inChar=getc(stdin);
```

is identical to

```
inChar=getchar();
```

and

```
putc(var, stdout);
```

is identical to

```
putchar(var);
```

The getchar() and putchar() functions are two of the most frequently used character I/O functions in C. Most I/O is performed on the keyboard and screen, and these two devices are generally routed to stdin and stdout by the operating system, unless you redirect them.

The getchar() and the getc() functions are both *buffered* input functions. That is, as you type characters, the data goes to a buffer rather than immediately to your program. The buffer is a section of memory managed by C (and has nothing to do with some computers' *typeahead buffers*).

Figure 21.2 shows you how this works. When your program gets to a getc() or a getchar(), the program temporarily waits as you type the input. The program does not see the characters because they are going to the buffer in memory. There is no limit to the size of the buffer; it keeps filling up with input until you press Enter. The Enter keypress signals the computer to release the buffer to your program.

## Figure 21.2

The *getc()* and *getchar()* input goes to a buffer, where it is held until you press Enter.

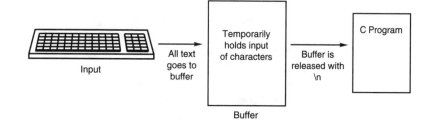

Both getchar() and putchar() use the stdio.h header file.

Most multiuser computers will buffer all input. Most PCs allow either buffered or nonbuffered input. The getch() function (shown later in this chapter) is nonbuffered. With getc() and getchar(), all input is buffered, and this affects the timing of your program's input. Your program receives no characters from a getchar() or getc() until you press Enter. Suppose that you ask a question such as the following:

```
Do you want to see the report again (Y/N)?
```

and use getchar() for input. If the user presses a Y, the program does not know this until the user presses Enter too. Then the Y and Enter keypresses are sent, one character at a time, to the program, where the input is processed. If you want immediate response to a user's typing (such as INKEY$ does, if you are familiar with BASIC), you must use getch().

> **Tip:** By using buffered input, the user can type a string of characters in response to repeated getc() requests, and correct the input with the Backspace key before pressing Enter. If the input is nonbuffered, the Backspace becomes just one more character of data.

## Examples

1. The following sample program illustrates getchar() and putchar(). The first getchar() gets a character from the keyboard; a second one gets the newline character produced when the user presses Enter. The putchar() echoes the typed character back to the screen. You might be able to see from this program why getchar() and putchar() are called *mirror-image functions*.

*Identify the program and include the necessary header file. This program will get a character from the user. Define an integer variable called myChar and use it to hold the character that the user types. Ask the user to type a character. Use the getChar function to store the typed character in the myChar variable. Call getChar again for the user's Enter keypress. Tell the user what they typed, by displaying the contents of myChar.*

```
/* Filename: C21GPC.C
   Illustrates simple getchar() and putchar() */
#include <stdio.h>
main()
{
   int myChar;                               /* Must be integer */

   printf("Please type a character... ");
   myChar = getchar();                       /* Get the character */
   getchar();                                /* Discard the newline */

   printf("You typed this: ");
   putchar(myChar);
   return;
}
```

Puts what
*getchar()* ———
got

When you get
characters, you
may need to
discard the newline
keypress.

This program must discard the newline character. It could have done so by assigning the input character—from getchar()—to an extra variable, as previous examples have done. Because we know that the user must press Enter after typing a character, we can ignore the second return value by not assigning getchar() to anything. You know the user must press Enter (to end the input), so it is all right to discard it with an unused getchar() function call.

**2.** The scanf() function has limited use when inputting strings such as names and sentences. The scanf() function allows only one word to be entered at a time. If you ask users for their full names with these lines:

```
printf("What are your first and last names? ");
scanf(" %s", names);            /* Get the name into the
                                   names character array */
```

the array called names would receive only the first name; scanf() ignores all data to the right of the first space.

Using getchar(), you can build an input function that does not have a single-word limitation. When you want to get a string of characters from users, such as their first and last names, you can call the getInStr() function shown in the next program.

```
/* Filename: C21IN.C
   Program that builds an input string array
   using getchar() */
#include <stdio.h>
```

```
#define MAX 25                        /* Size of character
                                         array to be typed in */
void getInStr(char str[], int len);

main()
{
   char inputStr[MAX];  /* Keyboard input will fill this */
   printf("What is your full name? ");
   getInStr(inputStr, MAX);     /* String from keyboard */
   printf("After return, your name is %s", inputStr);
   return 0;
}


/*************************************************************
The following function requires that a string and the
maximum length of the string be passed to it. It accepts
input from the keyboard, and sends keyboard input into the
string. Upon return, the calling routine has access to the
string.
*************************************************************/
void getInStr(char str[], int len)
{
   int i=0, inputChar;         /* Index and character typed */
   inputChar = getchar(); /* Get next character in string */
   while (i<(len-1) && (inputChar!='\n'))
     {
        str[i] = inputChar;        /* Build the string, one
                                      character at a time */
        i++;
        inputChar = getchar();   /* Get the next
                                    character in the string */
     }
   str[i]='\0';        /* Make the char array into a string */
   return;
}
```

Builds a string

The main() function defines an array and prompts the user for a name. After the prompt, the program calls the getInStr() function and uses getchar() to build the input array, one character at a time. The function keeps looping, using the while loop, until the user presses Enter (signaled by the newline character, \n) or types the maximum number of characters.

You might want to use this function in your own programs. Be sure to pass it a character array and an integer that holds the maximum array size (you don't want the input string to be longer than the character array that holds the string). When control returns to main()—or to whichever function called getInStr()—the array has the user's full input, spaces and all.

> **Note:** The loop checks for len-1 to save room for the null terminating zero at the end of the input string.

3. Because the getchar() function is used frequently for building strings (as the last example showed), many programmers have chosen to insert it directly inside the while test.

Here is a rewritten version of the getInStr() function shown in the last example. Notice that by putting the getchar() directly inside the while conditional test, you streamline the function. The while conditional test takes a little more room, but the improved efficiency is worth it. This is a common input procedure, and you should become familiar with seeing getchar() inside tests such as this. At first it may seem awkward and cumbersome, but many C programmers choose to use it because it gives them greater control over user input.

```c
void getInStr(char str[], int len)
{
    int i=0, inputChar;        /* Index and character typed */
    /* Get next character in string */
    while (i<(len-1) && ((inputChar=getchar()) != '\n') )
      {
          str[i] = inputChar;      /* Build the string, one
                                       character at a time */

          i++;
      }
    str[i]='\0';        /* Make the char array into a string */
    return;
}
```

## The *getch()* and *putch()* Functions

Both getch() and
putch() use the
conio.h header file.

The getch() and putch() functions are slightly different from the previous character I/O functions. Their formats are similar to getchar() and putchar(); they both assume that stdin and stdout are the standard input and output devices, and you cannot specify other devices (unless you redirect them with your operating system). The format of getch() and putch() follows:

```
inVar = getch();
```

and

```
putch(intVar);
```

Both getch() and
putch() offer
nonbuffered I/O
that "grabs"
characters
immediately after
they are typed.

The getch() and putch() functions are not ANSI C standard functions, but they are available on a large number of compilers and well worth mentioning. getch() and putch() are nonbuffered functions. However, many multiuser computer systems buffer getch(), even though the function was not designed for buffered input. The putch() character output function is a mirror-image of getch(); it is a nonbuffered output function. Because almost every output device (except screens and modems) is inherently buffered, putch() effectively does the same thing as putc().

As you type a
character in
response to
getch(), the
character is not
echoed to the
screen.

Another difference between getch() and the other character input functions is that getch() does not echo the input characters on-screen as it receives them. When you type characters in response to getchar(), you see the characters as you type them (as they are sent to the buffer). If you want to display on-screen the characters received by getch(), you must follow getch() with putch(). It is handy to echo the characters on-screen so that users can verify what they typed.

Both getch() and putch() assume that stdin and stdout are the standard input and output devices. When you want your program to respond immediately to keyboard input, use getch(). Some programmers want to make users press Enter after answering a prompt or selecting from a menu. They feel that buffered input gives users more time to decide if they really want to give that answer; users can press Backspace and correct the input before pressing Enter.

Other programmers like to "grab" the user's single-character answer (such as a menu response) and act on it immediately. They feel that pressing Enter is an added and unneeded burden for the user. The choice is yours. You should understand both buffered and nonbuffered input, so you can use either one.

**Tip:** Although getche() is not an ANSI C standard function, you can use it on most computer systems. The getche() function is a nonbuffered input function identical to getch(), except the input characters are echoed (displayed) to the screen as the user types them. Using getche() instead of getch() sometimes keeps you from having to echo the user's input to the screen.

## Example

The following program uses the getch() and putch() functions. The user is asked to enter five letters. These five letters are added to the character array named letters using a for loop. As you run this program, notice that the characters are not echoed to the screen as you type them. As you type the characters, the program receives each character, adds it to the array, and loops again, because getch() is unbuffered. (If this were buffered input, the program would not loop through the five iterations until you pressed Enter.)

A second loop uses putch() to print the five letters. A third loop uses putc() to print the five letters to the printer.

```
/* Filename: C21GCH1.C
      Uses getch() and putch() for input and output */
  #include <stdio.h>
  #include <conio.h>
  main()
  {
      int ctr;                        /* The for loop counter */
      char letters[5];      /* Holds five input characters. No
                               room is needed for the null zero
                               because this array will never be
                               treated like a string.          */
      printf("Please type five letters... \n");
      for (ctr=0; ctr<5; ctr++)
        {
            letters[ctr] = getch();      /* Add input to array */
        }
      for (ctr=0; ctr<5; ctr++)  /* Print them to the screen */
        {
            putch(letters[ctr]);
        }
      for (ctr=0; ctr<5; ctr++) /* Print them to the printer */
        {
            putc(letters[ctr], stdprn);
        }
      return;
  }
```

Gets five letters — (bracket)

Puts the five letters — (bracket)

When you run this program, don't press Enter after typing the five letters. The loop ends automatically after the fifth letter (due to the for loop). This is possible only because of the nonbuffered input allowed with getch().

## Summary

You now should understand the generic method that C programs use for input and output. By writing to standard I/O devices, C achieves portability. If you write a program for one computer, it will work on another. If C were to write directly to specific hardware, programs could not work on every computer.

If you still want to use formatted I/O functions, such as printf(), you can do so. The fprintf() function enables you to write formatted output to any device, including the printer.

Although the methods of character I/O are primitive, their flexibility allows you to build on them and create your own input functions. One of the most often used C functions, a string-building character I/O function, was demonstrated in this chapter (the C21IN.C program).

The next two chapters introduce many character and string functions, including string I/O functions. The string I/O functions build on the principles presented here. You may be surprised at the extensive character and string manipulation functions available in the C language.

## Review Questions

Answers to review questions are in Appendix B.

1. Why are there no input or output commands in C?

2. True or false: If you use the character I/O functions to send output to stdout, the output always goes to the screen.

3. What is the difference between getc() and getchar()?

4. What is the difference between getch() and getchar()?

5. What function sends formatted output to devices other than the screen?

6. What are the MS-DOS and UNIX redirection symbols?

7. What nonstandard function, most similar to getch(), echoes the input character to the screen as the user types it?

8. True or false: When you use getchar(), the program receives your input as you type it.

9. Which keypress releases buffered input to the program?

10. True or false: Using devices and functions described in this chapter, you could write one program that sends some output to the screen, some output to the printer, and some output to the modem.

## Review Exercises

**1.** Write a program that asks users for five letters and prints them backwards, first to the screen and then to the printer. (Note: If your compiler does not let you send output to the printer using fprintf(), ignore the last part of this exercise.)

**2.** Write a miniature typewriter program, using getc() and putc(). Loop to get a line of user input (until the user presses Enter), then write that line of characters to the printer. Because getc() is buffered, nothing goes to the printer until the user presses Enter at the end of each line of text. (Use the string-building input function shown in C21IN.C.)

**3.** Add a putch() inside the first loop of C21GCH1.C to echo the characters to the screen as the user types them. (This simulates the nonstandard getche() function offered with some C compilers.)

**4.** A *palindrome* is a word or phrase spelled (but not necessarily punctuated) the same way forward and backward. Here are two examples:

```
Madam, I'm Adam
Golf? No sir, prefer prison flog!
```

Write a C program that asks the user for a phrase. Build the input, one character at a time, using a character input function such as getchar(). After you have the full string (store it in a character array), test the phrase to see if it is a palindrome. You need to filter out special nonalphabetic characters, storing only alphabetic characters to a second character array. You must also convert the characters—as you store them—to uppercase. The first palindrome would become

```
MADAMIMADAM
```

Using one or more for or while loops, you can now test the phrase to see if it is a palindrome. Print the result of the test to the printer. Sample output should appear as follows:

```
"Madam, I'm Adam" is a palindrome.
```

# CHAPTER 22

# Character, String, and Numeric Functions

C provides many built-in functions in addition to the `printf()`, `scanf()`, and `strcpy()` functions you have seen so far throughout the book. These built-in functions increase your productivity and save you programming time. You don't need to write as much code because the built-in functions perform many useful tasks for you.

This chapter introduces you to the following:

♦ Character conversion functions

♦ Character and string testing functions

♦ String manipulation functions

♦ String I/O functions

♦ Mathematic, trigonometric, and logarithmic functions

♦ Random-number processing

# Character Functions

This section explores many of the character functions available in ANSI C. Generally, you pass character arguments to the functions, and the functions return values that you can store or print. By using these functions, you off-load much of your work to C and let it perform the more tedious manipulations of character and string data.

# Character Testing Functions

The character functions return True or False results based on characters you pass to them.

Several functions test for certain characteristics of your character data. You can test to see if your character data is alphabetic, digital, uppercase, lowercase, and much more. You must pass a character variable or constant argument to the function (by placing the argument in the function parentheses) when you call it. These functions all return a True or False result, so you can test their return values inside an `if` statement or a `while` loop.

> **Note:** All character functions presented in this section are prototyped in the ctype.h header file. Be sure to include ctype.h at the top of any program that uses them.

# Alphabetic and Digital Testing

The following functions test for alphabetic conditions:

- `isalpha(c)`: Returns True (nonzero) if `c` is an uppercase or lowercase letter. Returns False (0) if `c` is not a letter.

- `islower(c)`: Returns True (nonzero) if `c` is a lowercase letter. Returns False (0) if `c` is not a lowercase letter.

- `isupper(c)`: Returns True (nonzero) if `c` is an uppercase letter. Returns False (0) if `c` is not an uppercase letter.

Remember that any nonzero value is True in C, and 0 is always False. If you use the return values of these functions in a relational test, the True return value is not always 1 (it can be any nonzero value), but it is always considered True for the test.

The following functions test for digits:

- `isdigit(c)`: Returns True (nonzero) if `c` is a digit 0 through 9. Returns False (0) if `c` is not a digit.

> **Note:** Although some character functions test for digits, the arguments are still character data and cannot be used in mathematical calculations, unless you calculate using the ASCII values of characters.

♦ isxdigit(c): Returns True (nonzero) if c is any of the hexadecimal digits 0 through 9 or A, B, C, D, E, F, a, b, c, d, e, or f. Returns False (0) if c is anything else. (See Appendix A for more information on the hexadecimal numbering system.)

The following function tests for numeric or alphabetical arguments:

♦ isalnum(c): Returns True (nonzero) if c is a digit 0 through 9 or an alphabetic character (either uppercase or lowercase). Returns False (0) if c is not a digit or a letter.

> **Caution:** You can pass to these functions only a character value or an integer value holding the ASCII value of a character. You cannot pass an entire character array to character functions. If you want to test the elements of a character array, you must pass the array one element at a time.

## Example

The following program asks users for their initials. If a user types anything but alphabetic characters, the program displays an error and asks again.

*Identify the program and include the necessary header files. The program will ask the user for his or her first initial, so define the character variable* initial *to hold the user's answer.*

**1.** *Ask the user for his or her first initial, and get the user's answer.*

**2.** *If the answer was not an alphabetic character, tell the user this and repeat step 1.*

*Print a thank-you message on-screen.*

```
/* Filename: C22INI.C
   Asks for first initial and tests
   to ensure that it is correct */
#include <stdio.h>
#include <ctype.h>
main()
{
   char initial;
   printf("What is your first initial? ");
   scanf(" %c", &initial);
```

Ensures that
a character
was typed

```
while (! isalpha(initial))
  {
    printf("\nThat was not a valid initial! \n");
    printf("\nWhat is your first initial? ");
    scanf(" %c", &initial);
  }

printf("\nThanks!");
return;
}
```

This use of the not operator (!) is quite clear. The program continues to loop while the entered character is *not* alphabetic.

## Special Character Testing Functions

A few character functions become useful when you need to read from a disk file, a modem, or another operating system device that you route input from. These functions are not used as much as the character functions you saw in the last section, but they can be useful for testing specific characters for readability.

The character
testing functions
do not change
characters.

The remaining character testing functions follow:

◆ iscntrl(c): Returns True (nonzero) if c is a control character (any character from the ASCII table numbered 0 through 31). Returns False (0) if c is not a control character.

◆ isgraph(c): Returns True (nonzero) if c is any printable character (a noncontrol character) except a space. Returns False (0) if c is a space or anything other than a printable character.

◆ isprint(c): Returns True (nonzero) if c is a printable character (a noncontrol character) from ASCII 32 to ASCII 127, including a space. Returns False (0) if c is not a printable character.

◆ ispunct(c): Returns True (nonzero) if c is any punctuation character (any printable character other than a space, a letter, or a digit). Returns False (0) if c is not a punctuation character.

◆ isspace(c): Returns True (nonzero) if c is a space, newline (\n), carriage return (\r), tab (\t), or vertical tab (\v) character. Returns False (0) if c is anything else.

## Character Conversion Functions

Both `tolower()` and `toupper()` return lowercase or uppercase arguments.

Two remaining character functions can be very handy. Rather than test characters, these functions change characters to their lowercase or uppercase equivalents.

♦ `tolower(c)`: Converts *c* to lowercase. Nothing is changed if you pass `tolower()` a lowercase letter or a nonalphabetic character.

♦ `toupper(c)`: Converts *c* to uppercase. Nothing is changed if you pass `toupper()` an uppercase letter or a nonalphabetic character.

These functions return their changed character values.

These functions are very useful for user input. Suppose that you are asking users a yes-or-no question, such as the following:

```
Do you want to print the checks (Y/N)?
```

Before knowing `toupper()` and `tolower()`, you would need to check for both a *Y* and a *y* before printing the checks. Instead of testing for both conditions, you can convert the character to uppercase, and test for a *Y*.

### Example

Here is a program that prints an appropriate message if the user is a girl or a boy. The program tests for *G* and *B* after converting the user's input to uppercase. No check for lowercase needs to be done.

*Identify the program and include the necessary header files. The program will ask the user a question requiring an alphabetic answer, so define the character variable* ans *to hold the user's response.*

*Ask whether the user is a girl or a boy, and store the user's answer in* ans. *The user must press Enter, so get and then discard the Enter keypress. Change the value of* ans *to uppercase. If the answer is G, print a message. If the answer is B, print a different message. If the answer is something else, print another message.*

```
/* Filename: C22GB.C
   Tests whether the user typed a G or a B */
#include <stdio.h>
#include <ctype.h>
main()
{
   char ans;                    /* Holds user's response */
   printf("Are you a girl or a boy (G/B)? ");
   ans=getchar();                       /* Get answer */
   getchar();                        /* Discard newline */
```

Ensures uppercase——

```
    ans = toupper(ans);      /* Convert answer to uppercase */
    switch (ans)
    {   case ('G'): { printf("You look pretty today!\n");
                        break; }
        case ('B'): { printf("You look handsome today!\n");
                        break; }
        default :   { printf("Your answer makes no sense!\n");
                        break; }

    }
    return;
}
```

Here is the output from the program:

```
Are you a girl or a boy (G/B)? B
You look handsome today!
```

## String Functions

Some of the most powerful built-in C functions are the string functions. They perform much of the tedious work for which you have been writing code so far, such as inputting strings from the keyboard and comparing strings.

As with the character functions, there is no need to "reinvent the wheel" by writing code when built-in functions do the same task. Use these functions as much as possible.

Now that you have a good grasp of the foundations of C, you can master the string functions. They enable you to concentrate on your program's primary purpose, rather than spend time coding your own string functions.

### Useful String Functions

You can use a handful of useful string functions for string testing and conversion. You have already seen (in earlier chapters) the strcpy() string function, which copies a string of characters into a character array.

> **Note:** All string functions in this section are prototyped in the string.h header file. Be sure to include string.h at the top of any program that uses the string functions.

The string functions work on character arrays that contain strings or on string constants.

Some string functions that test or manipulate strings follow:

◆ strcat(s1, s2): Concatenates (merges) the s2 string to the end of the s1 character array. The s1 array must have enough reserved elements to hold both strings.

- strcmp(*s1*, *s2*): Compares the *s1* string with the *s2* string on an alphabetical, element-by-element basis. If s1 alphabetizes before *s2*, strcmp() returns a negative value. If *s1* and *s2* are the same strings, strcmp() returns 0. If *s1* alphabetizes after *s2*, strcmp() returns a positive value.

- strlen(*s1*): Returns the length of *s1*. Remember, the length of a string is the number of characters up to—but not including—the null zero. The number of characters defined for the character array has nothing to do with the length of the string.

> **Tip:** Before using strcat() to concatenate strings, use strlen() to ensure that the target string (the string being concatenated to) is large enough to hold both strings.

---

**For Related Information**

- "String-Constant Endings," p. 67
- "String Lengths," p. 69

---

## String I/O Functions

In previous chapters, you used a character input function, getchar(), to build input strings. Now you can begin to use the string input and output functions. Although the goal of the string-building functions has been to teach you the specifics of the language, these string I/O functions are much easier to use than writing a character input function.

The string input and output functions are listed as follows:

- gets(*s*): Stores input from stdin (usually directed to the keyboard) into the string named s.

- puts(*s*): Outputs the s string to stdout (usually directed to the screen by the operating system).

- fgets(*s*, *len*, *dev*): Stores input from the standard device specified by *dev* (such as stdin or stdaux) in the s string. If more than *len* characters are input, fgets() discards them.

*Both gets() and puts() input and output strings.*

- fputs(*s*, *dev*): Outputs the s string to the standard device specified by *dev*.

These four functions make the input and output of strings easy. They work in pairs. That is, strings input with gets() are usually output with puts(). Strings input with fgets() are usually output with fputs().

> **Tip:** gets() replaces the string-building input function you saw in earlier chapters.

Terminate gets() or fgets() input by pressing Enter. Each of these functions handles string-terminating characters in a slightly different manner, as follows:

| | |
|---|---|
| gets() | A newline input becomes a null zero (\0). |
| puts() | A null at the end of the string becomes a newline character (\n). |
| fgets() | A newline input stays, and a null zero is added after it. |
| fputs() | The null zero is dropped, and a newline character is not added. |

Therefore, when you enter strings with gets(), C places a string-terminating character in the string at the point where you press Enter. This creates the input string. (Without the null zero, the input would not be a string.) When you output a string, the null zero at the end of the string becomes a newline character. This is good because you typically prefer a newline at the end of a line of output (to put the cursor on the next line).

Because fgets() and fputs() can input and output strings from devices such as disk files and telephone modems, it may be critical that the incoming newline characters are retained for the data's integrity. When outputting strings to these devices, you do not want C inserting extra newline characters.

> **Caution:** Neither gets() nor fgets() ensures that its input strings are large enough to hold the incoming data. It is up to you to make sure enough space is reserved in the character array to hold the complete input.

One final function is worth noting, although it is not a string function. It is the fflush() function, which flushes (empties) whatever standard device is listed in its parentheses. To flush the keyboard of all its input, you would code as follows:

```
fflush(stdin);
```

When doing string input and output, sometimes an extra newline character gets into the keyboard buffer. A previous answer to gets() or getc() might have an extra newline you forgot to discard. When a program seems to ignore gets(), you might have to insert fflush(stdin) before gets().

Flushing the standard input device causes no harm, and using it can clear the input stream so that your next gets() works properly. You can also flush standard output devices with fflush() to clear the output stream of any characters you may have sent into it.

> **Note:** The header file for `fflush()` is in stdio.h.

> **For Related Information**
> ♦ "Printing Strings," p. 106

## Example

The following program shows you how easy it is to use `gets()` and `puts()`. The program requests the name of a book from the user using a single `gets()` function call, then prints the book title with `puts()`.

*Identify the program and include the necessary header files. The program will ask the user for the name of a book. Define the character array book with 30 elements to hold the user's answer. Ask the user for the book's title, and store the user's response in the book array. Display the string stored in book to an output device, probably your screen. Print a thank-you message.*

```
/* Filename: C22GPS1.C
   Gets and puts strings */
#include <stdio.h>
#include <string.h>
main()
{
   char book[30];

   printf("What is the book title? ");
   gets(book);                          /* Get an input string */
   puts(book);                          /* Display the string */
   printf("Thanks for the book!\n");
   return;
}
```

Gets a string ———
Puts a string ———

The output of the program follows:

```
What is the book title? Mary and Her Lambs
Mary and Her Lambs
Thanks for the book!
```

## Converting Strings to Numbers

Sometimes you need to convert numbers stored in character strings to a numeric data type. ANSI C provides three functions that let you do this:

- `atoi(s)`: Converts s to an integer. The name stands for alphabetic to integer.

- `atol(s)`: Converts s to a long integer. The name stands for alphabetic to long integer.

- `atof(s)`: Converts s to a floating-point number. The name stands for alphabetic to floating-point.

> **Note:** These three `ato()` functions are prototyped in the stdlib.h header file. Be sure to include stdlib.h at the top of any program that uses the `ato()` functions.

The string must contain a valid number. Here is a string that can be converted to an integer:

```
"1232"
```

The string must hold a string of digits short enough to fit in the target numeric data type. The following string could not be converted to an integer with the `atoi()` function:

```
"-1232495.654"
```

However, it could be converted to a floating-point number with the `atof()` function.

C cannot perform any mathematical calculation with such strings, even if the strings contain digits that represent numbers. Therefore, you must convert any string into its numeric equivalent before performing any arithmetic with it.

> **Note:** If you pass a string to an `ato()` function and the string does not contain a valid representation of a number, the `ato()` function returns 0.

These functions become more useful to you later, after you learn about disk files, pointers, and command-line arguments.

## Numeric Functions

This section presents many of the built-in C numeric functions. As with the string functions, these functions save you time by converting and calculating numbers instead of you having to write functions that do the same thing. Many of these are trigonometric and advanced math functions. You may use some of these numeric functions only rarely, but they are there if you need them.

This section concludes the discussion of C's standard built-in functions. After you master the concepts in this chapter, you will be ready to learn more about arrays and pointers. As you develop more skills in C, you may find yourself relying on these numeric, string, and character functions when you write more powerful programs.

## Useful Mathematical Functions

Several built-in numeric functions return results based on numeric variables and constants passed to them. Even if you write only a few science and engineering programs, some of these functions may be useful.

> **Note:** All mathematical and trigonometric functions are prototyped in the math.h header file. Be sure to include math.h at the top of any program that uses the numeric functions.

*These numeric functions return double-precision values.*

Here are the functions listed with their descriptions:

- `ceil(x)`: The `ceil()`, or ceiling, function rounds numbers up to the nearest integer.

- `fabs(x)`: Returns the absolute value of $x$. The absolute value of a number is its positive equivalent.

> **Tip:** Absolute value is used for distances (which are always positive), accuracy measurements, age differences, and other calculations that require a positive result.

- `floor(x)`: The `floor()` function rounds numbers down to the nearest integer.

- `fmod(x, y)`: Returns the floating-point remainder of $(x/y)$, with the same sign as $x$; $y$ cannot be zero. Because the modulus operator (%) works only with integers, this function is supplied to find the remainder of floating-point number divisions.

- `pow(x, y)`: Returns $x$ raised to the $y$ power, or $xy$. If $x$ is less than or equal to zero, $y$ must be an integer. If $x$ equals zero, $y$ cannot be negative.

- `sqrt(x)`: Returns the square root of $x$; $x$ must be greater than or equal to zero.

### The *n*th Root

No function returns the *n*th root of a number, only the square root. In other words, you cannot call a function that gives you the 4th root of 65,536. (By the way, 16 is the 4th root of 65,536, because 16 times 16 times 16 times 16 = 65,536.)

You can use a mathematical trick to simulate the *n*th root, however. Because C lets you raise a number to a fractional power—with the `pow()` function— you can raise a number to the *n*th root by raising it to the (1/*n*) power. For example, to find the 4th root of 65,536, you can type this:

```
root = pow(65536.0, (1.0/4.0));
```

Note that the decimal point keeps the numbers in floating-point format. If you leave them as integers, such as

```
root = pow(65536, (1,4));
```

C produces incorrect results. The `pow()` function and most other mathematical functions require floating-point values as arguments.

To store the 7th root of 78,125 in a variable called `root`, for example, you would type

```
root = pow(78125.0, (1.0/7.0));
```

This stores 5.0 in root because $5^7$ equals 78,125.

Knowing how to compute the *n*th root comes in handy in scientific programs and also in financial applications, such as time value of money problems.

## Example

The following program uses the `fabs()` function to compute the difference between two ages.

```
/* Filename: C22ABS.C
   Prints the difference between two ages */
#include <stdio.h>
#include <math.h>
main()
{
   float age1, age2, diff;
   printf("\nWhat is the first child's age? ");
   scanf(" %f", &age1);
   printf("What is the second child's age? ");
   scanf(" %f", &age2);
```

```
    /* Calculate the positive difference */
    diff = age1 - age2;
    diff = fabs(diff);      /* Determine the absolute value */

    printf("\nThey are %.0f years apart.", diff);
    return;
}
```

Converts *diff* to a positive value

The output from this program follows. Because of `fabs()`, the order of the ages doesn't matter. Without absolute value, this program would produce a negative age difference if the first age was less than the second. Because the ages are relatively small, floating-point variables are used in this example. C automatically converts floating-point arguments to double precision when passing them to `fabs()`.

```
What is the first child's age? 10
What is the second child's age? 12

They are 2 years apart.
```

## Trigonometric Functions

The following functions are available for trigonometric applications:

♦ `cos(x)`: Returns the cosine of the angle *x*, expressed in radians.

♦ `sin(x)`: Returns the sine of the angle *x*, expressed in radians.

♦ `tan(x)`: Returns the tangent of the angle *x*, expressed in radians.

These are probably the least-used functions. This is not to belittle the work of scientific and mathematical programmers who need them, however. Certainly they are grateful that C supplies these functions! Otherwise, programmers would have to write their own functions to perform these three basic trigonometric calculations.

Most C compilers supply additional trigonometric functions, including hyperbolic equivalents of these three functions.

**Tip:** If you need to pass an angle that is expressed in degrees to these functions, convert the angle's degrees to radians by multiplying the degrees by PI/180.0 (PI equals approximately 3.14159).

## Logarithmic Functions

Three highly mathematical functions are sometimes used in business and mathematics. They are listed as follows:

- `exp(x)`: Returns the base of natural logarithm (*e*) raised to a power specified by *x* (e*x*); *e* is the mathematical expression for the approximate value of 2.718282.

- `log(x)`: Returns the natural logarithm of the argument *x*, mathematically written as `ln(x)`. *x* must be positive.

- `log10(x)`: Returns the base-10 logarithm of argument *x*, mathematically written as `log10(x)`. *x* must be positive.

# Random-Number Processing

Random events happen every day. You wake up and it might be sunny or rainy. You might have a good day or a bad day. You might get a phone call or you might not. Your stock portfolio might go up or down in value.

Random events are especially important in games. Part of the fun in games is your luck with rolling dice or drawing cards, combined with your playing skills.

Simulating random events is an important task for computers. Computers, however, are finite machines; that is, given the same input, they *always* produce the same output. This can cause them to give you some very boring games!

The `rand()` function produces random integer numbers.

The designers of C knew this and found a way to overcome it. They wrote a random-number generating function called `rand()`. You can use `rand()` to compute a dice roll or draw a card, for example.

To call the `rand()` function and assign the returned random number to test, you use the following syntax:

```
test = rand();
```

The `rand()` function returns an integer from 0 to 32767. Never use an argument in the `rand()` parentheses.

Every time you call `rand()` in the same program, you get a different number. If you run the *same* program over and over, however, `rand()` returns the *same* set of random numbers. One way to get a different set of random numbers is to call the `srand()` function. The format of `srand()` follows:

```
srand(seed);
```

where *seed* is an integer variable or constant. If you don't call `srand()`, C assumes a *seed* value of 1.

> **Note:** The `rand()` and `srand()` functions are prototyped in the stdlib.h header file. Be sure to include stdlib.h at the top of any program that uses `rand()` or `srand()`.

The *seed* value reseeds, or resets, the random-number generator, so the *next* random number is based on the new *seed* value. If you call srand() with a different *seed* value at the top of a program, rand() returns a different random number each time you run the program.

---

**Why Do They Make Us Do This?**

There is considerable debate among C programmers concerning the random-number generator. Many think that the random numbers should be *truly* random, and that they should not have to seed the generator themselves. They think that C should do its own internal seeding when you ask for a random number.

However, many applications would no longer work if the random-number generator were randomized for you. Computers are used all the time in business, engineering, and research to simulate the pattern of real-world events. Researchers need to be able to duplicate these simulations, over and over. Even though the events inside the simulations might be random from each other, the running of the simulations cannot be random if researchers are to study several different effects. Mathematicians and statisticians also need to repeat random-number patterns for their analyses, especially when they work with risk, probability, and gaming theory.

Because so many computer users need to repeat their random-number patterns, the designers of C have wisely chosen to give you, the programmer, the option of keeping the same random patterns or changing them. The advantages far outweigh the disadvantage of including an extra srand() function call.

If you want to produce a different set of random numbers every time your program runs, you must find how your C compiler reads the computer's system clock. You can use the seconds count from the clock to seed the random-number generator so that it seems truly random.

---

## Summary

You have learned the character, string, and numeric functions that C provides. By including the ctype.h header file, you can test and convert characters that a user types. These functions have many useful purposes, such as converting a user's response to uppercase. This makes it easier for you to test user input.

The string I/O functions give you more control over both string and numeric input. You can get a string of digits from the keyboard and convert them to a number with the ato() functions. The string comparison and concatenation functions enable you to test and change the contents of more than one string.

Functions save you programming time because they take over some of your computing tasks, leaving you free to concentrate on your programs. C's numeric functions round and manipulate numbers, produce trigonometric and logarithmic results, and produce random numbers.

Now that you have learned most of C's built-in functions, you are ready to improve your ability to work with arrays. The following chapter extends your knowledge of character arrays and shows you how to produce arrays of any data type.

## Review Questions

Answers to review questions are in Appendix B.

1. How do the character testing functions differ from the character conversion functions?

2. What are the two string input functions?

3. What is the difference between `floor()` and `ceil()`?

4. What does the following nested function return?

```
isalpha(islower('s'));
```

5. If the character array str1 contains the string `Peter` and the character array str2 contains `Parker`, what does str2 contain after the following line of code executes?

```
strcat(str2, str1);
```

6. What is the output of the following `printf()`?

```
printf("%d %d", floor(8.5), ceil(8.5) );
```

7. True or false: The `isxdigit()` and `isgraph()` functions could return the same value, depending on the character passed to them.

8. Assume you define a character array with the following statement:

```
char ara[5];
```

Now suppose the user types `Programming` in response to the following statement:

```
fgets(ara, 5, stdin);
```

Would ara contain `Prog`, `Progr`, or `Programming`?

**9.** True or false: The following statements print the same results.

```
printf("%f", pow(64.0, (1.0/2.0) );
printf("%f", sqrt(64.0) );
```

# Review Exercises

**1.** Write a program that asks users for their ages. If a user types anything other than two digits, display an error message.

**2.** Write a program that stores a password in a character array called `pass`. Ask users for the password. Use `strcmp()` to let users know if they typed the proper password. Use the string I/O functions for all of the program's input and output.

**3.** Write a program that rounds up and rounds down the numbers –10.5, –5.75, and 2.75.

**4.** Ask users for their names. Print every name in reverse case; that is, print the first letter of each name in lowercase and the rest of the name in uppercase.

**5.** Write a program that asks users for five movie titles. Print the longest title. Use only the string I/O and manipulation functions presented in this chapter.

**6.** Write a program that computes the square root, cube root, and fourth root of the numbers from 10 to 25, inclusive.

**7.** Ask users for the titles of their favorite songs. Discard all the special characters in each title. Print the words in the title, one per line. For example, if they enter `My True Love Is Mine, Oh, Mine!`, you should output the following:

```
My
True
Love
Is
Mine
Oh
Mine!
```

**8.** Ask users for the first names of 10 children. Using `strcmp()` on each name, write a program to print the name that comes first in the alphabet.

# Part VI

*Arrays and Pointers*

# CHAPTER 23

# Introducing Arrays

This chapter discusses different types of arrays. You are already familiar with character arrays, which hold C character strings. A character array isn't the only kind of array you can use, however. There is an array for every data type in C. By learning how to process arrays, you greatly improve the power and efficiency of your programs.

This chapter introduces

- ♦ Array basics of names, data types, and subscripts

- ♦ Initializing an array at definition time

- ♦ Initializing an array during program execution

- ♦ Selecting elements from arrays

The sample programs in these next few chapters are some of the most advanced that you have seen in this book. Arrays are not difficult to use, but their power makes them well-suited to more advanced programming.

## Understanding Array Basics

An array is a list of more than one variable having the same name.

Although you have seen a special use of arrays as character strings, you still need a general review of arrays. An array is a *list* of more than one variable having the same name. Not all lists of variables are arrays. The following list of four variables, for example, does not qualify as an array:

```
sales      bonus_92      first_initial      ctr
```

This list contains four variables, but they don't make up an array because they each have different names. You might wonder how more than one variable can have the same name; this seems to violate the rules for variables. If two variables have the same name, how can C know which one you mean whenever you use that name?

You differentiate array variables, or array elements, by a *subscript*, which is a number inside brackets. Suppose you want to store a person's name in a character array called name. You know you can do this with

```
char name[] = "Ray Krebbs";
```

or

```
char name[11] = "Ray Krebbs";
```

Because C knows to reserve an extra element for the null zero at the end of every string, you don't need to specify the 11 as long as you initialize the array with a value. The variable name is an array because brackets follow its name. The array has a single name called name, and it contains 11 elements. The array is stored in memory, as shown in Figure 23.1. Each element is a character.

> **Note:** All array subscripts begin with 0.

You can manipulate individual elements in the array by their subscripts. For instance, the following printf() function prints Ray's initials.

**Figure 23.1**

Storing the *name* character array in memory.

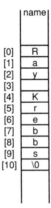

```
name
[0]   R
[1]   a
[2]   y
[3]
[4]   K
[5]   r
[6]   e
[7]   b
[8]   b
[9]   s
[10]  \0
```

*Print the first and fifth elements of the array called name.*

```
printf("%c. %c", name[0], name[4]);
```

You can define an array as any data type in C. You can have integer arrays, long integer arrays, double floating-point arrays, short integer arrays, and so on. C recognizes that you are defining an array, and not a single nonarray variable, when you put brackets, [], after the array name.

The following line defines an array called ages, consisting of five integers:

```
int ages[5];
```

The first element in the ages array is ages[0]. The second element is ages[1], and the last one is ages[4]. This definition of ages does not assign values to the elements, so you don't know what is *in* ages and your program cannot assume that it contains zeros or anything else.

Here are some more array definitions:

```
int weights[25], sizes[100];    /* Define two integer arrays */
float salaries[8];              /* Define a floating-point array */
double temps[50];    /* Define a double floating-point array */
char letters[15];               /* Define an array of letters */
```

When you define an array, you instruct C to reserve a specific number of memory locations for that array. C protects those elements. If you assign a value to letters[2] in the previous lines of code, you don't overwrite any data in weights, sizes, salaries, or temps. Also, if you assign a value to sizes[94], you don't overwrite data stored in weights, salaries, temps, or letters.

Array elements follow each other in memory, with nothing between them.

Each element in an array occupies the same amount of storage as a nonarray variable of the same data type. In other words, each element in a character array occupies one byte. Each element in an integer array occupies two or more bytes of memory—depending on the computer's internal architecture. The same is true for every other data type.

Your program may reference elements by using formulas for subscripts. As long as the subscript can evaluate to an integer, you can use a constant, a variable, or an expression for the subscript. The following are references to individual array elements:

```
ara[4]
sales[ctr+1]
bonus[month]
salary[month[i]*2]
```

C stores all array elements in a contiguous, back-to-back fashion. This is important to remember, especially as you write more advanced programs. You can *always* count on an array's first element preceding the second. The second element always appears immediately before the third, and so on. Memory is not "padded"; that is, C ensures and guarantees there is no extra space between array elements. This is true for character arrays, integer arrays, floating-point arrays, and every other type of array. If a floating-point value occupies four bytes of memory on your computer, the *next* element in a floating-point array *always* begins exactly four bytes after that previous element.

---

**The Size of Arrays**

The `sizeof()` function returns the number of bytes needed to hold its argument. If you request the size of an array name, `sizeof()` returns the number of bytes *reserved* for the entire array.

For example, suppose that you define an integer array of 100 elements called `scores`. If you were to find the size of the array, as in the following:

```
n = sizeof(scores);
```

n holds either 200 or 400, depending on the integer size of your computer. The `sizeof()` function always returns the reserved amount of storage, no matter what data is in the array. Therefore, a character array's contents— even if it holds a very short string—does *not* affect the size of the array that was originally reserved in memory.

If you request the size of an individual array element, however, as in the following:

```
n = sizeof(scores[6]);
```

n holds either 2 or 4, depending on the integer size of your computer.

---

You must never go out-of-bounds of any array. For example, suppose that you want to keep track of the exemptions and salary codes of five employees. You can reserve two arrays to hold such data like this:

```
int  exemptions[5];  /* Holds up to 5 employee exemptions */
char salCodes[5];        /* Holds up to 5 employee codes */
```

Figure 23.2 shows how C reserves memory for these arrays. The figure assumes a two-byte integer size, although this may differ on some computers. Notice that C "knows" to reserve five elements for `exemptions` from the array definition. C starts reserving memory for `salCodes` *after* it reserves all five elements for `exemptions`. If you define several *more* variables—either locally or globally—after these two lines, C always protects these reserved five elements for `exemptions` and `salCodes`.

**Figure 23.2**

Locating two
arrays in memory.

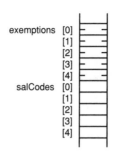

C protects only as
many array
elements as you
specify.

Because C does its part to protect the data in the array, so must you. If you reserve five elements for `exemptions`, you have five integer array elements referred to as `exemptions[0]`, `exemptions[1]`, `exemptions[2]`, `exemptions[3]`, and `exemptions[4]`. C *does not* protect more than five elements for `exemptions`! Suppose that you put a value into an `exemptions` element that you did not reserve:

```
exemptions[6] = 4; /* Assign a value to an out-of-range element */
```

C lets you do this—but the results are damaging! C overwrites *other* data (in this case, `salCodes[2]` and `salCodes[3]` because they are reserved where the sixth element of `exemptions` must be placed). Figure 23.3 shows the damaging results of assigning a value to an out-of-range element.

**Caution:** Unlike most programming languages, ANSI C lets you assign values to out-of-range (nonreserved) subscripts. You must be very careful *not* to do this; otherwise, you start overwriting your other data or code.

**Figure 23.3**

The arrays in
memory after
overwriting part of
*salCodes*.

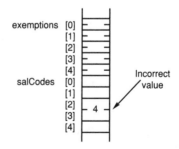

Although you can define an array of any data type, you cannot define an array of strings. A *string* is not a C variable data type. You learn how to hold multiple strings in an array-like structure in Chapter 27, "Pointers and Arrays."

> **For Related Information**
>
> ♦ "Character Arrays," p. 77
>
> ♦ "Character Arrays versus Strings," p. 81

# Initializing Arrays

You must assign values to array elements before using them. Here are the two ways to initialize elements in an array:

♦ Initialize the elements at definition time

♦ Initialize the elements in the program

> **Note:** C automatically initializes global arrays to null zeros. Therefore, global character array elements are all null, and numeric array elements all contain zero. You should limit your use of global arrays. If you use global arrays, explicitly initialize them to zero, even though C does this for you, to clarify your intentions.

## Initializing Elements at Definition Time

You already know how to initialize character arrays that hold strings when you define the arrays: you simply assign them a string. For example, the following definition reserves six elements in a character array called `city`:

```
char city[6];                    /* Reserve space for city */
```

If you also want to initialize `city` with a value, you can do it like this:

```
char city[6] = "Tulsa";          /* Reserve space and
                                    initialize city */
```

The 6 is optional because C counts the elements needed to hold `Tulsa`, plus an extra element for the null zero at the end of the quoted string.

You also can reserve a character array and initialize it—a single character at a time—by using braces around the character data. The following line of code defines an array called `initials` and initializes it with eight characters:

```
char initials[8] = {'Q', 'K', 'P', 'G', 'V', 'M', 'U', 'S'};
```

The array `initials` is *not a string*! Its data does not end in a null zero. There is nothing wrong with defining an array of characters such as this one, but you must remember that you cannot treat the array as if it were a string. Do not use string functions with it or attempt to print the array with the `%s printf()` format code.

By using braces, you can initialize any type of array. For example, if you want to initialize an integer array that holds your five children's ages, you can do it with the following definition:

```
int childAges[5] = {2, 5, 6, 8, 12};    /* Define and
                                            initialize array */
```

In another example, if you want to keep track of the last three years' total sales, you can define an array and initialize it at the same time with the following:

```
double sales[] = {454323.43, 122355.32, 343324.96};
```

As with character arrays, you do not need to state explicitly the array size when you define and initialize an array of any type. C knows, in this case, to reserve three double floating-point array elements for `sales`. Figure 23.4 shows the representation of `childAges` and `sales` in memory.

**Figure 23.4**

In-memory representation of two different types of arrays.

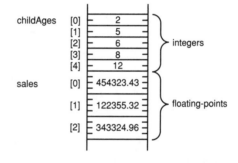

**Note:** You cannot initialize an array, using the assignment operator and braces, *after* you define it. You can initialize arrays in this manner only when you define them. If you want to fill an array with data after you define the array, you must do so element-by-element or by using functions as described in the next section.

C zeros all array values that you do not define explicitly.

Although C does not automatically zero-out (or initialize to *any* value) array elements, if you initialize some (but not all) of the elements when you define the array, C finishes the job for you by assigning the remainder to zero.

**Tip:** To initialize every element of a large array to zero at the same time, define the entire array and initialize its first value to zero. C finishes filling in the rest of the array to zero.

For instance, suppose you need to reserve array storage for profit figures of the three previous months as well as the three months to follow. You need to reserve six elements of storage, but you know values for only the first three of them. You can initialize the array as follows:

```
double profit[6] = {67654.43, 46472.34, 63451.93};
```

Because you explicitly initialized three of the elements, C initializes the rest to zero. If you use an appropriate `printf()` to print the entire array, one element per line, you get

```
67654.43
46472.34
63451.93
00000.00
00000.00
00000.00
```

**Caution:** Always define an array with the maximum number of subscripts, unless you initialize the array at the same time. The following array definition is illegal:

```
int count[];                 /* Bad array definition! */
```

C does not know how many elements to reserve for `count`, so it reserves *none*. If you then assign values to `count`'s nonreserved elements, you may (and probably would) overwrite other data.

The only time you can leave the brackets empty is if you also assign values to the array, such as the following:

```
int count[] = {15, 9, 22, -8, 12}; /* Good definition */
```

C can tell, from the list of values, how many elements to reserve. In this case, C reserves five elements for `count`.

## Examples

1. Suppose that you want to track the stock market averages for the last 90 days. Instead of storing them in 90 different variables, it is much easier to store them in an array. You can define the array like this:

```
float stock[90];
```

The rest of the program can assign values to the averages.

2. Suppose that you just finished taking classes at a local university and want to average your six class scores. The following program initializes one array for the school name and another for the six classes. The body of the program averages each of the six scores.

```
/* Filename: C23ARA1.C
   Averages six test scores */
#include <stdio.h>
main()
{
   char sName[] = "Tri Star University";
   float scores[6] = {88.7, 90.4, 76.0, 97.0, 100.0, 86.7};
   float average=0.0;
   int ctr;

   /* Compute total of scores */
   for (ctr=0; ctr<6; ctr++)
      { average += scores[ctr]; }

   /* Compute the average */
   average /= (float)6;

   printf("At %s, your class average is %.1f.", sName,
           average);
   return;
}
```

The 6 values in the *scores* array

The output follows:

```
At Tri Star University, your class average is 89.8.
```

Notice that using arrays makes processing lists of information much easier. Instead of averaging six differently named variables, you can use a `for` loop to step through each array element. If you have to average 1000 numbers, you can still do so with a simple `for` loop, as in this example. If the 1000 variables were not in an array, but were individually named, you would need to write a considerable amount of code just to add them.

**3.** The following program is an expanded version of the previous one. It prints the six scores before computing the average. Notice that you must print array elements individually; you cannot print an entire array in a single `printf()`. (You can print an entire character array with `%s`, but only if it holds a null-terminated string of characters.)

```
/* Filename: C23ARA2.C
   Prints and averages six test scores */
#include <stdio.h>
void prScores(float scores[]);
```

```
main()
{
    char sName[] = "Tri Star University";
    float scores[6] = {88.7, 90.4, 76.0, 97.0, 100.0, 86.7};
    float average=0.0;
    int ctr;

    /* Call function to print scores */
    prScores(scores);

    /* Compute total of scores */
    for (ctr=0; ctr<6; ctr++)
       { average += scores[ctr]; }

    /* Compute the average */
    average /= (float)6;

    printf("At %s, your class average is %.1f.",
            sName, average);
    return 0;
}

void prScores(float scores[6])
{
    /* Prints the six scores */
    int ctr;

    printf("Here are your scores:\n");               /* Title */
    for (ctr=0; ctr<6; ctr++)
      printf("%.1f\n", scores[ctr]);
    return;
}
```

Receives the array

To pass an array to a function, you need to specify only its name. In the receiving function's parameter list, you must state the array type and include its brackets, which tell the function that it is an array. (You do not explicitly need to state the array size in the receiving parameter list as shown in the prototype.)

4. To improve the maintainability of your programs, define all array sizes with the #define preprocessor directive. What if you took four classes next semester but still wanted to use the same program? You could modify it by

changing all the 6s to 4s, but if you had defined the array size with a
defined constant, you would have to change only one line in order to
change the program's subscript limits. Notice how the following program
uses a defined constant for the number of classes.

```c
/* Filename: C23ARA3.C
   Prints and averages six test scores */
#include <stdio.h>
void prScores(float scores[]);
#define CLASSNUM 6

main()
{
   char sName[] = "Tri Star University";
   float scores[CLASSNUM] = {88.7, 90.4, 76.0, 97.0,
                             100.0, 86.7};
   float average=0.0;
   int ctr;

   /* Call function to print scores */
   prScores(scores);

   /* Compute total of scores */
   for (ctr=0; ctr<CLASSNUM; ctr++)
      { average += scores[ctr]; }

   /* Compute the average */
   average /= (float)CLASSNUM;

   printf("At %s, your class average is %.1f.",
          sName, average);
   return 0;
}

void prScores(float scores[CLASSNUM])
{
   /* Prints the six scores */
   int ctr;

   printf("Here are your scores:\n");              /* Title */
   for (ctr=0; ctr<CLASSNUM; ctr++)
     printf("%.1f\n", scores[ctr]);
   return;
}
```

Makes array size
easy to change ——

For such a simple example, using a defined constant for the maximum subscript may not seem like a big advantage. If you were writing a larger program that processed several arrays, however, changing the defined constant at the top of the program would be much easier than searching the program for each occurrence of that array reference.

Using defined constants for array sizes has the added advantage of protecting you from going out of the subscript bounds. You do not have to remember the subscript when looping through arrays; you can use the defined constant instead.

## Initializing Elements in the Program

Rarely do you know the contents of arrays when you define them. Usually, you fill an array with user input or a disk file's data. The for loop is a perfect tool for looping through arrays when you fill them with values.

> **Caution:** An array name cannot appear on the left side of an assignment statement.

You cannot assign one array to another. Suppose that you want to copy an array called totalSales to a second array called savedSales. You *cannot* do so with the following assignment statement:

```
savedSales = totalSales;                    /* Invalid! */
```

Rather, you have to copy the arrays one element at a time, using a loop, such as the following section of code does.

*You want to copy one array to another. You have to do so one element at a time, so you need a counter. Initialize a variable called ctr to 0; the value of ctr will represent a position in the array.*

1. *Assign the element that occupies the position in the first array represented by the value of ctr to the same position in the second array.*

2. *If the counter is less than the size of the array, add 1 to the counter. Repeat step 1.*

```
for (ctr=0; ctr<ARRAYSIZE; ctr++)
        { savedSales[ctr] = totalSales[ctr]; }
```

The following examples illustrate methods for initializing arrays in a program. After learning about disk processing later in the book, you learn to read array values from a disk file.

## Examples

**1.** The following program uses the assignment operator to assign 10 temperatures to an array.

```
/* Filename: C23ARA4.C
   Fill an array with ten temperature values */
#include <stdio.h>
#define NUMTEMPS 10
main()
{
   float temps[NUMTEMPS];
   int ctr;

   temps[0] = 78.6;          /* Subscripts always begin at 0 */
   temps[1] = 82.1;
   temps[2] = 79.5;
   temps[3] = 75.0;
   temps[4] = 75.4;
   temps[5] = 71.8;
   temps[6] = 73.3;
   temps[7] = 69.5;
   temps[8] = 74.1;
   temps[9] = 75.7;

   /* Print the temps */
   printf("Daily temperatures for the last %d days:\n",
          NUMTEMPS);
   for (ctr=0; ctr<NUMTEMPS; ctr++)
      { printf("%.1f \n", temps[ctr]); }

   return;
}
```

Fill up the array

**2.** The following program uses a `for` loop and `scanf()` to assign eight integers entered individually by the user. The program then prints a total of all the numbers.

```
/* Filename: C23TOT.C
   Totals eight input values from the user */
#include <stdio.h>
#define NUM 8
main()
}
```

```
int nums[NUM];
int total = 0;          /* Holds total of user's 8 numbers */
int ctr;
for (ctr=0; ctr<NUM; ctr++)
  { printf("Please enter the next number...");
    scanf("%d", &nums[ctr]);
    total += nums[ctr]; }

printf("The total of the numbers is %d", total);
return;
}
```

3. You don't have to access an array in the same order as you initialized it. The next chapter, "Array Processing," shows you how to change the order of an array. You also can use the subscript to select items from an array of values.

The following program requests sales data for the preceding 12 months. Users can then type a month they want to see. That month's sales figure is then printed, without figures from other months getting in the way. This is how you begin to build a search program to find requested data: You store the data in an array (or in a disk file that you can read into an array, as you learn later) and then wait for a user's request to see specific pieces of the data.

```
/* Filename: C23SAL.C
   Stores twelve months of sales and
   prints selected ones */
#include <stdio.h>
#include <ctype.h>
#define NUM 12
main()
{
   float sales[NUM];
   int ctr, ans;
   int reqMonth;                    /* Holds user's request */

   /* Fill the array */
   printf("Please enter the twelve monthly sales values\n");
   for (ctr=0; ctr<NUM; ctr++)
     { printf("What are sales for month number %d\n", ctr+1);
       scanf("%f", &sales[ctr]); }
```

Gets each month's data in an array

```
/* Wait for a requested month */
for (ctr=0; ctr<25; ctr++)
{ printf("\n"); }                    /* Clear the screen */

printf("*** Sales Printing Program ***\n");
   printf("Prints any sales from the last %d months\n\n",
          NUM);
   do
     { printf("\nWhat month (1-%d) do you want to see a");
       printf(" sales value for?",NUM);
       scanf("%d", &reqMonth);
       /* Adjust for zero-based subscript */
       printf("\nMonth %d's sales are %.2f",reqMonth,
              sales[reqMonth-1]);
       printf("\nDo you want to see another (Y/N)? ");
       ans=getch();
       ans=toupper(ans);
     } while (ans == 'Y');
   return;
}
```

Notice the helpful screen-clearing routine that prints 23 newline characters. This scrolls the screen until it is blank. (Most compilers come with a better built-in screen-clearing function, but the ANSI C standard does not offer one because the compiler would be too closely linked with specific hardware.)

Figure 23.5 shows the second screen from this program. After you enter the 12 sales values into the array, you can request any or all of them, one at a time, simply by supplying the month's number (that is, the number of the subscript).

## Summary

You now know how to define and initialize arrays consisting of various data types. You can initialize an array either when you define it or in the body of your program. Array elements are much easier to process than many variables that each have a different name.

C has powerful sorting and searching techniques that make your programs even more serviceable. The next chapter introduces these techniques and shows you still other ways to access array elements.

**Figure 23.5**

Printing
individually
requested values
from an array.

```
*** Sales Printing Program ***
Prints any sales from the last 12 months


What month (1-12) do you want to see a sales value for?1

Month 1's sales are 3233.45
Do you want to see another (Y/N)?
What month (1-12) do you want to see a sales value for?5

Month 5's sales are 6535.64
Do you want to see another (Y/N)?
What month (1-12) do you want to see a sales value for?2

Month 2's sales are 6434.67
Do you want to see another (Y/N)?
What month (1-12) do you want to see a sales value for?8

Month 8's sales are 4598.79
Do you want to see another (Y/N)?
```

# Review Questions

Answers to review questions are in Appendix B.

1. True or false: A single array can hold several values of different data types.

2. How do C programs tell one array element from another if all elements have identical names?

3. Why must you initialize an array before using it?

4. Given the following definition of an array, called weights, what is the value of weights[5]?

   ```
   int weights[10] = {5, 2, 4};
   ```

5. If you pass an integer array to a function and change it, does the array get changed also in the calling function? (Hint: Remember how C passes character arrays to functions.)

6. How does C initialize global array elements?

# Review Exercises

1. Write a program to store the ages of six of your friends in a single array. Store each of the six ages using the assignment operator. Print the ages on-screen.

2. Modify the program in #1 to print the ages backwards.

**3.** Write a simple data program to track a radio station's ratings (1, 2, 3, 4, or 5) for the previous 18 months. Use `scanf()` to initialize the array with the ratings. Print the ratings on-screen with an appropriate title.

**4.** Write a program to store the numbers from 1 to 100 in an array of 100 integer elements. (Hint: The subscripts should begin at 0 and end at 99.)

**5.** Write a program that a small business owner could use to track customers. Assign each customer a number (starting at 0). Whenever a customer purchases something, store the sale in the element that matches the

# CHAPTER 24

# Array Processing

C provides many ways to access arrays. If you have programmed in other computer languages, you will find that some of C's array indexing techniques are different. Arrays in the C language are closely linked with *pointers.* Chapter 26, "Pointers," describes the many ways pointers and arrays interact. Because pointers are so powerful, and because learning arrays well provides a good foundation for learning about pointers, this chapter attempts to describe in detail how to reference arrays.

This chapter discusses the different types of array processing. You will learn how to search an array for one or more values, find the highest and lowest values in an array, and sort an array into numerical or alphabetical order.

This chapter introduces the following concepts:

♦ Searching arrays

♦ Finding the highest and lowest values in arrays

♦ Sorting arrays

♦ Advanced subscripting with arrays

Many programmers see arrays as a turning point. Gaining an understanding of array processing will make your programs more accurate and allow for more powerful programming.

## Searching Arrays

Array elements do not always appear in the order in which they are needed.

Arrays are one of the primary means by which data is stored in C programs. Many types of programs lend themselves to processing lists (arrays) of data, such as an employee payroll program, a scientific research of several chemicals, or customer account processing. As mentioned in the previous chapter, array data usually is read from a disk file. Later chapters describe disk file processing. For now, you should understand how to manipulate arrays so that you see the data exactly the way you want to see it.

Chapter 23, "Introducing Arrays," shows how to print arrays in the same order that you entered the data. This is sometimes done, but it is not always the most appropriate method of looking at data.

For instance, suppose that a high school used C programs for its grade reports. Suppose also that the school wanted to see a list of the top 10 grade-point averages. You could not print the first 10 grade-point averages in the list of student averages because the top 10 GPAs might not (and probably will not) appear as the first 10 array elements. Because the GPAs would not be in any sequence, the program would have to sort the array into numeric order, from high GPAs to low, or else search the array for the 10 highest GPAs.

You need a method for putting arrays in a specific order. This is called *sorting* an array. When you sort an array, you put that array in a specific order, such as in alphabetical or numerical order. A dictionary is in sorted order, and so is a phone book.

When you reverse the order of a sort, it is called a *descending sort*. For instance, if you wanted to look at a list of all employees in descending salary order, the highest-paid employees would be printed first.

Figure 24.1 shows a list of eight numbers in an array called unsorted. The middle list of numbers is an ascending sorted version of unsorted. The third list of numbers is a descending sorted version of unsorted.

**Figure 24.1**

A list of unsorted numbers sorted into an ascending and a descending order.

| Unsorted | Ascending order | Descending order |
|:---:|:---:|:---:|
| 6 | 1 | 8 |
| 1 | 2 | 7 |
| 2 | 3 | 6 |
| 4 | 4 | 5 |
| 7 | 5 | 4 |
| 8 | 6 | 3 |
| 3 | 7 | 2 |
| 5 | 8 | 1 |

Before you learn to sort, it would be helpful to learn how to search an array for a value. This is a preliminary step in learning to sort. What if one of those students received a grade change? The computer must be able to access that specific student's grade to change it (without affecting the others). As the next section shows, programs can search for specific array elements.

> **Note:** C provides a method for sorting and searching lists of strings, but you cannot understand how to do this until you learn about pointers, starting in Chapter 26, "Pointers." The sorting and searching examples and algorithms presented in this chapter demonstrate sorting and searching arrays of numbers. The same concepts will apply (and will actually be much more usable for "real-world" applications) when you learn how to store lists of names in C.

## Searching for Values

You do not have to sort an array to find its extreme values.

You do not need to know any new commands to search an array for a value. Basically, the `if` and `for` loop statements are all you need. To search an array for a specific value, look at each element in that array, comparing with the `if` statement to see whether they match. If they do not, keep searching down the array. If you run out of array elements before finding the value, it is not in the array.

You can perform several different kinds of searches. You might need to find the highest or the lowest value in a list of numbers. This is informative when you have much data and want to know the extremes of the data (such as the highest and lowest sales region in your division). You also can search an array to see whether it contains a matching value. For example, you can see whether an item is already in an inventory by searching a part number array for a match.

The following programs illustrate some of these array-searching techniques.

### Examples

1. To find the highest number in an array, compare each element with the first one. If you find a higher value, it becomes the basis for the rest of the array. Continue until you reach the end of the array and you will have the highest value, as the following program shows.

*Identify the program and include the I/O header file. We want to find the highest value in an array, so define the array size as a constant and then initialize the array.*

*Loop through the array, comparing each element to the highest value. If an element is higher than the highest value saved, store the element as the new high value. Print the highest value found in the array.*

```
/* Filename: C24HIGH.C
   Finds the highest value in the array */
#include <stdio.h>
#define SIZE 15
main()
{
   /* Puts some numbers in the array */
   int ara[SIZE]={5,2,7,8,36,4,2,86,11,43,22,12,45,6,85};
   int highVal, ctr;

   highVal = ara[0];                /* Initializes with first
                                       array element */
   for (ctr=1; ctr<SIZE; ctr++)
      {                      /* Stores current value if it is
                               higher than the highest so far */
         if (ara[ctr] > highVal)
            { highVal = ara[ctr]; }
      }

   printf("The highest number in the list is %d.", highVal);
   return;
}
```

Stores the high value if it's found

The output of the program is the following:

```
The highest number in the list is 86.
```

You have to save the element if and only if it is higher than the one you are comparing. Finding the smallest number in an array is just as easy, except that you compare to see whether each succeeding array element is less than the lowest value found so far.

2. The following example expands on the preceding one by finding the highest and the lowest value. First, store the first array element in *both* the highest and the lowest variable to begin the search. This ensures that each element after that one is tested to see whether it is higher or lower than the first.

This example also uses the rand() function from Chapter 22, "Character, String, and Numeric Functions," to fill the array with random values from 0 to 99 by applying the modulus operator (%) and 100 against whatever value rand() produces. The program prints the entire array before starting the search for the highest and the lowest.

```
/*   Filename: C24HILO.C
     Finds the highest and the lowest value in the array */
     #include <stdio.h>
     #include <stdlib.h>
     #define SIZE 15
     main()
     {
     int ara[SIZE];
     int highVal, lowVal, ctr;

     /* Fills array with random numbers from 0 to 99 */
     for (ctr=0; ctr<SIZE; ctr++)
       { ara[ctr] = rand() % 100; }

     /* Prints the array to the screen */
     printf("Here are the %d random numbers:\n",
            SIZE);                                        /* Title */
     for (ctr=0; ctr<SIZE; ctr++)
       {  printf("%4d\n", ara[ctr]); }

     printf("\n\n");                         /* Prints a blank line */

     highVal = ara[0];     /* Initializes first element to
                                     both high and low */
     lowVal  = ara[0];

     for (ctr=1; ctr<SIZE; ctr++)
       {                       /* Stores current value if it is
                                  higher than the highest so far */
         if (ara[ctr] > highVal)
           { highVal = ara[ctr]; }
         if (ara[ctr] < lowVal)
           { lowVal = ara[ctr]; }
       }

     printf("The highest number in the list is %d.\n",
            highVal);
     printf("The lowest number in the list is %d.\n",
            lowVal);
     return;
     }
```

Saves lowest
value if it's found

Figure 24.2 shows the output from this program.

**Figure 24.2**

Printing the highest and the lowest values in a list of random numbers.

```
Here are the 15 random numbers:
   46
   30
   82
   90
   56
   17
   95
   15
   48
   26
    4
   58
   71
   79
   92

The highest number in the list is 95.
The lowest number in the list is 4.
```

**3.** The next program fills an array with part numbers from an inventory. For this example, assignment statements initialize the array. The important idea from this program is not the array initialization, but the method for searching the array.

**Note:** If the newly entered part number is already on file, the program tells the user. Otherwise, the part number is added to the end of the array.

```c
/* Filename: C24SERCH.C
   Searches a part number array for the input value. If
   the entered part number is not in the array, it is
   added. If the part number is in the array, a message
   is printed. */
#include <stdio.h>
#define MAX 100
void fillParts(long int parts[MAX]);

main()
{
   long int searchPart;              /* Holds user request */
   long int parts[MAX];
   int ctr;
   int numParts=5;              /* Beginning inventory count */

   fillParts(parts);     /* Fills the first five elements */
   do
   {
```

```
        printf("\n\nPlease type a part number...");
        printf("(-9999 ends program) ");
        scanf("%ld", &searchPart);
        if (searchPart == -9999)
           { break; }                    /* Exits loop if user wants */
        /* Scan array to see whether part is in inventory */
        for (ctr=0; ctr<numParts; ctr++) /* Checks each item */
        { if (searchPart == parts[ctr])        /* If it is in
                                                   inventory...*/
             { printf("\nPart %ld is already in inventory",
                       searchPart);
               break;
             }
          else
           { if (ctr == (numParts-1) )      /* If not there,
                                               adds it */
             { parts[numParts] = searchPart;    /* Adds to
                                                   end of
                                                   array */
               numParts++;
               printf("\n%ld was added to inventory\n",
                       searchPart);
               break;
             }
           }
        }
     } while (searchPart != -9999);        /* Loops until user
                                              signals end */
     return 0;
}

void fillParts(long int parts[MAX])
{
   /* Assigns five part numbers to array for testing */
   parts[0] = 12345;
   parts[1] = 24724;
   parts[2] = 54154;
   parts[3] = 73496;
   parts[4] = 83925;
   return;
}
```

Looks for a match in the array

413

Figure 24.3 shows the output from this program.

**Figure 24.3**

Searching a table of part numbers.

```
Please type a part number...(-9999 ends program) 25432

25432 was added to inventory

Please type a part number...(-9999 ends program) 12345

Part 12345 is already in inventory

Please type a part number...(-9999 ends program) 65468

65468 was added to inventory

Please type a part number...(-9999 ends program) 25432

Part 25432 is already in inventory

Please type a part number...(-9999 ends program) 43234
```

# Sorting Arrays

*The lowest values in the list "float" to the top with the bubble sort algorithm.*

There are many times when you need to sort one or more arrays. Suppose that you were to take a list of numbers, write each number on a separate piece of paper, and throw all the pieces of paper into the air. The steps you would take—shuffling and changing the order of the pieces of paper, trying to put them in order—would be similar to what your computer goes through to sort numbers or character data into a sorted order.

Because sorting arrays requires exchanging values of elements back and forth, it helps if you first learn the technique for swapping variables. Suppose that you had two variables named score1 and score2. What if you wanted to reverse their values (putting score2 into the score1 variable, and vice versa)? You could not do this:

```
score1 = score2;   /* Does not swap the two values */
score2 = score1;
```

Why doesn't this work? In the first line, the value of score1 gets replaced with score2's value. When the first line finishes, both score1 and score2 contain the same value. Therefore, the second line cannot work as desired.

To swap two variables, you need to use a third variable to hold the intermediate result. (This is the only function of this third variable.) For instance, to swap score1 and score2, use a third variable (called holdScore in this code), as in

```
holdScore = score1;   /* These three lines properly */
score1 = score2;      /* swap score1 and score2     */
score2 = holdScore;
```

This exchanges the two values in the two variables.

There are several different ways to sort arrays. These methods include the *bubble sort*, the *quicksort*, and the *shell sort*. The basic goal of each method is to compare each array element to another array element and swap them if the higher one is less than the other.

The theory behind these sorts is beyond the scope of this book; however, the bubble sort is one of the easiest to understand. Values in the array are compared to each other, a pair at a time, and swapped if they are not in back-to-back order. The lowest value eventually "floats" to the top of the array, like a bubble in a glass of soda.

Figure 24.4 (p.417) shows a list of numbers before, during, and after a bubble sort. The bubble sort steps through the array, comparing pairs of numbers, to see whether they need to be swapped. The program might have to make several passes through the array before it is finally sorted (no more passes are needed). Other types of sorts improve on the bubble sort. The bubble sort procedure is easy to program, but it is slower compared to many of the other methods.

The following programs show the bubble sort in action.

## Examples

1. The following program assigns 10 random numbers between 0 and 99 to an array, then sorts the array. A nested `for` loop is perfect for sorting numbers in the array (as shown in the `sortArray()` function). Nested `for` loops provide a nice mechanism for working on pairs of values, swapping them if needed. As the outside loop counts down the list, referencing each element, the inside loop compares each of the remaining values to those array elements.

```
/* Filename: C24SORT1.C
   Sorts and prints a list of numbers */
#define MAX 10
#include <stdio.h>
#include <stdlib.h>
void fillArray(int ara[MAX]);
void printArray(int ara[MAX]);
void sortArray(int ara[MAX]);

main()
{
   int ara[MAX];

   fillArray(ara);      /* Puts random numbers in the array */

   printf("Here are the unsorted numbers:\n");
   printArray(ara);              /* Prints the unsorted array */

   sortArray(ara);                       /* Sorts the array */
```

```
      printf("\n\nHere are the sorted numbers:\n");
      printArray(ara);        /* Prints the newly sorted array */
      return 0;
}

void fillArray(int ara[MAX])
{
   /* Puts random numbers in the array */
   int ctr;
   for (ctr=0; ctr<MAX; ctr++)
      { ara[ctr] = (rand() % 100); }    /* Forces number to
                                           0-99 range */

   return;
}

void printArray(int ara[MAX])
{
   /* Prints the array */
   int ctr;
   for (ctr=0; ctr<MAX; ctr++)
      { printf("%d\n", ara[ctr]); }
   return;
}

void sortArray(int ara[MAX])
{
   /* Sorts the array */
   int temp;            /* Temporary variable to swap with */
   int ctr1, ctr2;            /* Need two loop counters to */
                              /*   swap pairs of numbers   */
   for (ctr1=0; ctr1<(MAX-1); ctr1++)
      { for (ctr2=(ctr1+1); ctr2<MAX; ctr2++)/* Test pairs */
          { if (ara[ctr1] > ara[ctr2])    /* Swap if this */
              { temp = ara[ctr1]; /* pair is not in order */
                ara[ctr1] = ara[ctr2];
                ara[ctr2] = temp;   /* "float" the lowest
                                        to the highest */
      }
             }
         }
      return;
}
```

Fills array with random values

Swaps if the pair is out of order

**Figure 24.4**

Sorting a list of numbers using the bubble sort.

First Pass

| | | | |
|---|---|---|---|
| 3 | 2 | 2 | 2 |
| 2 | 3 | 3 | 3 |
| 5 | 5 | 1 | 1 |
| 1 | 1 | 5 | 4 |
| 4 | 4 | 4 | 5 |

Second Pass

| | |
|---|---|
| 2 | 2 |
| 3 | 1 |
| 1 | 3 |
| 4 | 4 |
| 5 | 5 |

Third Pass

| | |
|---|---|
| 2 | 1 |
| 1 | 2 |
| 3 | 3 |
| 4 | 4 |
| 5 | 5 |

Fourth Pass

| |
|---|
| 1 |
| 2 |
| 3 |
| 4 |
| 5 |

Figure 24.5 shows the output from this program. If any two randomly generated numbers were the same, the bubble sort would work properly, placing them next to each other in the list.

**Figure 24.5**

Searching a table of part numbers.

```
Here are the unsorted numbers:
46
30
82
90
56
17
95
15
48
26


Here are the sorted numbers:
15
17
26
30
46
48
56
82
90
95
```

2. The following program is just like the last, except it prints the list of numbers in descending order.

A descending sort is as easy to write as an ascending sort. With the ascending sort (from low to high values), you compare pairs of values, testing to see whether the first is greater than the second. With a descending sort, you test to see whether the first is less than the second one.

To produce a descending sort, use the less-than (<) logical operator when swapping array elements.

```c
/* Filename: C24SORT2.C
   Sorts and prints a list of numbers in reverse
   and descending order */
#define MAX 10
#include <stdio.h>
#include <stdlib.h>
void fillArray(int ara[MAX]);
void printArray(int ara[MAX]);
void sortArray(int ara[MAX]);

main()
{
   int ara[MAX];

   fillArray(ara);      /* Puts random numbers in the array */

   printf("Here are the unsorted numbers:\n");
   printArray(ara);              /* Prints the unsorted array */

   sortArray(ara);                      /* Sorts the array */
```

```
   printf("\n\nHere are the sorted numbers:\n");
   printArray(ara);          /* Prints the newly sorted array */
   return 0;
}

void fillArray(int ara[MAX])
{
   /* Puts random numbers in the array */
   int ctr;
   for (ctr=0; ctr<MAX; ctr++)
      { ara[ctr] = (rand() % 100); }         /* Forces number
                                                to 0-99 range */
   return;
}

void printArray(int ara[MAX])
{
   /* Prints the array */
   int ctr;
   for (ctr=0; ctr<MAX; ctr++)
      { printf("%d\n", ara[ctr]); }
   return;
}

void sortArray(int ara[MAX])
{
   /* Sorts the array */
   int temp;                /* Temporary variable to swap with */
   int ctr1, ctr2;              /* Need two loop counters     */
                                /*   to swap pairs of numbers */
   for (ctr1=0; ctr1<(MAX-1); ctr1++)
      { for (ctr2=(ctr1+1); ctr2<MAX; ctr2++)/* Test pairs */
           /* Notice the difference in descending (here)
               and ascending */
              { if (ara[ctr1] < ara[ctr2]) /* Swap if this    */
                   { temp = ara[ctr1]; /* pair is not in order */
                     ara[ctr1] = ara[ctr2];
                     ara[ctr2] = temp;  /* "float" the lowest
                                           to the highest   */
                   }
              }
         }
   return;
}
```

Causes a descending sort

> **Tip:** You can save the previous programs' sort functions in two separate files named `sortAscend` and `sortDescend`. When you need to sort two different arrays, include these files inside your own programs. Even better, compile each of these routines separately and link the one you need to your program. (You must check your compiler's manual to learn how to do this.)

You can sort character arrays just as easily as you sort numeric arrays. C uses the ASCII table for its sorting comparisons. If you look at the ASCII table in Appendix C, you will see that numbers sort before letters and that uppercase letters sort before lowercase letters.

## Learning Advanced Referencing of Arrays

The array notation you have seen so far is common in computer programming languages. Most languages use subscripts inside brackets (or parentheses) to refer to individual array elements. For instance, you know that the following array references describe the first and fifth elements of the array called `sales` (remember that the starting subscript is always 0):

```
sales[0]
sales[4]
```

C provides another approach to referencing arrays. Even though the title of this section includes the word "advanced," this array-referencing method is not difficult. It is very different, however, especially if you are familiar with another programming language's approach.

*An array name is the address of the starting element of the array.*

There is nothing wrong with referring to array elements in the manner you have seen so far. However, the second approach, unique to C, will be helpful when you learn about pointers in upcoming chapters. Actually, C programmers who have programmed for several years rarely use the subscript notation you have seen.

In C, an array's name is not just a label for you to use in programs. To C, the array name is the actual address where the first element begins in memory. Suppose that you define an array called `amounts` with the following statement:

```
int amounts[6] = {4, 1, 3, 7, 9, 2};
```

Figure 24.6 shows how this array is stored in memory. The figure shows the array beginning at address 405,332. (The actual addresses of variables are determined by the computer when you load and run your compiled program.) Notice that the name of the array, `amounts`, is located somewhere in memory and contains the address of `amounts[0]`, or 405,332.

**Figure 24.6**

The array name
`amounts` holds
the address of
*amounts[0]*.

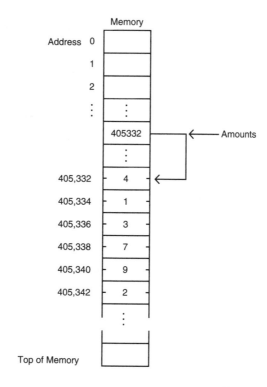

You can refer to an array by its regular subscript notation, or by modifying the address of the array. The following both refer to the third element of `amounts`:

```
amounts[3] and (amounts + 3)[0]
```

Because C considers the array name to be an address in memory that contains the location of the first array element, nothing keeps you from using a different address as the starting address and referencing from there. Taking this one step further, *each* of the following also refers to the third element of `amounts`:

```
(amounts+0)[3] and (amounts+2)[1] and (amounts-2)[5]
```

```
(1+amounts)[2] and (3+amounts)[0] and (amounts+1)[2]
```

You can print any of these array elements with a `printf()` function using the standard integer `%d` control code.

When you print strings inside character arrays, referencing the arrays by their modified addresses is more useful than with integers. Suppose that you stored three strings in a single character array. You could initialize this array with the following statement:

```
char names[]={'T','e','d','\0','E','v','a','\0','S',
              'a','m','\0'};
```

Figure 24.7 shows how this array might look in memory. The array name, names, contains the address of the first element, names[0] (the letter T).

**Figure 24.7**

Storing more than one string in a single character array.

| names | [0] | T |
|---|---|---|
| | [1] | e |
| | [2] | d |
| | [3] | \0 |
| | [4] | E |
| | [5] | v |
| | [6] | a |
| | [7] | \0 |
| | [8] | S |
| | [9] | a |
| | [10] | m |
| | [11] | \0 |

**Caution:** The hierarchy table in Appendix D shows that array subscripts have precedence over addition and subtraction. Therefore, you must enclose array names in parentheses if you want to modify the name as shown in these examples. The following two expressions are not equivalent:

```
(2+amounts)[1]
```

and

```
2+amounts[1]
```

The second example takes the value of amounts[1] (which is 1 in this example array) and adds 2 to it (resulting in a value of 3).

This second method of array referencing might seem like more trouble than it is worth, but learning to reference arrays in this fashion will make your transition to pointers much easier. An array name is actually a pointer itself, because the array contains the address of the first array element (it "points" to the start of the array).

You have yet to see a character array that holds more than one string, but C allows it. The problem with such an array is how you reference, especially how you print, the second and third strings. If you were to print this array using the %d string control code (as you have been doing) with the following printf():

```
printf("%s", names);
```

C would print the following:

```
Ted
```

The %s control
code prints
characters starting
at the array's
address until it
reaches a null
zero.

As mentioned in Chapter 7, "Simple Input and Output," (where this book introduces control codes) the %s control code prints the string starting at the address of the specified array. Without a different way to reference the array, you would have no way to print the three strings inside the single array (without resorting to printing them one element at a time).

Because the %s control code requires a starting address, you can print the three strings with the following printf() function calls:

```
printf("%s", names);          /* Prints Ted */
printf("%s", (names+4));       /* Prints Eva */
printf("%s", (names+8));       /* Prints Sam */
```

To test your understanding, what will the following printf() function calls print?

```
printf("%s", (names+1));
printf("%s", (names+6));
```

The first printf() prints ed. The %s prints the string starting at the address specified. The characters ed begin at (names+1) and the %s stops printing when it gets to the null zero. The second printf() prints a. Adding 6 to the address at names produces the address where the a is located. The "string" is only one character long because the null zero appears in the array immediately after the a.

To sum up character arrays, the following two expressions refer to individual array elements (single characters), and with such, you can print them with the %c control code, but not with %s:

```
names[2] and (names+1)[1]
```

The following two expressions refer to addresses only, and as such, you can print them with the %s control code but *not* with %c:

```
names and (names+4)
```

> **Caution:** Never use %c to print an address reference, even if that address contains a character. Print strings by specifying an address with %s, and single characters by specifying the character element with %c.

The following examples are a little different from most you have seen. They do not perform "real-world" work, but they are study examples for you to familiarize yourself with this new method of array referencing. The next few chapters expand on these methods.

## Examples

1. The following program stores the numbers from 100 to 600 in an array and then prints elements using the new method of array subscripting.

```c
/* Filename: C24REF1.C
   Print elements of an integer array in different ways */
#include <stdio.h>
main()
{
   int num[6] = {100, 200, 300, 400, 500, 600};

   printf("num[0] is \t%d \n", num[0]);
   printf("(num+0)[0] is \t%d \n", (num+0)[0]);
   printf("(num-2)[2] is \t%d \n\n", (num-2)[2]);

   printf("num[1] is \t%d \n", num[1]);
   printf("(num+1)[0] is \t%d \n", (num+1)[0]);
   printf("(num-4)[5] is \t%d \n\n", (num-4)[5]);

   printf("num[5] is \t%d \n", num[5]);
   printf("(num+5)[0] is \t%d \n", (num+5)[0]);
   printf("(num+2)[3] is \t%d \n\n", (num+2)[3]);

   printf("(3+num)[1] is \t%d \n", (3+num)[1]);
   printf("3+num[1] is \t%d \n", 3+num[1]);
   return;
}
```

An index into the array

Figure 24.8 shows the output of this program.

**Figure 24.8**

The output of various array references.

```
num[0] is        100
(num+0)[0] is    100
(num-2)[2] is    100

num[1] is        200
(num+1)[0] is    200
(num-4)[5] is    200

num[5] is        600
(num+5)[0] is    600
(num+2)[3] is    600

(3+num)[1] is    500
3+num[1] is      203
```

2. The following program prints strings and characters from a character array. The printf()s use %s and %c properly; you could not interchange any %s for %c (or %c for %s) and get correct output.

```
/* Filename: C24REF2.C
   Prints elements and strings from an array */
#include <stdio.h>
main()
{
   char names[]={'T','e','d','\0','E','v','a','\0','S',
                 'a','m','\0'};

   /* Must use extra percent (%) to print %s and %c */
   printf("names with %%s: %s\n", names);
   printf("names+0 with %%s: %s\n", names+0);
   printf("names+1 with %%s: %s\n", names+1);
   printf("names+2 with %%s: %s\n", names+2);
   printf("names+3 with %%s: %s\n", names+3);
   printf("names+5 with %%s: %s\n", names+5);
   printf("names+8 with %%s: %s\n\n", names+8);

   printf("(names+0)[0] with %%c: %c\n", (names+0)[0]);
   printf("(names+0)[1] with %%c: %c\n", (names+0)[1]);
   printf("(names+0)[2] with %%c: %c\n", (names+0)[2]);
   printf("(names+0)[3] with %%c: %c\n", (names+0)[3]);
   printf("(names+0)[4] with %%c: %c\n", (names+0)[4]);
   printf("(names+0)[5] with %%c: %c\n\n", (names+0)[5]);

   printf("(names+2)[0] with %%c: %c\n", (names+2)[0]);
   printf("(names+2)[1] with %%c: %c\n", (names+2)[1]);
   printf("(names+1)[4] with %%c: %c\n\n", (names+1)[4]);

   printf("(names-4)[6] with %%c: %c\n", (names-4)[6]);
   printf("(names-6)[11] with %%c: %c\n", (names-6)[11]);
   return;
}
```

Finds an address to print

Finds an array value to print

Study the output shown in Figure 24.9 by comparing it to the program. You will learn more about strings, characters, and character array referencing from studying this one example than from 20 pages of textual description.

**Figure 24.9**

The output of various character array references.

```
names with %s: Ted
names+0 with %s: Ted
names+1 with %s: ed
names+2 with %s: d
names+3 with %s:
names+5 with %s: va
names+8 with %s: Sam

(names+0)[0] with %c: T
(names+0)[1] with %c: e
(names+0)[2] with %c: d
(names+0)[3] with %c:
(names+0)[4] with %c: E
(names+0)[5] with %c: v

(names+2)[0] with %c: d
(names+2)[1] with %c:
(names+1)[4] with %c: v

(names-4)[6] with %c: d
(names-6)[11] with %c: v
```

## Summary

You are beginning to see the true power of programming languages. Arrays give you the ability to search and sort lists of values. Sorting and searching are what computers do best; computers can quickly scan through hundreds and even thousands of values, looking for a match. Scanning through files of paper by hand, looking for just the right number, takes much more time. By stepping through arrays, your program can quickly scan, print, sort, and calculate a list of values. You now have the tools to sort lists of numbers, as well as search for values in a list.

You will use the concepts learned here for sorting and searching lists of character string data as well, as soon as you learn a little more about the way C manipulates strings and pointers. To help build a solid foundation for this and more advanced material, you now know how to reference array elements without using conventional subscripts.

Now that you have mastered this chapter, the next one will be easy. Chapter 25, "Multidimensional Arrays," shows you how you can keep track of arrays in a different format called a *matrix*. Not all lists of data lend themselves to matrices, but you should be prepared for when you need them.

## Review Questions

Answers to review questions are in Appendix B.

1. True or false: You must access an array in the same order that you initialized it.

2. Where did the bubble sort get its name?

3. Are the following values sorted in ascending or descending order?

   33   55   78   78   90   102   435   859   976   4092

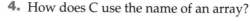

4. How does C use the name of an array?

5. Given the following array definition

```
char teams[] = {'E','a','g','l','e','s','\0','R',
                'a','m','s','\0'};
```

what is printed with each of these statements? (Answer "invalid" if the printf() is illegal.)

a. printf("%s", teams);

b. printf("%s", teams+7);

c. printf("%s", (teams+3);

d. printf("%s", teams[0]);

e. printf("%c", (teams+0)[0]);

f. printf("%c", (teams+5));

g. printf("%c", (teams-200)[202]);

## Review Exercises

1. Write a program to store six of your friends' ages in a single array. Assign the ages in random order. Print the ages, from low to high, on the screen.

2. Modify the program in Exercise 1 to print the ages in descending order.

3. Using the new approach of subscripting arrays, rewrite the programs in Exercises 1 and 2. Always put a 0 in the subscript brackets, modifying the address instead (use (ages+3)[0] rather than ages[3]).

4. Sometimes, programmers use *parallel arrays* in programs that must track more than one list of values that are related. For instance, suppose that you had to maintain an inventory, tracking the integer part numbers, prices, and quantities of each item. This would require three arrays: an integer part number array, a floating-point price array, and an integer quantity array. Each array would have the same number of elements (the total number of parts in the inventory). Write a program to maintain such an inventory, and reserve enough elements for 100 parts in the inventory. Present the user with an input screen. When the user enters a part number, search the part number array. As soon as you locate the position of the part, print the corresponding price and quantity. If the part does not exist, let the user add it to the inventory, along with the matching price and quantity.

# Multidimensional Arrays

Some data fits into lists, such as the data discussed in the previous two chapters, and other data is better suited for tables of information. This chapter takes arrays one step further. The previous chapters introduced single-dimensional arrays; that is, arrays that have only one subscript, which represent lists of values.

This chapter introduces arrays of more than one dimension, which are called *multidimensional arrays*. Multidimensional arrays, sometimes called *tables* or *matrices*, have at least two dimensions—rows and columns—and sometimes they have even more dimensions.

This chapter introduces the following concepts:

♦ What multidimensional arrays are

♦ Reserving storage for multidimensional arrays

♦ Putting data into multidimensional arrays

♦ Using nested for loops to process multidimensional arrays

If you understand single-dimensional arrays, you should have no trouble understanding arrays that have more than one dimension.

## Understanding Multidimensional Array Basics

A multidimensional array is an array with more than one subscript. Whereas a single-dimensional array is a list of values, a multidimensional array simulates a table of values, or even multiple tables of values. The most commonly used table is a two-dimensional table (an array with two subscripts).

Suppose that a softball team wanted to keep track of its players' batting record. The team played 10 games and there are 15 players on the team. Table 25.1 shows the team's batting record.

**Table 25.1. A softball team's batting record.**

| Player Name | Game 1 | Game 2 | Game 3 | Game 4 | Game 5 | Game 6 | Game 7 | Game 8 | Game 9 | Game 10 |
|---|---|---|---|---|---|---|---|---|---|---|
| Adams | 2 | 1 | 0 | 0 | 2 | 3 | 3 | 1 | 1 | 2 |
| Berryhill | 1 | 0 | 3 | 2 | 5 | 1 | 2 | 2 | 1 | 0 |
| Downing | 1 | 0 | 2 | 1 | 0 | 0 | 0 | 0 | 2 | 0 |
| Edwards | 0 | 3 | 6 | 4 | 6 | 4 | 5 | 3 | 6 | 3 |
| Franks | 2 | 2 | 3 | 2 | 1 | 0 | 2 | 3 | 1 | 0 |
| Grady | 1 | 3 | 2 | 0 | 1 | 5 | 2 | 1 | 2 | 1 |
| Howard | 3 | 1 | 1 | 1 | 2 | 0 | 1 | 0 | 4 | 3 |
| Jones | 2 | 2 | 1 | 2 | 4 | 1 | 0 | 7 | 1 | 0 |
| Martin | 5 | 4 | 5 | 1 | 1 | 0 | 2 | 4 | 1 | 5 |
| Powers | 2 | 2 | 3 | 1 | 0 | 2 | 1 | 3 | 1 | 2 |
| Smith | 1 | 1 | 2 | 1 | 3 | 4 | 1 | 0 | 3 | 2 |
| Smithtown | 1 | 0 | 1 | 2 | 1 | 0 | 3 | 4 | 1 | 2 |
| Townsend | 0 | 0 | 0 | 0 | 0 | 0 | 1 | 0 | 0 | 0 |
| Ulmer | 2 | 2 | 2 | 2 | 2 | 1 | 1 | 3 | 1 | 3 |
| Williams | 2 | 3 | 1 | 0 | 1 | 2 | 1 | 2 | 0 | 3 |

A three-dimensional table has three dimensions: depth, rows, and columns.

Do you see that the softball table is a two-dimensional table? It has rows (the first dimension) and columns (the second dimension). Therefore, you would call this a two-dimensional table with 15 rows and 10 columns. (Generally, the number of rows is specified first.)

Each row has a player's name, and each column has a game number associated with it, but these are not part of the actual data. The data consists of only 150 values (15 rows by 10 columns equals 150 data values). The data in a two-dimensional table, just as with arrays, always is the same type of data; in this case, every value is an integer. If it were a table of salaries, every element would be defined as floating-point.

The number of dimensions, in this case two of them, corresponds to the dimensions in the physical world. The single-dimensioned array is a line, or list of values. Two dimensions represent both length and width. You write on a piece of paper in two dimensions; two dimensions represent a flat surface. Three dimensions represent width, length, and depth. You have seen 3-D movies. Not only do the images have width and height, but they also appear to have depth. Figure 25.1 shows what a three-dimensional array looks like if it has a depth of four, six rows, and three columns. Notice that a three-dimensional table resembles a cube.

**Figure 25.1**

Representing a three-dimensional table (a cube).

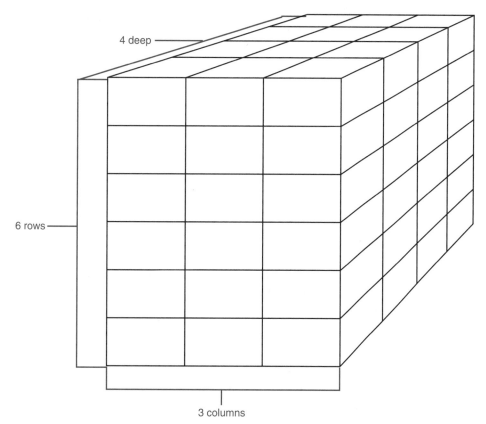

It is difficult to visualize more than three dimensions. However, you can think of each dimension after three as another occurrence. In other words, a list of one player's season batting record could be stored in an array. The team's batting record (as shown in Table 25.1) is two-dimensional. The league, made up of several teams' batting records, would represent a three-dimensional table. Each team (the depth of the table) would have rows and columns of batting data. If there is more than one league, that could be another dimension (another set of data).

C enables you to store several dimensions, although "real-world" data rarely requires more than two or three.

## Reserving Multidimensional Arrays

When you reserve a multidimensional array, you must let C know that the array has more than one dimension. Put more than one subscript in brackets after the array name. You must put a different number, in brackets, for each dimension in the table. For example, to reserve the team data from Table 25.1, you would use the following multidimensional array definition.

*Define an integer array called* teams *with 15 rows and 10 columns.*

```
int teams[15][10];  /* Reserves a two-dimensional table */
```

> **Caution:** Unlike other programming languages, C requires you to enclose each dimension in brackets. Do not reserve multidimensional array storage like this:
>
> ```
> int teams[15,10];   /* Invalid table definition */
> ```

The far-right dimension always represents columns, the next represents rows, and so on.

Properly reserving the teams table produces a table with 150 elements. Figure 25.2 shows what each element's subscript looks like.

Figure 25.2 shows this dimension's three occurrences of the teams table.

If you needed to track three teams, and each team had 15 players and played 10 games, you could dimension it as follows:

```
int teams[3][15][10]; /* Reserves a three-dimensional table */
```

When dimensioning a two-dimensional table, always put the maximum number of rows first, and the maximum number of columns second. C always uses 0 as the starting subscript of each dimension. The last element, the lower-right element of the teams table, would be teams[2][14][9].

**Figure 25.2**

Subscripts for the
softball table.

Columns

| | | | | | | | | | |
|---|---|---|---|---|---|---|---|---|---|
| [0] [0] | [0] [1] | [0] [2] | [0] [3] | [0] [4] | [0] [5] | [0] [6] | [0] [7] | [0] [8] | [0] [9] |
| [1] [0] | [1] [1] | [1] [2] | [1] [3] | [1] [4] | [1] [5] | [1] [6] | [1] [7] | [1] [8] | [1] [9] |
| [2] [0] | [2] [1] | [2] [2] | [2] [3] | [2] [4] | [2] [5] | [2] [6] | [2] [7] | [2] [8] | [2] [9] |
| [3] [0] | [3] [1] | [3] [2] | [3] [3] | [3] [4] | [3] [5] | [3] [6] | [3] [7] | [3] [8] | [3] [9] |
| [4] [0] | [4] [1] | [4] [2] | [4] [3] | [4] [4] | [4] [5] | [4] [6] | [4] [7] | [4] [8] | [4] [9] |
| [5] [0] | [5] [1] | [5] [2] | [5] [3] | [5] [4] | [5] [5] | [5] [6] | [5] [7] | [5] [8] | [5] [9] |
| [6] [0] | [6] [1] | [6] [2] | [6] [3] | [6] [4] | [6] [5] | [6] [6] | [6] [7] | [6] [8] | [6] [9] |
| [7] [0] | [7] [1] | [7] [2] | [7] [3] | [7] [4] | [7] [5] | [7] [6] | [7] [7] | [7] [8] | [7] [9] |
| [8] [0] | [8] [1] | [8] [2] | [8] [3] | [8] [4] | [8] [5] | [8] [6] | [8] [7] | [8] [8] | [8] [9] |
| [9] [0] | [9] [1] | [9] [2] | [9] [3] | [9] [4] | [9] [5] | [9] [6] | [9] [7] | [9] [8] | [9] [9] |
| [10] [0] | [10] [1] | [10] [2] | [10] [3] | [10] [4] | [10] [5] | [10] [6] | [10] [7] | [10] [8] | [10] [9] |
| [11] [0] | [11] [1] | [11] [2] | [11] [3] | [11] [4] | [11] [5] | [11] [6] | [11] [7] | [11] [8] | [11] [9] |
| [12] [0] | [12] [1] | [12] [2] | [12] [3] | [12] [4] | [12] [5] | [12] [6] | [12] [7] | [12] [8] | [12] [9] |
| [13] [0] | [13] [1] | [13] [2] | [13] [3] | [13] [4] | [13] [5] | [13] [6] | [13] [7] | [13] [8] | [13] [9] |
| [14] [0] | [14] [1] | [14] [2] | [14] [3] | [14] [4] | [14] [5] | [14] [6] | [14] [7] | [14] [8] | [14] [9] |

Rows

## Examples

**1.** Suppose that you wanted to keep track of utility bills for the year. You
could store 12 months of four utilities in a two-dimensional table of floating-point amounts, as the following array definition demonstrates:

```
float utilities[12][4];          /* Reserve 48 elements */
```

You can compute the total number of elements in a multidimensional array
by multiplying the subscripts. Because 12 times 4 is 48, there are 48 elements in this array (12 rows, 4 columns). Each of these elements is a
floating-point data type.

**2.** If you were keeping track of five years' worth of utilities, you would have to add an extra dimension. The first dimension would be the years, the second would be the months, and the last would be the individual utilities. Here is how you would reserve storage:

```
float utilities[5][12][4];      /* Reserve 240 elements */
```

# Mapping Arrays to Memory

C approaches multidimensional arrays a little differently than most programming languages do. When you use subscripts, you do not have to understand the internal representation of multidimensional arrays. However, most C programmers feel that a deeper understanding of these arrays is important, especially when programming advanced applications.

A two-dimensional array is actually an *array of arrays*. You program multidimensional arrays as though they were tables with rows and columns. A two-dimensional array is really a single-dimensional array, and each of its elements is not an integer, floating-point, or character, but another array.

Knowing that a multidimensional array is an array of other arrays is critical primarily when passing and receiving such arrays. C passes all arrays, including multidimensional arrays, by address. Suppose that you were using an integer array called `scores`, reserved as a 5-by-6 table. You can pass `scores` to a function called `printIt()` as follows:

```
printIt(scores);        /* Pass table to a function */
```

The function `printIt()` has to know the type of parameter being passed to it. The `printIt()` function must also know that the parameter is an array. If `table` were one-dimensional, you could receive it as

```
printIt(int scores[])      /* Works only if scores
                              are one-dimensional  */
```

or

```
printIt(int scores[10])    /* Assuming that scores
                              have 10 elements       */
```

If `scores` were a multidimensional table, you would have to designate each pair of brackets and put the maximum number of subscripts in its brackets, as in

```
printIt(int scores[5][6])   /* Let printIt() know
                               about dimensions     */
```

or

```
printIt(int scores[][6])    /* Let printIt() know
                               about dimensions     */
```

C stores
multidimensional
arrays in row
order.

Notice that you do *not* have to state explicitly the maximum subscript on the first dimension when receiving multidimensional arrays, but you must designate the second. If scores were a three-dimensional table, dimensioned as 10 by 5 by 6, you would receive it in printIt() as

```
printIt(int scores[][5][6])     /* Only first dimension
                                   is optional        */
```

or

```
printIt(int scores[10][5][6])     /* Let printIt() know
                                     about dimensions */
```

You should not need to worry too much about the way tables are physically stored. Even though a two-dimensional table is actually an array of arrays (and each of those arrays would contain another array if it were a three-dimensional table), you can use subscripts to program multidimensional arrays as if they were stored in row-an-column order.

Multidimensional arrays are stored in *row order*. Suppose that you want to keep track of a 4-by-4 table. The top of Figure 25.3 shows how that table (and its subscripts) could be visualized. Despite the two-dimensional table organization, your memory is still in sequential storage. C has to map multidimensional arrays to single-dimensional memory, and it does so in row order.

Each row fills memory before the next row is stored. Figure 25.3 shows how a 4-by-4 table is mapped to memory. The entire first row (table[0][0] through table[0][3]) is stored first in memory before any of the second row. A table is really an array of arrays, and, as you learned in previous chapters, array elements are always stored sequentially in memory. Therefore, the first row (array) completely fills memory before the second row. Figure 25.3 shows how two-dimensional arrays map to memory.

## Defining Multidimensional Arrays

C is not picky about the way you define a multidimensional array when you initialize it at definition time. As with single-dimensional arrays, you initialize multidimensional arrays with braces that designate dimensions. Because a multi-dimensional array is an array of arrays, you can nest braces when you initialize them.

The following three array definitions fill the three arrays ara1, ara2, and ara3, as shown in Figure 25.4:

```
int ara1[5] = {8, 5, 3, 25, 41};  /* One-dimensional array */
int ara2[2][4]={{4, 3, 2, 1},{1, 2, 3, 4}};
int ara3[3][4]={{1, 2, 3, 4},{5, 6, 7, 8},{9, 10, 11, 12}};
```

**Figure 25.3**

Mapping a two-
dimensional table
to memory.

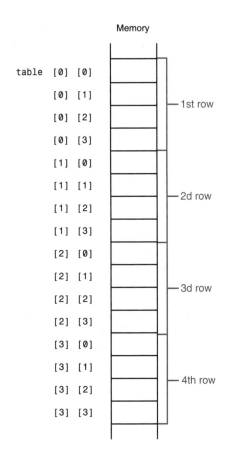

Notice that the multidimensional arrays are stored in row order. In ara3, the first row gets the first four elements of the definition (1, 2, 3, and 4).

**Tip:** To make a multidimensional array initialization match the array's subscripts, some programmers like to show how arrays are filled. Because C programs are free-form, you can initialize ara2 and ara3 as

```
int ara2[2][4]={{4, 3, 2, 1},   /* Does exactly the same */
                {1, 2, 3, 4}};  /* thing as before       */
int ara3[4][4]={{1, 2, 3, 4},
                {5, 6, 7, 8},
                    {9, 10, 11, 12},
            {13, 14, 15, 16}}; /* Visually more obvious */
```

**Figure 25.4**

After initializing a table.

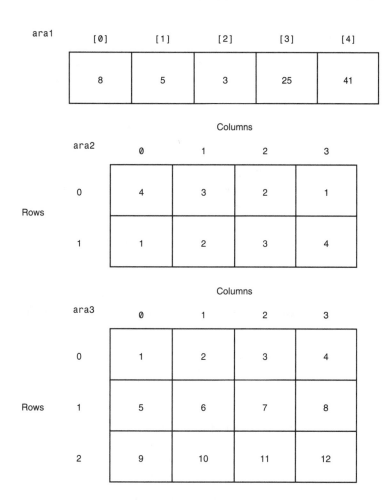

C does not mind if you initialize a multidimensional array as if it were single-dimensional. You must keep track of the row order if you do this. For instance, the following two definitions also reserve storage for and initialize ara2 and ara3:

```
int ara2[2][4]={4, 3, 2, 1, 1, 2, 3, 4};
int ara3[3][4]={1, 2, 3, 4, 5, 6, 7, 8, 9, 10, 11, 12, 13,
                14, 15, 16};
```

There is no difference in initializing ara2 and ara3 with and without the nested braces. The nested braces seem to show the dimensions and how C fills them a little better, but the choice of using nested braces is yours.

One last point to consider is how multidimensional arrays are viewed by your compiler. Many people program in C for years, but never understand how tables are really stored internally. As long as you use subscripts, a table's internal representation should not matter. As soon as you learn about pointer variables, however, you might want to know how C stores your tables in case you want to reference them using pointers (as shown in the next few chapters).

> **Tip:** Multidimensional arrays (unless they are global) are *not* initialized to specific values unless you assign them values at definition time or in the program. As with single-dimensional arrays, if you initialize one or more of the elements, but not all of them, C fills the rest with zeros. If you want to zero-out an entire multidimensional array, you can do so with the following:
>
> ```
> float sales[3][4][7][2] = {0};   /* Fills all of sales
>                                        with zeros */
> ```

Figure 25.5 shows the way C stores a 3-by-4 table in memory. Unlike single-dimensional arrays, each element is stored contiguously, but notice how C views the data. Because a table is an array of arrays, the array name contains the address of the start of the primary array. Each of those elements points to the arrays they contain (the data in each row). This coverage of table storage is for your information only, at this point. As you become more proficient in C, and write more powerful programs that manipulate internal memory, you might want to review this method C uses for table storage.

## Combining Tables and *for* Loops

As the following examples show, nested for loops are useful when you want to loop through every element of a multidimensional table.

For instance, the section of code

```
for (row=0; row<2; row++)
   { for (col=0; col<3; col++)
        { printf("%d   %d\n", row, col); }
   }
```

produces the following output:

```
0      0
0      1
0      2
1      0
1      1
1      2
```

*Nested loops work well with multidimensional arrays.*

These are exactly the subscripts, in row order, for a two-row by three-column table that is dimensional with

```
int table[2][3];
```

**Figure 25.5**

Internal
representation of
a two-dimensional
table.

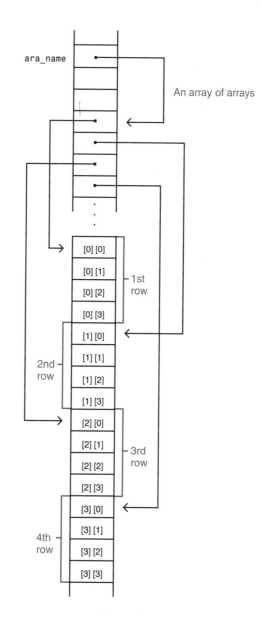

Notice that there are as many for loops as there are subscripts in the array (two). The outside loop represents the first subscript (the rows), and the inside loop represents the second subscript (the columns). The nested for loop steps through each element of the table.

You can use scanf(), gets(), getc(), and other input functions to fill a table, and you can also assign values to the elements when defining the table. More often, the data comes from data files on the disk. Regardless of what method actually stores values in multidimensional arrays, nested for loops are excellent control statements to step through the subscripts. The following examples demonstrate how nested for loops work with multidimensional arrays.

## Examples

1. The following statements reserve enough memory elements for a television station's ratings (A through D) for one week:

```
char ratings[7][48];
```

These statements reserve enough elements to hold seven days (the rows) of ratings for each 30-minute time slot (48 of them in a day).

Every element in a table is always the same type. In this case, each element in a character variable. Some could be initialized with the following assignment statements:

```
shows[3][12] = 'B';  /* Store B in 4th row, 13th column */
shows[1][5] = 'A' ;  /* Store C in 2nd row, 6th column */
shows[6][20] = getchar();
```

2. A computer company sells two sizes of disks: 3 1/2 inch and 5 1/4 inch. Each disk comes in one of four capacities: single-sided double-density, double-sided double-density, single-sided high-density, and double-sided high-density.

The disk inventory is well-suited for a two-dimensional table. The company determined that the disks have the following retail prices:

| Disk Size | Double-Density | | High-Density | |
|---|---|---|---|---|
| | Single-Sided | Double-2Sided | Single-Sided | Double-Sided |
| 3 1/2" | 2.30 | 2.75 | 3.20 | 3.50 |
| 5 1/4" | 1.75 | 2.10 | 2.60 | 2.95 |

The company wants to store the price of each disk in a table for easy access. The following program does that with assignment statements.

```
/* Filename: C25DISK1.C
   Assigns disk prices to a table */
#include <stdio.h>
main()
{
```

```
float disks[2][4];   /* Table of disk prices */
  int row, col;

  disks[0][0] = 2.30;       /* Row 1, column 1 */
  disks[0][1] = 2.75;       /* Row 1, column 2 */
  disks[0][2] = 3.20;       /* Row 1, column 3 */
  disks[0][3] = 3.50;       /* Row 1, column 4 */
  disks[1][0] = 1.75;       /* Row 2, column 1 */
  disks[1][1] = 2.10;       /* Row 2, column 2 */
  disks[1][2] = 2.60;       /* Row 2, column 3 */
  disks[1][3] = 2.95;       /* Row 2, column 4 */
  /* Print the prices */
  for (row=0; row<2; row++)
     { for (col=0; col<4; col++)
       { printf("$%.2f \n", disks[row][col]); }
     }

  return;
}
```

Fills the entire table (label pointing to the assignment block)

This program displays the prices as follows:

```
$2.30
$2.75
$3.20
$3.50
$1.75
$2.10
$2.60
$2.95
```

It prints them one line at a time, without any descriptive titles. Although the output is not labeled, it illustrates how you can use assignment statements to initialize a table, and how nested for loops can print the elements.

3. The preceding disk inventory would be displayed better if the output had descriptive titles. Before you add titles, it is helpful for you to see how to print a table in its native row and column format.

Typically, you use a nested for loop, such as the one in the previous example, to print rows and columns. You should not output a newline character with every `printf()`, however. If you do, you see one value per line, as in the previous program's output, which is not the row and column format of the table.

You do not want to see every disk price on one line, but you want each row of the table printed on a separate line. You must insert a `printf("\n");` to send the cursor to the next line each time the row number changes. Inserting newlines after each row prints the table in its row and column format, as this program shows:

```
/* Filename: C25DISK2.C
   Assigns disk prices to a table
   and prints them in a table format */
#include <stdio.h>
main()
{
    float disks[2][4];  /* Table of disk prices */
    int row, col;

    disks[0][0] = 2.30;        /* Row 1, column 1 */
    disks[0][1] = 2.75;        /* Row 1, column 2 */
    disks[0][2] = 3.20;        /* Row 1, column 3 */
    disks[0][3] = 3.50;        /* Row 1, column 4 */
    disks[1][0] = 1.75;        /* Row 2, column 1 */
    disks[1][1] = 2.10;        /* Row 2, column 2 */
    disks[1][2] = 2.60;        /* Row 2, column 3 */
    disks[1][3] = 2.95;        /* Row 2, column 4 */

    /* Print the prices */
    for (row=0; row<2; row++)
      { for (col=0; col<4; col++)
        { printf("$%.2f\t", disks[row][col]);
        }
        printf("\n");  /* Prints a new line each row */
      }

    return;
}
```

Causes each row in the table to print on a single line

Here is the output of the disk prices in their native table order:

```
$2.30    $2.75    $3.20    $3.50
$1.75    $2.10    $2.60    $2.95
```

**4.** To add the titles, simply print a row of titles before the first row of values, then print a new column title before each column, as shown in the following program:

```
/* Filename: C25DISK3.C
   Assigns disk prices to a table
   and prints them in a table format with titles */
#include <stdio.h>
main()
{
   float disks[2][4];   /* Table of disk prices */
   int row, col;

   disks[0][0] = 2.30;        /* Row 1, column 1 */
   disks[0][1] = 2.75;        /* Row 1, column 2 */
   disks[0][2] = 3.20;        /* Row 1, column 3 */
   disks[0][3] = 3.50;        /* Row 1, column 4 */
   disks[1][0] = 1.75;        /* Row 2, column 1 */
   disks[1][1] = 2.10;        /* Row 2, column 2 */
   disks[1][2] = 2.60;        /* Row 2, column 3 */
   disks[1][3] = 2.95;        /* Row 2, column 4 */

   /* Print the top titles */
   printf("\tSingle-sided,\tDouble-sided,\tSingle-sided,
   ➡    \tDouble-sided\n");
   printf("\tDouble-density\tDouble-density\tHigh-density
   ➡    \tHigh-density\n");

   /* Print the prices */
   for (row=0; row<2; row++)
      { if (row == 0)
      { printf("3-1/2\"\t"); }              /* Need \" to
                                               print quotation */
      else
         { printf("5-1/4\"\t"); }
      for (col=0; col<4; col++)    /* Print the current row */
      { printf("$%.2f\t\t", disks[row][col]);
         }
         printf("\n");            /* Prints a new line each row */
      }

   return;
}
```

Printing titles for the disk table ⎯

Figure 25.6 shows the output from this program.

**Figure 25.6**

The table of disk prices with titles.

```
            Single-sided,   Double-sided,   Single-sided,   Double-sided
            Double-density  Double-density  High-density    High-density
3-1/2"  $2.30           $2.75           $3.20           $3.50
5-1/4"  $1.75           $2.10           $2.60           $2.95
```

## Summary

You now know how to create, initialize, and process multidimensional arrays. Although not all data fits in the compact format of tables, much does. Using nested for loops makes stepping through a multidimensional array straightforward.

One of the limitations of a multidimensional array is that each element must be the same data type. This keeps you from being able to store several kinds of data in tables. Subsequent chapters show you how to store data in different ways to overcome this limitation of tables.

## Review Questions

Answers to the review questions are in Appendix B.

1. What statement reserves a two-dimensional table of integers called scores with five rows and six columns?

2. What statement reserves a three-dimensional table of four character arrays called initials with 10 rows and 20 columns?

3. In the following statement, which subscript (first or second) represents rows and which represents columns?

```
int weights[5][10];
```

4. How many elements are reserved with the following statement?

```
int ara[5][6];
```

5. The following table of integers is called ara:

| 4 | 1 | 3 | 5 | 9 |
|---|---|---|---|---|
| 10 | 2 | 12 | 1 | 6 |
| 25 | 42 | 2 | 91 | 8 |

What values do the following elements contain?

a. `ara[2][2]`

b. `ara[0][1]`

c. `ara[2][3]`

d. `ara[2][4]`

6. What control statement is best for stepping through multidimensional arrays?

7. Note the following section of a program:

```
int grades[3][5] = {80,90,96,73,65,67,90,68,92,84,70,
                    55,95,78,100};
```

What are the values of the following:

a. `grades[2][3]`

b. `grades[2][4]`

c. `grades[0][1]`

## Review Exercises

1. Write a program that stores and prints the numbers from 1 to 21 in a 3 by 7 table. (Hint: Remember that C begins subscripts at 0.)

2. Write a program that reserves storage for three years' worth of sales data for five salespeople. Use assignment statements to fill the table with data, then print it, one value per line.

3. Instead of using assignment statements, use the `scanf()` function to fill the salespeople data from Exercise 2.

4. Write a program that tracks the grades for five classes, each having 10 students. Input the data using the `scanf()` function. Print the table in its native row and column format.

# CHAPTER 26

# Pointers

C reveals its true power through *pointer variables.* Pointer variables (or *pointers*, as they generally are called) are variables that contain addresses of other variables. All variables you have seen so far have held data values. You understand that variables hold various data types: character, integer, floating-point, and so on. Pointer variables contain the location of regular data variables; they in effect *point* to the data because they hold the address of the data.

When first learning C, students of the language tend to shy away from pointers, thinking that they will be difficult. Pointers do not have to be difficult. In fact, after you work with them for a while, you will find that they are easier to use than arrays (and much more flexible).

This chapter introduces the following concepts:

♦ What pointers are

♦ Pointers of different data types

♦ The "address of" (&) operator

♦ The dereferencing (*) operator

♦ Arrays of pointers

Pointers offer a highly efficient means of accessing and changing data. Because pointers contain the actual address of your data, your compiler has less work to do when finding that data in memory. Pointers do not have to link data to specific variable names. A pointer can point to an unnamed data value. With pointers, you gain a "different view" of your data.

# Introduction to Pointer Variables

Pointers contain addresses of other variables.

Pointers are variables. They follow all the normal naming rules of regular, nonpointer variables. As with regular variables, you must define pointer variables before using them. There is a type of pointer for every data type in C; there are integer pointers, character pointers, floating-point pointers, and so on. You can define global pointers or local pointers, depending on where you define them.

About the only difference between pointer variables and regular variables is the data they hold. Pointers do not contain data in the usual sense of the word. Pointers contain addresses of data. If you need a quick review of addresses and memory, see Appendix A, "Memory Addressing, Binary, and Hexadecimal Review."

There are two pointer operators in C:

    &    The "address of" operator

    *    The dereferencing operator

Don't let these operators throw you; you have seen them before! The & is the bitwise AND operator (from Chapter 12, "Bitwise Operators") and the * means, of course, multiplication. These are called *overloaded* operators. They perform more than one function, depending on how you use them in your programs. C does not confuse * for multiplication when you use it as a dereferencing operator with pointers.

Any time you see the & used with pointers, think of the words "address of." The & operator always produces the memory address of whatever it precedes. The * operator, when used with pointers, either defines a pointer or dereferences the pointer's value. The next section explains each of these operators.

## Defining Pointers

Because you must define all pointers before using them, the best way to begin learning about pointers is to understand how to define and use them. Actually, defining pointers is almost as easy as defining regular variables. After all, pointers are variables.

If you need to define a variable that will hold your age, you can do so with the following variable definition:

```
int age=30;        /* Define a variable to hold my age */
```

Defining age like this does several things. C now knows that you will need a variable called age, so C reserves storage for that variable. C also knows that you will store only integers in age, not floating-point or double floating-point data. The definition also requests that C store the value of 30 in age after it reserves storage for age.

Where did C store age in memory? As the programmer, you do not really care where C decided to store age. You do not need to know the variable's address because you will never refer to age by its address. If you want to calculate or print with age, you will call it by its name, age.

> **Tip:** Make your pointer variable names meaningful. The name `filePtr` makes more sense than `x13` for a file-pointing variable, although either name is allowed.

Suppose that you want to define a pointer variable. This pointer variable will not hold your age, but it will point to age, the variable that holds your age. (Why you would want to do this is explained in this and the next few chapters.) pAge might be a good name for the pointer variable. Figure 26.1 illustrates what you want to do. The figure assumes that C stored age at the address 350,606; however, your C compiler arbitrarily determines the address of age, so it could be anything.

**Figure 26.1**

*pAge* contains the address of *age*; *pAge* points to the *age* variable.

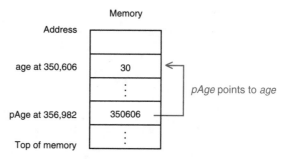

The name pAge by itself has nothing to do with pointers, except that is the name you made up for the pointer to age. You could just as easily have given pAge the name house, x43344, spaceTrek, or whatever else you wanted to call it, just as you can give variables any name (as long as the name follows the legal naming rules of variables). This reinforces the idea that a pointer is just a variable that you must reserve in your program. Make up meaningful variable names, even for pointer variables. pAge is a good name for a variable that points to age (as would be ptrAge and ptrToAge).

To define the pAge pointer variable, you must do the following:

```
int * pAge;              /* Define an integer pointer */
```

Similar to the definition for age, this definition reserves a variable called pAge. The pAge variable is not a normal integer variable, however. Because of the dereferencing operator, *, C knows that this is to be a pointer variable. Some C programmers prefer to define such a variable without a space after the *, as follows:

```
int *pAge;               /* Define an integer pointer */
```

Either method is okay, but you must remember that the * is *not* part of the name. When you later use pAge, you will not always prefix the name with the *, unless you are dereferencing it at the time (as later examples show).

> **Tip:** Whenever the dereferencing operator, *, appears in a variable definition, the variable being defined is *always* a pointer variable.

Consider the definition for pAge if the asterisk were not there: C would think you were defining a regular integer variable. The * is important because it tells C to interpret pAge as a pointer variable, not as a normal, data variable.

## Assigning Values to Pointers

*Pointers can point only to data of their own type.*

pAge is an integer pointer. This is very important. pAge can point only to integer values, never to floating-point, double floating-point, or even character variables. If you needed to point to a floating-point variable, you might do so with a pointer defined as

```
float *point;     /* Defines a floating-point pointer */
```

As with any automatic variable, C does not initialize pointers when you define them. If you defined pAge as previously described, and you wanted pAge to point to age, you would have to explicitly assign pAge to the address of age. The following statement does this:

```
pAge = &age;     /* Assign the address of age to pAge */
```

What value is now in pAge? You do not know exactly, but you know it is the address of age, wherever that is. Instead of assigning the address of age to pAge with an assignment operator, you can define and initialize pointers at the same time. These lines define and initialize both age and pAge:

```
int age=30;       /* Defines a regular integer
                     variable, putting 30 in it        */
int *pAge=&age;   /* Defines an integer pointer,
                     initializing it with the address
                     of pAge                           */
```

These lines produce the variables described in Figure 26.1.

If you want to print the value of age, you can do so with the following printf():

```
printf("%d", age);             /* Prints the value of age */
```

You also can print the value of age like this:

```
printf("%d", *pAge);                /* Dereferences pAge */
```

The dereference operator produces a value that tells the pointer where to point. Without the *, the last printf() would print an address (the address of age). With the *, the printf() prints the value at that address.

You can assign a different value to age with the following statement:

```
age=41;                          /* Assign a new value to age */
```

You also can assign a value to age like this:

```
*pAge=41;
```

This definition assigns 41 to the value to which pAge points.

> **Tip:** The * appears before a pointer variable in only two places—when you define a pointer variable, and when you dereference a pointer variable (to find the data it points to).

## Considering Pointers and Parameters

Now that you understand the pointer's * and & operators, you can finally see why scanf()'s requirements were not really as strict as they first appeared. While passing a regular variable to scanf(), you had to prefix the variable with the & operator. For instance, the following scanf() gets three integer values from the user:

```
scanf(" %d %d %d", &num1, &num2, &num3);
```

This scanf() does not pass the three variables, but passes the *addresses* of the three variables. Because scanf() knows the exact locations of these parameters in memory (because their addresses were passed), it goes to those addresses and puts the keyboard input values into those addresses.

This is the only way scanf() could work. If you passed these variables by copy, without putting the "address of" operator (&) before them, scanf() would get the keyboard input and fill a *copy* of the variables, but not the actual variables num1, num2, and num3. When scanf() then returned control to your program, you would not have the input values.

You might recall from Chapter 19, "Passing Values," that you can pass by address and override C's normal default of passing by copy (or "by value"). To pass by address, pass a variable preceded by an & and put an asterisk before the parameter everywhere it appears in the receiving function. The following function call passes tries by address to the receiving function called prIt():

```
prIt(&tries);    /* Pass integer tries to prIt() by
                    address (tries would normally pass
                    by copy)                          */
```

The following function, prIt(), receives the address of tries, in effect receiving tries by address:

```
prIt(int *tries)            /* Receive tries by address
                               (dereference its value)  */

{
*tries++;               /* This changes tries in calling
                           and receiving functions     */

   return;
}
```

Now that you understand the & and * operators, you can completely understand the passing of nonarray parameters by address to functions. (Arrays default to passing by address without requiring that you use & and *.)

---

**For Related Information**

♦ "Calling and Returning Functions," p. 286

♦ "Three Issues of Parameter Passing," p. 314

---

## Examples

1. The following section of a program defines three regular variables of three different data types, and pointers that point to those variables:

```
char initial= 'Q';    /* Defines three regular variables */
int num=40;               /* of three different types       */
float sales=2321.59;

char *pInitial=&initial;   /* Defines three pointers.     */
int * ptrNum=&num;          /* Pointer names and spacing  */
float * salesAdd = &sales; /* after * are not critical.   */
```

2. You can initialize pointers, just as with regular variables, with assignment statements. You do not have to initialize them when you define them. The next few lines of code are equivalent to the code in Example 1:

```
char initial;       /* Defines three regular variables */
int num;                /* of three different types       */
float sales;

char *pInitial;    /* Defines three pointers but does  */
int * ptrNum;       /* not initialize them yet          */
float * salesAdd;
```

```
initial='Q';        /* Initializes the regular variables */
num=40;             /* with values                       */
sales=2321.59;

pInitial=&initial;  /* Initializes the pointers with */
ptrNum=&num;        /* the addresses of their        */
salesAdd=&sales;    /* corresponding variables       */
```

Notice that you do not put the * operator before the pointer variable names when assigning them values. You would prefix a pointer variable with the * only if you were dereferencing it.

> **Note:** In this example, the pointer variables could have been assigned the addresses of the regular variables before the regular variables were assigned values. There would be no difference in the operation. The pointers are assigned the addresses of the regular variables regardless of the data in the regular variables.

Keep the data type of each pointer consistent. Do *not* assign a floating-point variable to an integer's address. For instance, you cannot make the following assignment statement:

```
pInitial = &sales;        /* Invalid pointer assignment */
```

because `pInitial` can point only to character data, not to floating-point data.

3. The following program is an example you should study closely. It shows more about pointers and the pointer operators, & and *, than several pages of text can do.

```
/* Filename: C26POINT.C
   Demonstrates the use of pointer definitions
   and operators */
#include <stdio.h>
main()
{
   int num=123;              /* A regular integer variable */
   int *pNum;                /* Defines an integer pointer  */

   printf("num is %d\n", num);     /* Prints value of num */
   printf("The address of num is %ld \n", &num); /* Prints
                                     num's location  */
```

Does not
store the
value of *num*

```
         pNum = &num;              /* Puts address of num in pNum,
                                      in effect making pNum point
                                      to num                         */
                                   /* No * in front of pNum)         */
         printf("*pNum is %d \n", *pNum);  /* Prints value of
                                              num                    */
         printf("pNum is %ld \n", pNum);   /* Prints location
                                              of num                 */

         return;
     }
```

Here is the output from this program:

```
num is 123
The address of num is 65522
*pNum is 123
pNum is 65522
```

If you run this program, you probably will get different results for the value of pNum because your compiler will place num at a different location, depending on your memory setup. The actual address is moot, however. Because the pointer pNum always contains the address of num, and because you can dereference pNum to get num's value, the actual address is not critical.

4. The following program includes a function that swaps the values of any two integers passed to it. You might recall that a function can return only a single value. Therefore, before now, you could not write a function that changed two different values and returned both values to the calling function.

To swap two variables (reversing their values for sorting, as you saw in Chapter 24, "Array Processing") you need the ability to pass both variables by address. Then, when the function reverses the variables, the calling function's variables also are swapped.

Notice the function's use of dereferencing operators before each occurrence of num1 and num2. You do not care which address num1 and num2 is stored at, but you must make sure that you dereference whatever addresses were passed to the function.

Be sure to pass arguments with the prefix & to functions that receive by address, as done here in main().

*Identify the program and include the I/O header file. This program will swap*
*two integers, so initialize two integer variables in* main()*. Pass the variables to*
*the swapping function, called* swapThem, *and then switch their values. Print the*
*results of the swap in* main()*.*

```
/* Filename: C26SWAP.C
   Program that includes a function that swaps
   any two integers passed to it */
#include <stdio.h>
void swapThem(int *num1, int *num2);

main()
{
    int i=10, j=20;
    printf("\n\nBefore swap, i is %d and j is %d\n\n",
            i, j);
    swapThem(&i, &j);
    printf("\n\nAfter swap, i is %d and j is %d\n\n",
            i, j);
    return 0;
}
void swapThem(int *num1, int *num2)
{
    int temp;                   /* Variable that holds
                                   in-between swapped value.   */
    temp = *num1;               /* The asterisks ensure that the  */
    *num1 = *num2;              /* calling function's variables    */
    *num2 = temp;               /* (and not copies of them) are    */
                                /* worked on in this function.     */

    return;
}
```

Lets *main()*'s values be swapped because arguments are passed by address

## Arrays of Pointers

If you need to reserve many pointers for many different values, you might want to
define an array of pointers. You know that you can reserve an array of characters,
integers, long integers, and floating-point values, as well as an array of every other
data type available. You also can reserve an array of pointers, with each pointer
being a pointer to a specific data type.

The following reserves an array of 10 integer pointer variables:

```
int *iptr[10]; /* Reserves an array of 10 integer pointers */
```

Figure 26.2 shows how C views this array. Each element holds an address (after being assigned values) that points to other values in memory. Each value pointed to must be an integer. You can assign an element from `iptr` an address just as you would for nonarray pointer variables. You can make `iptr[4]` point to the address of an integer variable named age by assigning it like this:

```
iptr[4] = &age;    /* Make iptr[4] point to address of age */
```

**Figure 26.2**

An array of 10
integer pointers.

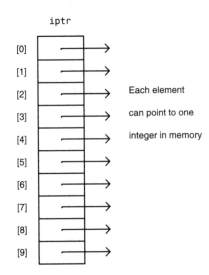

The following reserves an array of 20 character pointer variables:

```
char *cpoint[20];        /* Array of 20 character pointers */
```

Again, the asterisk is not part of the array name. The asterisk lets C know that this is an array of integer pointers and not just an array of integers.

Some beginning C students get confused when they see such a definition. Pointers are one thing, but reserving storage for arrays of pointers tends to bog novices down. However, reserving storage for arrays of pointers is easy to understand. Remove the asterisk from the last definition as follows

```
char cpoint[20];
```

and what do you have? You have just reserved a simple array of 20 characters. Adding the asterisk tells C to go one step further: rather than an array of character variables, you want an array of character pointing variables. Instead of having each element be a character variable, you have each element hold an address that points to characters.

Reserving arrays of pointers will be much more meaningful after you learn about structures in the next few chapters. As with regular, nonpointing variables, an array makes processing several variables much easier. You can use a subscript to reference each variable (element) without having to use a different variable name for each value.

## Summary

Defining and using pointers might seem like a lot of trouble at this point. Why assign *pNum a value when it is easier (and clearer) to assign a value directly to num? If you are asking yourself that question, you probably understand everything you should from this chapter and are ready to begin seeing the true power of pointers: combining pointers and array processing.

## Review Questions

Answers to review questions are in Appendix B.

1. What kind of variable is reserved in each of the following?

    a. `int *a;`

    b. `char * cp;`

    c. `float * dp;`

2. What words should come to mind when you see the & operator?

3. What is the dereferencing operator?

4. How would you assign the address of the floating-point variable `salary` to a pointer called `ptSal`?

5. True or false: You must define a pointer with an initial value when defining it.

6. In both of the following sections of code

```
int i;
int * pti;
i=56;
pti = &i;
```

and

```
int i;
int * pti;
pti = &i;          /* These two lines are reversed */
i=56;              /* from the preceding example    */
```

is the value of pti the same after the fourth line of each section?

**7.** In the following section of code:

```
float pay;
float *ptrPay;
pay=2313.54;
ptrPay = &pay;
```

Determine the value of each of the following (answer "invalid" if it cannot be determined):

a. pay

b. *ptrPay

c. *pay

d. &pay

**8.** What does the following define?

```
double *ara[4][6];
```

a. An array of double floating-point values

b. An array of double floating-point pointer variables

c. An invalid definition statement

> **Note:** Because this is a theory-oriented chapter, review exercises are saved until you master Chapter 27, "Pointers and Arrays."

# CHAPTER 27

# Pointers and Arrays

Arrays and pointers are closely related in the C programming language. You can address arrays as if they were pointers, and address pointers as if they were arrays. Being able to store and access pointers and arrays gives you the ability to store strings of data in array elements. Without pointers, you cannot store strings of data in arrays because there is no fundamental string data type in C (no string variables, only string constants).

This chapter introduces the following concepts:

- Array names and pointers

- Character pointers

- Pointer arithmetic

- Ragged-edge arrays of string data

This chapter introduces concepts you will use for much of your future programming in C. Pointer manipulation is very important to the C programming language.

## Array Names as Pointers

An array name is a pointer.

An array name is just a pointer, nothing more. To prove this, suppose that you have the following array definition:

```
int ara[5] = {10, 20, 30, 40, 50};
```

If you print ara[0], you see 10. Because you now fully understand arrays, this is the value you expect.

But what if you print *ara? Does *ara print anything? If so, what? Because an array name is a pointer, you also see 10 when you print *ara.

Recall how arrays are stored in memory. Figure 27.1 shows how ara would be mapped in memory. The array name, ara, is nothing more than a pointer that points to the first element of the array. Therefore, if you dereference that pointer, you dereference the value stored at the first element of the array, which is 10. Dereferencing ara is exactly the same thing as referring to ara[0], because they both produce the same value.

**Figure 27.1**

Storing the array called *ara* in memory.

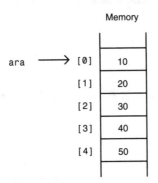

Memory

| ara ⟶ | [0] | 10 |
| | [1] | 20 |
| | [2] | 30 |
| | [3] | 40 |
| | [4] | 50 |

You now see that you can reference an array with subscripts or with pointer dereferencing. Can you use pointer notation to print the third element of ara? Yes, and you already have the tools to do so. The following printf() prints ara[2] (the third element of ara) without using a subscript:

```
printf("%d",C1 *(ara+2) );              /* Prints ara[2] */
```

The expression *(ara+2) is not vague at all if you remember that an array name is just a pointer that always points to the array's first element. *(ara+2) takes the address stored in ara, adds 2 to the address, and dereferences that location. The following holds true:

ara+0 points to ara[0]

ara+1 points to ara[1]

ara+2 points to ara[2]

ara+3 points to ara[3]

ara+4 points to ara[4]

Therefore, to print, store, or calculate with an array element, you can use either the subscript notation or the pointer notation. Because an array name contains the address of the array's first element, you must dereference the pointer to get the element's value.

**Internal Locations**

C knows the internal data size requirements of characters, integers, floating-points, and the other data types on your computer. Therefore, because `ara` is an integer array, and because each element in an integer array consumes 2 to 4 bytes of storage depending on the computer, C adds 2 or 4 bytes to the address if you reference arrays as just shown.

If you write `*(ara+3)` to refer to `ara[3]`, C adds 6 or 12 bytes to the address of `ara` to get the third element. C does not add an actual 3. You do not have to worry about this because C handles these internals. When you write `*(ara+3)`, you are actually requesting that C add three integer addresses to the address of `ara`. If `ara` were a floating-point array, C would add three floating-point addresses to `ara`.

**For Related Information**

♦ "Understanding Array Basics," p. 389

♦ "Array Processing," p. 407

# Pointer Advantages

An array name is a
pointer constant.

Although arrays are really pointers in disguise, they are special types of pointers. An array name is a *pointer constant,* not a pointer variable. You cannot change the value of an array name, because you cannot change constants. This explains why you cannot assign an array new values during a program's execution. For instance, even if `cname` is a character array, the following is not valid in C:

```
cname = "Christine Chambers";   /* Invalid array assignment */
```

You cannot change the array name, `cname`, because it is a constant. You would not attempt the following

```
5 = 4 + 8 * 21;                        /* Invalid assignment */
```

because you cannot change the constant 5 to any other value. C knows that you cannot assign anything to 5 and prints an error message if you attempt to change 5. C also knows that an array name is a constant and that you cannot change an array to another value. (You can assign values to an array only at definition time, one element at a time during execution, or by using functions such as `strcpy()`.)

This brings you to the most important reason to learn pointers: pointers (except arrays referenced as pointers) are variables. You *can* change a pointer variable, and being able to do so makes processing virtually any data, including arrays, much more powerful and flexible.

## Examples

**1.** By changing pointers, you make them point to different values in memory. The following program demonstrates how to change pointers. The program first defines two floating-point values. A floating-point pointer points to the first variable, v1, and is used in the printf(). The pointer is then changed so that it points to the second floating-point variable, v2.

```
/* Filename: C27PTRCH.C
   Changes the value of a pointer variable */
#include <stdio.h>
main()
{
    float v1=676.54;                        /* Defines two */
    float v2=900.18;               /* floating-point variables */
    float * pV;            /* Defines a floating-point pointer */

    pV = &v1;                         /* Makes pointer point to v1 */
    printf("The first value is %.2f \n", *pV);   /* Prints
                                                    676.54  */

    pV = &v2;                  /* Changes the pointer so that it
                                  points to v2                 */
    printf("The second value is %.2f \n", *pV);   /* Prints
                                                     900.18 */

    return;
}
```

*pv* points to *v1* first ⎯⎯⎯⎯⎯ pV = &v1;

*pv* then points to *v2* ⎯⎯⎯⎯⎯ pV = &v2;

Because they can change pointers, most C programmers use pointers rather than arrays. Because arrays are easy to define, C programmers sometimes define arrays and then use pointers to reference those arrays. If the array data changes, the pointer helps to change it.

**2.** You can use pointer notation and reference pointers as arrays with array notation. The following program defines an integer array and an integer pointer that points to the start of the array. The array and pointer values are printed using subscript notation. Afterward, the program uses array notation to print the array and pointer values.

Study this program carefully. You will see the inner workings of arrays and pointer notation.

```
/* Filename: C27ARPTR.C
   References arrays like pointers and
   pointers like arrays */
#include <stdio.h>
main()
{
   int ctr;
   int iara[5] = {10, 20, 30, 40, 50};
   int *iptr;

   iptr = iara;          /* Make iptr point to array's first
                             element. This would work also:
                             iptr = &iara[0];                  */

   printf("Using array subscripts:\n");
   printf("iara\tiptr\n");
   for (ctr=0; ctr<5; ctr++)
      { printf("%d\t%d \n", iara[ctr], iptr[ctr]);  }

   printf("\nUsing pointer notation:\n");
   printf("iara\tiptr\n");
   for (ctr=0; ctr<5; ctr++)
      { printf("%d\t%d \n", *(iara+ctr), *(iptr+ctr));  }

   return;
}
```

The pointer and the array refer to the same memory location

Here is the program's output:

```
Using array subscripts:
iara    iptr
10      10
20      20
30      30
40      40
50      50
```

```
Using pointer notation:
iara    iptr
10      10
20      20
30      30
40      40
50      50
```

# Character Pointers

Character pointers can point to the first character of a string.

The ability to change pointers is best seen when working with character strings in memory. You can store strings in character arrays, or point to them with character pointers. Consider the following two string definitions:

```
char cara[] = "C Is fun";    /* An array holding a string */
char *cptr = "C by Example";   /* A pointer to the string */
```

Figure 27.2 shows how C stores these two strings in memory. C stores both in basically the same way. You are familiar with the array definition. When assigning a string to a character pointer, C finds enough free memory to hold the string and assigns the address of the first character to the pointer. The previous two string definition statements do almost exactly the same thing; the only difference between them is the changeability of the two pointers (the array name and the character pointers).

Because the %s control code prints strings, starting at the array or pointer name until the null zero is reached, you can print each of these strings with the following printf() statements:

```
printf("String 1: %s \n", cara);
printf("String 2: %s \n", cptr);
```

Notice that you print strings in arrays and pointed-to strings in the same way. You might wonder what advantage one method of storing strings has over the other. The seemingly minor difference between these stored strings makes a big difference when you change them.

Suppose that you want to store the string Hello in the two strings. You *cannot* assign the string to the array like this:

```
cara = "Hello";                              /* Invalid */
```

Because you cannot change the array name, you cannot assign it a new value. The only way to change the contents of the array is by assigning the array characters from the string an element at a time, or by using a built-in function such as strcpy(). You can, however, make the character array point to the new string like this:

```
cptr = "Hello";         /* Change the pointer so that
                            it points to the new string */
```

**Figure 27.2**

Storing two
strings: one in an
array and one
pointed to.

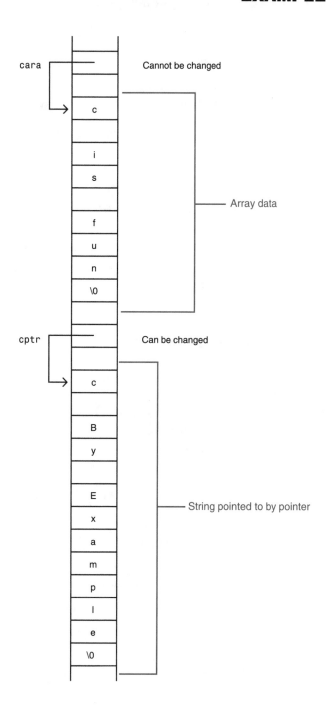

cara     Cannot be changed

c

i

s

       Array data

f

u

n

\0

cptr     Can be changed

c

B

y

E

x

a

m

p

l

e

\0

String pointed to by pointer

> **Tip:** If you want to store user input in a string pointed to by a pointer, first you must reserve enough storage for that input string. The easiest way to do this is to reserve a character array and then assign a character pointer to the beginning element of that array like this:
>
> ```
> char input[81];    /* Holds a string as long
>                        as 80 characters */
>
> char *iptr=input; /*            Could also have done this:
>                                 char *iptr=&input[0];      */
> ```
>
> Now you can input a string by using the pointer:
>
> ```
> gets(iptr); /*            Make sure that iptr points to
>                           the string typed by the user */
> ```
>
> You can use pointer manipulation, arithmetic, and modification on the input string.

## Examples

1. Suppose that you want to store your sister's full name and print it. Instead of using arrays, you can use a character pointer. The following program does just that.

```
/* Filename: C27CP1.C
   Stores a name in a character pointer */
#include <stdio.h>
main()
{
    char *c="Bettye Lou Horn";

    printf("My sister's name is %s", c);
    return;
}
```

Points to the *B* in *Bettyc*

This prints the following:

```
My sister's name is Bettye Lou Horn
```

**2.** Suppose that you need to change a string pointed to by a character pointer. If your sister changed her last name to Henderson by marriage, your program could show both strings in the following manner:

*Identify the program and include the I/O header file. This program uses a character pointer to point to a string literal in memory. We'll call the character pointer c. Point to the string literal and then print the string. Make the character pointer point to a new string literal and then print the new string.*

Name stored with a pointer ⸺

Name stored in an array ⸺

```
/* Filename: C27CP2.C
   Illustrates changing a character string */
#include <stdio.h>
main()
{
    char *c="Bettye Lou Horn";

    printf("My sister's maiden name was %s \n", c);

    c = "Bettye Lou Henderson"; /* Assigns new string to c */

    printf("My sister's married name is %s \n", c);
    return;
}
```

The output is as follows:

```
My sister's maiden name was Bettye Lou Horn
My sister's married name is Bettye Lou Henderson
```

**3.** Do not use character pointers to change string constants. Doing so can confuse the compiler, and you probably will not get the results you expect. The following program is similar to those you just saw. Instead of making the character pointer point to a new string, this example attempts to change the contents of the original string.

```
/* Filename: C27CP3.C
   Illustrates changing a character string improperly */
#include <stdio.h>
main()
{
    char *c="Bettye Lou Horn";

    printf("My sister's maiden name was %s \n", c);
```

Changes the pointer ─────────
```
                                c += 11; /* Makes c point to the last name (the 12th
                                            character)*/
                            c = "Henderson";              /* Assigns a new string to c */

                            printf("My sister's married name is %s \n", c);
                            return;
                        }
```

The program seems to change the last name from Horn to Henderson, but it does not. Here is the output of this program:

```
My sister's maiden name was Bettye Lou Horn
My sister's married name is Henderson
```

Why didn't the full string print? Because the address pointed to by c was incremented by 11, c still points to Henderson, so that was all that printed.

**4.** You might guess at a way to fix the last program. Instead of printing the string stored at c after assigning it to Henderson, you might want to decrement it by 11 so that it points to its original location, the start of the name. The code to do this follows, but it does not work as expected. Study the program before reading the explanation.

```
/* Filename: C27CP4.C
   Illustrates changing a character string improperly */
#include <stdio.h>
main()
{
    char *c="Bettye Lou Horn";

    printf("My sister's maiden name was %s \n", c);

    c += 11;                        /* Makes c point to the last
                                        name (the 12th character) */
    c = "Henderson";                /* Assigns a new string to c */
    c -= 11;                        /* Makes c point to its
                                        original location (???) */

    printf("My sister's married name is %s \n", c);
    return;
}
```

Does not work the way ─────────
you might think!

This program produces garbage at the second printf(). There are actually two string constants in this program. When you first assign c to Bettye Lou Horn, C reserves space in memory for the constant string and puts the starting address of the string in c.

When the program then assigns c to Henderson, C finds room for *another* character constant, as shown in Figure 27.3. If you subtract 11 from the location of c, after it points to the new string Henderson, c points to an area of memory that your program is not using. There is no guarantee that printable data appears before the string constant Henderson. If you want to manipulate parts of the string, you must do so an element at a time, just as you must with arrays.

**Figure 27.3**

Two string constants appear in memory because two string constants are used in the program.

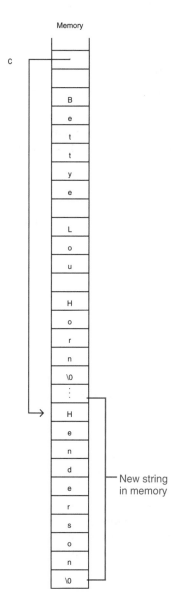

# Pointer Arithmetic

You saw an example of pointer arithmetic when you accessed array elements with pointer notation. By now you should be comfortable with the fact that both of these array or pointer references are identical:

```
ara[sub] and *(ara + sub)
```

You can increment or decrement a pointer. If you increment a pointer, the address inside the pointer variable increments. The pointer does not always increment by 1, however.

Suppose that fPtr is a floating-point pointer that points to the first element of an array of floating-point numbers. You can initialize fPtr as follows:

```
float fara[] = {100.5, 201.45, 321.54, 389.76, 691.34};
fPtr = fara;
```

Figure 27.4 shows what these variables look like in memory. Each floating-point value in this example takes four bytes of memory.

**Figure 27.4**

A floating-point array and a pointer.

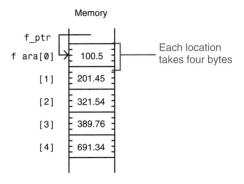

If you print the value of *fPtr, you see 100.5. Suppose that you increment fPtr by 1 with the following statement:

*Incrementing a pointer can add more than one byte to the pointer.*

```
fPtr++;
```

C does *not* add 1 to the address in fPtr, even though it seems as though 1 should be added. In this case, because floating-point values take four bytes each on this machine, C adds 4 to fPtr. How does C know how many bytes to add to fPtr? C knows from the pointer's definition how many bytes of memory pointers take. This is why the data type of pointers is so important.

After incrementing fPtr, if you print *fPtr, you see 201.45, the second element in the array. If C adds only 1 to the address in fPtr, fPtr points only to the second byte of 100.5. This outputs garbage to the screen.

**Note:** When you increment a pointer, C adds one data type size (in bytes) to the pointer, not 1. When you decrement a pointer, C subtracts one data type size (in bytes) from the pointer.

## Examples

1. The following program defines an array with five values. An integer pointer is then initialized to point to the first element in the array. The rest of the program prints the dereferenced value of the pointer and then increments the pointer so that it points to the next integer in the array.

   Just to show you what is going on, the size of integer values is printed at the bottom of the program. Because (in this case) integers take two bytes, C increments the pointer by 2 so that it points to the next integer. (The integers are two bytes apart from each other.)

```
/* Filename: C27PTI.C
   Increments a pointer through an integer array */
#include <stdio.h>
main()
{
   int iara[] = {10,20,30,40,50};
   int *ip = iara;                   /* The pointer points to
                                        the start of the array */

   printf("%d \n", *ip);
   ip++;                             /* 2 is actually added */
   printf("%d \n", *ip);
   ip++;                             /* 2 is actually added */
   printf("%d \n", *ip);
   ip++;                             /* 2 is actually added */
   printf("%d \n", *ip);
   ip++;                             /* 2 is actually added */
   printf("%d \n\n", *ip);
   printf("The integer size is %d \n",sizeof(int));
   printf("bytes on this machine");
   return;
}
```

Makes pointer move ahead in memory

Here is the output from the program:

```
10
20
30
40
50

The integer size is 2 bytes on this machine
```

**2.** Here is the same program using a character array and a character pointer. Because a character takes only one byte of storage, incrementing a character pointer actually adds just 1 to the pointer; only 1 is needed because the characters are only one byte apart from each other.

```
/* Filename: C27PTC.C
   Increments a pointer through a character array */
#include <stdio.h>
main()
{
   char cara[] = {'a', 'b', 'c', 'd', 'e'};
   char *cp = cara;              /* The pointers points to
                                    the start of the array */

   printf("%c \n", *cp);
   cp++;                         /* 1 is actually added */
   printf("%c \n", *cp);
   cp++;                         /* 1 is actually added */
   printf("%c \n", *cp);
   cp++;                         /* 1 is actually added */
   printf("%c \n", *cp);
   cp++;                         /* 1 is actually added */
   printf("%c \n\n", *cp);
   printf("The character size is %d ",sizeof(char));
   printf("bytes on this machine");
   return;
}
```

Moves pointer ahead by the size of a character

**3.** The next program shows the many ways you can add to, subtract from, and reference arrays and pointers. The program defines a floating-point array and a floating-point pointer. The body of the program prints the values from the array using array and pointer notation.

```
/* Filename: C27ARPT2.C
   Comprehensive reference of arrays and pointers */
#include <stdio.h>
```

```
main()
{
   float ara[] = {100.0, 200.0, 300.0, 400.0, 500.0};
   float *fptr;                        /* Floating-point pointer */

   /* Make pointer point to array's first value */
   fptr = &ara[0];             /* Could also have been this:
                                    fptr = ara; */


   printf("%.1f \n", *fptr);              /* Prints 100.0 */
   fptr++;          /* Points to next floating-point value */
   printf("%.1f \n", *fptr);              /* Prints 200.0 */
   fptr++;          /* Points to next floating-point value */
   printf("%.1f \n", *fptr);              /* Prints 300.0 */
   fptr++;          /* Points to next floating-point value */
   printf("%.1f \n", *fptr);              /* Prints 400.0 */
   fptr++;          /* Points to next floating-point value */
   printf("%.1f \n", *fptr);              /* Prints 500.0 */


   fptr = ara;             /* Points to first element again */
   printf("%.1f \n", *(fptr+2) ); /* Prints 300.00 but
                                      does not change fptr */


   /* References both array and pointer using subscripts   */
   printf("%.1f  %.1f \n", (fptr+0)[0],
          (ara+0)[0]);                    /* 100.0  100.0 */
   printf("%.1f  %.1f \n", (fptr+1)[0],
          (ara+1)[0]);                    /* 200.0  200.0 */
   printf("%.1f  %.1f \n", (fptr+4)[0],
          (ara+4)[0]);                    /* 500.0  500.0 */


   /* References both array and pointer using subscripts.
      Notice that subscripts are based from addresses that
      begin before the data in the array and the pointer. */
   printf("%.1f  %.1f \n", (fptr-1)[2],
          (ara-1)[2]);                    /* 200.0  200.0 */
   printf("%.1f  %.1f \n", (fptr-20)[23],
          (ara-20)[23]);                  /* 400.0  400.0 */
   return;
}
```

Array is referenced using several kinds of pointer notations

The following is the output from this program:

```
100.0
200.0
300.0
400.0
500.0
300.0
100.0   100.0
200.0   200.0
500.0   500.0
200.0   200.0
400.0   400.0
```

# Arrays of Strings

*An array that a character pointer defines is a ragged-edge array.*

You now are ready for one of the most useful applications of character pointers: storing arrays of strings. Actually, you cannot store an array of strings, but you can store an array of character pointers, and each character pointer can point to a string in memory.

By defining an array of character pointers, you define a *ragged-edge array*. A ragged-edge array is similar to two-dimensional tables, except that instead of each row being the same length (the same number of elements), each row contains a different number of characters.

The term *ragged-edge* derives from the use of word processors. A word processor typically can print text fully justified or with a ragged-right text format. This paragraph is fully justified: the text aligns evenly with both the left and right margins. Letters you write by hand and type on typewriters (remember what a typewriter is?) generally have ragged-right edges. It is very difficult to type so that each line aligns exactly with the right margin.

All two-dimensional tables you have seen so far have been fully justified. For example, if you define a character table with 5 rows and 20 columns, each row contains the same number of characters. You can define the table with the following statement:

```
char names[5][20]={ {"George"},
                    {"Michelle"},
                    {"Joe"},
                    {"Marcus"},
                    {"Stephanie"} };
```

This table is shown in Figure 27.5. Notice that much of the table is wasted space. Each row takes 20 characters, even though the data in each row takes far fewer characters. The unfilled elements contain null zeros because C zeros out all elements you do not initialize in arrays. This type of table uses too much memory.

**Figure 27.5**

A fully justified table.

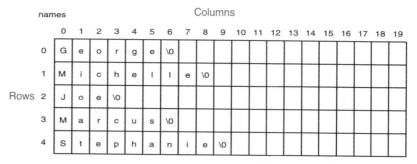

Most of the table is wasted

To fix the memory-wasting problem of fully justified tables, you should define a single-dimensional array of character pointers. Each pointer points to a string in memory, and the strings do *not* have to be the same length.

Here is the definition for such an array:

```
char *names[5]={ {"George"},
                 {"Michelle"},
                 {"Joe"},
                 {"Marcus"},
                 {"Stephanie"} };
```

This array is single-dimensional. The definition should not confuse you although it is something you have not seen. The asterisk before names makes this an array of pointers. The type of pointers is character. The strings are *not* being assigned to the array elements, but they are being *pointed to* by the array elements. Figure 27.6 shows this array of pointers. The strings are stored elsewhere in memory. Their actual locations are not critical because each pointer points to the starting character. The strings waste no data. Each string takes only as much memory as needed by the string and its terminating zero. This gives the data its ragged-right appearance.

To print the first string, you use this printf():

```
printf("%s", *names);              /* Prints George */
```

To print the second string, you use this printf():

```
printf("%s", *(names+1));          /* Prints Michelle */
```

Whenever you dereference any pointer element with the * dereferencing operator, you access one of the strings in the array. You can use a dereferenced element any place you would use a string constant or character array (with strcpy(), strcmp(), and so on).

**Figure 27.6**

The array that
points to each of
the five strings.

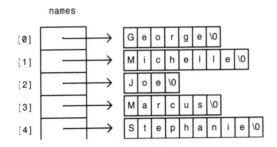

names

[0] → George\0

[1] → Michelle\0

[2] → Joe\0

[3] → Marcus\0

[4] → Stephanie\0

**Tip:** Working with pointers to strings is *much* more efficient than working with the strings. For instance, sorting a list of strings takes a lot of time if they are stored as a fully justified table. Sorting strings pointed to by a pointer array is much faster. You swap only pointers during the sort, not entire strings.

## Examples

**1.** Here is a full program that uses the pointer array with five names. The `for` loop controls the `printf()` function, printing each name in the string data. Now you can see why learning about pointer notation for arrays pays off!

```
/* Filename: C27PTST1.C
   Prints strings pointed to by an array */
#include <stdio.h>
main()
{
    char *name[5]={ {"George"},    /* Defines a ragged-edge */
                    {"Michelle"},  /* array of pointers to  */
                    {"Joe"},       /* strings               */
                    {"Marcus"},
                    {"Stephanie"} };
    int ctr;

    for (ctr=0; ctr<5; ctr++)
        { printf("String #%d is %s \n", (ctr+1), *(name+ctr)); }

    return;
}
```

Each name consumes
a different number
of memory locations

The following is the output from this program:

```
String #1 is George
String #2 is Michelle
String #3 is Joe
String #4 is Marcus
String #5 is Stephanie
```

2. The following program stores the days of the week in an array. When the user types a number from 1 to 7, the day of the week that matches that number (with Sunday being 1) displays by dereferencing the pointer that points to that string.

```
/* Filename: C27PTST2.C
   Prints the day of the week based on an input value */
#include <stdio.h>
main()
{
   char *days[] = {"Sunday",    /* The seven separate sets */
                   "Monday",    /* of braces are optional. */
                   "Tuesday",
                   "Wednesday",
                   "Thursday",
                   "Friday",
                   "Saturday"};
   int dayNum;

   do
     { printf("What is a day number (from 1 to 7)? ");
       scanf(" %d", &dayNum);
     } while ((dayNum<1) || (dayNum>7));      /* Ensures
                                                 an accurate
                                                 number */


   dayNum--;                           /* Adjusts for subscript */
   printf("The day is %s\n", *(days+dayNum));
   return;
}
```

Derefences the array value

**Note:** All of the examples in this chapter explain how to store data in ragged-edge arrays using assignment statements. You cannot accept user input directly into a character ragged-edge array element until you learn how to *dynamically allocate memory* in Chapter 29. Although dynamic memory allocation sounds difficult, it is relatively easy and provides the most important reason for learning pointers.

## Summary

You deserve a break! You now understand the foundation of C's pointers and array notation. As soon as you have mastered this section, you are on your way to thinking in C as you design your programs. C programmers know that C's arrays are pointers in disguise, and they program them accordingly.

Being able to use ragged-edge arrays offers two advantages: you can hold arrays of string data without wasting extra space, and you can quickly change the pointers without having to move the string data around in memory.

As you progress into advanced C concepts, you will appreciate the time you spend mastering pointer notation. The next chapter introduces a new topic called *structures*. Structures enable you to store data in a more unified manner than simple variables have allowed.

## Review Questions

Answers to review questions are in Appendix B.

1. What is the difference between an array name and a pointer?

2. Assume that `ipointer` points to integers that take four bytes of memory. If you perform the following statement

   ```
   ipointer += 2;
   ```

   how many bytes are added to `ipointer`?

3. Which of the following are equivalent, assuming that `iary` is an integer array and `iptr` is an integer pointer that points to the start of the array?

   a. `iary` and `iptr`

   b. `iary[1]` and `*iptr+1`

   c. `iary[3]` and `*(iptr + 3)`

   d. `(iary-4)[9]` and `iary[5]`

   e. `*iary` and `iary[0]`

   f. `iary[4]` and `*iptr+4`

4. Why is it more efficient to sort a ragged-edge character array than a fully justified string array?

5. Given the following array and pointer definition

```
int ara[] = {1, 2, 3, 4, 5, 6, 7, 8, 9, 10};
int *ip1, *ip2;
```

which of the following is allowed?

a. `ip1 = ara;`

b. `ip2 = ip1 = &ara[3];`

c. `ara = 15;`

d. `*(ip2 + 2) = 15;   /* Assuming ip2 and ara are equal */`

# Review Exercises

1. Write a program to store your family members' names in a character array of pointers. Print the names.

2. Write a program that asks the user for 15 daily stock market averages and stores those averages in a floating-point array. Using only pointer notation, print the array forward and backward. Using only pointer notation, print the highest and lowest stock market quote in the list.

3. Modify the bubble sort shown in Chapter 24, "Array Processing," so that it sorts using pointer notation. Add this bubble sort to the program in exercise 2 to print the stock market averages in ascending order.

4. Write a program that defines an array named `songs` and initialize each element in the array to 25 blanks at the top of `main()`. (The blanks reserve some space for user input, and you learn how to get around the up-front memory reservation in Chapter 29.) Request 10 song titles from the user. Store the titles in an array of character pointers (a ragged-edge array). Print the original titles, print the alphabetized titles, and print the titles in backward alphabetical order (from Z to A).

# Part VII

*Structures and File I/O*

# CHAPTER 28

# Structures

Using structures, you have the ability to group data and work with that data as a whole. Business data processing uses the structure concept in almost every program. Being able to manipulate several variables as a single group makes your programs easier to manage.

This chapter introduces the following concepts:

- Structure definitions

- Initializing structures

- The dot operator (.)

- Structure assignment

- Nested structures

This chapter is one of the last in the book to present brand new concepts. The rest of the book builds on the structure concepts you learn in this chapter.

## Introducing Structures

Structures can have members of different data types.

A *structure* is a collection of one or more variable types. As you know, each element in an array must be the same data type, and you must refer to the entire array by its name. Each element (called a *member*) in a structure can be a different data type.

Suppose you want to keep track of your CD music collection. You might want to track the following pieces of information about each CD:

Title

Artist

Number of songs

Cost

Date bought

There would be five members in this CD structure.

> **Tip:** For those who have programmed in other computer languages or used a database program, C structures are analogous to file records, and members are analogous to fields in those records.

After deciding on the members, you must decide what data type each member is. The title and artist both will be character arrays, the number of songs will be integer, the cost will be floating-point, and the date will be another character array. This information is represented like this:

| Member Name | Data Type |
| --- | --- |
| Title | Character array of 25 characters |
| Artist | Character array of 20 characters |
| Number of songs | Integer |
| Cost | Floating-point |
| Date bought | Character array of eight characters |

Each structure you define can have an associated structure name called a *structure tag*. Structure tags are not required in most cases, but it is generally best to define one for each structure in your program. The structure tag is *not* a variable name. Unlike array names that reference the array as variables, a structure tag is just a label for the structure's format.

You name structure tags yourself, using the same naming rules for variables. If you give the CD structure a structure tag named cdCollection, you are telling C that the tag called cdCollection looks like two character arrays, followed by an integer, a floating-point value, and a final character array.

A structure tag is a label for the structure's format.

A structure tag is actually a newly defined data type that you, the programmer, define. When you want to store an integer, you do not have to define to C what an integer is. C already knows what an integer is. When you want to store a CD collection's data, however, C does not know what format your CD collection will take. You have to tell C (using the example being described here) that you need a new data type. That data type is your structure tag, called cdCollection in this example, and it looks like the structure previously described (two character arrays, integer, floating-point, and character array).

> **Note:** No memory is reserved for structure tags. A structure tag is your own data type. C does not reserve memory for the integer data type until you define an integer variable. C does not reserve memory for a structure until you define a structure variable.

Figure 28.1 shows the CD structure, graphically representing the data types within the structure. Notice that there are five members and that each member is a different data type. The entire structure is called cdCollection because that is the structure tag.

**Figure 28.1**

The layout of the *cdCollection* structure.

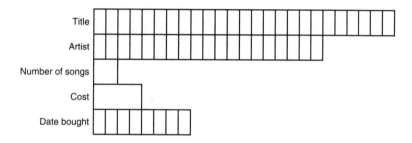

## Examples

**1.** Suppose that you are asked to write a program for a company's inventory system. The company has been using a card-file inventory system that tracks the following items:

>    Item name

>    Quantity in stock

>    Quantity on order

>    Retail price

>    Wholesale price

This is a perfect use for a structure containing five members. Before defining the structure, you have to determine the data types of each member. After asking questions about the range of data (you must know the largest item name and the largest quantity that would ever be on order to ensure that your data types will hold the data), you decide to use the following structure tag and data types:

| Structure tag: inventory Member | Data Type |
|---|---|
| Item name | Character array of 20 characters |
| Quantity in stock | `long int` |
| Quantity on order | `long int` |
| Retail price | `double` |
| Wholesale price | `double` |

**2.** Suppose that the same company also wants you to write a program that keeps track of monthly and annual salaries, printing a report at the end of the year that includes both the monthly and annual data.

What would the structure look like? Be careful! This type of data probably does not need a structure. Because all the salaries require the same data type, a floating-point or a double floating-point array can hold the salaries nicely without the complexity of a structure.

Structures are very useful for keeping track of data that must be grouped, such as inventory data, customer name and address data, or employee data.

# Defining Structures

To define a structure, you must use the `struct` statement. The `struct` statement defines a new data type, with more than one member, for your program. The format of the `struct` statement is this:

```
struct [structure tag]
    {
        member definition;
        member definition;
            :
        member definition;
    } [one or more structure variables];
```

As mentioned earlier, the *structure tag* is optional (hence the brackets in the format). Each *member definition* is a normal variable definition, such as `int i;` or `float sales[20];` or any other valid variable definition, including variable pointers if the structure requires a pointer as a member. At the end of the structure's definition, before the final semicolon, you can specify one or more structure variables.

**Note:** Structure tags are required when you define structure variables later in the program instead of immediately before the `struct`'s closing semicolon. (See the "Initializing Structure Data" section later in this chapter.)

If you specify a structure variable, you request C to reserve space for that variable. C knows that the variable is not integer, character, or any other internal data type; C knows the variable will be a type that looks like the structure. It might seem strange that the members themselves do not reserve storage, but they don't. The structure variables do. This is made very clear in the examples that follow.

Here is the way you define the CD structure and variables:

```
struct cdCollection
    {
       char title[25];
       char artist[20];
       int numSongs;
       float price;
       char dateBought[9];
    } cd1, cd2, cd3;
```

Before going any further, you should be able to answer the following questions about this structure:

♦ What is the structure tag?

♦ How many members are there?

♦ What are the member data types?

♦ What are the member names?

♦ How many structure variables are there?

♦ What are their names?

The structure tag is called `cdCollection`. There are five members, two character arrays, an integer, a floating-point value, and a character array. The member names are `title`, `artist`, `numSongs`, `price`, and `dateBought`. There are three structure variables—`cd1`, `cd2`, and `cd3`.

**Tip:** Many times, you can visualize structure variables as looking like a card-file inventory system. Figure 28.2 shows how you might keep your CD collection in a 3-by-5 card file. Each CD takes one card (representing one structure variable), and the information for the CD (the structure members) is on that card.

**Figure 28.2**

Using a card-file
CD inventory
system.

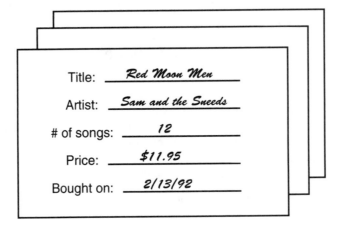

If you have 1000 CDs, you have to define 1000 structure variables. Obviously, you do not want to list that many structure variables at the end of a structure definition. To help define structures for a large number of occurrences, you must define an *array of structures*. Chapter 29, "Arrays of Structures," shows you how to do that. For now, however, concentrate on familiarizing yourself with structure definitions.

## Examples

1. Here is a structure definition of the inventory application described earlier in this chapter.

```
struct inventory
{
    char itemName[20];
    long int inStock;
    long int orderQty;
    float retail;
    float wholesale;
} item1, item2, item3, item4;
```

Four inventory structure variables are defined. Each structure variable—item1, item2, item3, and item4—looks like the structure.

2. Suppose that a company wants to track its customers and personnel. The following two structure definitions create five structure variables for each structure. This example, having five employees and five customers, is very limited, but serves to show how structures can be defined.

```
struct employees
{
```

```
    char empName[25];                  /* Employee's full name */
    char address[30];                   /* Employee's address */
    char city[10];
    char state[2];
    long int zip;
    double salary;                            /* Annual salary */
} emp1, emp2, emp3, emp4, emp5;

struct customers
{
    char custName[25];                 /* Customer's full name */
    char address[30];                   /* Customer's address */
    char city[10];
    char state[2];
    long int zip;
    double balance;                /* Balance owed to company */
} cust1, cust2, cust3, cust4, cust5;
```

Each structure has very similar data. A little later in this chapter, you learn how to consolidate similar member definitions by creating nested structures.

**Tip:** Put comments to the right of members to document their purposes.

# Initializing Structure Data

You can define a structure's data when you define the structure.

There are two ways to initialize members of a structure. You can initialize members when you define a structure variable, and you can initialize a structure within the body of the program. Most programs lend themselves to the latter method because you do not always know structure data when you write your program.

Here is an example of a structure variable defined and initialized at the same time:

```
struct cdCollection
    {
    char title[25];
    char artist[20];
    int numSongs;
    float price;
    char dateBought[9];
    } cd1 = {"Red Moon Men", "Sam and the Sneeds",
            12, 11.95, "02/13/92"};
```

When first learning about structures, you might be tempted to initialize members individually inside the structure, such as

```
char artist[20]="Sam and the Sneeds";      /* Invalid */
```

You cannot initialize individual members, however, because they are *not* variables. You can assign only values to variables. The only structure variable in this structure is cd1. The braces must enclose the data you initialize in the structure variables, just as they enclose data when you initialize arrays.

This method of initializing structure variables gets tedious when there are several structure variables (as there usually are). Putting the data into several variables, each set of data enclosed in braces, gets messy and takes too much space in your code.

More importantly, you usually do not even know the contents of the structure variables. Generally, the user enters data to be stored in structures, or you read them from a disk file.

**Use the dot operator to initialize structure members.**

A better approach to initializing structures is to use the *dot operator* (.). The dot operator provides one way to initialize individual members of a structure variable within the body of your program. With the dot operator, you can treat each structure member almost as if it were a regular nonstructure variable.

The format you use with the dot operator is

```
structureVariableName.memberName
```

A structure variable name must *always* precede the dot operator, and a member name must always appear after the dot operator. Using the dot operator is very easy, as the following examples show.

## Examples

1. Here is a simple program that uses the CD collection structure and the dot operator to initialize the structure. Notice that the program treats members as if they were regular variables when combined with the dot operator.

*Identify the program and include the necessary header file. Define a CD structure variable with five members. Fill the CD structure variable with data, and then print it.*

```
/* Filename: C28ST1.C
   Structure initialization with the CD collection */
#include <stdio.h>
#include <string.h>
main()
{
```

```
            ┌── struct cdCollection
            │    {
            │      char title[25];
Declares a ─┤      char artist[20];
structure   │      int numSongs;
            │      float price;
            └──    char dateBought[9];
                 } cd1;
Defines a ─────────┘
structure
variable           /* Initialize members here */
                   strcpy(cd1.title, "Red Moon Men");
                   strcpy(cd1.artist, "Sam and the Sneeds");
                   cd1.numSongs=12;
                   cd1.price=11.95;
                   strcpy(cd1.dateBought, "02/13/92");

                   /* Print the data to the screen */
            ┌──  printf("Here is the CD information:\n\n");
            │    printf("Title: %s \n", cd1.title);
Prints individual  printf("Artist: %s \n", cd1.artist);
members of the ─┤  printf("Songs: %d \n", cd1.numSongs);
same structure  │  printf("Price: %.2f \n", cd1.price);
            └──  printf("Date bought: %s \n", cd1.dateBought);

                   return;
                 }
```

Here is the output from this program:

```
Here is the CD information:

Title: Red Moon Men
Artist: Sam and the Sneeds
Songs: 12
Price: 11.95
Date bought: 02/13/92
```

**2.** By using the dot operator, you can get structure data from the keyboard with any of the data-input functions you know, such as scanf(), gets(), and getchar().

The following program asks the user for student information. To keep the example reasonably short, only two students are defined in the program.

```
/* Filename: C28ST2.C
   Structure input with student data */
#include <stdio.h>
#include <string.h>
main()
{
   struct students
   {
     char name[25];
     int age;
     float average;
   } student1, student2;

   /* Get data for two students */
   printf("What is first student's name? ");
   gets(student1.name);
   printf("What is the first student's age? ");
   scanf(" %d", &student1.age);
   printf("What is the first student's average? ");
   scanf(" %f", &student1.average);

   fflush(stdin);      /* Clear input buffer for next input */

   printf("\nWhat is second student's name? ");
   gets(student2.name);
   printf("What is the second student's age? ");
   scanf(" %d", &student2.age);
   printf("What is the second student's average? ");
   scanf(" %f", &student2.average);

   /* Print the data */
   printf("\n\nHere is the student information you
   ➥ entered:\n\n");
   printf("Student #1:\n");
   printf("Name:    %s\n", student1.name);
   printf("Age:     %d\n", student1.age);
   printf("Average: %.1f\n", student1.average);

   printf("\nStudent #2:\n");
   printf("Name:    %s\n", student2.name);
   printf("Age:     %d\n", student2.age);
   printf("Average: %.1f\n", student2.average);

   return;
}
```

*scanf()* always needs & for nonarray data

Figure 28.3 shows the output from this program.

**Figure 28.3**

The user is filling
structure variables
with values.

```
What is first student's name? Joe Sanders
What is the first student's age? 13
What is the first student's average? 78.4

What is second student's name? Mary Reynolds
What is the second student's age? 12
What is the second student's average? 98.9


Here is the student information you entered:

Student #1:
Name:    Joe Sanders
Age:     13
Average: 78.4

Student #2:
Name:    Mary Reynolds
Age:     12
Average: 98.9
```

**3.** Structure variables are passed by copy, not by address as with arrays. Therefore, if you fill a structure in a function, you must return it to the calling function for the calling function to recognize it, or use global structure variables, which is generally not recommended.

Define structures globally and structure variables locally.

A good solution to the local/global structure problem is this: Define your structures globally without *any* structure variables. Define all your structure variables locally to the functions that need them. As long as your structure definition is global, you can define local structure variables from that structure. All subsequent examples in this book use this method.

This is where structure tag plays an important role. Use the structure tag to define local structure variables. The following program is similar to the previous one. Notice that the student structure is defined globally with *no structure variables*. In each function, local structure variables are defined by referring to the structure tag. The structure tag keeps you from having to redefine the structure members every time you define a new structure variable.

```c
/* Filename: C28ST3.C
   Structure input with student data passed to functions */
#include <stdio.h>
#include <string.h>
struct students fillStructs(struct students studentVar);
void prStudents(struct students studentVar);

struct students                        /* A global structure */
```

```
{
    char name[25];
    int age;
    float average;
};                              /* No memory reserved yet */

main()
{
    struct students student1, student2;    /* Defines two
                                               local variables */

    /* Call function to fill structure variables */
    student1 = fillStructs(student1);    /* student1 is passed by
                                            copy, so it must be
                                            returned for main()
                                            to recognize it */

    student2 = fillStructs(student2);

    /* Print the data */
    printf("\n\nHere is the student information you");
    printf(" entered:\n\n");
    prStudents(student1);   /* Print first student's data */
    prStudents(student2);   /* Print second student's data */

    return 0;
}

struct students fillStructs(struct students studentVar)
{
    /* Get student's data */
    fflush(stdin);     /* Clear input buffer for next input */
    printf("What is student's name? ");
    gets(studentVar.name);
    printf("What is the student's age? ");
    scanf(" %d", &studentVar.age);
    printf("What is the student's average? ");
    scanf(" %f", &studentVar.average);

    return (studentVar);
```

Must tell function the entire data type ——

```
    }

void prStudents(struct students studentVar)
{
    printf("Name:    %s\n", studentVar.name);
    printf("Age:     %d\n", studentVar.age);
    printf("Average: %.1f\n", studentVar.average);
    return;
}
```

The prototype and definition of the fillStructs() function might seem complicated, but it follows the same pattern you have seen throughout this book. Before a function name, you must define void or put the return data type if the function returns a value. fillStructs() does return a value, and the type of value it returns is struct students.

**4.** Because structure data is nothing more than regular variables grouped together, feel free to calculate using structure members. As long as you use the dot operator, you can treat structure members just as you treat other variables.

The following example asks for a customer's balance and uses a discount rate (included in the customer's structure) to calculate a new balance. To keep the example short, the structure's data is initialized at variable definition time.

This program does not actually require structures because only one customer is used. Individual variables could have been used, but they would not illustrate calculating with structures.

```
/* Filename: C28CUST.C
   Updates a customer balance in a structure */
#include <stdio.h>

struct customerRec
    {
        char custName[25];
        double balance;
        float disRate;
    } ;

main()
{
    struct customerRec customer = {"Steve Thompson",
                                   2431.23, .25};
```

Stores data when structure variable is defined

```
printf("Before the update, %s", customer.custName);
   printf(" has a balance of $%.2f\n", customer.balance);

   /* Update the balance */
   customer.balance *= (1.0-customer.disRate);

   printf("After the update, %s", customer.custName);
   printf(" has a balance of $%.2f\n", customer.balance);
   return;
}
```

5. You can copy the members of one structure variable to the members of another as long as both structures have the same format. Some older versions of C require you to copy each member individually when you want to copy one structure variable to another, but ANSI C makes duplicating structure variables easy.

Being able to copy one structure variable to another will seem more meaningful when you read Chapter 29, "Arrays of Structures."

The following program defines three structure variables, but initializes only the first one with data. The other two are then initialized by assigning the first structure variable to them.

```
/* Filename: C28STCPY.C
   Demonstrates assigning one structure to another */
#include <stdio.h>

struct student
{
   char stName[25];
   char grade;
   int age;
   float average;
};

main()
{
   struct student std1 = {"Joe Brown", 'A', 13, 91.4};
   struct student std2, std3;               /* Not initialized */

   std2 = std1;                   /* Copies each member of std1 */
   std3 = std1;                   /* to std2 and std3           */
```

Each copies an entire structure

```
    printf("The contents of std2:\n");
        printf("%s, %c, ", std2.stName, std2.grade);
        printf("%d, %.1f\n\n", std2.age, std2.average);

        printf("The contents of std3:\n");
        printf("%s, %c, ", std3.stName, std3.grade);
        printf("%d, %.1f\n", std3.age, std3.average);
        return;
    }
```

Here is the output from the program:

```
The contents of std2
Joe Brown, A, 13, 91.4

The contents of std3
Joe Brown, A, 13, 91.4
```

Notice that each member of std1 was assigned to std2 and std3 with two single assignments.

## Nesting Structures

C gives you the ability to nest one structure definition within another. This saves time when you are writing programs that use similar structures. You have to define the common members only once in their own structure and then use that structure as a member in another structure.

The following two structure definitions illustrate this point:

```
struct employees
{
   char empName[25];              /* Employee's full name */
   char address[30];               /* Employee's address */
   char city[10];
   char state[2];
   long int zip;
   double salary;                      /* Annual salary */
};

struct customers
{
   char custName[25];             /* Customer's full name */
   char address[30];               /* Customer's address */
```

```
      char city[10];
      char state[2];
      long int zip;
      double balance;              /* Balance owed to company */
};
```

These structures hold different data. One structure is for employee data and the other holds customer data. Even though the data should be kept separate (you don't want to send a customer a paycheck!), the structure definitions have a lot of overlap and can be consolidated by creating a third structure.

Suppose that you create the following structure:

```
struct addressInfo
{
   char address[30];        /* Common address information */
   char city[10];
   char state[2];
   long int zip;
};
```

You can then use this structure as a member in the other structures like this:

```
struct employees
{
   char empName[25];              /* Employee's full name */
   struct addressInfo eAddress;    /* Employee's address */
   double salary;                       /* Annual salary */
};

struct customers
{
   char custName[25];              /* Customer's full name */
   struct addressInfo cAddress;    /* Customer's address */
   double balance;              /* Balance owed to company */
};
```

It is important to realize that there is a total of three structures and that they have the tags addressInfo, employees, and customers. How many members does the employees structure have? If you answered three, you are correct. There are three members in both employees and customers. The employees structure has the structure of a character array, followed by the addressInfo structure, followed by the double floating-point member salary. Figure 28.4 shows how these structures look.

**Figure 28.4**

Defining a nested
structure.

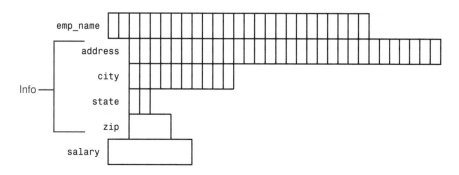

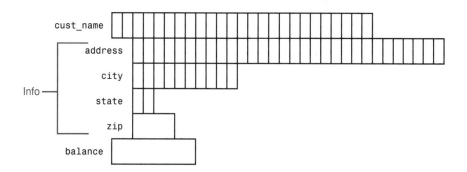

As soon as you define a structure, that structure is then a new data type in the program and can be used anywhere a data type (such as int, float, and so on) can appear.

You can assign members values using the dot operator. To assign the customer balance a number, you can type something like this:

```
customer.balance = 5643.24;
```

The nested structure might seem to pose a problem. How can you assign a value to one of the nested members? By using the dot operator, you must nest the dot operator just as you nest the structure definitions. You assign a value to the customer's ZIP code like this:

```
customer.cAddress.zip = 34312;
```

To assign a value to the employee's ZIP code, you do this:

```
employee.eAddress.zip = 59823;
```

## Summary

With structures, you have the ability to group data in more flexible ways than arrays allow. Your structures can contain members of different data types. You can initialize the structures either at definition time or during the program with the dot operator.

Structures become even more powerful when you define arrays of structure variables. Chapter 29, "Arrays of Structures," shows you how to define several structure variables without giving them each a different name. This lets you step through structures much quicker with loop constructs.

## Review Questions

Answers to review questions are in Appendix B.

1. What is the difference between structures and arrays?

2. What are the individual elements of a structure called?

3. What are the two ways to initialize members of a structure?

4. Do you pass structures by copy or by address?

5. True or false: The following structure definition reserves storage in memory:

```
struct crec
   { char name[25];
     int age;
     float sales[5];
     long int num;
   }
```

6. Should you define a structure globally or locally?

7. Should you define a structure variable globally or locally?

8. How many members does the following structure definition contain?

```
struct item
   {
     int quantity;
     struct partRec itemDesc;
     float price;
     char dateBought[8];
   };
```

# Review Exercises

1. Write a structure that a video store can use in a program that tracks its video tape inventory. Make sure that the structure includes the tape title, the length of the tape (in minutes), the cost of the tape, the rental price of the tape, and the date of the movie's release.

2. Write a program that uses the structure you defined in exercise 1. Define three structure variables and initialize them *when you define the variables* with data. Print the data to the screen.

3. Write a teacher's program that keeps track of 10 students' names, ages, letter grades, and IQs. Use 10 different structure variable names and get the data for the students in a `for` loop from the keyboard. Print the data on the printer when the teacher finishes entering the information for all the students.

# CHAPTER 29

# Arrays of Structures

This chapter builds on the preceding one by showing you how to create many structures for your data. After creating an array of structures, you can store many occurrences of your data values.

Arrays of structures are good for storing a complete employee file, inventory file, or any other set of data that fits within the structure format. Whereas arrays provide a handy way to store several values that are the same type, with arrays of structures you can store several values of different types together, grouped as structures.

Finally, *dynamic memory allocation* is important so you can step up to the next level of C programming. Dynamic memory allocation lets you reserve memory when you need it for your data instead of having to define variables in advance.

This chapter introduces the following concepts:

- ◆ Creating arrays of structures
- ◆ Initializing arrays of structures
- ◆ Referencing elements from a structure array
- ◆ Dynamic memory allocation with `malloc()` and `free()`

Many C programmers use arrays of structures as a prelude to storing their data in a disk file. You can input and calculate your disk data in arrays of structures and then store those structures in memory. Arrays of structures also provide a means of holding data you read from the disk.

# Defining Arrays of Structures

It is very easy to define an array of structures. Specify the number of reserved structures, inside array brackets, when you define the structure variable. Consider the following structure definition:

```
struct stores
    { int employees;
          int registers;
          double sales;
    } store1, store2, store3, store4, store5;
```

This structure should pose no problem for you to understand because there are no new commands used in the structure definition. This structure definition creates five structure variables. Figure 29.1 shows how C stores these five structures in memory. Each of the structure variables has three members—two integers followed by a double floating-point value.

**Figure 29.1**

The structure of *store1, store2, store3, store4*, and *store5*.

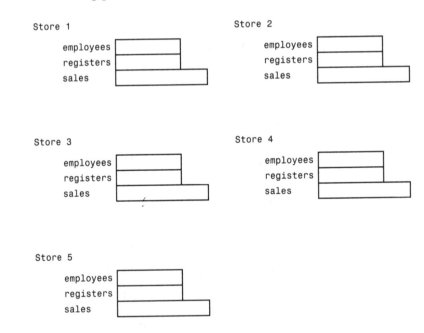

If the fourth store increases its employee count by three, you can update the store's employee number with the following assignment statement:

```
store4.employees += 3;        /* Add 3 to this store's
                                 employee count */
```

Suppose that the fifth store just opened and you want to initialize its members with data. If the stores are a chain and the new store is similar to one of the others, you might begin initializing the store's data by assigning each of its members the same data as another store's like this:

```
store5 = store2;              /* Define initial values
                                 for the store5 members */
```

Arrays of structures make working with large numbers of structure variables manageable.

Such structure definitions are fine for a small number of structures, but if the stores were a national chain, five structure variables would not be enough. Suppose there are 1000 stores. You do not want to create 1000 different store variables and work with each one individually. It is much easier to create an array of store structures.

Consider the following structure definition:

```
struct stores
     { int employees;
          int registers;
          double sales;
     } store[1000];
```

In one quick definition, this code creates 1000 store structures, each one containing three members. Figure 29.2 shows how these structure variables appear in memory. Notice the name of each individual structure variable: store[0], store[1], store[2], and so on.

**Figure 29.2**

An array of the *store* structures.

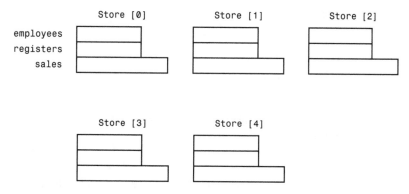

**Caution:** Be careful that your computer does not run out of memory when you create a large number of structures. Arrays of structures quickly consume valuable memory. You might have to create fewer structures, storing more data in disk files and less data in memory.

The element `store[2]` is an array element. This array element, unlike the others you have seen, is a *structure variable*. Therefore, it contains three members, each of which you can reference with the dot operator.

The dot operator works the same way for structure array elements as it does for regular structure variables. If the number of employees for the fifth store (`store[4]`) increases by three, you can update the structure variable like this:

```
store[4].employees += 3;      /* Add 3 to this store's
                                 employee count */
```

You can assign complete structures to one another using array notation also. To assign all the members of the 20th store to the 45th store, you do this:

```
store[44] = store[19];     /* Copy all members from the
                              20th store to the 45th */
```

The rules of arrays are still in force here. Each element of the array called `store` is the *very same data type*. The data type of `store` is `struct stores`. As with any array, each element must be the same data type; you cannot mix data types within the same array. This array's data type happens to be a structure you created containing three members. The data type for `store[316]` is the same for `store[981]` and `store[74]`.

The name of the array, `store`, is a pointer constant to the starting element of the array, `store[0]`. Therefore, you can use pointer notation to reference the stores. To assign `store[60]` the same value as `store[23]`, you can reference the two elements like this:

```
*(store+60) = *(store+23);
```

You also can mix array and pointer notation, such as

```
store[60] = *(store+23);
```

and get the same results.

You can increase the `sales` of `store[8]` by 40 percent using pointer or subscript notation as well, as in

```
store[8].sales = (*(store+8)).sales * 1.40;
```

The extra pair of parentheses are required because the dot operator has precedence over the dereferencing symbol in C's hierarchy of operators (see Appendix D). Of course, in this case, the code is not helped by the pointer notation. The following is a much clearer way to increase the `sales` by 40 percent:

```
store[8].sales *= 1.40;
```

---

**Keep Your Array Notation Straight**

You never access the member `sales` like this:

```
store.sales[8] = 3234.54;          /* Invalid */
```

Array subscripts follow only array elements. `sales` is not an array; it was defined as being a double floating-point number. `store` can never be used *without* a subscript (unless you are using pointer notation).

Here is a corrected version of the previous assignment statement:

```
store[8].sales=3234.54;          /* Correctly assigns
                                    the value          */
```

---

The following examples build an inventory data-entry system for a mail-order firm using an array of structures. There is very little new you have to know when working with arrays of structures. Concentrate on the notation used when accessing arrays of structures and their members to get comfortable with the arrays of structures notation.

---

**For Related Information**

♦ "Understanding Array Basics," p. 389

♦ "Searching for Values," p. 409

---

## Examples

1. Suppose that you work for a mail-order company that sells disk drives. You are given the task of writing a tracking program for the 125 different drives you sell. You must keep track of the following information:

> Storage capacity in megabytes
>
> Access time in milliseconds
>
> Vendor code (A, B, C, or D)
>
> Cost
>
> Price

Because there are 125 different disk drives in the inventory, the data will fit nicely into an array of structures. Each array element is a structure containing the five members described in the list.

The following structure definition defines the inventory:

```
struct inventory
{
    long int storage;
    int accessTime;
    char vendorCode;
    double code;
    double price;
} drive[125]; /* Defines 125 occurrences of the structure */
```

**2.** When working with a large array of structures, your first concern should be how the data will be input into the array elements. The application determines the best method of data entry.

For instance, if you are converting from an older computerized inventory system, you have to write a conversion program that reads the inventory file in its native format and saves it to a new file in the format needed by your C programs. This is no easy task. It requires that you have extensive knowledge of the system from which you are converting.

If you are writing a computerized inventory system for the first time, your job is a little easier because you do not need to worry about converting the old files. You still must realize that someone has to type the data into the computer. You have to write a data-entry program that receives each inventory item from the keyboard and saves it to a disk file. You should give the user a chance to edit inventory data to correct any data that he or she originally might have typed incorrectly.

One of the reasons this book waits until the last chapters to introduce disk files is that disk-file formats and structures share a common bond. As soon as you store data in a structure, or more often, in an array of structures, you can very easily write that data to a disk file using straightforward disk I/O commands.

The following program takes the array of disk drive structures shown in the previous example and adds a data-entry function so that the user can enter data into the array of structures. The program is menu-driven. The user has a choice, when starting the program, to add data, print data to the screen, or exit the program. Because you have yet to see disk I/O commands, the data in the array of structures goes away when the program ends. As mentioned earlier, saving those structures to disk is an easy task after you learn C's disk I/O commands. For now, concentrate on the manipulation of the structures.

This program is longer than many you have seen in this book, but if you have followed the discussion of structures and the dot operator, you should have little trouble following the code.

*Identify the program and include the necessary header files. Define a structure that describes the format of each inventory item. Create an array of structures called* disk. *Display a menu that gives the user the choice of entering new inventory data, displaying the data on-screen, or quitting the program.*

*If the user wants to enter new inventory items, prompt the user for each item and store the data into the array of structures. If the user wants to see the inventory, loop through each inventory item in the array, displaying each one on-screen.*

```c
/* Filename: C29DSINV.C
   Data-entry program for a disk drive company */
#include <stdio.h>
#include <stdlib.h>

struct inventory              /* Global structure definition */
{
   long int storage;
   int accessTime;
   char vendorCode;
   float cost;
   float price;
};                /* No structure variables defined globally */

void dispMenu(void);
struct inventory enterData();
void seeData(struct inventory disk[125], int numItems);

main()
{
struct inventory disk[125];  /* Local array of structures */
   int ans;
   int numItems=0;                    /* Number of total items
                                         in the inventory */

   do
      {
         do
           { dispMenu();    /* Display menu of user choices */
             scanf(" %d", &ans);        /* Get user's request
*/
```

```
                } while ((ans<1) || (ans>3));

          switch (ans)
        { case (1): { disk[numItems] = enterData(); /* Enter
                                                       disk data */
                numItems++; /* Increment number of items */
                break; }
          case (2): { seeData(disk, numItems);  /* Display
                                                    disk data */
                break; }
          default : { break; }
        }
        } while (ans!=3);               /* Quit program
                                           when user is through */

     return 0;
}

void dispMenu(void)
{

   printf("\n\n*** Disk Drive Inventory System ***\n\n");
   printf("Do you want to:\n\n");
   printf("\t1. Enter new item in inventory\n\n");
   printf("\t2. See inventory data\n\n");
   printf("\t3. Exit the program\n\n");
   printf("What is your choice? ");
   return;
}

struct inventory enterData()
{
   struct inventory diskItem;   /* Local variable to fill
                                    with input */

   printf("\n\nWhat is the next drive's storage in bytes? ");
   scanf(" %ld", &diskItem.storage);
   printf("What is the drive's access time in ms? ");
   scanf(" %d", &diskItem.accessTime);
   printf("What is the drive's vendor code (A, B, C, or D)? ");
   fflush(stdin);   /* Discard input buffer
                       before getting character */
```

Calls a function and stores the return value

```
      diskItem.vendorCode = getchar();
      getchar();  /* Discard carriage return */
      printf("What is the drive's cost? ");
      scanf(" %f", &diskItem.cost);
      printf("What is the drive's price? ");
      scanf(" %f", &diskItem.price);

      return (diskItem);
}

void seeData(struct inventory disk[125], int numItems)
{
   int ctr;
   printf("\n\nHere is the inventory listing:\n\n");
   for (ctr=0;ctr<numItems;ctr++)
      {
      printf("Storage: %ld\t", disk[ctr].storage);
      printf("Access time: %d\n", disk[ctr].accessTime);
      printf("Vendor code: %c\t", disk[ctr].vendorCode);
      printf("Cost: $%.2f\t", disk[ctr].cost);
      printf("Price: $%.2f\n", disk[ctr].price);
      }
   return;
}
```

Figure 29.3 shows an item being entered into the inventory file. Figure 29.4 shows the inventory listing being displayed to the screen. There are many features and error-checking functions you can add, but this program is the foundation of a more comprehensive inventory system. You can easily adapt it to a different type of inventory, a video tape collection, a coin collection, or any other tracking system just by changing the structure definition and the member names throughout the program.

# Using Arrays as Members

Members of structures themselves can be arrays. Array members pose no new problems, but you have to be careful when you access individual array elements. Keeping track of arrays of structures that contain array members might seem like a great deal of work on your part, but there is really nothing to it.

**Figure 29.3**

Entering inventory
information.

```
*** Disk Drive Inventory System ***

Do you want to:

        1. Enter new item in inventory

        2. See inventory data

        3. Exit the program

What is your choice? 1


What is the next drive's storage in bytes? 120000
What is the drive's access time in ms? 17
What is the drive's vendor code (A, B, C, or D)? A
What is the drive's cost? 121.56
What is the drive's price? 240.00
```

**Figure 29.4**

Displaying the
inventory data.

```
What is your choice? 2


Here is the inventory listing:

Storage: 120000 Access time: 17
Vendor code: A   Cost: $121.56    Price: $240.00
Storage: 320000 Access time: 21
Vendor code: D   Cost: $230.85    Price: $409.57
Storage: 280000 Access time: 19
Vendor code: C   Cost: $210.84    Price: $398.67


*** Disk Drive Inventory System ***

Do you want to:

        1. Enter new item in inventory

        2. See inventory data

        3. Exit the program

What is your choice? 3
```

Consider the following structure definition. This statement defines an array of
100 structures, each structure holding payroll information for a company. Two of
the members, name and department, are arrays.

```
struct payroll
   { char name[25];                      /* Employee name array */
     int dependents;
     char department[10];        /* Department name array */
     float salary;
   } employee[100];              /* An array of 100 employees */
```

Figure 29.5 shows what these structures look like. The first and third members are arrays. name is an array of 25 characters, and department is an array of 10 characters.

Suppose that you need to save the 25th employee's initial in a character variable. Assuming that initial is already defined as a character variable, the following statement assigns the employee's initial to initial:

```
initial = employee[24].name[0];
```

The double subscripts might look confusing, but the dot operator requires a structure variable on its left (employee[24]) and a member on its right (name's first array element). Being able to refer to member arrays makes the processing of character data in structures simple.

## Examples

1. Suppose that an employee gets married and wants her name changed in the payroll file. (She happens to be the 45th employee in the array of structures.) Given the payroll structure described in the previous section, this assigns a new name to her structure:

```
strcpy(employee[44].name, "Mary Larson");   /* Assign
                                              a new name */
```

When you refer to a structure variable using the dot operator, you can use regular commands and functions to process the data in the structures.

2. Here is a very comprehensive example of the steps you might go through to write a C program. You are getting to the point where you understand enough of the C language to start writing some advanced programs. Sadly, this book is coming to an end. I hope it is fulfilling its goal of introducing the C language in a conversational style with many examples along the way.

**Figure 29.5**
The payroll data.

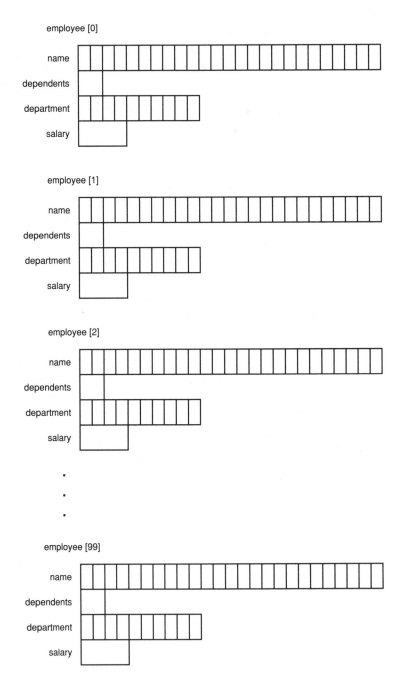

Assume that you have been hired by a local bookstore to write a magazine inventory system. You need to track the following:

Magazine title (at most, 25 characters)

Publisher (at most, 20 characters)

Month (1, 2, 3,…12)

Publication year

Number of copies in stock

Number of copies on order

Price of magazine (dollars and cents)

Suppose that there is a projected maximum of 1000 magazine titles that the store will ever carry. This means that you need 1000 occurrences of the structure, not 1000 magazines total. Here is a good structure definition for such an inventory:

```
struct magInfo
    { char title[25];
      char pub[25];
      int month;
      int year;
      int stockCopies;
      int orderCopies;
      float price;
    } mags[1000];                    /* Define 1000 occurrences */
```

Because this program will consist of more than one function, it is best to define the structure globally and the structure variables locally within the functions that need them.

This program needs three basic functions: a main() controlling function, a data-entry function, and a data printing function. You can add much more, but this is a good start for an inventory system. To keep the length of this example reasonable, assume that the user will want to enter several magazines and then print them. (To make the program more "usable," you want to add a menu so that the user can control when he or she adds and prints the information, as well as add more error-checking and editing capabilities.)

Here is an example of the complete data-entry and printing program with prototypes. The arrays of structures are passed between the functions from main().

```
/* Filename: C29MAG.C
   Magazine inventory program for adding and displaying
   a bookstore's magazines */
#include <stdio.h>
#include <ctype.h>

struct magInfo
   { char title[25];
     char pub[25];
     int month;
     int year;
     int stockCopies;
     int orderCopies;
     float price;
   };

struct magInfo fillMags(struct magInfo mag);
void printMags(struct magInfo mags[], int magCtr);

main()
{
   struct magInfo mags[1000];
   int magCtr=0;                /* Number of magazine titles */
   char ans;

   do
   {                            /* Assumes that there will be
                                   at least one magazine filled */
     mags[magCtr] = fillMags(mags[magCtr]);
     printf("Do you want to enter another magazine? ");
     fflush(stdin);
     ans = getchar();
     fflush(stdin);             /* Discard carriage return */
     if (toupper(ans) == 'Y')
       { magCtr++; }
       } while (toupper(ans) == 'Y');
     printMags(mags, magCtr);
     return 0;                  /* Return to operating system */
}

void printMags(struct magInfo mags[], int magCtr)
{
```

Simple *main()* loop makes function do all the work

```
        int i;
        for (i=0;  i<=magCtr; i++)
          { printf("\n\nMagazine %d:\n", i+1);    /* Adjust for
                                                    subscript */
            printf("\nTitle: %s \n", mags[i].title);
            printf("\tPublisher: %s \n", mags[i].pub);
            printf("\tPub. Month: %d \n", mags[i].month);
            printf("\tPub. Year: %d \n", mags[i].year);
            printf("\tIn-stock: %d \n", mags[i].stockCopies);
            printf("\tOn order: %d \n", mags[i].orderCopies);
            printf("\tPrice: %.2f \n", mags[i].price);
          }
        return;
      }

struct magInfo fillMags(struct magInfo mag)
{
    puts("\n\nWhat is the title? ");
    gets(mag.title);
    puts("Who is the publisher? ");
    gets(mag.pub);
    puts("What is the month (1, 2, ..., 12)? ");
    scanf(" %d", &mag.month);
    puts("What is the year? ");
    scanf(" %d", &mag.year);
    puts("How many copies in stock? ");
    scanf(" %d", &mag.stockCopies);
    puts("How many copies on order? ");
    scanf(" %d", &mag.orderCopies);
    puts("How much is the magazine? ");
    scanf(" %f", &mag.price);
    return (mag);
}
```

# Using *malloc()* and *free()* for Dynamic Memory Allocation

The difference between a beginning C programmer and an expert C programmer is the knowledge of *dynamic memory allocation*. Using dynamic memory allocation, you can request memory when you need it. Instead of giving the memory names as you do with variables, you create pointers that point to the newly allocated memory. Although you must define the pointers in advance, the memory that the pointers point to (such as an array of structures) doesn't consume memory until you need the memory.

The pool of memory your program draws from is called the *heap*. The heap is the unused memory not taken up by DOS, your programs, and your program variables.

> **Note:** Local variables are reserved before your program ever begins, just as global variables are. Some people mistakenly believe that local variables are just as good as dynamically allocated data, but you must remember that local variables are not *visible* throughout an entire program. Local variables are reserved at the very beginning, when the program first begins running.

Dynamic memory allocation is extremely important in networked and windowing environments.

The size of the heap grows and shrinks as your program runs. Without using the heap and dynamic memory allocation, your program consumes the same amount of memory space for its entire run. Therefore, if a regular program uses a huge array of long character arrays in only a single function, that array consumes memory for the entire program. If you dynamically allocate the array space, however, the memory is only consumed for the lines that need the memory and the memory is released after the program is finished with it.

Dynamic memory allocation is especially important when you program in networked and windowed environments, as is more common every day. All the users and program tasks need to share the same computer's memory, so programs shouldn't reserve memory until they need it.

The `malloc()` function allocates memory from the heap and assigns it to your programs; `free()` releases your program memory back to the heap. The concept and use of `malloc()` is not difficult, but the syntax of `malloc()` looks intimidating to newcomers.

## Looking at *malloc()* and *free()*

Here are the formats of `malloc()` and `free()`:

```
void * malloc(sizeToReserve)

free(pointerToheap)
```

Of the two, `malloc()` takes a little more time to understand. Remember that both `malloc()` and `free()` are functions, not commands. `malloc()` returns a `void` pointer. A `void` *pointer* is a special kind of pointer that you *must* typecast. You've never typecast pointers before in this book, only regular data types such as `int`.

Here is an example of code that uses `malloc()`:

```
int * countPtr;      /* Defines an integer pointer */
countPtr = (int *)malloc(sizeof(int));
```

> **Tip:** Read `malloc()` function calls from right to left.

Here is what the second statement does: `malloc()` needs to know exactly how much heap memory you want to grab. Because this code allocates a single integer from the heap, the `sizeof()` an `int` is requested. (Integers take different amounts of memory on different computers, so you must use `sizeof` for any data allocated.)

After `malloc()` does its job grabbing enough heap memory to hold an integer, `malloc()` returns a `void` pointer that you must typecast to an integer pointer. The `(int *)` typecasts the pointer to an integer. (Without the `*`, the typecast can work only on nonpointer data.) Figure 29.6 shows what the `malloc()` function accomplished.

**Figure 29.6**

After allocating a single integer.

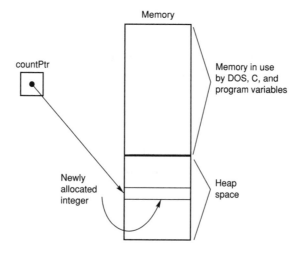

> **Note:** If you reserve a `float` or a `double`, you have to allocate the size of those data types instead of `int` as done here.

The integer pointer is your only access to the heap memory. `malloc()` does not assign a variable name to the allocated data, but returns only a pointer to the data. Therefore, if you want to store a value such as 17 in the heap's newly allocated value, you must do so through the pointer like this:

```
*countPtr = 17;   /* Store a 17 on the heap */
```

If you want to print the value on the heap, you can do so like this:

```
printf("The value is %d.\n", *countPtr);
```

After your program finishes with the heap value, it's much easier to give the memory back to the heap than it was to allocate it. Use `free()` like this:

```
free(countPtr);    /* Gives the memory back to the heap */
```

**What Have We Saved?**

You might not think that much has happened, except that you've learned a difficult function. Although you've seen how to reserve an integer when you need it, the pointer *to* that integer (`countPtr`) had to be reserved for the entire program.

Remember that a pointer is no different from an array name. Therefore, with a single pointer, you can dynamically allocate an entire array when you need it!

Suppose that you needed an array of 100 floating-point values. Here is how to dynamically allocate the array (assuming that `fPtr` is already defined to be a `float` pointer):

```
fPtr = (float *)malloc(100 * sizeof(float));
```

Notice that `malloc()` is being instructed to reserve 100 floating-point values on the heap and to return, after the typecast, a floating-point pointer to the first of the 100 values. You now have an array! Here are a few things you can do:

```
for (i=0; i<100; i++)
   { fPtr[i] = 0.0; } /* Zero the whole array on the heap */

fPtr[20] = 23.54;    /* Store a value in the 21st element */

*(fPtr+20) = 23.54;    /* Store a value in the 21st element */
```

The last two statements both do the same thing, except that one uses array subscript notation and the other uses pointer notation.

When you are through with the heap array, you can release the entire array back to the heap with this single `free()` function call:

```
free(fPtr);    /* The free heap space will now grow */
```

**Note:** C remembers how much memory you allocated with `malloc()` so that when you `free()` with the same pointer, the entire memory space is freed.

You can even allocate structures and arrays of structures! Just be sure to include the sizeof() whatever data element you want to reserve in the heap.

> **Caution:** If you do not call free(), C frees the allocated memory back to the heap when your program ends. If, however, you are going to keep unused space allocated after you are done with it, making other tasks and users strain more for resources, you might as well not use dynamic memory allocation to begin with.

This section has only scratched the surface of dynamic memory allocation, but some examples that follow will help clear things up. The bottom line is this: use dynamic allocation when you don't know in advance how many array elements you need, when you are getting user input into an array of ragged-right edge array elements, or when you are working in a multitasking or multiuser environment. For example, you can declare an array of 100 structure pointers, but not waste the memory for each of the actual structures until the user is ready to enter data into the next structure.

> **Tip:** Be sure to include stdlib.h in all programs that call malloc() and free().

## Examples

**1.** This example first defines three pointer variables and then stores data on the heap at the location of those pointers. If a pointer points to several heap values, you can treat the pointer as though it were a dynamically allocated array as done with this program's myName pointer.

```
/* Filename: C29DYN1.C */
/* Dynamically allocate simple variables on the heap
   then deallocate them */
#include <stdio.h>
#include <stdlib.h>
main()
{
   int *iPtr;
   float *fPtr;
   char *myName;
   iPtr = (int *)malloc(sizeof(int));
   fPtr = (float *)malloc(sizeof(float));
```

Grabs memory from heap

Grabs 20
characters
from heap

```
/* The name stored in myName can be as long as 20 characters */
myName = (char *)malloc(20 * sizeof(char));
*iPtr = 25;    /* Stores in the reserved heap */
*fPtr = 3.14159;
printf("What is your first name? ");
/* Ordinarily, you couldn't gets() into a character pointer
   unless the pointer were originally defined as an array
   with ample space reserved */
gets(myName);    /* User's name goes to the heap */
printf("Here are the values:\n");
printf("iPtr points to the heap at value %d.\n", *iPtr);
printf("fPtr points to the heap at value %f.\n", *fPtr);
/* No dereference on myName because it's printed with %s */
printf("myName points to the heap at value %s.\n", myName);
/* Always free everything back to the free heap space */
free(iPtr);
free(fPtr);
free(myName);
return 0;   /* Return to DOS */
}
```

2. In the fourth review exercise at the end of Chapter 27, you were asked to write a program to accept 10 of the user's favorite songs into an array of character pointers (a ragged-edge array). Until you learned dynamic memory allocation, you had to first fill the array with enough blanks to hold the songs.

Now that you know about dynamic memory allocation, you only have to reserve the array of pointers and *then* allocate space for each song when the user enters that song.

The following program does just that. The program allocates the character-pointer array and an extra character array that is 80 characters long. The extra array is used to grab a total of five song titles (up to 79 characters maximum with an 80th element for the null zero). The actual length of the song entered determines exactly how much heap space to allocate.

The most important thing to remember about this code is that the space for each song is not reserved until the song is ready to be stored.

```
/* Filename: C29DYN2.C */
/* Dynamically allocate favorite songs of the user */
#include <stdio.h>
#include <stdlib.h>
#include <string.h>
main()
{
   #define TOTALSONGS 5      /* For more songs, change this 5
*/
   char * songs[10];  /* Ragged-edge array for the songs */
   char newSong[80];  /* Temporary holding place for user's
                          song */
   int i;
   for (i=0;i<TOTALSONGS;i++)
     { printf("What is your favorite song #%d? ", (i+1));
       gets(newSong);
       /* sizeof() tells the length of the song */
       songs[i] = (char *)malloc((strlen(newSong)+1) *
                                  sizeof(char));
       strcpy(songs[i], newSong);
     }
   printf("Here are the songs in reverse order:\n");
   for (i=(TOTALSONGS-1);i>=0;i--)
     { printf("Song #%d: %s\n", (i+1), songs[i]);
       free(songs[i]); } /* Dynamically deallocate when done
*/
   return 0;
}
```

Be sure to deallocate all heap space

Here is the output from this program:

```
What is your favorite song #1? Cinque Terre, My Italian
Riviera
What is your favorite song #2? My Bride's Gone
What is your favorite song #3? Red as a Rose
What is your favorite song #4? O' Say Can You C?
What is your favorite song #5? Don't Mouse Around With My PC!
Here are the songs in reverse order:
Don't Mouse Around With My PC!
O' Say Can You C?
Red as a Rose
My Bride's Gone
Cinque Terra, My Italian Riviera
```

The songs take only as much memory (inside the heap) as the song titles consume, plus the character pointer in the songs array that points to each song. Also, even though as the program is close to ending, it does free each song.

There is a lot to dynamic memory allocation. Many beginning C books don't even cover the topic. However, mastering malloc() and free() is about all you have left to mastering C.

# Summary

You have mastered structures and arrays of structures. Many useful inventory and tracking programs are ready to be written using structures. By being able to create arrays of structures, you can now create several occurrences of data.

You've also managed to learn one of the most complex features of C: dynamic memory allocation. Although you only saw the tip of the dynamic memory iceberg in this chapter, you are well on your way to mastering a difficult subject.

The next step in the process of learning C is to save those structures and other data to disk files. The next two chapters explore the concepts of disk file processing.

# Review Questions

Answers to review questions are in Appendix B.

1. True or false: Each element in an array of structures must be the same type.

2. What is the advantage of creating an array of structures instead of using individual variable names for each structure variable?

3. Given the following structure definition:

```
struct item
  { char partNo[8];
    char descr[20];
    float price;
    int inStock;
  } inventory[100];
```

   a. How do you assign a price of 12.33 to the 33d item's in-stock quantity?

   b. How do you assign the first character of the 12th item's part number the value of X?

   c. How do you assign the 97th inventory item the same values as the 63d?

4. Given the following structure definition:

```
struct item
  { char desc[20];
    int num;
    float cost;
  } inventory[25];
```

a. What is wrong with the following statement?

```
item[1].cost = 92.32;
```

b. What is wrong with the following statement?

```
strcpy(inventory.desc, "Widgets");
```

c. What is wrong with the following statement?

```
inventory.cost[10] = 32.12;
```

5. Which consumes the most memory when a program is first loaded to run: an array of integers, or an array of pointers to integers that will be allocated later?

6. True or false: If you define nonarray variables such as integer variables on the heap, you don't save memory but actually consume more memory.

## Review Exercises

1. Write a program that stores an array of friends' names, phone numbers, and addresses and that prints them two ways: with their full name and address, or with just their name and phone number for a phone listing.

2. Add a sort function to the program in exercise 1 so that you can print your friends' names in alphabetical order. (Hint: You have to make the member holding the names a character pointer.)

3. Expand on the book data-entry program C29MAG.C by adding features to make it more usable (such as search book by author, by title, and be able to print an inventory of books on order).

4. Write a program that keeps a customer contact book in arrays. Define an array of character pointers for each person's name, an array of floating-point pointers for the person's sales-to-date total, and a third array of character pointers for each person's phone number. As the user enters each customer, allocate that customer's data on the heap. When the user is finished entering all the data, print the contact list and free the allocated memory.

# CHAPTER 30

# Sequential Files

So far, every example in this book has processed data that resided inside the program listing or came from the keyboard. You assigned constants and variables to other variables and created new data values from expressions. The programs also received input with scanf(), gets(), and the character input functions.

The data that is created by the user and assigned to variables with assignment statements is sufficient for some applications. With the large volumes of data that most real-world applications need to process, however, you need a better way of storing that data. For all but the smallest computer programs, disk files offer the solution.

After storing data on the disk, the computer helps you enter, find, change, and delete the data. The computer and C are simply tools to help you manage and process data. This chapter focuses on disk and file processing concepts and teaches you the first of two methods of disk access, *sequential file access.*

This chapter introduces you to the following concepts:

♦ An overview of disk files

♦ The types of files

♦ Processing data on the disk

♦ Sequential file access

♦ File I/O functions

After this chapter, you will be ready to tackle the more advanced random file access methods covered in Chapter 31, "Random Access Files." If you have programmed computerized data files with another programming language, you might be surprised at how C borrows from other programming languages, especially BASIC, when working with disk files. If you are new to disk file processing, be assured that disk files are simple to create and read.

## Why Use a Disk?

The typical computer system has much less memory storage than hard disk storage. Your disk drive holds much more data than can fit in your computer's RAM. This is the primary reason for using the disk drive for your data. The disk memory, because it is nonvolatile, also lasts longer. When you power-off your computer, the disk memory is not erased, but RAM is erased. Also, when your data changes, you (or more important, your users) do not have to edit the program and look for a set of assignment statements. Instead, the users run previously written programs that make changes to the disk data.

This makes programming more difficult at first because programs have to be written to change the data on the disk. However, nonprogrammers then can use the programs and modify the data without knowing how to program.

Disks hold more data than computer memory.

The capacity of your disk makes it a perfect place to store your data as well as your programs. Think about what would happen if all data had to be stored with a program's assignment statements. What if the Social Security office in Washington, D.C., asked you to write a C program to compute, average, filter, sort, and print the name and address of each person in their office's computer data files? Would you want your program to include millions of assignment statements? Not only would you not want the program to hold that much data, but it could not do so because only relatively small amounts of data fit in a program before you run out of RAM.

By storing data on your disk, you are much less limited because you have more storage. Your disk can hold as much data as you have disk capacity. Also, if your disk requirements grow, you usually can increase your disk space, whereas you cannot always add more RAM to your computer.

> **Note:** ANSI C cannot access the special extended memory or expanded memory that some computers have.

When working with disk files, C does not have to access much RAM because C reads data from your disk drive and processes the data only parts at a time. Not all your disk data has to reside in RAM for C to process it. C reads some data, processes it, and then reads some more. If C requires disk data a second time, it rereads that place on the disk.

## Understanding Types of Disk File Access

Your programs can access files two ways: through sequential access or random access. Your application determines the method you should choose. The access mode of a file determines how you read, write, change, and delete data from the file.

Some of your files can be accessed in both ways, sequentially and randomly, as long as your programs are written properly and the data lends itself to both types of file access.

A sequential file must be accessed in the same order the file was written. This is analogous to cassette tapes: You play music in the same order it was recorded. (You can quickly fast-forward or rewind through songs that you do not want to listen to, but the order of the songs dictates what you do to play the song you want.) It is difficult, and sometimes impossible, to insert data in the middle of a sequential file. How easy is it to insert a new song in the middle of two other songs on a tape? The only way to truly add or delete records from the middle of a sequential file is to create a completely new file that combines both old and new records.

It might seem that sequential files are limiting, but it turns out that many applications lend themselves to sequential file processing.

Unlike with sequential files, you can access random access files in any order you want. Think of data in a random access file as you would think of songs on a compact disc or a record; you can go directly to any song you want without having to play or fast-forward through the other songs. If you want to play the first song, the sixth song, and then the fourth song, you can do so. The order of play has nothing to do with the order in which the songs appear on the recording. Random file access sometimes takes more programming but rewards that effort with a more flexible file access method. Chapter 31, "Random Access Files," discusses how to program for random access files.

# Learning Sequential File Concepts

There are three operations you can perform on sequential disk files. You can

◆ Create disk files

◆ Add to disk files

◆ Read from disk files

Your application determines what you need to do. If you are creating a disk file for the first time, you must create the file and write the initial data to it. Suppose that you wanted to create a customer data file. You would create a new file and write your current customers to that file. The customer data might originally be in arrays, arrays of structures, pointed to with pointers, or typed into regular variables by the user.

Over time, as your customer base grows, you can add new customers to the file. When you add to the end of a file, you *append* to that file. As your customers entered your store, you would read their information from the customer data file.

Customer disk processing brings up one disadvantage of sequential files, however. Suppose that a customer moves and wants you to change his or her address in your files. Sequential access files do not lend themselves well to changing data stored in them. It is also difficult to remove information from sequential files. Random files, described in the next chapter, provide a much easier approach to changing and removing data. The primary approach to changing or removing data from a sequential access file is to create a new one from the old one with the updated data. Because of the updating ease provided with random access files, this chapter concentrates on creating, reading, and adding to sequential files.

> **Note:** All file functions described in this chapter use the stdio.h header file.

## Opening and Closing Files

Before you can create, write to, or read from a disk file, you must open the file. This is analogous to opening a file cabinet before working with a file stored in the cabinet. As soon as you are done with a cabinet's file, you close the file door. You must also close a disk file when you finish with it.

When you open a disk file, you must inform C only of the file name and what you want to do (write to, add to, or read from). C and your operating system work together to make sure that the disk is ready, and they create an entry in your file directory (if you are creating a file) for the file name. When you close a file, C writes any remaining data to the file, releases the file from the program, and updates the file directory to reflect the file's new size.

> **Caution:** If you use a PC, you must ensure that the FILES= statement in your CONFIG.SYS file is large enough to hold the maximum number of disk files you *have* open, with one left over for your C program itself. If you are unsure of how to do this, check your DOS reference manual or a beginner's book about DOS.

To open a file, you must call the fopen() function (for "file open"). To close a file, call the fclose() function. Here is the format of these two function calls:

```
filePtr = fopen(fileName, access);
```

and

```
fclose(filePtr);
```

The filePtr is a special type of pointer that points only to files, not to data variables. You must define a file pointer with FILE *, a definition in the stdio.h header file. The examples that follow show you how to define a file pointer.

Your operating system handles the exact location of your data in the disk file. You do not want to worry about the exact track and sector number of your data on the disk. Therefore, you let the filePtr point to the data you are reading and writing. Your program only has to generically manage the filePtr while C and the operating system take care of locating the actual physical data.

The *fileName* is a string (or a character pointer that points to a string) containing a valid file name for your computer. If you are using a PC or a UNIX-based computer, the *fileName* can contain a complete disk and directory path name. If you are using a mainframe, you must use the complete dataset name in the *fileName* string. Generally, you can specify the file name in uppercase or lowercase letters, as long as your operating system does not have a preference.

> **Caution:** Typically, UNIX is the only operating system that specifies that a lowercase file name is different from an uppercase (or mixed case) file name. Therefore, if a file is named UNIXfile.Dat, your **fopen()** command must use UNIXfile.Dat, not unixfile.dat, UNIXFILE.DAT, or any other combination of upper- or lowercase.

The access can be one of the mode values from Table 30.1. The updating access modes (those with a plus sign) are not discussed here. Rather, file updating is saved for random access files in the next chapter.

**Table 30.1. Possible access modes.**

| Mode | Description |
| --- | --- |
| "r" | Opens a file for reading |
| "w" | Opens a file for writing (creating it) |
| "a" | Opens a file for appending (adding to it) |
| "r+" | Opens a file for update (reading and writing) |
| "w+" | Opens a file for update (create it, then allow reading and writing) |
| "a+" | Opens a file for update (read the entire file, or write to the end of it) |

Sometimes you see programs that contain a *t* or a *b* in the access mode, such as "rt" or "wb+". The *t* means *text file* and is the default mode; each of the access modes listed in Table 30.1 is equivalent to using *t* after the access mode letter ("rt" is identical to "r", and so on). A text file is an ASCII file, compatible with most other programming languages and applications. Text files do not always contain text, in the word processing sense of the word. Any data you need to store can go in a text file. Programs that read ASCII files can read data you create as C text files. The *b* in the access mode means *binary mode*. See the "Binary Modes" box that follows for a discussion of the binary file modes.

> **Binary Modes**
>
> If you specify *b* inside the access mode rather than *t*, C creates or reads the file in a binary format. Binary data files are "squeezed"—that is, they take less space than text files. The disadvantage of using binary files is that other programs cannot always read the data files. Only C programs written to access binary files (using the *b* access mode) can read and write to them. The advantage of binary files is that you save disk space because your data files are more compact. Other than the access mode in the `fopen()` function, you use no additional commands to access binary files with your C programs.
>
> The binary format is a system-specific file format. In other words, not all computers can read a binary file created on another computer.
>
> Here is a complete list of binary file access modes:
>
>     "rb" "wb" "ab" "ab+" "a+b" "wb+" "w+b" "ab+" "a+b"

If you open a file for writing (using access modes of "w", "wt", "wb", or "w+"), C creates the file. If a file by that name already exists, C overwrites the old file with no warning. When opening files, you must be careful that you do not overwrite existing data you want to save.

If an error occurs during the opening of a file, C does not return a valid file pointer. Instead, C returns a file pointer equal to the value NULL, which is defined in stdio.h. For example, if you open a file for output, but use a disk name that is invalid, C cannot open the file and will make the file pointer point to NULL. Always check the file pointer when writing disk file programs to ensure that the file opened properly.

> **Tip:** Beginning programmers like to open all files at the beginning of their programs and close them at the end. This is not always best. Open files immediately before you access them and close them when you are done with them. This protects the files, keeping them open only as long as needed. A closed file is more likely to be protected in the unlikely (but possible) event of a power failure or a computer breakdown.

This section has contained much file access theory. The following examples help illustrate these concepts.

## Examples

1. Suppose that you want to create a file for storing your house payment records for the last year. Here are the first few lines in the program that would create a file called house.dat on your disk.

*Include the stdio.h header file. Start the program with the main() function. Define the filePtr variable with FILE, found in stdio.h. Open the house.dat file for writing and creating.*

```
#include <stdio.h>

main()
{
    FILE *filePtr;                 /* Defines a file pointer */
    filePtr = fopen("house.dat", "w"); /* Creates the file */
```

The rest of the program writes data to the file. The program never has to refer to the file name again. The program uses the `filePtr` variable to refer to the file. Examples in the next few sections illustrate how. There is nothing special about `filePtr`, other than its name (although the name is meaningful in this case). You can name file pointer variables XYZ or a908973 if you like, but these names are not meaningful.

You must include the stdio.h header file because it contains the definition for the `FILE *definition`. You do not have to worry about the physical `FILE`'s specifics. The `filePtr` "points" to data in the file as you write it. Put the `FILE *definitions` in your programs where you define other variables and arrays.

> **Tip:** Because files are not part of your program, you might find it useful to define file pointers globally. Unlike data in variables, there is rarely a reason to keep file pointers local.

Before finishing with the program, you should close the file. The following `fclose()` function closes the house file:

```
    fclose(filePtr);          /* Closes the house payment file */
```

**2.** If you like, you can put the complete path name in the file name. The following opens the household payment file in a subdirectory on the D disk drive:

```
    filePtr = fopen("d:\mydata\house.dat", "w");  /* Creates
                                                     the file */
```

**3.** If you like, you can store a file name in a character array or point to it with a character pointer. Each of the following sections of code is equivalent:

```
char fn[] = "house.dat";    /* File name in character array */
filePtr = fopen(fn, "w");               /* Creates the file */
char *myfile="house.dat";        /* File name pointed to */
filePtr = fopen(myfile, "w");           /* Creates the file */
/* Let the user enter the file name */
printf("What is the name of the household file? ");
gets(filename);               /* Filename must be an
                                 array or character pointer */
filePtr = fopen(filename, "w");        /* Creates the file */
```

No matter how you specify the file name when opening the file, close the file with the file pointer. This `fclose()` function closes the open file, no matter which method you used to open the file:

```
fclose(filePtr);         /* Closes the house payment file */
```

**4.** You should check the return value from `fopen()` to ensure that the file opened properly. Here is code after `fopen()` that checks for an error:

```
#include <stdio.h>

main()
{
   FILE *filePtr;                  /* Defines a file pointer */
   filePtr = fopen("house.dat", "w"); /* Creates the file */
   if (filePtr == NULL)
      { printf("Error opening file.\n"); }
   else
      { /* Rest of output commands go here */ }
```

**5.** You can open and write to several files in the same program. Suppose that you wanted to read data from a payroll file and create a backup payroll data file. You would have to open the current payroll file using the "r" reading mode, and the backup file in the output "w" mode.

For each open file in your program, you must define a different file pointer. The file pointers that your input and output statements use determine which file they operate on. If you have to open many files, you can define an array of file pointers.

Here is a way you can open the two payroll files:

```
#include <stdio.h>
FILE *fileIn;                                        /* Input file */
FILE *fileOut;                                       /* Output file */

main()
{
   fileIn = fopen("payroll.dat", "r");  /* Existing file */
   fileOut = fopen("payroll.BAK", "w");       /* New file */
```

When you finish with these files, be sure to close them with these two
fclose() function calls:

```
fclose(fileIn);
fclose(fileOut);
```

# Writing to a File

Any input or output function that requires a device performs input and output with
files. You have seen most of these already. The most common file I/O functions are

getc() and putc()

fprintf()

fgets() and fputs()

There are a few more, but the most common I/O function left that you have not
seen is the fscanf() function. fscanf() is to scanf() as fprintf() is to printf(). The
only difference between fscanf() and scanf() is its first parameter. The first
parameter to fscanf() must be a file pointer (or any C device, such as stdin and
stdaux).

The following function reads three integers from a file pointed to by filePtr:

```
fscanf(filePtr, "%d %d %d", &num1, &num2, &num3);
```

As with scanf(), you do not have to specify the & before array variable names.
The following fscanf() reads a string from the disk file:

```
fscanf(filePtr, "%s", name);
```

The fscanf() is not as potentially dangerous as the scanf() function. scanf() gets
input from the user. The user does not always enter data in the format that scanf()
expects. When you get data from a disk file, however, you can be more certain about
the format because you probably wrote the program that created the file in the first
place. Errors still can creep into a data file, and you might be wrong about the file's
format when using fscanf(), but generally, fscanf() is more secure than scanf().

There is always more than one way to write data to a disk file. Most of the time, more than one function will work. For instance, if you write many names to a file, both fputs() and fprintf() will work. You also can write the names using putc(). You should use whichever function you are most comfortable with for the data being written. If you want a newline character (\n) at the end of each line in your file, the fprintf() and fputs() probably are easier than putc(), but all three will do the job.

> **Tip:** Each line in a file is called a *record*. By putting a newline character at the end of file records, you make the input of those records easier.

## Examples

1. The following program creates a file called NAMES.DAT. The program writes five names to a disk file using fputs().

*Identify the program and include the I/O header file. Open a new data file called NAMES.DAT. Write five names to the file, and then close the file and return to the operating system.*

```
/* Filename: C30WR1.C
   Writes five names to a disk file */
#include <stdio.h>

FILE *fp;

main()
{
    fp = fopen("NAMES.DAT", "w");     /* Creates a new file */

    fputs("Michael Langston\n", fp);
    fputs("Sally Redding\n", fp);
    fputs("Jane Kirk\n", fp);
    fputs("Stacy Grady\n", fp);
    fputs("Paula Hiquet\n", fp);

    fclose(fp);                        /* Release the file */
    return;
}
```

These strings go to file

To keep this first example simple, no error checking was done on the fopen(). The next few examples check for the error.

NAMES.TXT is a text data file. If you like, you can read this file into your word processor (use your word processor's command for reading ASCII files) or use an operating system command to display this file on-screen (such as the MS-DOS TYPE command or the UNIX cat command). If you display NAMES.TXT, you see

```
Michael Langston
Sally Redding
Jane Kirk
Stacy Grady
Paula Hiquet
```

**2.** The following file writes the numbers from 1 to 100 to a file called NUMS.1.

```
/* Filename: C30WR2.C
   Writes 1 to 100 to a disk file */
#include <stdio.h>
#include <stdlib.h>

FILE *fp;

main()
{
   int ctr;
   fp = fopen("NUMS.1", "wt");        /* Creates a new file */
   if (fp == NULL)
      { printf("Error opening file.\n"); }
   else
      { for (ctr=1; ctr<101; ctr++)
         { fprintf(fp, "%d ", ctr); }   /* Writes the data */
      }
   fclose(fp);
   return;
}
```

Makes sure there is no problem ———— (points to `{ printf("Error opening file.\n"); }`)

The numbers are not written one per line, but with a space between each of them. The format of the fprintf() control string determines the format of the output data. When writing data to disk files, keep in mind that you have to read the data later. You have to use "mirror-image" input functions to read data you output to files.

Notice that this program opens the file using the "wt" access mode. This is equivalent to the "w" access mode because C opens all files as text files unless you specify a binary override access.

# Writing to a Printer

The fopen() and other output functions were not designed to just write to files. They were designed to write to any device, including files, the screen, and the printer. If you need to write data to a printer, you can treat the printer as if it were a file. The following program opens a FILE pointer using the MS-DOS name for a printer located at LPT1 (the MS-DOS name for the first parallel printer port):

Prepares the printer just as if it were a file

```
/* Filename: C30PRNT.C
   Prints to the printer device */
#include <stdio.h>
FILE *prnt;  /* Points to the printer */

main()
{
    prnt = fopen("LPT1", "w");
    fprintf(prnt, "Printer line 1\n");  /* 1st line printed */
    fprintf(prnt, "Printer line 2\n");  /* 2nd line printed */
    fprintf(prnt, "Printer line 3\n");  /* 3rd line printed */

    fclose(prnt);
    return;
}
```

Make sure that your printer is turned on and that it has paper before you run this program. When you run the program, you see this printed on paper:

```
Printer line 1
Printer line 2
Printer line 3
```

# Adding to a File

You can easily add data to an existing file or create new files by opening the file in append access mode. Data files on the disk rarely are static; they grow almost daily due to (with luck!) increased business. Being able to add to data already on the disk is very useful indeed.

Files you open for append access (using "a", "at", "ab", "a+b", and "ab+") do not have to exist. If the file exists, C appends data to the end of the file when you write the data. If the file does not exist, C creates the file (as is done when you open a file for write access).

## Example

The following program adds three more names to the NAMES.DAT file created in an earlier example.

```
/* Filename: C30AP1.C
   Adds three names to a disk file */
#include <stdio.h>

FILE *fp;

main()
{
   fp = fopen("NAMES.DAT", "a");              /* Adds to file */

   fputs("Johnny Smith\n", fp);
   fputs("Laura Hull\n", fp);
   fputs("Mark Brown\n", fp);

   fclose(fp);                                /* Release the file */
   return;
}
```

Sends strings to file

If the file did not exist, C would create it and store the three names to the file. Here is what the file now looks like:

```
Michael Langston
Sally Redding
Jane Kirk
Stacy Grady
Paula Hiquet
Johnny Smith
Laura Hull
Mark Brown
```

Basically, you have to change only the fopen() function's access mode to turn a file creation program into a file appending program.

# Reading from a File

As soon as the data is in a file, you must be able to read that data. You must open the file in a read access mode. There are several ways to read data. You can read character data a character at a time or a string at a time. The choice depends on the format of the data. If you stored numbers using fprintf(), you might want to use a mirror-image fscanf() to read the data.

Files you open for read access (using `"r"`, `"rt"`, and `"rb"`) must exist already, or C gives you an error. You cannot read a file that does not exist. `fopen()` returns NULL if the file does not exist when you open it for read access.

> **Tip:** You can read one word at a time from a file using `fscanf()` with the `%s` control code.

Another event happens when reading files. Eventually, you read all the data. Subsequent reading produces errors because there is no more data to read. C provides a solution to the end-of-file occurrence. If you attempt to read from a file that you have completely read the data from, C returns the value EOF, defined in stdio.h. To find the end-of-file condition, be sure to check for EOF when performing input from files.

> **Note:** Because some compilers return –1 when the end-of-file condition is reached, ANSI C requires that you define input variables as integers. If the end-of-file is not reached, you can treat the integer as if it were a character, as always.

## Examples

1. This program asks the user for a file name and prints the contents of the file to the screen. If the file does not exist, the program displays an error message.

```
/* Filename: C30RE1.C
   Reads and displays a file */
#include <stdio.h>
#include <stdlib.h>

FILE *fp;

main()
{
    char filename[12];              /* Holds user's filename */
    int inChar;                          /* Input character */

    printf("What is the name of the file you want to see? ");
    gets(filename);

    if ((fp=fopen(filename, "r"))==NULL)
```

Let user
determine the ——— file name

```
      { printf("\n\n*** That file does not exist ***\n");
        exit(0);                                /* Exits program */
      }

    inChar = getc(fp);              /* Reads first character */
    while (inChar != EOF)
      { putchar(inChar);
        inChar = getc(fp);
      }
    fclose(fp);
    return;
}
```

Notice that the program reads the input character in two places. It is possible, although rare, that a file with no data could exist. In such a file, the first character read would result in the end-of-file condition. Therefore, this program reads the first character and prints it as long as it is not EOF.

Although the program is written to help illustrate file input, most C programmers combine the file input with the test for EOF. This might seem like too much to do at once, but it is so common in C programs that you should become familiar with the algorithm. Here is a rewritten version of the previous program's I/O routine that is more common:

```
while ((inChar = getc(fp)) != EOF)        /* Reads first */
  { putchar(inChar); }                    /* character   */
```

Figure 30.1 shows what happens when the NAMES.DAT file is requested. Because newline characters are in the file at the end of each name, the names appear on-screen one per line. If you attempt to read a file that does not exist, the program displays the following message:

```
*** That file does not exist ***
```

**2.** This program reads one file and copies it to another. You might want to use such a program to back up important data in case the original file gets damaged.

The program must open two files—the first for reading and the second for writing. The file pointer determines which of the two files is being accessed.

```
/* Filename: C30RE2.C
   Makes a copy of a file */
```

```
#include <stdio.h>
#include <stdlib.h>

FILE *inFp;
FILE *outFp;

main()
{
   char inFilename[12];          /* Holds original filename */
   char outFilename[12];          /* Holds backup filename */

   int inChar;                          /* Input character */

   printf("What is the name of the file you want to back up? ");
   gets(inFilename);

   printf("What is the name of the file ");
   printf("you want to copy %s to? ", inFilename);
   gets(outFilename);

   if ((inFp=fopen(inFilename, "r"))==NULL)
     { printf("\n\n*** %s does not exist ***\n",
             inFilename);
       exit(0);                               /* Exits program */
     }
   if ((outFp=fopen(outFilename, "w"))==NULL)
     { printf("\n\n*** Error opening %s ***\n",
             outFilename);
       exit(0);                               /* Exits program */
     }

   printf("\nCopying...\n");              /* Waiting message */
   while ((inChar = getc(inFp)) != EOF)     /* Gets input
                                                character */
     { putc(inChar, outFp); }   /* Writes the character
                                    to the backup file */

   printf("\nThe files are copied.\n");
```

Opens
both
files

Closes both files ———

```
        ┌ fclose(inFp);
        └ fclose(outFp);
          return;
    }
```

**Figure 30.1**

Reading and
displaying a disk
file.

```
What is the name of the file you want to see? names.dat
Michael Langston
Sally Redding
Jane Kirk
Stacy Grady
Paula Hiquet
Johnny Smith
Laura Hull
Mark Brown
```

## Summary

You can now perform one of the most important requirements of data processing: writing and reading to and from disk files. Before completing this chapter, you could only store data in variables. The short life of variables (they last only as long as your program is running) makes long-term storage of data impossible. You can now save large amounts of data in disk files to process them later.

Reading and writing sequential files involves learning more concepts than actual commands or functions. The fopen() and fclose() are the most important functions you learned in this chapter. You are familiar with most of the I/O functions needed to get data to and from disk files.

The next chapter concludes this book's discussion of disk files. You will learn how to create and use random access files. By programming with random file access, you can read selected data from a file, as well as change data without having to rewrite the entire file.

## Review Questions

Answers to review questions are in Appendix B.

**1.** What are the three ways to access sequential files?

**2.** What advantages do disk files have over holding data in memory?

**3.** How do sequential files differ from random access files?

4. What happens when you open a file for read access and the file does not exist?

5. What happens when you open a file for write access and the file already exists?

6. What happens when you open a file for append access and the file does not exist?

7. How does C inform you that you have reached the end-of-file condition?

8. Why must you use an integer variable for performing character input?

# Review Exercises

1. Write a program that creates a file that contains the following data:

   Your name

   Your address

   Your phone number

   Your age

2. Write a second program that reads and prints the data file you created in exercise 1.

3. Write a program that takes the data you created in exercise 1 and writes it to the screen, one word per line. (Hint: Use the fscanf() function and the %s control code.)

4. Write a program for PCs that backs up two important files: AUTOEXEC.BAT and CONFIG.SYS. Call the backup files AUTOEXEC.SAV and CONFIG.SAV.

5. Write a program that reads a file and creates a new file with the same data, but reverse the case on the second file. Everywhere uppercase letters appear in the first file, write lowercase letters to the new file, and everywhere lowercase letters appear in the first file, write uppercase letters to the new file.

# CHAPTER 31

# Random Access Files

This chapter introduces the concept of random file access. Random file access enables you to read or write any data in your disk file without having to read or write every piece of data before it. You can quickly search for, add, retrieve, change, and delete information in a random access file. Although you need a few new functions to access files randomly, you will find that the extra effort pays off in flexibility, power, and speed of disk access.

This chapter introduces the following concepts:

♦ Random access files

♦ File records

♦ The `fseek()` function

♦ Special-purpose file I/O functions

This chapter concludes *C By Example,* Special Edition. With C's sequential and random access files, you can do everything you would ever want to do with disk data.

**For Related Information**

♦ "Understanding Types of Disk File Access," p. 528

♦ "Learning Sequential File Concepts," p. 529

# Understanding Random File Records

Random files exemplify the power of data processing with C. Sequential file processing is slow unless you read the entire file into arrays and process them in memory. As explained in the last chapter, however, you have much more disk space than RAM, and most disk files do not even fit in your RAM at one time. Therefore, you need a way to quickly read individual pieces of data from a file in any order needed and process them one at a time.

*A record is to a file what a structure is to a variable.*

Generally, you read and write file *records*. A record to a file is analogous to a C structure. A record is a collection of one or more data values (called *fields*) that you read and write to disk. Generally, you store data in structures and write the structures to disk, where they are called records. When you read a record from disk, you generally read that record into a structure variable and process it with your program.

Unlike most programming languages, not all disk data has to be stored in record format. Typically, you write a stream of characters to a disk file and access that data either sequentially or randomly by reading it into variables and structures.

The process of randomly accessing data in a file is simple. Consider the data files of a large credit card organization. When you make a purchase, the store calls the credit card company to get an authorization. Millions of names are in the credit card company's files. There is no quick way the credit card company could read every record sequentially from the disk that comes before yours. Sequential files do not lend themselves to quick access. In many situations, looking up individual records in a data file with sequential access is not feasible.

The credit card companies must use a random file access so that their computers can go directly to your record, just as you go directly to a song on a compact disc or a record album. The functions you use are different from the sequential functions, but the power that results from learning the added functions is worth the effort.

*You do not have to rewrite the entire file to change random access file data.*

Reading and writing files randomly is similar to thinking of the file as a big array. With arrays, you know that you can add, print, or remove values in any order. You do not have to start the first array element, sequentially looking at the next one, until you get the element you need. You can view your random access file in the same way, accessing the data in any order.

Most random file records are fixed-length records. That is, each record (usually a row in the file) takes the same amount of disk space. Most sequential files you read and wrote in the previous chapter were variable-length records. When you are reading or writing sequentially, there is no need for fixed-length records because you input each value one character, word, string, or number at a time, looking for the data you want. With fixed-length records, your computer can better calculate exactly where the search record is located on the disk.

Although you waste some disk space with fixed-length records (because of the spaces that pad some of the fields), the advantages of random file access compensate for the "wasted" disk space.

> **Tip:** With random access files, you can read or write records in any order. Therefore, even if you want to perform sequential reading or writing of the file, you can use random access processing and "randomly" read or write the file in sequential record number order.

## Opening Random Access Files

Just as with sequential files, you must open random access files before reading or writing to them. You can use any of the read access modes mentioned in the last chapter (such as "r", "rt", and "rb") if you are only going to read a file randomly. To modify data in a file, however, you must open the file in one of the update modes, which Table 31.1 reviews.

**Table 31.1. Random access update modes.**

| Mode | Description |
|------|-------------|
| "r+" | Opens a file for update (reading and writing) |
| "w+" | Opens a file for update (creates it, then allows reading and writing) |
| "a+" | Opens a file for update (reads the entire file, or writes to the end of it) |
| "r+t" | Opens a text file for update (reading and writing; same as "r+") |
| "w+t" | Opens a text file for update (creates it, then allows reading and writing; same as "w+") |
| "a+t" | Opens a text file for update (reads the entire file or writes to the end of it; same as "a+") |
| "r+b" | Opens a binary file for update (reading and writing) |
| "w+b" | Opens a binary file for update (creates it, then allows reading and writing) |
| "a+b" | Opens a binary file for update (reads the entire file or writes to the end of it) |

You can randomly read a file, even if the file was opened without an update +. Therefore, there is really no physical difference between sequential files and random files in C. However, the methods you use to access and update them differ.

## Examples

1. Suppose that you want to write a program to create a file of friends' names. The following `fopen()` function call will suffice, assuming that `fp` is declared as a file pointer:

```
if ((fp = fopen("NAMES.DAT", "w"))==NULL)
    { printf("\n*** Cannot open file ***\n"); }
```

No update `fopen()` access mode is needed if you are only creating the file. However, what if you wanted to create the file, write names to it, and give the user a chance to change any of the names before closing the file? You would have to open the file like this:

```
if ((fp = fopen("NAMES.DAT", "w+"))==NULL)
    { printf("\n*** Cannot open file ***\n"); }
```

This lets you create the file, then change data that you wrote to the file.

2. As with sequential files, the only difference between using a binary `fopen()` access mode and a text `fopen()` access mode is that the file you create with the binary `fopen()` is more compact and will save disk space. You could not, however, read that file from other programs as an ASCII text file. The previous `fopen()` function can be rewritten to create and allow updating of a binary file. All other file-related commands and functions work for binary files just as they do for text files.

```
if ((fp = fopen("NAMES.DAT", "w+t"))==NULL)
    { printf("\n*** Cannot open file ***\n"); }
```

3. Suppose that you want to read a binary inventory file, and want to change some of the data to reflect new pricing. The following `fopen()` function call suffices for such a file that you want to read and update:

```
if ((fp = fopen("INVENT.JUN", "r+b"))==NULL)
    { printf("\n*** Cannot open file ***\n"); }
```

# Using the *fseek()* Function

You can read forward or back-ward from any point in the file with `fseek()`.

C provides a function that enables you to read to a specific point in a random access data file. This is the `fseek()` function. The format of `fseek()` is

```
fseek(filePtr, longNum, origin);
```

The filePtr is the pointer to the file that you want to access, initialized with an fopen() statement. The longNum is the number of bytes in the file you want to skip. C does not read this many bytes, but literally skips the data by the number of bytes specified in longNum. Skipping the bytes on the disk is much faster than reading them. If longNum is negative, C skips backward in the file (this allows for rereading of data several times). Because data files can be large, you must declare longNum as a long integer to hold a large number of bytes.

The origin is a value that tells C where to begin skipping bytes specified by longNum. The origin can be any of the three values shown in Table 31.2.

**Table 31.2. Possible origin values.**

| Description | Equivalent | origins |
| --- | --- | --- |
| Beginning of file | SEEK_SET | 0 |
| Current file position | SEEK_CUR | 1 |
| End of file | SEEK_END | 2 |

The words SEEK_SET, SEEK_CUR, and SEEK_END are defined in stdio.h as the constants 0, 1, and 2, respectively. That is why it does not matter which (the defined constants or the numeric constants) you use as the origin.

> **Note:** Actually, the file pointer plays a much more important role than just "pointing to the file" on the disk. The file pointer continually points to the exact location of the *next byte to read or write*. In other words, as you read data, from either a sequential or a random access file, the file pointer increments with each byte read. By using fseek(), you can move the file pointer forward or backward in the file.

## Examples

**1.** No matter how far into a file you have read, the following fseek() function positions the file pointer back at the beginning of a file:

```
fseek(fp, 0L, SEEK_SET); /* Positions the file pointer
                                    at the beginning */
```

The constant 0L passes a long integer 0 to the fseek() function. Without the L, C would pass a regular integer that would not match the fseek() prototype, which is located in stdio.h. Chapter 4, "Variables and Constants," explains the use of data type suffixes on numeric constants, but the suffixes have not been used since then, until now.

This `fseek()` function literally reads "move the file pointer 0 bytes from the beginning of the file."

2. The following example reads a file named MYFILE.TXT twice, once to send the file to the screen and once to send the file to the printer. Three file pointers are used, one for each device (the file, the screen, and the printer). The device names for the screen and the printer are MS-DOS compatible. If you run this program on a minicomputer or a mainframe, substitute your operating system's code for your local screen and printer in the `fopen()` function calls for these devices.

```c
/* Filename: C31TWIC.C
   Writes a file to the screen, rereads it,
   and sends it to the printer */
#include <stdio.h>
#include <stdlib.h>
FILE *inFile;                        /* Input file pointer */
FILE *scrn;                           /* Screen pointer */
FILE *prnt;                           /* Printer pointer */

main()
{
   int inChar;
   if ((inFile = fopen("MYFILE.TXT", "r"))==NULL)
     { printf("\n*** Error opening MYFILE.TXT ***\n");
       exit(0);  }

   scrn = fopen("CON", "w");         /* Open screen device */
   while ((inChar=getc(inFile))!=EOF)
      { putc(inChar,scrn); }          /* Output characters
                                         to the screen */

   fclose(scrn);                     /* Close screen because
                                        it is no longer needed */

   fseek(inFile, 0L, SEEK_SET);         /* Reposition
                                           file pointer */
   prnt = fopen("LPT1", "w");        /* Open printer device */
   while ((inChar=getc(inFile))!=EOF)
      { putc(inChar,prnt); }           /* Output characters
                                          to the printer */
```

File pointer is now at beginning again

```
      fclose(prnt);            /* Always close all open files */
      fclose(inFile);

      return;
}
```

You also can close then reopen a file to position the file pointer back at the beginning, but using fseek() is a more efficient method.

Of course, you could have used regular I/O functions such as printf() to write to the screen, instead of having to open the screen as a separate device.

3. The following fseek() function positions the file pointer at the 30th byte in the file. (The next byte read is the 31st byte.)

```
fseek(filePtr, 30L, SEEK_SET); /* Positions file pointer
                                    at the 30th byte */
```

This fseek() function literally reads "move the file pointer 30 bytes from the beginning of the file."

If you write structures to a file, you can quickly seek any structure in the file by using the sizeof() function. Suppose that you want the 123rd occurrence of the structure tagged with inventory. You would search using the following fseek() function:

```
fseek(filePtr, (123L * sizeof(struct inventory)), SEEK_SET);
```

4. The following program writes the letters of the alphabet to a file called ALPH.TXT. The fseek() function is then used to read and display the 9th and 17th letters (I and Q).

*Identify the program and include the I/O header file. This program will read some letters from a file. We need to store the alphabet in a file, so open the ALPH.TXT file for output. Loop through the letters of the alphabet, from A to Z, writing each to the file.*

*Position the file pointer so that it points to the 9th character in the file (the letter I). Read the character, and then print it. Position the file pointer so that it points to the 17th character in the file (the letter Q). Read the character, and then print it. Close the file and return to DOS.*

```
/* Filename: C31ALPH.C
   Stores the alphabet in a file,
   then reads two letters from it */
#include <stdio.h>
#include <stdlib.h>
FILE *fp;
main()
{
   int ch;                              /* Holds A through Z */

   /* Opens in update mode so that you can read
      the file after writing to it */
   if ((fp=fopen("alph.txt", "w+"))==NULL)    /* Create
                                                 alphabet
                                                 file */
     { printf("\n*** Error opening file ***\n");
       exit(0); }

   for (ch=65; ch<=90; ch++)
     { putc(ch, fp); }                   /* Writes letters */

   fseek(fp, 8L, SEEK_SET);              /* Skips 8 letters,
                                            points to I */
   ch=getc(fp);
   printf("The first character is %c\n",ch);
   fseek(fp, 16L, SEEK_SET);            /* Skips 16 letters,
                                            points to Q */
   ch=getc(fp);
   printf("The second character is %c\n",ch );

   fclose(fp);
   return;
}
```

Finds individual letters ———— (marks `fseek(fp, 8L, SEEK_SET);` line)

Finds individual letters ———— (marks `fseek(fp, 16L, SEEK_SET);` line)

**5.** To point to the end of a data file, you can use the fseek() function to position the file pointer at the last byte. Subsequent fseek()s should then use a negative longNum value to skip backward in the file. The following fseek() function makes the file pointer point to the end of the file:

```
fseek(filePtr, 0L, SEEK_END);  /* Positions file pointer
                                   at the end */
```

This `fseek()` function literally reads "move the file pointer 0 bytes from the end of the file." The file pointer now points to the end-of-file marker, but you can then `fseek()` backward to get to other data in the file.

6. The following program reads the ALPH.TXT file (created in example 4) backward, printing each character as it skips back in the file.

```
/* Filename: C31BACK.C
   Reads and prints a file backward */
#include <stdio.h>
#include <stdlib.h>
FILE *fp;
main()
{
    int ctr;    /* Steps through the 26 letters in the file */
    int inChar;

    if ((fp = fopen("ALPH.TXT", "r"))==NULL)
      { printf("\n*** Error opening file ***\n");
        exit(0); }

    fseek(fp, 1L, SEEK_END);      /* Points to the last byte
                                     in the file */
    for (ctr=0;ctr<26;ctr++)
      {
        inChar = getc(fp);
        fseek(fp, -2L, SEEK_CUR);
        putchar(inChar); }

    fclose(fp);
    return;
}
```

Reads one and backs up two

This program also uses the SEEK_CUR origin value. The last `fseek()` in the program seeks two bytes backward from the *current position,* not from the beginning or the end as the previous examples do. The `for` loop toward the end of the program performs a "skip 2 bytes back, read 1 byte forward" method to skip through the file backward.

7. The following program performs the same actions as example 4 (C31ALPH.C), with one addition. When the letters *I* and *Q* are found, an `fputc()` writes the letter *x* over the *I* and *Q*. The `fseek()` must be used to back up one byte in the file to overwrite the letter just read.

```
/* Filename: C31CHANG.C
   Stores the alphabet in a file, reads two letters from
   it, and changes those letters to x's */
#include <stdio.h>
#include <stdlib.h>
FILE *fp;
main()
{
   int ch;                              /* Holds A through Z */

   /* Opens in update mode so that you can read
      the file after writing to it */
   if ((fp=fopen("alph.txt", "w+"))==NULL)       /* Creates
                                                    alphabet
                                                    file */

     { printf("\n*** Error opening file ***\n");
       exit(0); }

   for (ch=65; ch<=90; ch++)
     { putc(ch, fp); }                   /* Writes letters */

   fseek(fp, 8L, SEEK_SET);            /* Skips 8 letters,
                                          points to I */

   ch=getc(fp);

   /* Changes the I to an x */
   fseek(fp, -1L, SEEK_CUR);
   fputc('x', fp);

   printf("The first character is %c\n",ch);
   fseek(fp, 16L, SEEK_SET);          /* Skips 16 letters,
                                         points to Q */
   ch=getc(fp);
   printf("The second character is %c\n",ch );

   /* Changes the Q to an x */
   fseek(fp, -1L, SEEK_CUR);
   fputc('x', fp);

   fclose(fp);
   return;
}
```

Overwrites the *I* ——— `fputc('x', fp);`

Overwrites the *Q* ——— `fputc('x', fp);`

The file named ALPH.TXT now looks like this:

```
ABCDEFGHxJKLMNOPxRSTUVWXYZ
```

This program forms the basis of a more complete data file management program. After you master the `fseek()` functions and become more familiar with disk data files, you will begin to write programs that store more advanced data structures and access them.

# Learning Other Helpful I/O Functions

Several more disk I/O functions are available that you might find useful. They are mentioned here for completeness. As you write more powerful programs in C, you will find a use for many of these functions when performing disk I/O. Each of these functions is prototyped in the stdio.h header file.

- ♦ `feof(fp)` can be used to test for an end-of-file condition when reading binary files. Unlike text files, C can mistake the binary data for the end-of-file marker. The `feof()` function ensures that the end-of-file condition is properly tested.

- ♦ `fread(array, size, count, fp)` reads the amount of data specified by the integer count, each data size being `size` in bytes (use the `sizeof()` function), into the array or pointer specified by array. `fread()` is called a buffered I/O function. `fread()` enables you to read much data with a single function call.

- ♦ `fwrite(array, size, count, fp)` writes count array elements, each being size *size*, to the file specified by `fp`. `fwrite()` uses a buffered I/O function. `fwrite()` enables you to write much data in a single function call.

- ♦ `remove(fp)` erases the file pointed to by `fp`. `remove()` returns 0 if the file was erased successfully and –1 if an error occurred.

- ♦ `rewind(fp)` positions the file pointer at the beginning of the file.

Many of these (and other built-in I/O functions that you will learn in your C programming career) are helpful functions that you can duplicate using what you already know. For instance, the `rewind()` function simply positions the file pointer at the beginning of a file. `rewind()` is the third method you have seen that does this. These three methods all position the file pointer at the beginning of the file:

```
fclose(fp);
fopen(fp, "r");              /* Reopening a file always
                                reinitializes the pointer */
```

and

```
fseek(fp, 0L, SEEK_SET);
```

and

```
rewind(fp);
```

The buffered I/O file functions enable you to read and write entire arrays (including arrays of structures) to the disk in a single function call.

## Examples

1. The following program requests a file name from the user and uses the remove() function to erase the file from the disk:

```
/* Filename: C31ERAS.C
   Erases the file specified by the user */
#include <stdio.h>
FILE *fp;
main()
{
   char filename[12];

   puts("What is the filename you want me to erase? ");
   gets(filename);

   if (remove(filename) == -1)
      { printf("\n*** I could not remove the file ***\n"); }
   else
      { printf("\nThe file %s is now removed\n", filename);
}
   return;
}
```

Erases the file

2. The following program reads a binary file, a character at a time, until feof() returns a true condition. (The regular end-of-file defined constant works only for text files.)

```
/* Filename: C31READ.C
   Reads and displays a binary file */
#include <stdio.h>
#include <stdlib.h>

FILE *fp;

main()
```

```
{
    char filename[12];              /* Holds user's filename */
    int inChar;                         /* Input character */

    printf("What is the name of the file you want to see? ");
    gets(filename);

    if ((fp=fopen(filename, "rb"))==NULL)
      { printf("\n\n*** That file does not exist ***\n");
        exit(0);                        /* Exits program */
      }

    while (!feof(fp))
        { inChar = getc(fp);
          putchar(inChar); }

    fclose(fp);
    return;
}
```

Check for end-of-file ⎯⎯⎯⎯⎯

**3.** The following function is part of a larger program that gets inventory data, in an array of structures, from the user. This function is passed the array name and the number of elements (structure variables) in the array. The fwrite() function then writes the complete array of structures to the disk file pointed to by fp.

```
void writeStr(struct inventory items[], int invCnt)
{
    fwrite(items, sizeof(struct inventory), invCnt, fp);
    return;
}
```

If the inventory array had 1,000 elements, this one-line function would still write the entire array to the disk file. You could use the fread() function to read the entire array of structures from the disk in a single function call.

## Summary

C supports random access files with several functions. These functions include error-checking, file-pointer positioning, and the opening and closing of files. You now have the tools you need to save your C program data to disk for storage and retrieval.

# Review Questions

Answers to review questions are in Appendix B.

1. What is the difference between records and structures?

2. True or false: You have to create a random access file before reading from it randomly.

3. What happens to the file pointer as you read from a file?

4. What are the two buffered file I/O functions?

5. What are two methods for positioning the file pointer at the beginning of a file?

6. What are the three starting positions (the `origins`) in the `fseek()` function?

7. What is wrong with this program?

```
#include <stdio.h>
FILE *fp;
main()
{
  int inChar;
  fopen(fp, "rb");
  if((inChar=getc(fp))!=EOF)
      { putchar(inChar); }      /* Writes to the screen */
  fclose(fp);
  return;
}
```

# Review Exercises

1. Write a program that asks the user for a list of five names, then writes the names to a file. Rewind the file and display its contents on-screen by using the `fseek()` and `getc()` functions.

2. Rewrite the program in exercise 1 so that it displays every other character in the file of names.

3. Write a program that reads characters from a file. If the input character is a lowercase letter, change it to uppercase. If the input character is uppercase, change it to lowercase. Do not change other characters in the file.

4. Write a program that displays the number of nonalphabetic characters in a file.

**5.** Write a grade-keeping program for a teacher. Let the teacher enter as many as 10 students' grades. Each student has three grades for the semester. Store the students' names and their three grades in an array of structures and store the data on the disk. Make the program menu-driven. Let the teacher have the option of adding more students, viewing the file's data, or printing the grades to the printer with a calculated class average.

# Memory Addressing, Binary, and Hexadecimal Review

You do not have to understand the concepts in this appendix to become well-versed in C. You can master C, however, only if you spend some time learning about the "behind-the-scenes" roles played by binary numbers. The material presented here is not difficult, but many programmers do not take the time to study it; hence, there are a handful of C masters who learn this material and understand how C works "under the hood," and there are those who will never be as expert in the language as they could be.

You should take the time to learn about addressing, binary numbers, and hexadecimal numbers. These fundamental principles are presented here for you to learn, and although a working knowledge of C is possible without knowing them, they will greatly enhance your C skills (and your skills in every other programming language).

After reading this appendix, you will better understand why different C data types hold different ranges of numbers. You also will see the importance of being able to represent hexadecimal numbers in C, and you will better understand C array and pointer addressing.

# Computer Memory

Each memory location inside your computer holds a single character called a *byte*. A byte is any character, whether it is a letter of the alphabet, a numeric digit, or a special character such as a period, question mark, or even a space (a blank character). If your computer contains 640K of memory, it can hold a total of approximately 640,000 bytes of memory. This means that as soon as you fill your computer's memory with 640K, there is no room for an additional character unless you overwrite something else.

Before describing the physical layout of your computer's memory, it might be best to take a detour and explain exactly what 640K means.

## Memory and Disk Measurements

By appending the K (from the metric word *kilo*) to memory measurements, the manufacturers of computers do not have to attach as many zeros to the end of numbers for disk and memory storage. The K stands for approximately 1000 bytes. As you will see, almost everything inside your computer is based on a power of 2. Therefore, the K of computer memory measurements actually equals the power of 2 closest to 1000, which is 2 to the 10th power, or 1024. Because 1024 is very close to 1000, computerists often think of K as meaning 1000, even though they know it only approximately equals 1000.

Think for a moment about what 640K equals exactly. Practically speaking, 640K is about 640,000 bytes. To be exact, however, 640K equals 640 times 1024, or 655,360. This explains why the PC DOS command CHKDSK returns 655,360 as your total memory (assuming that you have 640K of RAM) rather than 640,000.

Because extended memory and many disk drives can hold such a large amount of data, typically several million characters, there is an additional memory measurement shortcut called *M*, which stands for *meg*, or *megabytes*. The M is a shortcut for approximately one million bytes. Therefore, 20M is approximately 20,000,000 characters, or bytes, of storage. As with K, the M literally stands for 1,048,576 because that is the closest power of 2 (2 to the 20th power) to one million.

How many bytes of storage are 60 megabytes? It is approximately 60 million characters, or 62,914,560 characters to be exact.

## Memory Addresses

Each memory location in your computer, just as with each house in your town, has a unique *address*. A memory address is simply a sequential number, starting at 0, that labels each memory location. Figure A.1 shows how your computer memory addresses are numbered if you have 640K of RAM.

By using unique addresses, your computer can keep track of memory. When the computer stores a result of a calculation in memory, it finds an empty address, or one matching the data area where the result is to go, and stores the result at that address.

**Figure A.1**

Memory
addresses for a
640K computer.

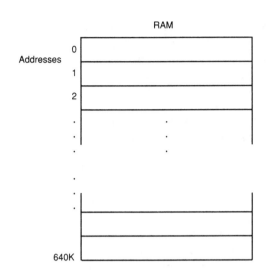

Your C programs and data share computer memory with DOS. DOS must always reside in memory while you operate your computer. Otherwise, your programs would have no way to access disks, printers, the screen, or the keyboard. Figure A.2 shows computer memory being shared by DOS and a C program. The exact amount of memory taken by DOS and a C program is determined by the version of DOS you use, how many DOS extras (such as device drivers and buffers) your computer uses, and the size and needs of your C programs and data.

**Figure A.2**

DOS, your C
program, and your
program's data
share the same
memory.

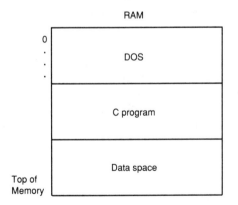

## Bits and Bytes

You now know that a single address of memory might contain any character, called a byte. You know that your computer holds many bytes of information, but it does not store those characters in the same way that humans think of characters.

For example, if you type a letter *W* on your keyboard while working in your C editor, you see the *W* on-screen, and you also know that the *W* is stored in a memory location at some unique address. Actually, your computer does not store the letter *W*; it stores electrical impulses that stand for the letter *W*.

Electricity, which is what runs through the components of your computer, making it understand and execute your programs, can exist in only two states—on or off. As with a light bulb, electricity is either flowing (it is on) or it is not flowing (it is off). Even though you can dim some lights, the electricity is still either on or off.

Today's modern digital computers employ this on-or-off concept. Your computer is nothing more than millions of on and off switches. You might have heard about integrated circuits, transistors, and even vacuum tubes that computers have contained over the years. These electrical components are nothing more than switches that rapidly turn electrical impulses on and off.

This two-state, on-and-off mode of electricity is called a *binary* state of electricity. Computer people use a 1 to represent an on state (a switch in the computer that is on) and a 0 to represent an off state (a switch that is off). These numbers, 1 and 0, are called *binary digits.* The term binary digits is usually shortened to *bits.* A bit is either a 1 or a 0 representing an on or an off state of electricity. Different combinations of bits represent different characters.

Several years ago, someone listed every single character that can be represented on a computer, including all uppercase letters, all lowercase letters, the digits 0 through 9, the many other characters (such as %, *, {, and +), and some special control characters. When you add the total number of characters that a PC can represent, you get 256 of them. The first 128 of these characters are found on all PCs and are listed in the ASCII (pronounced *ask-ee*) table in Appendix C. The remaining 128 characters can only be found on IBM-compatible computers and are not shown in Appendix C.

The order of the ASCII table's 256 characters is basically arbitrary, just as the telegraph's Morse code table is arbitrary. With Morse code, a different set of long and short beeps represents different letters of the alphabet. In the ASCII table, a different combination of bits (1s and 0s strung together) represents each of the 256 ASCII characters. The ASCII table is a standard table used by almost every PC in the world. ASCII stands for American Standard Code for Information Interchange. (Some minicomputers and mainframes use a similar table called the EBCDIC table.)

It turns out that if you take every different combination of eight 0s strung together, to eight 1s strung together (that is, from 00000000, 00000001, 00000010, and so on until you get to 11111110, and finally, 11111111), you will have a total of 256 of them. (256 is 2 to the 8th power.) Each memory location in your computer holds eight bits. These bits can be any combination of eight 1s and 0s. This brings us to the following fundamental rule of computers.

> **Note:** Because it takes a combination of eight 1s and 0s to represent a character, and because each byte of computer memory can hold exactly one character, eight bits equal one byte.

To bring this into better perspective, consider that the bit pattern needed for the uppercase letter *A* is 01000001. No other character in the ASCII table "looks" like this to the computer because each of the 256 characters is assigned a unique bit pattern.

Suppose that you press the *A* key on your keyboard. Your keyboard does *not* send a letter *A* to the computer; rather, it looks in its ASCII table for the on and off states of electricity that represent the letter *A*. As Figure A.3 shows, when you press the *A* key, the keyboard actually sends 01000001 (as on and off impulses) to the computer. Your computer simply stores this bit pattern for *A* in a memory location. Even though you can think of the memory location as holding an *A*, it really holds the byte 01000001.

**Figure A.3**

Your computer keeps track of characters by their bit patterns.

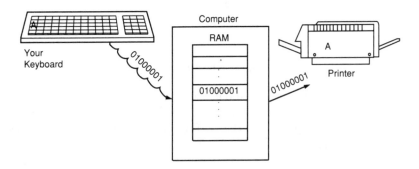

If you were to print that *A*, your computer would not send an *A* to the printer; it would send the 01000001 bit pattern for an *A* to the printer. The printer receives that bit pattern, looks up the correct letter in the ASCII table, and prints an *A*.

From the time you press the *A* until the time you see it on the printer, it is *not* a letter *A*! It is the ASCII pattern of bits that the computer uses to represent an *A*. Because a computer is electrical, and because electricity is easily turned on and off, this is a nice way for the computer to manipulate and move characters, and it can do so very quickly. Actually, if it was up to the computer, you would enter everything by its bit pattern, and look at all results in their bit patterns. This would not be good, so devices such as the keyboard, screen, and printer know that they have to work part of the time with letters as we know them. That is why the ASCII table is such an integral part of a computer.

There are times when your computer treats two bytes as a single value. Even though memory locations are typically eight bits wide, many CPUs access memory two bytes at a time. If this is the case, the two bytes are called a *word* of memory. On other computers (commonly mainframes), the word size can be four bytes (32 bits) or even eight bytes (64 bits).

---

**Summarizing Bits and Bytes**

A bit is a 1 or a 0 representing an on or an off state of electricity.

Eight bits represents a byte.

A byte, or eight bits, represents one character.

Each memory location of your computer is eight bits (a single byte) wide. Therefore, each memory location can hold one character of data. Appendix C provides the first 128 characters of the ASCII table.

If the CPU accesses memory two bytes at a time, those two bytes are called a word of memory.

---

# The Order of Bits

To further understand memory, you should understand how programmers refer to individual bits. Figure A.4 shows a byte and a two-byte word. Notice that the bit on the far right is called bit 0. From bit 0, keep counting by ones as you move left. For a byte, the bits are numbered 0 to 7, from right to left. For a double-byte (a 16-bit word), the bits are numbered from 0 to 15, from right to left.

**Figure A.4**

The order of bits in a byte and a two-byte word.

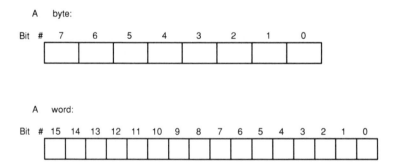

Bit 0 is called the *least-significant bit*, or sometimes the *low-order bit*. Bit 7 (or bit 15 for a two-byte word) is called the *most-significant bit*, or sometimes the *high-order bit*.

# Binary Numbers

Because a computer works best with 1s and 0s, its internal numbering method is limited to a *base-2* (binary) numbering system. People work in a *base-10* numbering system in the real world. The base-10 numbering system is sometimes called the decimal numbering system. There are always as many different digits as the base in a numbering system. For example, in the base-10 system, there are ten digits, 0 through 9. As soon as you count to 9 and run out of digits, you have to combine some that you already used. The number 10 is a representation of ten values, but it combines the digits 1 and 0.

The same is true of base 2. There are only two digits, 0 and 1. As soon as you run out of digits, after the second one, you have to reuse digits. The first seven binary numbers are 0, 1, 10, 11, 100, 101, and 110.

It is okay if you do not understand how these numbers were derived; you will see how in a moment. For the time being, you should realize that no more than two digits, 0 and 1, can be used to represent any base-2 number, just as no more than 10 digits, 0 through 9, can be used to represent any base-10 number in the regular "real-world" numbering system.

You should know that a base-10 number, such as 2981, does not really mean anything by itself. You must assume what base it is. You get very used to working with base-10 numbers because that is what the world uses. However, the number 2981 actually represents a quantity based on powers of 10. For example, Figure A.5 shows what the number 2981 actually represents. Notice that each digit in the number represents a certain number of a power of 10.

**Figure A.5**

The base-10 breakdown of the number 2981.

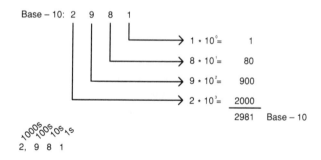

This same concept applies when you work in a base-2 numbering system. Your computer does this, because the power of 2 is just as common to your computer as the power of 10 is to you. The only difference is that the digits in a base-2 number represent powers of 2 and not powers of 10. Figure A.6 shows you what the binary numbers 10101 and 10011110 are in base-10. This is how you convert any binary number to its base-10 equivalent.

**Figure A.6**

The base-2
breakdown of the
numbers 10101
and 10011110.

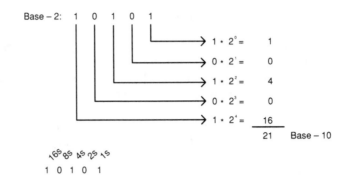

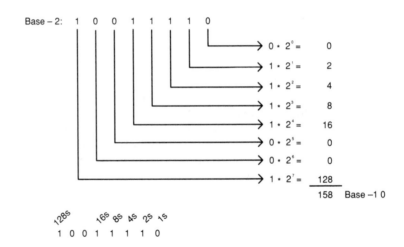

A base-2 number contains only 1s and 0s. To convert any base-2 number to base-10, add each power of 2 everywhere a 1 appears in the number. The base-2 number 101 represents the base-10 number 5. (There are two 1s in the number, one in the 2 to the 0 power, which equals 1, and one in the 2 to the second power, which equals 4.) Table A.1 shows the first 18 base-10 numbers and their matching base-2 numbers.

**Table A.1. The first 17 base-10 and base-2 (binary) numbers.**

| Base-10 | Base-2 |
| --- | --- |
| 0 | 0 |
| 1 | 1 |
| 2 | 10 |

| Base-10 | Base-2 |
| --- | --- |
| 3 | 11 |
| 4 | 100 |
| 5 | 101 |
| 6 | 110 |
| 7 | 111 |
| 8 | 1000 |
| 9 | 1001 |
| 10 | 1010 |
| 11 | 1011 |
| 12 | 1100 |
| 13 | 1101 |
| 14 | 1110 |
| 15 | 1111 |
| 16 | 10000 |
| 17 | 10001 |

You do not have to memorize this table; you should be able to figure the base-10 numbers from their matching binary numbers by adding the powers of two for each 1 (on) bit. Many programmers do memorize the first several binary numbers, however, because it comes in handy in advanced programming techniques.

What is the largest binary number a byte can hold? The answer is all 1s, or 11111111. If you add the first eight powers of 2, you get 255.

A byte holds either a number or an ASCII character, depending on how it is accessed. For example, if you were to convert the base-2 number 01000001 to a base-10 number, you would get 65. However, this also happens to be the ASCII bit pattern for the uppercase letter *A*. If you check the ASCII table, you will see that the *A* is ASCII code 65. Because the ASCII table is so closely linked with the bit patterns, the computer knows whether to work with a number 65 or a letter *A*—by the context of how the patterns are used.

A binary number is not limited to a byte, as an ASCII character is. Sixteen or 32 bits at a time can represent a binary number (and usually do). There are more powers of 2 to add when converting that number to a base-10 number, but the process is the same. By now you should be able to figure out that 1010101010101010 is 43,690 in the base-10 decimal numbering system (although it takes a little time to calculate).

To convert from decimal to binary takes a little more effort. Luckily, you rarely need to convert in that direction. Converting from base-10 to base-2 is not covered in this appendix.

## Binary Arithmetic

At their lowest level, computers can only add and convert binary numbers to their negative equivalents. Computers cannot truly subtract, multiply, or divide, although they simulate these operations through judicious use of the addition and negative-conversion techniques.

If a computer were to add the numbers 7 and 6, it could do so (at the binary level). The result is 13. If, however, the computer were instructed to subtract 7 from 13, it could not do so. It can, however, take the negative value of 7 and add that to 13. Because –7 plus 13 equals 6, the result is a simulated subtraction.

To multiply, computers perform repeated addition. To multiply 6 by 7, the computer adds seven 6s together and gets 42 as the answer. To divide 42 by 7, a computer keeps subtracting 7 from 42 repeatedly until it gets to a 0 answer (or less than 0 if there is a remainder), then counts the number of times it took to reach 0.

Because all math is done at the binary level, the following additions are possible in binary arithmetic:

$0 + 0 = 0$

$0 + 1 = 1$

$1 + 0 = 1$

$1 + 1 = 10$

Because these are binary numbers, the last result is not the number 10, but the binary number 2. (Just as the binary 10 means "no ones, and carry an additional power of 2," the decimal number 10 means "no ones, and carry a power of 10.") No binary digit represents a 2, so you have to combine the 1 and the 0 to form the new number.

Because binary addition is the foundation of all other math, you should learn how to add binary numbers. You will then understand how computers do the rest of their arithmetic.

Using the binary addition rules shown previously, look at the following binary calculations:

```
  01000001        (65 decimal)
 +00101100        (44 decimal)
 ---------
  01101101        (109 decimal)
```

The first number, 01000001, is 65 decimal. This also happens to be the bit pattern for the ASCII A, but if you add with it, the computer knows to interpret it as the number 65 rather than the character A.

The following binary addition requires a carry into bit 4 and bit 6:

```
  00101011      (43 decimal)
 +00100111      (39 decimal)

  01010010      (82 decimal)
```

Typically, you have to ignore bits that carry past bit 7, or bit 15 for double-byte arithmetic. For example, both of the following binary additions produce incorrect positive results:

```
 10000000  (128 decimal)      1000000000000000  (65536 decimal)
+10000000  (128 decimal)     +1000000000000000  (65536 decimal)

 00000000  (0 decimal)        0000000000000000  (0 decimal!)
```

There is no 9th or 17th bit for the carry, so both of these seem to produce incorrect results. Because the byte and 16-bit word cannot hold the answers, the magnitude of both these additions is not possible. The computer must be programmed, at the bit level, to perform *multiword arithmetic*, which is beyond the scope of this book.

## Binary Negative Numbers

Because subtracting requires understanding binary negative numbers, you need to learn how computers represent them. The computer uses *2's complement* to represent negative numbers in binary form. To convert a binary number to its 2's complement (to its negative) you must

**1.** Reverse the bits (the 1s to 0s and the 0s to 1s).

**2.** Add 1.

This seems a little strange at first, but it works very well for binary numbers. To represent a binary –65, you need to take the binary 65 and convert it to its 2's complement, such as

```
 01000001  (65 decimal)
 10111110  (Reverse the bits)
+1         (Add 1)

 10111111  (-65 binary)
```

By converting the 65 to its 2's complement, you produce –65 in binary. You wonder what makes 10111111 mean –65, but by the 2's complement definition it means –65.

If you were told that 10111111 is a negative number, how would you know which binary number it is? You perform the 2's complement on it. Whatever number you produce is the positive of that negative number. For example:

```
10111111   (-65 decimal)
01000000   (Reverse the bits)
+1         (Add 1)
_____
01000001   (65 decimal)
```

Something might seem wrong at this point. You just saw that 10111111 is the binary −65, but isn't 10111111 *also* 191 decimal (adding the powers of 2 marked by the 1s in the number, as explained earlier)? It depends whether the number is a *signed* or an *unsigned* number. If a number is signed, the computer looks at the most-significant bit (the bit on the far left), called the *sign bit*. If the most-significant bit is a 1, the number is negative. If it is 0, the number is positive.

Most numbers are 16 bits long; that is, two-byte words are used to store most integers. This is not always the case for all computers, but it is true for most PCs.

In the C programming language, you can designate numbers as either signed integers or unsigned integers (they are signed by default if you do not specify otherwise). If you designate a variable as a signed integer, the computer interprets the high-order bit as a sign bit. If the high-order bit is on (1), the number is negative. If the high-order bit is off (0), the number is positive. If, however, you designate a variable as an unsigned integer, the computer uses the high-order bit as just another power of 2. That is why the range of unsigned integer variables goes higher (generally from 0 to 65535, but it depends on the computer) than for signed integer variables (generally from −32768 to +32767).

After so much description, a little review is in order. Assume that the following 16-bit binary numbers are unsigned:

0011010110100101

1001100110101010

1000000000000000

These numbers are unsigned, so the bit 15 is not the sign bit, but just another power of 2. You should practice converting these large 16-bit numbers to decimal. The decimal equivalents are

13733

39338

32768

If, on the other hand, these numbers are signed numbers, the high-order bit (bit 15) indicates the sign. If the sign bit is 0, the numbers are positive and you convert them to decimal in the usual manner. If the sign bit is 1, you must convert the numbers to their 2's complement to find what they equal. Their decimal equivalents are

+13733

−26198

−32768

To compute the last two binary numbers to their decimal equivalents, take their 2's complement and convert it to decimal. Put a minus sign in front of the result and you find what the original number represents.

> **Tip:** To make sure that you convert a number to its 2's complement correctly, you can add the 2's complement to its original positive value. If the answer is 0 (ignoring the extra carry to the left), you know that the 2's complement number is correct. This is like saying that decimal opposites, such as −72 + 72, add up to zero.

## Hexadecimal Numbers

All those 1s and 0s get confusing. If it were up to your computer, however, you would enter *everything* as 1s and 0s! This is unacceptable to people because we do not like to keep track of all those 1s and 0s. Therefore, a *hexadecimal* numbering system (sometimes called *hex*) was devised. The hexadecimal numbering system is based on base-16 numbers. As with other bases, there are 16 unique digits in the base-16 numbering system. Here are the first 19 hexadecimal numbers:

0 1 2 3 4 5 6 7 8 9 A B C D E F 10 11 12

Because there are only 10 unique digits (0 through 9), the letters A through F represent the remaining six digits. (Anything could have been used, but the designers of the hexadecimal numbering system decided to use the first six letters of the alphabet.)

To understand base-16 numbers, you should know how to convert them to base-10 so that they represent numbers people are familiar with. Perform the conversion to base-10 from base-16 the same way you did with base-2, but instead of using powers of 2, represent each hexadecimal digit with powers of 16. Figure A.7 shows how to convert the number 3C5 to decimal.

**Figure A.7**

Converting hexadecimal 3C5 to its decimal equivalent.

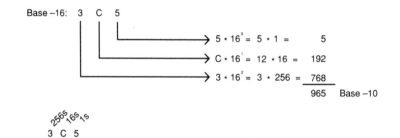

**Tip:** There are calculators available that convert numbers between base-16, base-10, and base-2, and also perform 2's complement arithmetic.

You should be able to convert 2B to its decimal 43 equivalent, and E1 to decimal 225 in the same manner. Table A.2 shows the first 20 decimal, binary, and hexadecimal numbers.

**Table A.2. The first 20 base-10, base-2 (binary), and base-16 (hexadecimal) numbers.**

| Base-10 | Base-2 | Base-16 |
|---------|--------|---------|
| 0 | 0 | 0 |
| 1 | 1 | 1 |
| 2 | 10 | 2 |
| 3 | 11 | 3 |
| 4 | 100 | 4 |
| 5 | 101 | 5 |
| 6 | 110 | 6 |
| 7 | 111 | 7 |
| 8 | 1000 | 8 |
| 9 | 1001 | 9 |
| 10 | 1010 | A |
| 11 | 1011 | B |
| 12 | 1100 | C |
| 13 | 1101 | D |

| Base-10 | Base-2 | Base-16 |
|---------|--------|---------|
| 14 | 1110 | E |
| 15 | 1111 | F |
| 16 | 10000 | 10 |
| 17 | 10001 | 11 |
| 18 | 10010 | 12 |
| 19 | 10011 | 13 |
| 20 | 10100 | 14 |

# Why Learn Hexadecimal?

Because of its close association to the binary numbers your computer uses, hexadecimal notation is extremely efficient for describing memory locations and values. It is much easier for you (and more important at this level, for your computer) to convert from base-16 to base-2 than from base-10 to base-2. Therefore, you sometimes want to represent data at the bit level, but using hexadecimal notation is easier (and requires less typing) than using binary numbers.

To convert from hexadecimal to binary, convert each hex digit to its four-bit binary number. You can use Table A.2 as a guide for this. For example, the following hexadecimal number

   5B75

can be converted to binary by taking each digit and converting it to four binary numbers. If you need leading zeroes to "pad" the four digits, use them. The number becomes

   0101 1011 0111 0101

It turns out that the binary number 0101101101110101 is exactly equal to the hexadecimal number 5B75. This is much easier than converting them both to decimal first.

To convert from binary to hexadecimal, reverse this process. If you were given the following binary number

   1101000011110111111010

you could convert it to hexadecimal by grouping the bits into groups of four, starting with the bit on the far right. Because there is not an even number of groups of four, pad the one on the far left with zeroes. You then have the following:

   0011 0100 0011 1101 1111 1010

Now you only have to convert each group of four binary digits into their hexadecimal number equivalent. You can use Table A.2 to help. You then get the following base-16 number:

343DFA

The C programming language also supports the base-8 *octal* representation of numbers. Because octal numbers are rarely used with today's computers, they are not covered in this appendix.

# How Binary and Addressing Relates to C

The material presented here may seem foreign to many programmers. The binary and 2's complement arithmetic reside deep in your computer, shielded from most programmers (except assembly language programmers). Understanding this level of your computer, however, explains everything else you learn.

Many C programmers learn C before delving into binary and hexadecimal representation. For them, much about the C language seems strange, but it could be explained very easily if they understood the basic concepts.

For example, a signed integer holds a different range of numbers than an unsigned integer. You now know that this is due to the sign bit being used in two different ways, depending on whether the number is designated as signed or unsigned.

The ASCII table also should make more sense to you after this discussion. The ASCII table is an integral part of your computer. Characters are not actually stored in memory and variables; rather, their ASCII bit patterns are. That is why C can move easily between characters and integers. The following two C statements are allowed, whereas they probably would not be in another programming language:

```
char c = 65;    /* Puts the ASCII letter A in c */
int ci = 'A';   /* Puts the number 65 in ci */
```

The hexadecimal notation taught to many C programmers also makes much more sense if they truly understand base-16 numbers. For example, if you see the following line in a C program

```
char a = '\x041';
```

you can convert the hex 41 to decimal (65 decimal) if you want to know what is being assigned. Also, C systems programmers find that they can better interface with assembly language programs when they understand the concepts presented in this appendix.

If you gain only a cursory knowledge of this material at this point, you will be very much ahead of the game when you program in C.

# Answers to Review Questions

## Chapter 1 Answers

1. BCPL or Algol

2. 1970s

3. False. C's compact size makes it an excellent programming language for smaller computers.

4. The hard disk

5. A modem

6. b. Input. By moving the mouse, you give cursor-direction commands to the computer.

7. Num Lock

8. UNIX

9. When you turn off the computer, the contents of RAM are destroyed.

10. True

11. 524,288 (512 times 1,024)

12. *Modulate demodulate*

# Chapter 2 Answers

1. A set of detailed instructions that tells the computer what to do

2. Buy one or write it yourself.

3. False

4. The program produces the output.

5. A program editor

6. The .C extension

7. You must first plan the program by deciding which steps you will take to produce the final program.

8. To get the errors out of your program

9. So that your programs work with various compilers and computer equipment

10. False. You must compile a program before linking it. Many compilers link the program automatically.

# Chapter 3 Answers

1. /* and */

2. A holding place for data that can be changed

3. A value that cannot be changed

4. False. ANSI C does not support nested comments.

5. The +, -, *, and / operators

6. The = assignment operator

7. False. There are floating-point, double floating-point, short integers, long integers, and many more variable data types.

8. `printf()`

9. `city` must be a variable name because it is not enclosed in quotation marks.

10. All C commands must be in lowercase.

# Chapter 4 Answers

1. `myName` and `sales_89`

2. Characters: `'X'` and `'0'`

   Strings: `"2.0"` and `"X"`

   Integer: `0` and `-708`

   Floating-point: `-12.0` and `65.4`

3. Seven variables are defined: three integers, three characters, and one floating-point variable.

4. A null zero, also called a binary zero or an ASCII zero

5. True

6. 1

7. As a series of ASCII values, representing the characters and blanks in the string, ending in an ASCII 0

8. A single ASCII 0

# Chapter 5 Answers

1. `char myName[] = "This is C";`

2. 9 characters

3. 10

4. Binary zero

5. Two character arrays are defined, each with 25 elements.

6. False. The keyword char must precede the variable name.

7. True. The binary zero terminates the string.

8. False. The characters do not represent a string because there is no terminating zero.

# Chapter 6 Answers

1. False. You can define only constants with the `#define` preprocessor directive.

2. `#include`

3. `#define`

4. True

5. The preprocessor changes your source code before the compiler sees the source code.

6. Use angled brackets when the `include` files reside in the compiler's `include` subdirectory. Use quotation marks when the `include` file resides in the same subdirectory as the source program.

7. Defined constants are easier because you have to change only the line with `#define` and not several other lines in the program.

8. stdio.h

9. False. You cannot define constants enclosed in quotation marks (as `"MESSAGE"` is in the `printf()` function).

10. `Amount is 4` (If you got something else, you are treating `AMT1` and `AMT2` as variables and not as constants as the chapter explained.)

# Chapter 7 Answers

1. `printf()` sends output to the screen, and `scanf()` gets input from the keyboard.

2. The prompt tells the user what is expected.

3. Four values are entered: two integers, a floating-point, and a string.

4. True

5. Arrays

6. The `scanf()` function gets its values from the keyboard.
The assignment statement gets its value from data in the program.

7. `The backslash, "\" character is special`

8. The following value prints, with one leading space: 123.456

9. False

10. 1234000    .000001234    −1234000    −.000001234

# Chapter 8 Answers

1. a. 5

   b. 6

   c. 5

2. a. 2

   b. 7

3. a. a = (3+3) / (4+4);

   b. x = (a-b)*( (a-c) * (a-c));

   c. d = ( (8-x*x)/(x-9) ) - ((4*2-1) / (x*x*x));

4. 
```
#include <stdio.h>

#define PI 3.14159
main()
{
   printf("%f", (PI*(4*4)));
   return;
}
```

5. 
```
r = 100%3;

printf("%d", r);
```

# Chapter 9 Answers

1. The == operator

2. a. False

   b. True

   c. True

   d. True

3. True

4. The if statement determines what code executes when the relational test is true. The if-else statement determines what happens for both the True and the False relational test.

**5.** No

**6.** a. True

b. False

c. True

# Chapter 10 Answers

**1.** The `&&`, `¦¦`, and `!` operators

**2.** a. False

b. False

c. True

d. True

**3.** a. True

b. True

c. True

**4.** `g` is 25 and `f` got changed to 8

**5.** a. True

b. True

c. False

d. True

**6.** Yes

# Chapter 11 Answers

**1.** The `if-else` statement

**2.** The conditional operator is the only C operator with three arguments.

**3.** Yes

```
if (a == b)
   { ans = c + 2; }
else
   { ans = c + 3; }
```

4. True

5. The increment and decrement operators compile into single assembly instructions.

6. A comma operator (,) that forces a left-to-right execution of the statements on either side

7. The output cannot be determined reliably. Do not pass an increment operator as an argument.

8. `The size of name is 20`

# Chapter 12 Answers

1. Bitwise logical operators: !, &, ^, and ¦
   Compound bitwise logical operators: &=, ^=, and ¦=
   Bitwise shift operators: << and >>

2. a. 1

   b. 1

   c. 0

   d. 0

3. True

4. The 2's complement converts a number to its negative. The 1's complement simply reverses the bit pattern.

# Chapter 13 Answers

1. The `while` loop tests for a true condition at the top of the loop. The `do-while` tests at the bottom.

2. A counter variable increments by one. A total variable increments by the addition to the total you are performing.

3. The ++ operator

4. If the body of the loop is a single statement, the braces are not required. However, braces are always recommended.

5. There are no braces. The second `printf()` will always execute, regardless of the result of the `while` loop's relational test.

6. stdlib.h

**7.** One time

**8.** By returning a value inside the `exit()` function's parentheses

**9.** `This is the outer loop`

`This is the outer loop`

`This is the outer loop`

`This is the outer loop`

# Chapter 14 Answers

**1.** A sequence of one or more instructions executed repeatedly

**2.** False

**3.** A loop within a loop

**4.** Because the expressions might be initialized elsewhere, such as before the loop or in the body of the loop

**5.** The inner loop

**6.** `10`

`7`

`4`

`1`

**7.** True

**8.** The body of the `for` loop stops repeating.

**9.** False, due to the semicolon after the first `for` loop

**10.** There is no output. The value of `start` is already less than `end` when the loop begins; therefore, the `for` loop's test is immediately False.

# Chapter 15 Answers

**1.** If the `continue` and `break` statements were unconditional, there would be little use for them.

**2.** Because of the unconditional `continue` statement, there is no output.

**3.** `*****`

# Chapter 16 Answers

1. The program does not execute sequentially, as it would without goto.

2. The switch statement

3. A break statement

4. False

```
switch (num)
{ case (1) : { printf("Alpha");
               break; }
  case (2) : { printf("Beta");
               break; }
  case (3) : { printf("Gamma");
               break; }
  default :  { printf("Other");
               break; }
}

do
  { printf("What is your first name? ");
    scanf(" %s", name);
  } while ((name[0] < 'A') || (name[0] > 'Z'));
```

# Chapter 17 Answers

1. True

2. main()

3. Several smaller functions are better because each function can perform a single task

4. Function names always end with a pair of parentheses.

5. By putting separating comments between functions

6. The function sq25() cannot be nested in calcIt().

7. A function call (a prototype)

8. True

# Chapter 18 Answers

1. True

2. Local variables are passed as arguments.

3. False

4. The variable data types

5. Static

6. You should never pass global variables—they do not need to be passed.

7. 2 arguments

# Chapter 19 Answers

1. Arrays

2. Nonarray variables are always passed by value, unless you override the default with & before each variable name.

3. True

4. No

5. Yes

6. The data types of variables x, y, and z are not defined in the receiving parameter list.

7. c

# Chapter 20 Answers

1. By putting the return type to the left of the function name

2. 1

3. To prototype built-in functions

4. Integer

5. False

6. Prototypes ensure that the correct number of parameters is being passed.

7. Global variables are already known across functions.

8. The return type is float. Three parameters are passed: a character, an integer, and a floating-point variable.

# Chapter 21 Answers

1. For portability between different computers

2. False. The standard output can be redirected to any device through the operating system.

3. `getchar()` assumes `stdin` for the input device.

4. `getch()` does not wait for the Enter keypress.

5. `fprintf()`

6. `>` and `<`

7. `getche()`

8. False. The input from `getchar()` goes to a buffer as you type it.

9. Enter

10. True

# Chapter 22 Answers

1. The character-testing functions do not change the character passed to them.

2. `gets()` and `fgets()`

3. `floor()` rounds down and `ceil()` rounds up.

4. False. The inner function returns 1.

5. `PeterParker`

6. `8 9`

7. True

8. `Prog` with a null zero at the end

9. True

# Chapter 23 Answers

1. False

2. The array subscripts differentiate array elements.

3. C does not initialize, or "zero out," arrays for you.

**4.** 0

**5.** Yes. All arrays are passed by address because an array name is nothing more than an address to that array.

**6.** C initializes all global variables (and every other static variable in your program) to zero or null zero.

# Chapter 24 Answers

**1.** False

**2.** From the low numbers "floating" to the top of the array like bubbles

**3.** Ascending order

**4.** The name of an array is an address to the starting element of that array.

**5.** a. Eagles

   b. Rams

   c. les

   d. Invalid

   e. E

   f. Invalid

   g. g

# Chapter 25 Answers

**1.** int scores[5][6];

**2.** char initials[4][10][20]

**3.** The first subscript represents rows and the last represents columns.

**4.** 30 elements

**5.** a. 2

   b. 1

   c. 91

   d. 8

6. Nested `for` loops step through multidimensional tables very easily.

7. a. 78

   b. 100

   c. 90

# Chapter 26 Answers

1. a. Integer pointer

   b. Character pointer

   c. Floating-point pointer

2. "Address of "

3. The * operator

4. `ptSal = &salary;`

5. False

6. Yes

7. a. 2313.54

   b. 2313.54

   c. Invalid

   d. Invalid

8. b

# Chapter 27 Answers

1. Array names are pointer constants, not pointer variables.

2. 8

3. a, c, d, e. Parentheses are needed around `iptr+1` and `iptr+4` to make b and f valid.

4. You have to move only pointers, not entire strings.

5. a and d

## Chapter 28 Answers

1. Structures hold groups of more than one value, each of which can be a different data type.

2. Members

3. At definition time and at run time

4. Structures pass by copy.

5. False. Memory is reserved only when structure variables are defined.

6. Globally

7. Locally

8. 4

## Chapter 29 Answers

1. True

2. Arrays are easier to manage.

3. a. `inventory[32].price = 12.33;`

   b. `inventory[11].partNo[0] = 'X';`

   c. `inventory[96] = inventory[62];`

4. a. `item` is not a structure variable.

   b. `inventory` is an array and must have a subscript.

   c. `inventory` is an array and must have a subscript.

5. The array of integer pointers.

6. True. You must define a pointer as well as allocate the value on the heap. However, when you allocate arrays, dynamically-allocating the arrays can save much more space than using regular arrays that must be defined from the beginning.

## Chapter 30 Answers

1. Write, append, and read

2. Disks hold more data than memory.

3. You can access sequential files only in the same order that they were originally written.

4. An error condition occurs.

5. The old file is overwritten.

6. The file is created.

7. C returns the EOF constant, defined in stdio.h, when an end-of-file condition is met.

8. The EOF return value might be a negative number.

# Chapter 31 Answers

1. Records are stored in files and structures are stored in memory.

2. False

3. The file pointer continually updates to point to the next byte to read.

4. `fwrite()` and `fread()`

5. `rewind()` and `fseek(fp, 0, SEEK_SET);`

6. SEEK_SET (or 0), SEEK_CUR (or 1), and SEEK_END (or 2)

7. You must use the `feof()` function to check for the end-of-file condition in binary files.

# ASCII Table

| Dec $X_{10}$ | Hex $X_{16}$ | Binary $X_2$ | ASCII Character |
|---|---|---|---|
| 000 | 00 | 0000 0000 | null |
| 001 | 01 | 0000 0001 | ☺ |
| 002 | 02 | 0000 0010 | ● |
| 003 | 03 | 0000 0011 | ♥ |
| 004 | 04 | 0000 0100 | ◆ |
| 005 | 05 | 0000 0101 | ♣ |
| 006 | 06 | 0000 0110 | ♠ |
| 007 | 07 | 0000 0111 | ● |
| 008 | 08 | 0000 1000 | ■ |
| 009 | 09 | 0000 1001 | ○ |
| 010 | 0A | 0000 1010 | ■ |
| 011 | 0B | 0000 1011 | ♂ |
| 012 | 0C | 0000 1100 | ♀ |
| 013 | 0D | 0000 1101 | ♪ |
| 014 | 0E | 0000 1110 | ♪♪ |
| 015 | 0F | 0000 1111 | ☼ |
| 016 | 10 | 0001 0000 | ► |
| 017 | 11 | 0001 0001 | ◄ |
| 018 | 12 | 0001 0010 | ↕ |
| 019 | 13 | 0001 0011 | ‼ |
| 020 | 14 | 0001 0100 | ¶ |
| 021 | 15 | 0001 0101 | § |
| 022 | 16 | 0001 0110 | ▬ |
| 023 | 17 | 0001 0111 | ↨ |

| Dec $X_{10}$ | Hex $X_{16}$ | Binary $X_2$ | ASCII Character |
|---|---|---|---|
| 024 | 18 | 0001 1000 | ↑ |
| 025 | 19 | 0001 1001 | ↓ |
| 026 | 1A | 0001 1010 | → |
| 027 | 1B | 0001 1011 | ← |
| 028 | 1C | 0001 1100 | ∟ |
| 029 | 1D | 0001 1101 | ↔ |
| 030 | 1E | 0001 1110 | ▲ |
| 031 | 1F | 0001 1111 | ▼ |
| 032 | 20 | 0010 0000 | Space |
| 033 | 21 | 0010 0001 | ! |
| 034 | 22 | 0010 0010 | " |
| 035 | 23 | 0010 0011 | # |
| 036 | 24 | 0010 0100 | $ |
| 037 | 25 | 0010 0101 | % |
| 038 | 26 | 0010 0110 | & |
| 039 | 27 | 0010 0111 | ' |
| 040 | 28 | 0010 1000 | ( |
| 041 | 29 | 0010 1001 | ) |
| 042 | 2A | 0010 1010 | * |
| 043 | 2B | 0010 1011 | + |
| 044 | 2C | 0010 1100 | ' |
| 045 | 2D | 0010 1101 | - |
| 046 | 2E | 0010 1110 | . |
| 047 | 2F | 0010 1111 | / |
| 048 | 30 | 0011 0000 | 0 |
| 049 | 31 | 0011 0001 | 1 |
| 050 | 32 | 0011 0010 | 2 |
| 051 | 33 | 0011 0011 | 3 |
| 052 | 34 | 0011 0100 | 4 |
| 053 | 35 | 0011 0101 | 5 |
| 054 | 36 | 0011 0110 | 6 |
| 055 | 37 | 0011 0111 | 7 |
| 056 | 38 | 0011 1000 | 8 |
| 057 | 39 | 0011 1001 | 9 |
| 058 | 3A | 0011 1010 | : |

| Dec $X_{10}$ | Hex $X_{16}$ | Binary $X_2$ | ASCII Character |
|---|---|---|---|
| 059 | 3B | 0011 1011 | ; |
| 060 | 3C | 0011 1100 | < |
| 061 | 3D | 0011 1101 | = |
| 062 | 3E | 0011 1110 | > |
| 063 | 3F | 0011 1111 | ? |
| 064 | 40 | 0100 0000 | @ |
| 065 | 41 | 0100 0001 | A |
| 066 | 42 | 0100 0010 | B |
| 067 | 43 | 0100 0011 | C |
| 068 | 44 | 0100 0100 | D |
| 069 | 45 | 0100 0101 | E |
| 070 | 46 | 0100 0110 | F |
| 071 | 47 | 0100 0111 | G |
| 072 | 48 | 0100 1000 | H |
| 073 | 49 | 0100 1001 | I |
| 074 | 4A | 0100 1010 | J |
| 075 | 4B | 0100 1011 | K |
| 076 | 4C | 0100 1100 | L |
| 077 | 4D | 0100 1101 | M |
| 078 | 4E | 0100 1110 | N |
| 079 | 4F | 0100 1111 | O |
| 080 | 50 | 0101 0000 | P |
| 081 | 51 | 0101 0001 | Q |
| 082 | 52 | 0101 0010 | R |
| 083 | 53 | 0101 0011 | S |
| 084 | 54 | 0101 0100 | T |
| 085 | 55 | 0101 0101 | U |
| 086 | 56 | 0101 0110 | V |
| 087 | 57 | 0101 0111 | W |
| 088 | 58 | 0101 1000 | X |
| 089 | 59 | 0101 1001 | Y |
| 090 | 5A | 0101 1010 | Z |
| 091 | 5B | 0101 1011 | [ |
| 092 | 5C | 0101 1100 | \ |
| 093 | 5D | 0101 1101 | ] |

| Dec $X_{10}$ | Hex $X_{16}$ | Binary $X_2$ | ASCII Character |
|---|---|---|---|
| 094 | 5E | 0101 1110 | ^ |
| 095 | 5F | 0101 1111 | – |
| 096 | 60 | 0110 0000 | ` |
| 097 | 61 | 0110 0001 | a |
| 098 | 62 | 0110 0010 | b |
| 099 | 63 | 0110 0011 | c |
| 100 | 64 | 0110 0100 | d |
| 101 | 65 | 0110 0101 | e |
| 102 | 66 | 0110 0110 | f |
| 103 | 67 | 0110 0111 | g |
| 104 | 68 | 0110 1000 | h |
| 105 | 69 | 0110 1001 | i |
| 106 | 6A | 0110 1010 | j |
| 107 | 6B | 0110 1011 | k |
| 108 | 6C | 0110 1100 | l |
| 109 | 6D | 0110 1101 | m |
| 110 | 6E | 0110 1110 | n |
| 111 | 6F | 0110 1111 | o |
| 112 | 70 | 0111 0000 | p |
| 113 | 71 | 0111 0001 | q |
| 114 | 72 | 0111 0010 | r |
| 115 | 73 | 0111 0011 | s |
| 116 | 74 | 0111 0100 | t |
| 117 | 75 | 0111 0101 | u |
| 118 | 76 | 0111 0110 | v |
| 119 | 77 | 0111 0111 | w |
| 120 | 78 | 0111 1000 | x |
| 121 | 79 | 0111 1001 | y |
| 122 | 7A | 0111 1010 | z |
| 123 | 7B | 0111 1011 | { |
| 124 | 7C | 0111 1100 | ¦ |
| 125 | 7D | 0111 1101 | } |
| 126 | 7E | 0111 1110 | ~ |
| 127 | 7F | 0111 1111 | Delete |

# C Precedence Table

## Precedence

| Level | Symbol | Description | Associativity |
|-------|--------|-------------|---------------|
| 1 | ++ | Prefix increment | Left to right |
| | -- | Prefix decrement | |
| | ( ) | Function call and subexpression | |
| | [ ] | Array subscript | |
| | -> | Structure pointer | |
| | . | Structure member | |
| 2 | ! | Logical negation | Right to left |
| | ~ | 1's complement | |
| | - | Unary negation | |
| | + | Unary plus | |

**Precedence Continued**

| Level | Symbol | Description | Associativity |
|-------|--------|-------------|---------------|
| 2 | (type) | Type cast | |
| | * | Pointer dereference | |
| | & | Address of | |
| | sizeof | Size of | |
| 3 | * | Multiplication | Left to right |
| | / | Division | |
| | % | Modulus (integer remainder) | |
| 4 | + | Addition | Left to right |
| | - | Subtraction | |
| 5 | << | Bitwise left shift | Left to right |
| | >> | Bitwise right shift | |
| 6 | < | Less than | Left to right |
| | <= | Less than or equal to | |
| | > | Greater than | |
| | >= | Greater than or equal to | |
| 7 | == | Equal test | Left to right |
| | != | Not equal test | |
| 8 | & | Bitwise AND | Left to right |
| 9 | ^ | Bitwise exclusive OR | Left to right |
| 10 | ¦ | Bitwise inclusive OR | Left to right |
| 11 | && | Logical AND | Left to right |

| Level | Symbol | Description | Associativity |
|-------|--------|-------------|---------------|
| 12 | ¦¦ | Logical inclusive OR | Left to right |
| 13 | ?: | Conditional test | Right to left |
| 14 | = | Assignment | Right to left |
| | += | Compound add | |
| | -= | Compound subtract | |
| | *= | Compound multiply | |
| | /= | Compound divide | |
| | %= | Compound modulus | |
| | <<= | Compound bitwise left shift | |
| | >>= | Compound bitwise right shift | |
| | &= | Compound bitwise AND | |
| | ^= | Compound bitwise exclusive OR | |
| | ¦= | Compound bitwise inclusive OR | |
| 15 | , | Sequence point | Left to right |
| | ++ | Postfix increment | |
| | -- | Postfix decrement | |

Technically, the postfix and prefix operators appear in different locations in C's precedence table (levels 1 and 2 respectively). To interpret ambiguous expressions like this: n = ++a++b;, the designers of C had to decide how to interpret such expressions (ones that shouldn't be written anyway). You will find that the *practical* order presented here makes the most sense.

# Keyword and Function Reference

These are the 32 ANSI C standard keywords:

| | | | |
|---|---|---|---|
| auto | double | int | struct |
| break | else | long | switch |
| case | enum | register | typedef |
| char | extern | return | union |
| const | float | short | unsigned |
| continue | for | signed | void |
| default | goto | sizeof | volatile |
| do | if | static | while |

The following are the built-in function prototypes, listed by their header files. The prototypes describe the parameter data types that each function requires.

## `<stdio.h>`

```
int fclose(FILE *stream);
int feof(FILE *stream);
int ferror(FILE *stream);
int fflush(FILE *stream);
int fgetc(FILE *stream);
char *fgets(char *, int, FILE *stream);
FILE *fopen(const char *filename, const char *mode);
int fprintf(FILE *stream, const char *format, ...);
int fputc(int, FILE *stream);
int fputs(const char *, FILE *stream);
size_t fread(void *, size_t, size_t, FILE *stream);
int fscanf(FILE *stream, const char *format, ...);
int fseek(FILE *stream, long offset, int origin);
size_t fwrite(const void *, size_t, size_t, FILE *stream);
int getc(FILE *stream);
int getchar(void);
char *gets(char *);
void perror(const char *);
int putc(int, FILE *stream);
int putchar(int);
int puts(const char *);
int remove(const char *filename);
void rewind(FILE *stream);
int scanf(const char *format, ...);
```

## `<ctype.h>`

```
int isalnum(unsigned char);
int isalpha(unsigned char);
int iscntrl(unsigned char);
int isdigit(unsigned char);
int isgraph(unsigned char);
int islower(unsigned char);
int isprint(unsigned char);
int ispunct(unsigned char);
int isspace(unsigned char);
int isupper(unsigned char);
int isxdigit(unsigned char);
int tolower(int);
int toupper(int);
```

## <string.h>

```
char *strcat(char *, char *);
int strcmp(char *, char *);
int strcpy(char *, char *);
size_t strlen(char *);Ce
```

## <math.h>

```
double ceil(double);
double cos(double);
double exp(double);
double fabs(double);
double floor(double);
double fmod(double, double);
double log(double);
double log10(double);
double pow(double, double);
double sin(double);
double sqrt(double);
double tan(double);
```

## <stdlib.h>

```
double atof(const char *);
int atoi(const char *);
long atol(const char *);
void exit(int);
int rand(void);
void srand(unsigned int);
```

# Glossary

**address**   Each memory (RAM) location (each byte) has a unique address. The first address in memory is 0, the second RAM location's address is 1, and so on until the last RAM location (which comes thousands of bytes later).

**argument**   The value sent to a *function*. An argument is *constant* or a *variable* enclosed in parentheses.

**array**   A list of *variables*, sometimes called a table of variables.

**ASCII**   An acronym for American Standard Code for Information Interchange.

**ASCII file**   A file containing characters that can be used by any program on most computers. Sometimes it is called a text file or an ASCII text file.

**AUTOEXEC.BAT**   An optional *batch file* that executes a series of commands whenever you start or reset the computer.

**backup file**   A duplicate copy of a file that preserves your work in case you damage the original file. Files on a *hard disk* are commonly backed up onto *floppy disks* or *tape*.

**batch file**   An ASCII text file containing *DOS* commands.

**binary**   A numbering system based on two digits. The only valid digits in a binary system are 0 and 1. See also *bit*.

**binary zero**   Another name for *null zero*.

**bit**   Binary digit, the smallest unit of storage on a computer. Each bit can have a value of 0 or 1, indicating the absence or presence of an electrical signal. See also *binary*.

**bitwise operators**   C operators that manipulate the binary representation of values.

**block**   One or more statements treated as though they are a single statement.

**bubble sort**   An easy-to-code *sorting* routine that orders arrays of values.

**bug**   An error in a program that prevents the program from running correctly. This term originated when a moth short-circuited a connection in one of the first computers and prevented the computer from working.

**byte**   A basic unit of data storage and manipulation. A byte is equivalent to eight *bits* and can contain a value ranging from 0 to 255.

**cathode ray tube (CRT)**   The television-like screen of the computer, also called the *monitor*. It is one place to which the output of the computer can be sent.

**central processing unit (CPU)**   The *microprocessor* responsible for operations within the computer. These operations generally include system timing, logical processing, and logical operations. The CPU controls every operation of the computer system.

**code**   A set of instructions written in a *programming language*. See also *source code*.

**compile**   The process of translating a program written in a *programming language*, such as C or Pascal, into machine code your computer understands.

**concatenation**   The process of attaching one string to the end of another or combining two or more strings into a longer string.

**conditional loop**   A series of C instructions that occurs a fixed number of times.

**constant**   Data that remain the same during a program run.

**CPU**   See *central processing unit*.

**CRT**   See *cathode ray tube*.

**data**   Information stored in the computer as numbers, letters, and special symbols (such as punctuation marks). Data also refers to the characters you input into your program so that the program can produce meaningful information.

**data processing**   When a computer takes data and manipulates it into meaningful output, which is called *information*.

**data validation**   The process of testing the values input into a program—for instance, ensuring that a number is within a certain range.

**debug**   The process of locating an error (*bug*) in a program and removing it.

**default**  A predefined action or command that the computer chooses unless you specify otherwise.

**dereference**  The process of finding a value pointed to by a *pointer* variable.

**digital computer**  A term that comes from the fact that your computer operates on *binary* (**on** and **off**) digital impulses of electricity.

**directory**  A list of files stored on a disk. Directories within existing directories are called *subdirectories*.

**disk**  A round, flat magnetic storage medium. *Floppy disks* are made of flexible material and enclosed in 5 1/4-inch or 3 1/2-inch protective cases. *Hard disks* consist of a stack of rigid disks housed in a single unit. A disk is sometimes called *external memory*. Disk storage is non*volatile*. When you turn off your computer, the disk's contents do not go away.

**disk drive**  A device that reads and writes data to a *floppy disk* or a *hard disk*.

**diskette**  Another name for a removable *floppy disk*.

**display**  A screen or *monitor*.

**display adapter**  Located in the *system unit*, the display adapter determines the amount of *resolution* and the possible number of colors on-screen.

**DOS**  Disk operating system.

**dot-matrix printer**  One of the two most common PC printers. The laser printer is the other. A dot-matrix printer is inexpensive and fast; it uses a series of small dots to represent printed *text* and *graphics*. See also *laser printer*.

**element**  An individual *variable* in an *array*.

**execute**  To run a program.

**expanded memory**  See *extended memory*.

**extended memory**  The amount of *RAM* that is above and beyond the basic 640K in most PCs. The two kinds of high RAM are *extended* and *expanded*. You cannot access this extra RAM without special programs.

**external modem**  A modem that sits in a box outside your computer. See also *internal modem*.

**file**  A collection of data stored as a single unit on a *floppy disk* or *hard disk*. A file always has a *file name* that identifies it.

**file extension**  A suffix to a *file name* consisting of a period followed by up to three characters. The extension denotes what kind of file it is.

**file name**   A unique name that identifies a file. File names can be up to eight characters long and can have a period followed by a *file extension* (which is normally three characters long).

**fixed disk**   See *hard disk*.

**fixed-length records**   A record in which each field takes the same amount of disk space, even if that field's data value does not fill the field. Fixed strings are typically used for fixed-length records.

**floppy disk**   See *disk*.

**format**   To create a "map" on the *disk* that tells the operating system how the disk is structured. This is how the operating system keeps track of where *files* are stored.

**function**   A self-contained coding segment designed to do a specific task. All C programs must have at least one function called `main()`. Some functions are built-in routines that manipulate numbers, strings, and output.

**function keys**   Keys labeled F1 through F12 (some keyboards go only to F10) that provide special *functions*.

**global variable**   A variable that can be seen from (and used by) every statement in the program.

**hard copy**   The printout of a program (or its output). Hard copy also refers to a safe backup copy for a program in case the disk is erased.

**hard disk**   Sometimes called a *fixed disk*. A hard disk holds much more data and is many times faster than a *floppy disk*. See also *disk*.

**hardware**   The physical parts of the machine. Hardware, which has been defined as "anything you can kick," consists of the things you can see.

**hexadecimal**   A numbering system based on 16 *elements*. Digits are numbered 0 through F, as follows: 0, 1, 2, 3, 4, 5, 6, 7, 8, 9, A, B, C, D, E, F.

**hierarchy of operators**   See *order of operators*.

**indeterminate loop**   A loop in which you do not know in advance how many cycles of the loop will be made (unlike with the `for-next` loop).

**infinite loop**   The never-ending repetition of a *block* of C statements.

**information**   The meaningful product of a program. Data goes into a program to produce meaningful output (information).

**input**   The data entered into a computer through a device such as the keyboard.

**input-process-output**  This model is the foundation of everything that happens in your computer. *Data* is input and then processed by your *program* in the computer. Finally, *information* is output.

**integer variables**  *Variables* that can hold integers.

**internal modem**  A modem that resides inside the system unit. See also *external modem*.

**I/O**  An acronym for input/output.

**kilobyte (K)**  A unit of measurement that refers to 1,024 *bytes*.

**laser printer**  A type of printer that in general is faster than a dot-matrix printer. Laser printer output is much sharper than that of a dot-matrix printer, because a laser beam actually burns toner ink into the paper. Laser printers are more expensive than dot-matrix printers. See also *dot-matrix printer*.

**least significant bit**  The extreme-right bit of a *byte*. For example, a *binary* 00000111 has a 1 as the least significant bit.

**line printer**  Another name for your printer.

**local variable**  A *variable* that can be seen from (and used by) only the *code* in which it is defined (within a *function*).

**loop**  The repeated circular execution of one or more statements.

**machine language**  The series of *binary* digits that a *microprocessor* executes to perform individual tasks. People seldom (if ever) program in machine language. Instead, they program in assembly language, and an assembler translates their instructions into machine language.

**main module**  The first *function* in every C program called `main()` that controls the execution of the other functions.

**maintainability**  The computer industry's word for the ability to change and update programs that were written in a simple style.

**math operator**  A symbol used for addition, subtraction, multiplication, division, or other calculations.

**megabyte (M)**  In computer terminology, about a million *bytes*.

**member**  A piece of a structure variable that holds a specific type of data.

**memory**  Storage area inside the computer, used to temporarily store data. The computer's memory is erased when the power is turned off.

**menu**  A list of commands or instructions displayed on-screen. These lists organize commands and make a program easier to use.

**menu-driven**  Describes a program that provides menus for choosing commands.

**microchip**  A small wafer of silicon that holds computer components and occupies less space than a postage stamp.

**microcomputer**  A small version of a computer that can fit on a desktop. The *microchip* is the heart of the microcomputer. Microcomputers are much less expensive than their larger counterparts.

**microprocessor**  The chip that does the calculations for the computer. Sometimes it is called the *central processing unit* (*CPU*).

**modem**  A piece of *hardware* that *modulates* and *demodulates* signals so that your PC can communicate with other computers over telephone lines. See also *external modem* and *internal modem*.

**modular programming**  The process of writing your programs in several modules rather than as one long program. By breaking a program into several smaller program-line routines, you can isolate problems better, correct programs faster, and produce programs that are much easier to maintain.

**modulate**  Before your computer can transmit data over a telephone line, via a *modem*, the information to be sent must be converted (modulated) into *analog signals*. See also *modem*.

**modulus**  The integer remainder of division.

**monitor**  A television-like screen that lets the computer display information. It is known as an *output device*. See also *cathode ray tube*.

**mouse**  A hand-held device that you move across the desktop to move an indicator, called a mouse pointer, across the screen. The mouse is used rather than the keyboard to select and move items (such as *text* or *graphics*), execute commands, and perform other tasks.

**MS-DOS**  An operating system for IBM and IBM-compatible computers.

**multidimensional arrays**  Arrays with more than one subscript. Two-dimensional arrays, which have rows and columns, are sometimes called tables or matrices.

**nested loop**  A loop within a loop.

**null zero**  The string-terminating character. All C string constants and strings stored in character *arrays* end in null zero. The *ASCII* value for the null zero is 0.

**null string**  An empty string, the first character of which is the null zero and the length of which is zero.

**numeric functions**  Built-in routines that work with numbers.

**object code**   A "halfway step" between *source code* and executable *machine language*. Object code consists mostly of machine language, but is not directly executable by the computer. It must first be linked to resolve external references and *address* references.

**order of operators**   Sometimes called the *hierarchy of operators* or the *precedence of operators*, it determines exactly how C computes formulas.

**output device**   Where the results of a program are output, such as the screen, the printer, or a disk file.

**parallel arrays**   Two *arrays* working side by side. Each *element* in each array corresponds to one in the other array.

**parallel port**   A connector used to plug a device such as a printer into the computer. Transferring data through a parallel port is much faster than transferring data through a *serial port*.

**parameter**   A list of *variables* enclosed in parentheses that follow the name of a *function*. Parameters indicate the number and type of *arguments* that will be sent to the function.

**passing by address**   When an argument (a *local variable*) is passed by *address*, the variable's address in *memory* is sent to, and is assigned to, the receiving routine's *parameter* list. (If more than one *variable* is passed by address, each of their addresses is sent to and assigned to the receiving *function*'s parameters.) A change made to the parameter within the routine also changes the value of the argument variable.

**passing by copy**   Another name for *passing by value*.

**passing by value**   By default, all C variables are passed by value. When the value contained in a *variable* is passed to the *parameter* list of a receiving routine, changes made to the parameter within the routine do not change the value of the *argument* variable. Also called *passing by copy*.

**path**   The route the computer travels from the root *directory* to any *subdirectories* when locating a *file*. The path also refers to the subdirectories that *MS-DOS* examines when you type a command that requires it to find and access a file.

**peripheral**   A device attached to the computer—such as a *modem, disk drive, mouse,* or *printer*.

**personal computer**   A *microcomputer*, sometimes called a PC.

**pointer**   A *variable* that holds the address of another variable.

**precedence of operators**   See *order of operators*.

**preprocessor directive**   A command, preceded by a #, that you place in your *source code* that directs the compiler to modify the source code in some fashion. The two most common preprocessor directives are #define and #include.

**printer**   A device that prints data from the computer to paper.

**program**   A group of instructions that tells the computer what to do.

**programming language**   A set of rules for writing instructions for the computer. Popular programming languages include BASIC, QBasic, Visual Basic, C, C++, and Pascal.

**RAM**   See *random-access memory*.

**random-access file**   A file in which *records* can be accessed in any order you choose.

**random-access memory (RAM)**   What your computer uses to temporarily store data and programs. RAM is measured in *kilobytes* and *megabytes*. Generally, the more RAM a computer has, the more powerful the programs it can run.

**read-only memory (ROM)**   A permanent type of computer memory. ROM contains the BIOS (basic input/output system), a special chip used to provide instructions to the computer when you turn on the computer.

**real number**   A number that has a decimal point and a fractional part to the right of the decimal. Real numbers are represented as float and double in C.

**record**   An individual row in a file.

**relational operators**   *Operators* that compare data; they tell how two *variables* or *constants* relate to each other. They tell you whether two variables are equal or not equal, or which one is less than or more than the other.

**ROM**   See *read-only memory*.

**scientific notation**   A shortcut method of representing numbers of extreme values.

**sector**   A pattern of pie-shaped wedges on a *disk*. Formatting creates a pattern of *tracks* and sectors where your data and programs are stored.

**sequential file**   A file that has to be accessed one *record* at a time beginning with the first record.

**serial port**   A connector used to plug in serial devices, such as a *modem* or a *mouse*.

**single-dimensional arrays**   Arrays that have only one *subscript*. Single-dimensional arrays represent a list of values.

**software** The *data* and *programs* that interact with your hardware. The C language is an example of software. See also *hardware*.

**sorting** A method of putting *arrays* in a specific order (such as alphabetical or numerical order), even if that order is not the same order in which the *elements* were entered.

**source code** The C language instructions, written by humans, that the C compiler translates into *object code*.

**spaghetti code** A term used when there are too many gotos in a program. If a program branches all over the place, it is difficult to follow; the logic resembles a "bowl of spaghetti."

**stream** Literally, a stream of characters, one following another, flowing between devices in your computer.

**string constant** One or more groups of characters that end in a *null zero*.

**string literal** Another name for a *string constant*.

**structure** An aggregate unit of related data containing one or more numbers, such as an employee number, employee name, employee address, employee pay rate, and so on.

**subdirectory** A *directory* within another directory.

**subscript** A number inside brackets that differentiates one *element* of an *array* from another.

**syntax error** The most common error a programmer makes. Usually a misspelled word.

**system unit** The large box component of the computer. The system unit houses the PC's *microchip* (the *CPU*).

**track** A pattern of *paths* on a *disk*. Formatting creates a pattern of tracks and *sectors* where your data and programs go.

**truncation** When the fractional part of a number (the part of the number to the right of the decimal point) is taken off the number. No rounding is done.

**two's complement** A method your computer uses to take the negative of a number. This method, plus addition, enables the computer to simulate subtraction.

**unary operator** The addition or subtraction *operator* used by itself.

**user-defined functions** Functions that the user writes. See also *functions*.

**user-friendliness** A program is user-friendly if it makes the user comfortable and simulates what the user is already familiar with.

**UNIX**   A multiuser operating system used by minicomputers.

**variable**   Data that can change as the program runs.

**variable-length record**   A *record* that wastes no space on the *disk*. As soon as a field's data value is saved to the file, the next field's data value is stored immediately after it. There is usually a special separating character between the fields so that your programs know where the fields begin and end.

**variable scope**   Sometimes called the *visibility of variables*, this describes how variables are "seen" by your program. See also *global variables* and *local variables*.

**volatile**   Refers to something temporary. For example, data in your computer's *RAM* is volatile: when you turn off the computer, all of it is erased.

**word**   In general computer usage, two consecutive bytes (16 bits) of data. On a minicomputer or mainframe, the word size can be larger.

# Index

# NOTES

# NOTES

# NOTES

## Character Tests: <ctype.h>

```
int isalnum(unsigned char);
int asalpha(unsigned char);
int iscntrl(unsigned char);
int isdigit(unsigned char);
int isgraph(unsigned char);
int islower(unsigned char);
int isprint(unsigned char);
int ispunct(unsigned char);
int isspace(unsigned char);
int isupper(unsigned char);
int isxdigit(unsigned char);
```

## Character Conversion Functions: <ctype.h>

```
int tolower(int);
int toupper(int);
```

## String Functions: <string.h>

```
char *strcpy(char *, char *);
char *strcat(char *, char *);
int strcmp(char *, char *);
size_t strlen(char *);
```

## Mathematical Functions: <math.h>

```
double ceil(double);
double cos(double);
double exp(double);
double fabs(double);
double floor(double);
double fmod(double, double);
double log(double);
double log10(double);
double pow(double, double);
double sin(double);
double sqrt(double);
double tan(double);
```

## Utility Functions: <stdlib.h>

```
double atof(const char *);
int atoi(const char *);
long atol(const char *);
void exit(int);
int rand(void);
```